URBAN RENAISSANCE?

New Labour, community a
urban policy

D0353403

Edited by Rob Imrie and Mike Raco

First published in Great Britain in May 2003 by

The Policy Press
Fourth Floor, Beacon House
Queen's Road
Bristol BS8 1QU

Tel +44 (0)117 331 4054
Fax +44 (0)117 331 4093
e-mail tpp-info@bristol.ac.uk
www.policypress.org.uk

Reprinted 2004

British Library Cataloguing in Publication Data

A catalogue record for this book is available from the British Library

ISBN 1 86134 380 9 paperback

A hardcover version of this book is also available

Rob Imrie is Professor of Human Geography in the Department of Geography at Royal Holloway, University of London and **Mike Raco** is Lecturer in Economic Geography in the Department of Geography at the University of Reading.

Cover design by Qube Design Associates, Bristol
Front cover: photograph supplied by kind permission of www.third-avenue.co.uk
Printed and bound in Great Britain by MPG Books, Bodmin

Contents

Acknowledgements   v

Notes on the editors   vi

Notes on the contributors   vii

Preface   x

Part One   **New Labour and the turn to community regeneration**   1

one   Community and the changing nature of urban policy   3
                 Rob Imrie and Mike Raco

two   Social capital, regeneration and urban policy   37
                 Ade Kearns

three   Visions of 'urban renaissance': the Urban Task Force report   61
                 and the Urban White Paper
                 Loretta Lees

Part Two   **Community involvement in urban policy**   83
four   Strategic, multilevel neighbourhood regeneration: 85
                 an outward-looking approach at last?
                 Annette Hastings

five   Addressing urban social exclusion through community   101
                 involvement in urban regeneration
                 Rob Atkinson

six   Communities at the heart? Community action and urban   121
                 policy in the UK
                 Peter North

seven   Cultural justice and addressing 'social exclusion': a case study   139
                 of a Single Regeneration Budget project in Blackbird Leys,
                 Oxford
                 Zoë Morrison

eight   Disability and the discourses of the Single Regeneration   163
                 Budget
                 Claire Edwards

nine   Citizenship, community and participation in small towns: 181
                 a case study of regeneration partnerships
                 Bill Edwards, Mark Goodwin and Michael Woods

ten   Economy, equity or empowerment? New Labour, communities   205
                 and urban policy evaluation
                 Stuart Wilks-Heeg

Part Three   The future of community in urban policy   **221**

eleven   The new urban policy: towards empowerment or   223
                 incorporation? The practice of urban policy
                 Allan Cochrane

twelve   New Labour, community and the future of Britain's urban   235
                 renaissance
                 Mike Raco

References   251

Index   287

Acknowledgements

We would like to thank the individual contributors for their willingness to be involved in the project, and for their responsiveness to our many requests. We are particularly grateful to the referees of the book proposal for their encouraging comments and useful advice about the structure and substance of the book. This helped us to rethink aspects of the overall rationale of the endeavour. A team of responsive and insightful referees vetted the initial submissions of chapters, and returned their comments in record times. In this respect, we would particularly like to thank Mark Boyle, Martin Jones, Gordon MacLeod, Nick Phelps, Andy Pratt and Dave Valler. Thanks are also due to two anonymous readers of the final draft of the book for helping us to reshape parts of the text. The book could not have been produced without the support and encouragement of a number of other individuals and we would like to acknowledge comments on draft chapters by Sarah Fielder and Marian Hawkesworth, and to thank Dawn Rushen of The Policy Press for her encouragement and guidance.

Rob Imrie and Mike Raco

Notes on the editors

Rob Imrie (r.imrie@rhul.ac.uk) is Professor of Human Geography in the Department of Geography at Royal Holloway, University of London. He has published widely on subjects such as urban policy, geographies of disability, inclusive design and industrial networks. He is co-author (with Peter Hall) of *Inclusive design: Designing and developing accessible environments* (Spon Press: London, 2001), and author of *Disability and the city* (London: Sage Publications, 1996) and *Housing quality* (London: Routledge, 2004: forthcoming). He also co-edited *British urban policy – An evaluation of the Urban Development Corporations* (with Huw Thomas; London: Sage Publications, 1999).

Mike Raco (m.raco@reading.ac.uk) is Lecturer in Economic Geography in the Department of Geography at the University of Reading. He has published a wide range of academic papers on urban policy, community mobilisation and the governance of economic development. Although his doctoral subject was geography, his background also includes planning and urban studies. Between 1997 and 2000 he was a lecturer in the Department of Urban Studies, University of Glasgow.

Notes on the contributors

Rob Atkinson is Urban Research Director of the Cities Research Centre, Faculty of the Built Environment, University of the West of England. His primary research interests are cross-national work on urban regeneration, community participation in urban regeneration partnerships, urban social exclusion and European urban policy. He has lectured throughout Europe on these subjects, and has published widely.

Allan Cochrane is Professor of Public Policy at the Open University. He has published research on a wide range of topics relating to urban policy and urban (and local) politics, and is particularly interested in the ways in which they connect into wider processes of political and social change. His most recent research includes the reshaping and reimagining of Berlin that has taken place over the last decade, as well as a contemporary redefinition of British urban policy. He is co-author of *Re-thinking the region* (with John Allen and Doreen Massey; London: Routledge, 1998) and joint editor of *Comparing welfare states* (with John Clarke and Sharon Gewirtz; London: Sage Publications, 2001).

Bill Edwards is Lecturer in Geography at the University of Wales. His publications have focused on the subjects of community leadership, citizen participation and power relations in small towns and the countryside. He has undertaken research on community action and community development for a wide range of agencies. Most recently, he has completed work for the Economic and Social Research Council (ESRC) concerning participation in rural community leadership (with Michael Woods), and for the Joseph Rowntree Foundation on partnership working in rural regeneration (with Mark Goodwin and Michael Woods).

Claire Edwards is a research officer in the Social Research Division of the Department for Work and Pensions. Between 1997 and 2000 her doctoral research explored how disabled people are being involved in urban regeneration schemes. Upon its completion, she spent one year at the Disability Rights Commission. Her current post involves managing research projects on a range of disability issues, including the provision of support and services to disabled people and the evaluation of the New Deal for Disabled People Programme. She has had her papers published in many journals, including *Urban Studies*, *Local Economy* and *Sociology*.

Mark Goodwin is Professor of Human Geography at the University of Wales. He has published extensively in the subject areas of the local state, changing forms of governance and regulation theory. His work is informed by research in both urban and rural Britain. More recently, he has been involved in two major research projects (funded by the Joseph Rowntree Foundation and the ESRC, respectively) investigating partnership working and regional devolution in the UK. He is co-editor with Paul Cloke and Philip Crang of *Introducing human geographies* (London: Arnold, 2000).

Annette Hastings is Lecturer in Urban Regeneration in the Department of Urban Studies, University of Glasgow. Her research focuses on the governance of urban regeneration at the neighbourhood and city scales. She has a particular interest in the implications of how language is used in the urban policy process. She has published on community participation and partnership working in regeneration, the linguistic turn in urban studies and 'image management' in neighbourhood renewal. She is currently researching the role of public services in neighbourhood decline.

Ade Kearns is Professor of Urban Studies in the Department of Urban Studies, University of Glasgow. His research interests include neighbourhood change and social processes, housing, residence and health, and urban policy. He is co-director of the ESRC Centre for Neighbourhood Research, which aims to provide evidence for policy making through the conduct of systematic reviews, secondary analysis of data sets and primary research.

Loretta Lees is Lecturer in Human Geography at King's College London. She is Chair of the Royal Geographical Society–Institute of British Geographers' Urban Geography Research Group. Her research interests are urbanism and the cultural politics of urban space. She has published on gentrification, urban public space, the geography of architecture, urban sociocultural theory, planning discourse and the city more generally. She is currently researching the concept of 'urban community'. She is editor of *The emancipatory city: Paradoxes and possibilities* (London: Sage Publications, 2003).

Zoë Morrison is Lecturer in Human Geography at St Peter's College, Oxford. She is also a research fellow in the School of Geography, Oxford University.

Peter North is Lecturer in Geography at the University of Liverpool. His research interests are urban regeneration, partnership working and urban management, urban protest and urban social movements. His contribution to this book was written while he was a research fellow at the Local Economy Policy Unit at South Bank University and a member of Elephant Links Community Forum.

Stuart Wilks-Heeg is Lecturer in Social Policy at the University of Liverpool. He has published widely on aspects of urban policy and local, as well as regional, governance, and has considerable personal experience of undertaking urban policy evaluation. He is co-author (with Hugh Atkinson) of *Local government* *from Thatcher to Blair: The politics of creative autonomy* (Cambridge: Polity Press, 2000).

Michael Woods is Lecturer in Human Geography at the University of Wales. His research interests are local politics and governance, participation and citizenship, and the politics of rurality. He has recently completed research with Bill Edwards for the ESRC on participation in rural community leadership, and co-directed a Joseph Rowntree Foundation study on partnership working in rural regeneration (with Bill Edwards and Mark Goodwin).

Preface

This book seeks to understand the nature of urban policy in the UK through the context of its main object and subject of regulation; that is, the community. Since the inception of the first formal urban policy in 1968, discourses of community have been pivotal to the development and implementation of a host of urban policy programmes. From the Community Development Projects of the early 1970s to the Challenge Fund Programmes of the late 1990s, the community has been the target and recipient of various forms of government intervention. Such intervention has tended to define target communities as part of geographically bounded areas, characterised by a deficiency of jobs, social skills, educational attainment, high incomes, and social mobility and opportunity. In turn, target communities have often been understood as comprising the socially excluded – or deviant and dysfunctional people – characterised by problems all of their own making. Urban policy programmes, in their various ways, have sought to integrate such people into the norms and values of mainstream liberal society, where the virtues of good parenting, stable family units and self-responsible citizens have been paramount.

The advent of New Labour to power has brought a renewed emphasis on the active involvement and development of communities as core to the successful regeneration of British cities. For New Labour, communities and the individuals that comprise them have been cast as part of the process of urban renaissance and core to the success of urban policy. As the Urban White Paper of 2000 states, communities "must be fully engaged in the process from the start and ... everyone must be included" (p 32). Such engagement is envisaged as part of a new mode of governance, whereby communities are not only the recipients of policy but are active in policy programmes.

This book explores the meaning, and relevance, of New Labour's focus on community as the basis for urban renaissance. In doing so, its contributors interrogate the conceptual and ideological content of New Labour's conceptions of community, and evaluate how far, and with what effects, such conceptions are shaping contemporary urban policy and practice.

Part One
New Labour and the turn to community regeneration

ONE

Community and the changing nature of urban policy

Rob Imrie and Mike Raco

Introduction

Throughout the 1980s and early 1990s, urban policy was dominated by property-led regeneration. Behind this regeneration lay the diagnosis of our cities' problems as a shortfall of physical infrastructure to support the activities of global corporate investors. The removal of supply-side constraints to investment in cities, including the minimisation of local government and community involvement in planning for regeneration and its implementation, was the mantra of Margaret Thatcher and her governments (see Thornley, 1993). Regeneration, Thatcher-style, was characterised by the use of public subsidies, tax breaks, and the reduction in planning and other regulatory controls, as mechanisms to create a context to encourage corporate capital to invest in cities. Cities were, in the words of Michael Heseltine, Minister of the Environment in the early 1980s, to be "incentivised". This, the government argued, would generate investment and create a 'trickle-down' of wealth into local communities so that all would benefit (DoE, 1985).

For many commentators, however, the consequence of Thatcher's social and economic agenda was the intensification of inequality and poverty in the cities (Fainstein et al, 1992; Pacione, 1997; Imrie and Thomas, 1999; Schoon, 2001). As Logan et al (1992) indicate, inequalities in household incomes in London became substantially greater between 1977 and 1988. The ratio of the income of the lowest quartile to the median fell "from 54% in 1980 to 39% in 1988, and that of the lowest docile from 30% to 20%" (Logan et al, 1992, p 132). Other data confirm such trends. For instance, Burgess and Propper (2002) demonstrate that during the 1960s 10% of the British population was in poverty, a figure that declined to 6% by 1977 and then rose sharply to 20% by the early 1990s[1]. Poverty was more evident in some places than in others. In 1991, for instance, Liverpool City Council reported that 40% of Liverpool's population lived in poverty in the previous year, a figure that translated into 6 out of every 10 households in the inner-city wards (see also Merrifield, 1996).

Such data formed part of a recognition that benefits were not necessarily accruing to local communities, and that economic development and related programmes were by-passing the inner cities (Holman, 2000). Various reports and commentaries on the state of British cities highlighted an intensification of geographical inequalities between the wealthy and poor, the advantaged and disadvantaged (Pacione, 1997; Turok and Edge, 1999; Robson et al, 2000). By the end of the 1990s, despite decades of urban policy, British cities were characterised by stark inequalities between rich and poor neighbourhoods. Significant neighbourhood differences, in levels of mortality, educational attainment and per capita incomes, were evidence of policy failure or, as Schoon suggests, "100 years of policy initiatives [that] had almost no impact in the pattern of inequality" (2001, p 83). This was particularly so in relation to ethnic groups, and others, that were geographically segregated and socially excluded from mainstream opportunities and denied access to decent housing and services.

The Labour government came to power in 1997 with a commitment to regenerate Britain's cities by recourse to social inclusion, neighbourhood renewal and community involvement. As Prime Minister Tony Blair said:

> Over the last two decades the gap between these worst estates and the rest of the country has grown.... It shames us as a nation, it wastes lives and we all have to pay the costs of dependency and social division. (Blair, 1998a, p 1)

Such observations were part of a broader consensus that past policies had failed to deliver, and that they were part of the problem of inner-city decline (SEU, 1998; 2000). As the Social Exclusion Unit (SEU) notes, there has been "too much reliance on short-term regeneration", with governments failing "to harness the knowledge and energy of local people" (SEU, 2000, p 7). The SEU also suggests that urban decline was attributable to factors such as "lack of leadership", "a failure to spread what works and encourage innovation" and "too little attention to the problems of worklessness, crime, and poor education" (2000, p 7).

These observations have been translated into a bewildering myriad of policies since the Labour Party came to power. They range in scale from national welfare-to-work programmes, to local, neighbourhood initiatives, such as Inner City 100 Project (www.theinnercity100.org), a scheme that encourages enterprise in disadvantaged communities. In particular, discourses of community are pivotal in framing the policy agenda for cities, and the core of Labour's approach to the revitalisation of cities is the revival of citizenship and the activation of communities to spearhead urban change. As Tony Blair has said, "unless the community is fully engaged in shaping and delivering regeneration, even the best plans on paper will fail to deliver in practice" (SEU, 2000, p 5). In part, this statement recognised, as others had done before, that previous periods of policy had stifled local initiative. Declining neighbourhoods were a feature of cities because little or nothing had been done to empower residents or provide them with the means "to develop their own solutions" (SEU, 2001, p 2).

For Tony Blair and his advisers, the attainment of such solutions depends on the re-scaling of government and the devolution of power to new layers of community governance. Geoff Mulgan, chief adviser to the Prime Minister, has argued:

> To the extent that powers and responsibilities can be passed down to smaller scales, politics and government can be freed to concentrate on what they alone can do ... of thinking strategically, while leaving citizens and communities to govern themselves. (Mulgan, 1998a, p 200)

In particular, Richard Caborn, the Local Regeneration Minister, suggested that "success depends on giving communities the responsibility for making things better, the skills and confidence to get involved, and the power to really achieve their aims" (Caborn, 1999, p 3). Communities, then, are arguably part of the reinvention of government (urban) policy programmes, or where there is a focus on rebuilding the "social in a manner which operationalises the capacities of diverse associations, movements, and groups" (Dean, 1999, p 207; see also Cruikshank, 1999; Raco and Imrie, 2000).

Such rebuilding is to revolve around the *community*, which is, according to the Labour government, the key scale of meaningful human interaction and the basis for the distribution of social obligations and responsibilities. For the Prime Minister, it is not sufficient for people to treat citizenship as solely the conferral of legal rights (which may or may not be exercised). Rather, citizenship is defined by the duty to cooperate with others for the greater public good, as Blair suggests. The responsibility to engage actively in civic affairs as a "self-governing member of a self-governed community" (Dagger, 2000, p 26) is seen by Labour as a prerequisite for the economic revival of cities (see also Rose, 1993; 2000a). In Blair's terms, "for neighbourhood renewal to succeed, individuals also have to take responsibility for the environment in which they live" (Blair, 2001, p 1). For some commentators, such as Etzioni, this conjures up "a society based on its members' voluntary compliance" and the commitment "to a social order that is well balanced with socially secured autonomy" (Etzioni, 1996, p 87).

This chapter sets the context for this volume by documenting the nature of contemporary – that is, New Labour – urban policy and its emphasis on community, citizenship and rights. To do so, we have divided the chapter into three main parts. First, the Labour government's concerns with community are briefly situated within the context of the rise and popularisation of communitarian views on society (see Etzioni, 1996; Newman, 2001). In particular, we explore how far, and in what ways, discourses of community and citizenship have informed previous periods of public policy, with the focus on urban policy programmes. Our argument is that the substance of urban policy has always been associated with particular discourses of community. That is, they variously refer to 'the community' either as an *object* of policy (in other words, a thing to be worked on), a policy *instrument* (that is, the means by which policies become devised and activated), or a thing to be created (an end in itself).

Second, we describe the plethora of approaches to the regeneration of cities adopted by the Labour government and its various policy programmes. We refer to these as part of a degenerate policy culture, and the social construction of issues and target populations as 'deserving' and 'undeserving' groups (see Schneider and Ingram, 1997). These constructions are evident in the ways in which urban problems are defined, labelled and problematised by government, and "made amenable to authoritative action in terms of features of communities and their strengths, cultures, and pathologies" (Rose, 1996a, p 334). It is our contention that one consequence of 'government through community' in British cities is likely to be the creation of new social divisions between those considered to be competent (or active) citizens, "from those who are not" (Rose, 1996a, p 335). Indeed, the potential for people and/or places to be labelled 'inactive' (or dependent or deviant) is part of the policy design which is being applied by the Labour government to the 'renaissance' of Britain's cities.

These arguments are developed in our final part of the chapter, which is a substantive discussion of how far, and in what ways, Labour's focus on 'the community' is contributing to this renaissance. Here we ask (after Foucault, 1977), how does the concept of community function in and through the context of urban policy? Thus, how far are Labour's pronouncements about devolution of power and self-help being translated into settings for individuals and their social networks to influence the regeneration of the cities? What types of communities, and with what resources, motivations and powers, are being cultivated through the context of urban policy? And more, is Labour's emphasis on regeneration through community a genuine break with the past or, as the Audit Commission suggests, just "more of the same" (2002, p 10)? We will attempt to answer these questions before outlining the themes of this volume's individual chapters.

Public policy and discourses of community

Active citizens, through the context of community, represent the mode of governance favoured in the pronouncements of the Labour government. As Tony Blair has said:

> Our policies, programmes and structures of governance are about engaging
> local people in a partnership for change and enabling communities to take
> a decisive role in their future. (Blair, 1998a, p 2)

Such statements are based on a rejection of either the market or the state as the means for organising people's welfare. Rather, the Labour Party has shed its image as a defender of the state, as is well documented. Labour has rejected it as a mode of governance that is "too universal, expensive and bureaucratic" and that stifles "devolved management or individual choice" (Driver and Martell, 1997, p 33; also, see Deakin, 2001; Newman, 2001). Likewise, Labour claims not to support competitive individualism or the operations of unfettered markets, on the basis that they erode social interaction and civic engagement. For Labour, social fragmentation and economic inequalities can only be solved by the pursuit of partnerships between government and civil society. Such partnerships revolve around the development of a society based on connecting individuals with the plurality of broader social networks (Cruikshank; 1998; Dean, 1999), or what the Labour government understands to be communities: that is, the context in which individuals and their actions are tied to society, or where the individual is

> both self responsible and subject to certain emotional bonds of affinity to a circumscribed network of other individuals – unified by family ties, by locality, by moral commitment to environmental protection or animal welfare. (Rose, 1996a, p 334)

Such bonds, as Bowring (2000, p 308) suggests, are crucial to the healthy functioning of society and a recognition that individuals cannot exist or act outside of their mutual obligations to others. Indeed, for Tony Blair, community "is the method through which we can build a society that does not subsume our individuality but allows it to develop healthily" (1998a, p 1).

The pursuit of government through community is based on the Labour government counterposing the positive attributes of personal choice and morality in a community setting with the alleged dehumanising actions of professionals and experts in the context of centralised authority. Whereas the latter is projected as a part of insensitive and remote government, the former is evidence of government by people through the context of civic interaction and engagement. Such views chime with Labour's agenda for change, which is premised, in part, on releasing the energies of people by providing opportunities for participative politics, "local empowerment, and engagement of residents in decisions over their own lives" (Rose, 1996a, p 335). Thus, for Tony Blair:

> After years of intervention centrally ... I want power devolved down in our public services, so that the creative energy of our teachers, doctors, nurses, police officers is incentivised and released. They are the social entrepreneurs of the future. (Blair, 2001, p 1)

These observations are related to a broader series of normative goals of government through community envisaged by Blair. In particular, Labour's policy agenda is closely aligned to the values and views of *communitarianism* (see, for example, Etzioni, 1996; Mulgan, 1998a). Communitarian views are premised on overcoming social fragmentation and the (alleged) breakdown of core aspects of communities, such as parenting, family, voluntary associations and intermediary institutions in civil society. In part, communitarianism represents a tradition concerned with the revival of social structures that will enable strong bonds to be forged between individuals and broader collectives (of which they are a part). Therefore, it laments the loss of consensus and cooperation, and mutuality and civic responsiveness, which, for communitarians, bind society together. Such sentiments are typified by Putnam's observation that "the ebbing of community over the last several decades has been silent and deceptive. We notice its effects ... in the degradation of our public life" (Putnam, 2000, p 403).

Putnam's views, however, are nothing new, and they draw on a long tradition (see also Mumford, 1938; Wirth, 1938). For instance, in the mid-19th century, Benjamin Disraeli (1845, p 6) noted that "in the great cities, men are brought together by the desire of gain. They are not in a state of co-operation ... they are careless of neighbours". Similarly, Louis Wirth's (1938) description of anomie in the industrial city, and Jane Jacobs' (1961) observations about the decline of sociability in American cities, have become perennial themes in urban studies (Robins, 1995; Sandercock, 1998). More recently, Atkinson's work on the decline of Britain's cities offers a familiar story line, linking moral decay and social degeneration to the decline of cities:

> The extended family has shrunk.... The good neighbour is now a scarce
> commodity. Both street and park have become places where horrific crimes
> against young children, women and the elderly spread fear. (Atkinson, 1995,
> p 1)

Such sentiments are evident in New Labour's statements concerning what constitutes the elements of a moral order. At its crux is the restoration of the family as "the basis of a more moral, dutiful and cohesive community" (Driver and Martell, 2002, p 47). Thus, as the government has said, "family life is the foundation on which our communities, our societies, and our country are built" (Straw, 1998). 'Community', given this interpretation, is the aggregation of families connected through social networks, in and through which a cohesive or organic society, with "common goals and a shared vision" (Home Office, 1999, p 3), can emerge. For Labour, 'community' is a natural and desirable social formation, based on the diminution of difference and conflict, and the inculcation of shared values. These values construct 'community' as something that ought to be based on culturally homogeneous social relationships, and what Amin refers to as "a unitary sense of space" (2002a). Indeed, as the Home Office suggests, for community to function, divided groups "should occupy a common sense of place" (2001a, p 70).

Labour's views, therefore, are part of a long tradition, in which organic conceptions of 'community' have been propagated as a basis for the development and delivery of social policy. For instance, the 19th-century American social commentator, Charles Brace, noted that policies to redress social problems in cities ought to provide a "link of sympathy" (1868, p 8) between the classes. For Brace, the American city in the mid-19th century was characterised by social fragmentation, and poverty and dependency were perceived as a threat to community. The social disintegration of the family and the powerlessness of the church were, so it was alleged, at the root of crime and disorder, and necessitated the use of new mechanisms to maintain social order and community cohesion. Such mechanisms emphasised the importance of 'urban charity', and the use of volunteers in conjunction with professionals to develop and deliver the means for (community) self-help (see Bender, 1975). As Brace (1868, p 8) argued, "without volunteers from the respectable classes in personal contact with the unfortunate, community was impossible".

Other documents, predating Blair's administration, note that the 'community' is something to be defined, activated and empowered in the pursuit of specific ends and (policy) objectives (see, for example, Ross, 1955; South East Asian Treaty Organisation, 1966). For instance, a publication by the British Colonial Office defined 'community' as comprising organic coherence with the capacity "for spontaneous self help and regulation and its willingness to participate actively and intelligently in the betterment of plans" (1958, p 2). Likewise, the UN defined the parameters of community development as the potential to create "the conditions whereby the vast under-utilised human resources of local communities may be developed and brought into more effective play" (United Nations, 1967, p 5). In doing so, the UN was advocating policy programmes with objectives that parallel Labour's recent statements, such as "developing the capacity of the average individual ... at the same time that the community as a whole is being renovated" (United Nations, 1967, p 5).

Urban policy in the UK, post-1968, has been characterised by the adoption and absorption of similar policy discourses about community and the regeneration of people and places (DoE, 1972; Higgens et al, 1983). For instance, in 1968 the Home Office argued that the regeneration of British cities depended on "the growth of persons in community" and the need to develop "the awareness of interdependence" (Home Office, 1968, p 3). In a striking resemblance to the policy pronouncements of the Labour government today, urban decline in the 1960s was attributed, in part, to the loss of community, which, as the Home Office suggested, was responsible for "the rising rate of vandalism, child neglect, or isolation among the elderly" (1968, p 2). What was required, the Home Office argued, were policies to supplement the work of social services in neighbourhoods, in order to encourage "the personal and moral growth of individuals" (Higgens et al, 1983, p 16).

Thus, in July 1969, the Home Secretary announced that the local authorities of Coventry, Liverpool and Southwark would be taking part in neighbourhood-based action research experiments. These experiments, known as the Community Development Projects (CDPs), were an attempt to propagate joined-up government by seeking to combine the efforts of national and local government, voluntary groups and universities in finding new ways of supporting (deficient) people and neighbourhoods. For Derek Morrell, architect of the CDPs, they were nothing less than an "experiment in social growth" (quoted in Higgens et al, 1983, p 23). The emphasis was on citizen involvement and self-help, better integration and coordination of government services, and the use of research to provide information for action and for the monitoring and evaluation of policies. The CDPs also reflected the concerns of the Secretary of State for Social Services, Richard Crossman; that is, that policy ought to help communities to "stand more on their own in the future by their own efforts" (quoted in Topping and Smith, 1977, p 9).

By the early 1970s, the number of CDPs had grown to 12, and they were operating alongside the main part of urban policy at that time, the Urban Programme (UP). Both the CDPs and UP projects operated in areas of designated 'special social need', and resources were concentrated on educational projects, refuges for physically and mentally abused women, nursery care and provision, and environmental schemes (see Atkinson and Moon, 1994, for a more detailed account). Their remit was similar: to strengthen community involvement in projects by the formation of resident (and other) groups with the capacity to carry out particular tasks. However, as the documented histories of the period suggest, communities were often difficult to find or to cultivate and operationalise in particular places (Higgens et al, 1983). Even where particular groupings or associations were located and harnessed, it was usually through the context of top-down agencies, such as the local authority.

Indeed, the main difficulties of the early phases of urban policy, in relation to mobilising and responding to inner-city communities, were manifold (Stewart et al, 1976). These included what are now seen as common problems relating to community development. For instance, Stewart et al (1976, pp 3-4) highlighted problems with recruiting experienced or high-quality professionals; the partial nature of policy by tailoring programmes to 'standard' families and communities; difficulties faced by communities in communicating with development agencies; apathy and low take-up rates for particular services; and an unequal distribution of power and influence weighted against particular community groups. Government-imposed targets and stringent deadlines were also anathema to the incorporation of communities into policy programmes. Thus, a government evaluation of partnerships in the UP noted that, in Liverpool, "they have had no time to involve the public but there will be greater community involvement in future years" (DoE, 1981, p 24).

These considerations were of less importance by the late 1970s because of a shift from the CDPs towards policy focused "not on people and communities but on property and physical regeneration" (Colenutt and Cutten, 1994, p 237). Discourses of community in the 1980s were premised, in part, on the understanding that community capacity ought to be developed as a means of reducing government expenditure. As Tom King, then Secretary of State, said, "voluntary groups can do more to tap the resources of the private sector and free government money for the projects that would otherwise not go ahead" (King, 1980). However, the broader political objective of the Conservative governments of the 1980s was a moralisation of individuals in ways that were not dissimilar to the UP, or the policies that have since been put into place by the current Labour government. Pre-empting the pronouncements of Tony Blair, Margaret Thatcher argued that society is not an abstraction, "but a living structure of individuals, families, neighbours and voluntary associations" (1993, p 626). She claimed that "it is our duty to look after ourselves, and then to look after our neighbour" (1987, p 10).

These views were aligned to policies that defined the individual as a sovereign consumer, whose interests were best served by minimal government and the facilitation of choice through the context of the market. Bureaucracy and dependency were to be emasculated through the "establishment of a culture of enterprise and responsible autonomy" (Dean, 1999, p 210). An implication for urban policy was that expenditure on the UP was reduced over the course of the 1980s, and diverted into the Urban Development Corporations (UDCs) and related initiatives that were seeking to provide development opportunities for the (enterprising) private sector. In particular, funding was made available for property-led projects that tended to prioritise economic development and business interests over those of local residents and community groups. In Tiesdell and Allmendinger's terms, the "Thatcher government did not have a comprehensive strategy for neighbourhood regeneration", because it was assumed that a liberalised economy "would provide benefits that would inevitably trickle down" (2001, p 907).

By the late 1980s, however, much dissatisfaction was being expressed by commentators about the partial nature of urban regeneration projects and the failure of benefits to 'trickle down' to poorer neighbourhoods (Cochrane, 1999). For instance, the House of Commons Public Accounts Committee (1989, p 8) criticised urban policy for its lack of social content. Likewise, the House of Commons Select Committee on Employment (1989) noted that UDCs were failing to respond to local need. As it suggested, "UDCs cannot be regarded as a success if buildings and land are regenerated but the local community are bypassed and do not benefit from regeneration" (1989, p 3). Others noted that the neoliberal policies of the 1980s, in encouraging strong central direction and limited local political autonomy, failed to provide a context for communities to exercise "the duty to look after themselves" (Colenutt, 1999, p 234). Rather, regeneration was led from the top and was characterised by partnerships between powerful corporate interests that had little interest in encouraging grass-roots participation.

The effect, for some, was a polarisation of incomes, and an intensification of social disadvantage and poverty in particular parts of the British cities (Logan et al, 1992; Pacione, 1997). Regeneration projects tended to encourage gentrification and rising land values, but did little to tackle an endemic shortage of affordable housing, job insecurity, and the proliferation of low-waged employment. In particular, the persistence of social fragmentation and the intensification of social disadvantage in 'sink estates' were cited as evidence of policy failures and of the difficulties for poorer people to exercise their citizenship through Thatcher's preferred route – as dutiful consumers (Schoon, 2001). Thatcher's referral to individuals, families and voluntary associations as the basis of society rarely translated into active policy programmes to support them, and evidence suggests that 'community' "became a metaphor for the absence or withdrawal of services by the state" (Hoggett, 1997, p 10)

Throughout the early 1990s, a shift towards community participation, partnership and empowerment occurred in urban policy, reflecting new discourses of participation, albeit within the context of competitive bidding programmes. These were dominated by City Challenge and the Single Regeneration Budget (SRB) Challenge Fund, initiatives that required successful bidders to be comprised of partnerships between local authorities, communities, and private sector and voluntary interests (see Oatley, 1998a). As the Conservative government of the time remarked, regeneration could best be achieved by talking "to the people who live and work in those areas" (DoE, 1991). For Michael Heseltine, Secretary of State of the Environment, the partnership approach to regeneration was akin to a new philanthropy. As he said, "it is today's equivalent of that Victorian sense of competitive drive linked with social obligation" (Heseltine, 1991, p 9), an observation that would be later fleshed out by the Labour Party as one of its own defining principles of government.

However, challenge programmes did not fundamentally alter much and had little "impact on the levels of alienation felt by communities in the most deprived urban areas" (Foley and Martin, 2000, p 481). For some, the emerging arrangements were little more than the 'corporatist-style' coalitions redolent of the Thatcher years, developed with the objective of responding to the competitive rules of urban policy. 'Community', in this interpretation, was no more than a means of developing and delivering neoliberal policies based on the inculcation of 'the habits of workfare' among often reticent and disaffected individuals (Eisenschitz and Gough, 1993). Others, such as Lovering (1995), saw little in the way of real empowerment or resources being given to community participants in urban policy. Too often, community groups were "given a mere presence rather than a voice" (Cameron and Davoudi, 1998, p 250), a sentiment that led various commentators to conclude that partnership was a largely discredited notion by the late 1990s (see for example, Colenutt, 1999).

Degenerate policy cultures and the renaissance of British cities

Labour's accession to power in May 1997 was predicated on the modernisation of government by continuing the process, first started in the late 1970s, of dismantling the cornerstones of the postwar welfare state. For Labour, state reform was necessary, in the words of the Home Secretary because of "declining popular confidence in the ability of institutions to do their job, and to respond to the needs of the communities that they are supposed to serve" (Blunkett, 2001, p 109). Labour's agenda for change was based on the understanding that there was too much reliance by individuals on the power of the state, or that individuals and communities "still often expect government to deliver as though we were in a by-gone era" (Blunkett, 2002a, p 1). Rather, for Blunkett, as well as others in the Labour Party, "government never could do it all.... We have deluded ourselves if we believed we could simply deliver from the centre" (Blunkett, 2002a, p 1; see also Etzioni, 1996; Giddens, 1998; Mulgan, 1998a).

Such views have underpinned Labour's promotion of selected imaginations of the prewar era as the basis for the reform of the welfare state. For instance, Blunkett has emphasised a historical ethos of mutualism in Britain, which, so he alleges, has been undermined by the welfare state (also, see Mulgan, 1998b). As he suggests:

> Britain has a history of people working together but all too often government policies – like regeneration initiatives – have been focused too much on building physical infrastructure and imposing services on people rather than engaging them in decision-making. (Blunkett, 2002b, p 1)

Rather, it is the responsibility of individuals and communities, working in "joint endeavour" with government, to develop their own risk-minimising welfare strategies (Blunkett, 2002a, p 1). This shift in responsibilities requires a new, flexible state that puts policy efficiency and delivery above all else, so that, in Blair's much quoted aphorism, 'what matters is what works'.

Not surprisingly, policy reforms since 1997 have been underpinned by the notion that the state should take on a facilitating role in which it "should exercise only limited powers of its own, steering and regulating rather than rowing and providing" (Rose, 2000c, pp 323-24). In Blair's terms, this involves a 'hand-up, not a hand-out', in which communities and individuals should be encouraged to help themselves rather than depend on others – that is, the state – to lift them out of their difficulties. Accordingly, Labour's approach to urban regeneration is based, first and foremost, on policies designed to provide people with the skills and capacities to reduce (their) poverty and dependence on welfare. Thus, benefit reforms have been combined with job subsidies to shift people from welfare to work and, following the Urban White Paper (DETR, 2000e), and the SEU report on Neighbourhood Renewal (2000), government spending is increasingly targeted towards assisting those living in alleged problem communities (see Chapter Four of this volume). In particular, the practice of 'bending' mainstream spending programmes – health, education and housing – has become a core component of the government's approach to tackling disadvantage and deprivation in cities. As a Home Office brief argues:

> [R]eal improvements will be achieved in these areas by raising the standard of public services in the country's most deprived areas, by dramatically lifting standards of employment, educational attainment, housing, health, and lowering crime rates. (Home Office, 2001a, p 1)

This reflects, in part, a recognition that local initiatives have been undermined in the past by broader government spending, which has at times transferred greater resources to more affluent places (for example, those specialising in the defence industry) at the expense of others (see Lovering, 1995). In seeking to redress this, the result is a plethora of policy programmes. As Figure 1.1 indicates, it seems as though any government initiative, in whatever sphere of public policy, qualifies as an 'urban policy'.

Figure 1.1: Policy programmes that have 'some relevance to urban policy'

Business and Investment

- Partnership Investment Programme
- Business Improvement Districts
- Coalfields Enterprise Fund
- Community Development Venture Fund
- Community Investment Credit
- English Cities Fund; English Partnerships and Regional Development Agency Coalfield Programme
- Heritage Economic Regeneration Schemes
- Higher Education Innovation Fund
- Inner City 100 Project
- Local Tax Re-investment Programme
- Network Space
- New Entrepreneur Scholarships
- 100% capital allowances for flats over shops for letting
- 100% tax credit for contaminated land clean-up
- Phoenix Fund; Public Sector Research Establishment Fund
- Reducing Business Rates for small businesses
- Regional Innovation Fund
- Regional Venture Capital Funds
- Remove VAT burden on sale of renovated houses empty for 10 plus years; Research and Development Tax Credit
- Science Enterprise Challenge
- Small Firms Loan Guarantee Scheme
- Stamp Duty exemption in certain disadvantaged communities
- UK High Technology Fund; University Challenge
- University for Industry (learndirect)
- VAT reduced to 5% for residential conversions

Community

- Active Community – match funding for volunteering
- Active Community Funding Package Experience Corps; Better Government for Older People Programme
- Business Improvement Districts
- City Academies
- Coalfields Enterprise Fund
- Coalfields Regeneration Trust
- Community Chests
- Community Development Venture Fund
- Community Investment Credit
- Education Action Zones
- English Cities Fund
- English Partnerships and RDA Coalfield Programme
- Ethnic Minority Achievement Grant Programme
- Fuel Duty Rebate for Community Transport
- Health Action Zones
- Health Improvement Programmes
- Healthy Living Centres
- Heritage Economic Regeneration Schemes
- Home Zones
- Housing Renewal Areas
- Inner City 100 Project
- Local Tax Re-investment Programme

- Mentoring Fund; Millennium Communities
- Neighbourhood Renewal Fund
- Neighbourhood Support Fund
- Neighbourhood Wardens
- Network Space
- New Deal for Communities
- New Opportunities Fund
- Green Spaces and Sustainable Communities Programme
- Transforming Communities Programme
- New Strategy for Rough Sleeping
- Pilot Clear Zones

- Safer Communities Housing Fund
- School Sport Co-ordinators
- Space for Sport and the Arts scheme
- Special Grants Programme
- Sports Action Zones
- Area-based Stamp Duty exemption
- Supporting People Programme
- Sure Start local programmes
- Urban Bus Challenge Fund
- VAT relief for listed buildings that are places of worship
- Reallocation of Lottery Community Projects Fund

Crime and Community Safety

- Crime and Disorder Partnerships
- Crime Reduction Programme
- Expansion of Closed Circuit Television

- Neighbourhood Wardens
- Projects to Reduce Domestic Burglary
- Safer Communities Housing Fund

Education and Training

- Advanced Modern Apprenticeships
- Catch-up Programmes
- Childcare Tax Credit payments to increase employment take-up
- City Academies
- ConneXions Services
- Creative Partnerships
- Education Action Zones
- Employment Zones
- Environment Task Force option of the New Deal for Young People
- Ethnic Minority Achievement Grant Programme
- Excellence in Cities and Excellence Challenge
- Extended Mortgage Interest Income Support run on
- Higher Education Innovation Fund

- Job Grant
- National Child Care Strategy
- Neighbourhood Support Fund
- New Deal for Schools Capital Funding
- New Deal Programme for the 50+
- New Entrepreneur Scholarships
- Paid time off to pursue qualifications
- Pilot Education Maintenance Allowance
- Public Sector Research Establishment Fund
- RDA Regional Skills Development Funds
- Science Enterprise Challenge
- School Sport Co-ordinators
- Space for Sport and the Arts scheme
- Sure Start local programmes
- University Challenge
- University for Industry (learndirect)

Figure 1.1 contd.../

Environment

- English Partnerships and RDA Coalfield Programme
- Environmental Action Fund
- Environment Task Force option of the New Deal for Young People
- Heritage Economic Regeneration Schemes
- Heritage Lottery Fund Urban Parks + Townscape Heritage Initiatives
- Home Energy Efficiency Scheme
- Home Zones

- Millennium Communities
- New Opportunities Fund
- Green Spaces and Sustainable Communities Programme
- New Opportunities Fund Transforming Communities Programme
- Pilot Clear Zones
- Special Grants Programme

Health and Well-Being

- Health Action Zones
- Health Improvement Programmes
- Healthy Living Centres
- Reallocation of Lottery Community Projects Fund

- Remove VAT burden on sale of renovated houses empty for 10 plus years
- School Sport Co-ordinators
- Space for Sport and the Arts scheme
- Sports Action Zones

Homes and Housing

- Homebuy and Shared Ownership Schemes
- Home Energy Efficiency Scheme
- Housing Renewal Areas
- New Strategy for Rough Sleeping
- 100% capital allowances for flats over shops for letting

- Safer Communities Housing Fund
- Stamp Duty Exemption in Disadvantaged Communities
- Starter Home Initiative for key workers
- Supporting People Programme
- VAT reduced or refurbishment of empty homes

Land and Planning

- Alternatives to the Partnership Investment Programme
- English Cities Fund, English Partnerships and RDA Coalfield Programme

- 100% Tax Credit for contaminated land clean-up
- VAT reduced to 5% for residential conversions

Leisure and Sport

- Creative Partnerships
- Heritage Lottery Fund Urban Parks + Townscape Heritage Initiatives
- New Opportunities Fund (NOF) Green Spaces and Sustainable Communities Programme

- Reallocation of Lottery Community Projects Fund
- School Sport Co-ordinators
- Space for Sport and the Arts scheme
- Sports Action Zones

Transport and Traffic

- Fuel Duty Rebate for community transport
- Home Zones

- Pilot Clear Zones
- Road maintenance and street lighting
- Urban Bus Challenge Fund

In central government, the drive towards 'mainstreaming' is being spearheaded by the Neighbourhood Renewal Unit (NRU) in the Office of the Deputy Prime Minister (ODPM), and institutionalised through a range of Public Service Agreements (PSAs) drawn up between Whitehall departments and the Treasury. Figure 1.2 outlines the PSA targets for deprived areas, which are designed to tailor programmes to local needs and requirements. In seeking to justify the approach, the government has stated in its Spending Review that "in future, core public services like schools and the police should be equipped to become the main weapons against deprivation" (HM Treasury, 2000, para 23.3). This requires nothing less than "re-focusing main programmes to ensure that improving life in deprived neighbourhoods is one of their key objectives", while simultaneously "creating new and stronger co-ordinating mechanisms at the local level to enable services to work together more effectively" (HM Treasury, 2000, para 23.3).

Such sentiments reflect the Labour government's desire to avoid the mistakes of past policies. As the SEU (1998) has suggested, these mistakes included – among others – 'parachuting in' solutions instead of involving communities, a failure to 'bend' mainstream programmes to benefit the poorest communities, and the absence of a long-term political commitment to the regeneration of the cities. In seeking to avoid these, the NRU has been joined by a range of other institutions to create an institutionally thick arena in order that the development and filtration of policy between different policy scales can be coordinated. Their remit is to shift:

> more responsibility for policy delivery away from central government departments, and to allow local flexibility in policy implementation. Devolution and delegation to more local levels means that those with the best knowledge of what is needed have the freedom to implement the most appropriate policies for their area, leaving the scope for creative and innovative solutions that are focused on local needs. (HM Treasury, 2002, para 4.8)

However, at the local level, responsibility for policy development has not reverted to local authorities, as was the case in earlier rounds of urban policy. Instead, it has shifted to a range of supra-local organisations based on partnerships, including Neighbourhood Renewal Teams, Local Strategic Partnerships (LSPs) and Regional Development Agencies (RDAs), all operating under central government control and guidance. For instance, the Treasury notes that "government views the RDAs, rather than local authorities, as the key strategic drivers of economic development and regeneration in the regions" (HM Treasury, 2000, para 23.8). Likewise, the establishment of 12 Urban Regeneration Companies (URCs) is indicative of a quango-led approach to regeneration, not unlike that pursued by Thatcher in the 1980s. Thus, the URCs "should be capable of acting swiftly, as a single purpose delivery body to lead and co-ordinate the regeneration of neighbourhoods in accordance with the objectives of a wider local strategy" (Urban Task Force, 1999, pp 147-9).

Figure 1.2: Public service agreement targets

Issue	Government lead department	Local lead	Target
Employment	DfES/DWP	Employment Service, New Deal Partnerships, Action Teams for Jobs	Increase employment rates of 30 local authority districts with the poorest initial labour market conditions and narrow the gap between these and the overall rates
	DTI	Small Business Service	Generate more sustainable enterprise in disadvantaged communities
	DfES/ODPM	Regional Development Agencies	Increase the employment rates of disabled people, lone parents, ethnic minorities and over 55s, and narrow the gap between these rates and the overall rate
Crime	Home Office	Crime and disorder reduction partnerships	Reduce domestic burglary by 25%, with no local authority district having a rate more than three times the national average by 2005
Education	DfES	Schools and Local Education Authorities (LEAs)	Increase the percentage of pupils obtaining 5 or more GCSEs at A*-C, with at least 38% to achieve this standard in every LEA, and 25% in every school
Health	DH	Health authorities/care trusts/local authorities	To narrow the health gap between socioeconomic groups and between the most deprived areas and the rest of the country
Housing and the environment	ODPM	Local authorities and social landlords	Reduce by 33% the number of households living in non-decent social housing by 2004
Environment	ODPM/DEFRA	Local authorities	Improve air quality in most deprived neighbourhoods
	ODPM/DEFRA	Local authorities	Improve by 2003 the recycling and composting of household waste

Notes: DfES = Department for Education and Skills, DWP = Department for Work and Pensions, DTI = Department of Trade and Industry, ODPM = Office of the Deputy Prime Minister, DH = Department of Health, DEFRA = Department for the Environment, Food and Rural Affairs

Source: Adapted from Social Exclusion Unit (2000)

Interestingly, the plethora of new institutions, operating at a range of spatial scales, seems to suggest that the emphasis on mainstreaming has not supplanted the staple approach of urban policy: that is, the alleviation of deprivation and poverty in neighbourhoods by use of area-based initiatives (ABIs). As Figure 1.3 shows, Labour's first term was characterised by a proliferation of spatial initiatives, such as Health Action Zones (HAZs), Employment Action Zones and Education Zones, that sought to put into practice a series of measures targeted on what were alleged to be problem communities and places. Indeed, within months of coming into power, the government issued a set of new guidelines that promoted ABIs as a critical element, alongside 'mainstreaming', in "a concerted attack against the multiple causes of social and economic decline" in the cities (DETR, 1997, pp 1-2). This set the tenor for pronouncements by the Treasury, which subsequently said that government must ensure "that area-targeted initiatives play a role that is genuinely additional to main services, rather than attempting to compensate for their failings" (HM Treasury, 2000, para 23.3).

The development of ABIs is indicative in part of Labour's commitment to a political agenda, which enables the locality to become "the subject rather than the object of development" (Eisenschitz and Gough, 1993, p 11). Of most significance in this respect is the New Deal for Communities (NDC), launched in 1998 to increase the number of people in work, improve education levels, reduce crime and improve people's health (see Benjamin, 2001). The NDC has a budget of £2 billion to be spent over 10 years in 39 neighbourhoods of between 1,000 and 4,000 households. Each scheme comprises a local partnership involving residents, community organisations, local authorities and local businesses. The NDC differs from previous initiatives in that executive boards are not given the bulk of their funding until they have engaged local communities in the development of wide-ranging regeneration plans. Advocates argue that this gives residents a new level of responsibility that inspires communities "by their real influence over decisions and budgets" (Dwelly, 2001, p 1).

The NDC has been backed up by other major initiatives, such as the extension of the SRB (see Chapters Seven and Eight of this volume). The SRB, first started in 1994, has been reshaped to target 80% of its resources on the 65 most deprived areas in Britain, with the funding of projects conditional on the direct involvement of local communities. Likewise, the £800 million Neighbourhood Renewal Fund (NRF) was set up in 2000 to provide resources, primarily to LSPs, to improve housing, raise school standards, reduce crime and improve health in deprived areas. As John Prescott, the Deputy Prime Minister, said when announcing the NRF:

> This fund will help our most deprived communities ... tackle their main concerns, creating stronger more inclusive communities for everyone. (Prescott, 2000, p 1)

Figure 1.3: Key government Action Zone Programmes

Programme	Date	Objectives	Resources
Education Action Zones	2000 (onwards)	Allows deprived areas to set up partnerships to target areas of need and to develop innovative and radical solutions for raising educational standards	73 large zones, 58 small zones. Small zones receive up to £350,000 per year in public and private funds
Education in Cities Action Zones (EiCAZs)	2002	To establish local partnerships of schools, parents, businesses, local communities and local authorities to address the educational problems of major cities, to target action and to develop innovative and radical solutions to raise educational standards	102 EiCAZs, each receives £250,000/ year for three years
Health Action Zones	1998-2002 (onwards)	To tackle inequalities in health in the most deprived areas of England through health and social care modernisation programmes, and address other interdependent and wider determinants of health, such as housing, education and employment and linking with other initiatives	26 zones, £270 million
Home Zones	2001 (onwards)	To improve the quality of life in residential areas of England	£30 million over three years
Pilot Clear Zones	2001 (onwards)	This programme helps to create liveable, accessible and lively urban centres where traffic congestion, pollution, noise, stress and other negative effects of mobility are eliminated or reduced. It does this through a package of transport-related measures using innovative technologies	Nine pilots selected, no separate funding
Sports Action Zones (SAZs)	2001 (onwards)	Aims to improve sporting provision in areas of high social, economic and sporting deprivation	12 SAZs identified, five-year programme, funded £70,000 from Sport England

Source: Adapted from ODPM (2002); HM Treasury (2002)

However, the fund comes with 'strings attached': eligible authorities, such as LSPs, can only access it if they have an approved local neighbourhood renewal strategy.

The development and implementation of such policy programmes is predicated on communities having the capacity to engage as democratic agents. This was the view of the Urban White Paper, which stated that "we intend to build the capacity of communities to help themselves and bring about social cohesion right across the country" (DETR, 2000e, p 6). The SEU reinforced this by noting that "the most effective (policy) interventions are often where communities are actively involved in their design and delivery, and, where possible, in the driving seat" (SEU, 2000, para 1.19). To this end, Labour has identified capacity building as core to the success of urban policy, or where communities are to be provided with the skills and knowledge to become active in eradicating (their) poverty and deprivation. Communities are to be worked on, (re)shaped, and improved (in Foucault's terms) and, as Mulgan suggests, to be made "stronger, more responsible, more capable of making decisions and understanding the world in which they live" (1998a, p 11).

The propagation of the active society is, in part, the particular remit of the Orwellian-sounding Active Community Unit (ACU), set up in the Home Office in 1998 to spearhead the government's initiatives to promote community self-help as a basis of neighbourhood renewal. The unit was given specific responsibility to develop and deliver an action plan for community self-help to enable an increase in "the amount of volunteering and community activity in poor neighbourhoods" (Boateng, 1999, p iii). By 2005-6 it will be funded, at a cost of £65 million per year. The ACU aims to support and nurture community organisations through the provision of small grants, support and advice, and to boost their capacities to engage with policy-making processes and practices. As Blunkett suggests, the ACU is designed to play a catalytic role in bringing about change within communities, primarily by involving one million people "actively in their communities" by 2004 (Blunkett, 2002a, p 6).

The activities of the ACU are occurring alongside other programmes that, Labour claims, will provide local citizens with the skills to act as equal partners with councils and other agencies (see Figure 1.4). In particular, the government notes that one of the significant problems faced by citizens is their estrangement from, and lack of involvement in, technocratic/bureaucratic decision-making processes. In trying to redress this, the SEU has introduced a Community Empowerment Fund of £35 million to provide residents with training and consultation support. Likewise, Community Chests, launched in 2002, seek to support "the activities of formal and informal community groups in the 88 most deprived areas ... as a first step towards their more formal involvement in neighbourhood renewal" (ODPM, 2002, p 1). A Voluntary Sector Investment Fund, to "tackle barriers to effective service delivery and modernise the sector for the future" (HM Treasury, 2002, para 30.7), has also been established to empower local communities, by enhancing their capacities to assist in the delivery of welfare services.

Figure 1.4: Key community-focused initiatives under New Labour

Programme	Date	Objectives	Resources
Active Community Unit (ACU)	2002 onwards	To develop and deliver an action plan for community self-help to enable an increase in the amount of volunteering and community activity in poor neighbourhoods	£120 million
ACU Experience Corps Scheme	2002 onwards	Establish 'Experience Corps' for the over 50s, which will allow them to pass on their skills and experience to help others. The initiative will provide marketing to encourage volunteers and a network of local fieldworkers to develop volunteering opportunities	Not a grant programme
Community Chests	2002 onwards	This programme supports the activities of formal and informal community groups in the 88 most deprived areas. This is a first step towards their more formal involvement in neighbourhood renewal	Not yet announced
Community Development Venture Fund	2000 onwards	Aims to increase community business ventures in deprived areas	£10 million per year
Community Empowerment Fund	2000 onwards	To support residents with training and consultation support to allow them to act as equal partners with councils and other agencies locally	£35 million for grants
Community Finance and Learning Initiative	2001 onwards	To improve the basic financial literacy and access to final services of communities in deprived areas to tackle financial exclusion	–
Health Improvement Programmes		HImPs are local health strategies developed by health and local authorities and other key stakeholders, such as Primary Care Groups and NHS Trusts. They include local communities, which set out national health priorities in a local context. It includes local targets to tackle issues which are judged important locally, with particular emphasis on health inequality in local communities	No specific funding
Healthy Living Centres	2002 onwards	This initiative aims to develop a network of healthy living centres across the UK, accessible to the most disadvantaged 20% of the population and complementing the government's wider public health policy and social exclusion agenda. Healthy living centres will offer a range of services, focusing on wider health factors and reflecting the needs of local communities	£300 million

Figure 1.4: continued

Programme	Date	Objectives	Resources
Millennium Communities	1999 onwards	Four initiatives in Greenwich (London); Allerton Bywater (Leeds); Cardroom Estate (Manchester); and Nar Ouse (Kings Lynn). Advice on developing land as sustainable mixed use development	No specific funding
Neighbourhood Renewal Fund/ National Strategy Action Plan	2000-2003	To provide support for 88 local authorities in England to enable them to improve services in their most deprived areas	£900 million
New Deal for Communities	2000-2010 (Round One), 2001-2011 (Round Two)	To support the regeneration of individual deprived neighbourhoods of between 2,000 and 4,000 residents, through 39 community-based inclusive partnerships across England	£774 million committed to support 17 Round One partnerships; total including Round Two approaching £10 billion over 10 years
Single Regeneration Budget (SRB) (Rounds One to Six)	1994-2005	To enhance the quality of life of local people in areas of need by reducing the gap between deprived and other areas and between different groups To harness the talent, resources and experience of local businesses, the voluntary sector and the local community	900 schemes, £5.5 billion
New Opportunities Fund – Transforming Community Programme	2001 onwards	This programme promotes environmental renewal and community regeneration. It also supports recycling and the development of renewable energy sources	£159 million to be made available

Source: Adapted from ODPM (2002); HM Treasury (2002)

23

However, such measures are problematic for assuming that a lack of civic participation is the problem to be addressed, rather than the often exclusive character of policy decision-making processes, for instance. Moreover, organisations such as the ACU are part of an apparatus directed towards the development of policy that is both voluntary and coercive. In particular, Labour's programmes for an urban renaissance are underpinned by an analysis of urban populations that does not deny that individual apathy and docility may, in some ways, be responsible for poverty and deprivation. Thus, measures such as the Working Families' Tax Credit, the National Childcare Strategy and the Out of School Childcare Initiative are designed as incentives for paid employment, and threaten those unwilling or unable to take up new 'opportunities' with the restriction of benefit entitlement. Labour's aim is to remove barriers to paid employment for those drawing benefits (primarily single mothers and low-income households) and living in deprived areas, so that they can actively engage with paid work and thus bring themselves – and their communities – out of poverty (Scott et al, 2002).

The focus on individual deficiency is, arguably, at the core of other programmes that propagate Labour's belief that poor communities will only make progress if their members become informed and knowledgeable citizens (as empowered consumers) who can then make personal decisions to overcome whatever problems that they have. For instance, the Community Finance and Learning Initiative (CFLI), a programme that is being piloted by the Department for Education and Skills (DfES) at the time of writing, aims to encourage individuals and communities to improve their basic financial literacy skills and access financial services, such as bank accounts and debt management. In doing so, the DfES notes that the initiative will "help people understand how best to manage their finances, get on top of their debts and begin to think about saving" (DfES, 2002, p 1). Explaining the background to the CFLI, Oatley suggests that financial exclusion will be tackled "by promoting learning opportunities in adult literacy and numeracy (including financial literacy) and facilitating better access to mainstream financial services" (2002, p 163).

Despite its merits, the policy runs the risk of blaming the victims for their plight. Such potential pathologising of the urban poor is also evident in measures that seek to inculcate 'good habits' and forge character and wellbeing in individuals in deprived places. For instance, government has argued that poor health in urban communities is not a consequence of socioeconomic deprivation, but rather its cause (through poor productivity, poor take-up on training and employment schemes, and so on). Thus, poor health is a problem of place, of local cultures and dietary habits, which requires policy action to bring about changing modes of living within the locality. As Figure 1.5 indicates, initiatives such as the HAZs and Healthy Living Centres are being conducted through the actions of citizens and communities who are required to change their patterns of behaviour and social practices to tackle the problem of poor health. Parallel shifts in policies to tackle crime, antisocial behaviour and training provision have also taken place.

Figure 1.5: Nottingham's Health Action Zone

East's (2002) study of a HAZ in the district of Sneinton, Nottingham, is an example of the development of an ABI. Sneiton is a typical inner-urban location, characterised by housing built during the area's industrial heyday of the 19th century, and possessing a range of socioeconomic problems. It is an area of ethnic and social diversity and was subject to a City Challenge project between 1992 and 1997. It has subsequently been declared a key part of Nottingham's HAZ, drawing on a three-way partnership between government, communities and individuals to improve the health of the local population.

The original policy statement declared that improving health rates "is a challenge for every individual ... though, in particular, the health inequalities experienced by those who reside in areas of deprivation" (Nottinghamshire County Council, 2000, p 10). East's study highlights a series of difficulties that have emerged about the definition of health issues, and the differences of opinion within local communities in relation to health priorities. There are differences between experts, who categorise local health priorities in technocratic-bureaucratic ways, and local lay communities, which have their own agendas and priorities. The latter tend to focus on perceived threats to local health (such as the potential for pollution from a local incinerator), whereas the former are concerned with improving the health of local communities in order to facilitate enhanced socioeconomic regeneration.

In the development of the local strategy, lay perspectives were frequently marginalised as they conflicted with expert opinion and failed to address the government's wider directives for HAZs, namely the promotion of healthy urban spaces. Within local communities, different views, over the form and character of the neighbourhood, have also undermined efforts to develop a local consensus-based approach. Some, for example, have adopted explicitly racist agendas, whereas others have argued that the regeneration programmes for the area ought to focus on different priorities.

For East, the case study shows "that very different world views can share the same geographical space ... divisions based on age, gender, class and ethnicity proved to be more important in shaping the lives of local residents" (2002, pp 169-70). The operationalisation of the HAZ has, therefore, become an increasingly bureaucratic exercise, designed to fulfil particular targets, rather than seeking to uncover, and respond to, the range of health issues in the locality.

Source: East (2002)

What we have here, then, is a policy design that targets a population (in this case, the poor) along the lines of an entrenched stereotype – that is, the poor are a problem because they are dependent and deviant. This, for Schneider and Ingram (1997), is a characteristic of a degenerate policy design (where social constructions separate the 'deserving' from the 'undeserving', and where the latter are subject to policy tools that become increasingly punitive). Such constructions are also dependent on economic incentives and disincentives as policy tools, which "reinforce self interest as the dominant human motivation and create contexts in which other motivations, such as public regardedness, are destined to lose" (Schneider and Ingram, 1997, pp 193-4). This is something of an irony given Labour's intent to enhance social capital, or individuals' capacities to interact and network as the basis for the renewal of sociability in cities (see Chapter Two of this volume).

Towards an evaluation of the urban renaissance

The Labour government has embarked on a series of urban policy initiatives that, even if they overlap and contradict one another at times, do represent something of a commitment to the regeneration of Britain's cities. There is genuine willingness in parts of the Labour government to tackle urban problems such as poverty and poor housing, a willingness that is reflected in a renewed political emphasis in pursuing an urban renaissance (see Tiesdell and Allmendinger, 2001). This emphasis has led to an appraisal of the relationship between state and citizen, with the government seeking to adopt particular mentalities, in which citizens'"rights in the city are as much about [the fulfilment] of duties as they are about entitlements" (Osborne and Rose, 1999, p 752). While it is too early to assess, empirically, much of the impact and effectiveness of such statements in contributing to the renaissance of British cities, some of the tensions and contradictions that underpin aspects of the emergent policy programmes have become apparent.

First and foremost are the paradoxical, even contradictory, ways in which communities, and their involvement in urban regeneration, have been conceived by the Labour government. Thus, for Labour, communities are characterised as being beyond politics – apolitical entities – while simultaneously being the vehicle in and through which urban policy agendas are to be mobilised and delivered (Rose 2000a). They are portrayed, in pathological-underclass terms, as entities that inculcate individuals with the values of immoral behaviour, disorder and (welfare-state) dependency, while simultaneously being promoted as a source of moral good, whose corrosion lies at the heart of urban problems and disorder (Blair, 1998a). Communities are also an object and instrument of policy, as a key part of technocratic policy design and, at the same time, the alleged subject of programmes of empowerment and self-actualisation (Kogan, 1999; Southern, 2001).

Alongside this, new managerial practices that espouse rational solutions to urban policy problems have, paradoxically, reinforced and expanded the role of experts and expert knowledge, rather than, in many instances, making policy more responsive to community needs and aspirations. Thus, the requirement to institutionalise community views is designed to empower planners and decision makers by providing them with increased knowledge of targeted populations and places. For instance, the Urban Task Force Report and the Urban White Paper note that the key to urban regeneration is not to be found by recourse to lay viewpoints per se; rather, it is to draw on the knowledge of architects, designers and planners to enhance urban spaces and the lives of communities (see Chapter Three of this volume). Not surprisingly, large sums of government money have been spent on hiring 'expert' consultants from the private sector – indeed, one critic has dubbed the NDC "the new deal for consultants" (Jones, quoted in Weaver, 2002a, p 1).

The enhanced role for experts is reinforced by managerial systems that require local agencies and communities to open themselves up to bureaucratic scrutiny. Communities are required to be transparent, accountable for their actions, and to be judged on their ability to match targets and objectives imposed from above. Guidelines adopted by the DETR, concerning tenant involvement in the management of housing estates for example, note that once local communities establish an input into policy-making processes, they then have a responsibility to "comply with public service principles of accountability, confidentiality, financial propriety and working within the relevant statutory and regulatory constraints" (DETR, 1999a, p 4). Although the guidelines are voluntary and supposed to reflect the wishes of local agents, they state that communities must adhere to disciplinary frameworks established by central government. Thus, communities are expected to "take a realistic and practical view of what is appropriate if they wish to increase their levels of involvement" (DETR, 1999a, p 14).

Not surprisingly, designing policy to facilitate particular practices and technologies of government is not necessarily congruent with the expectations, needs and perceptions of individuals and communities. East states that "as residents we do not see our lives in terms of problems to be addressed and solutions to be achieved within a specified time-scale" (2002, p 170). Others concur, with the Audit Commission noting that communities' interest in neighbourhood renewal is limited and, as a topic, is unlikely "to engage with disengaged and disaffected people" (2002, p 3). Monbiot (2001) also notes that decisions about regeneration are more likely than not to be 'stitched up' by powerful players behind closed doors. Indeed, despite the repeated assertions that urban policy is now community-focused, and oriented towards the involvement and activation of local knowledge in the policy process, the practices of urban governance remain highly centralised and output-focused. Communities are often 'shoehorned' on to local policy initiatives according to central government guidelines, and this is limiting the effectiveness of programmes on the ground.

For instance, Weaver (2002) recounts an NDC initiative in north-east London in which community tenants proposed plans for the improvement of local housing through local authority-led action (see Figure 1.6). These were rejected by central government because they were counter to Labour's policy of transferring homes to housing associations. The community was told to go back and come up with an 'appropriate' (that is, Labour government-approved) solution. Likewise, Edwards' research on the SRB notes that "there was little real involvement of voluntary and community groups in projects" (Chapter

Eight of this volume). Similarly, the Urban Forum (1997) identified substantial variation in the quality of the voluntary and community sectors' involvement in the SRB. This evidence suggests that regeneration initiatives are driven by a "policy of inclusion but on terms which have already been defined and set outside the community" (Diamond, 2001, p 277). In this sense, the role of community in urban policy appears to be not much more than "a key construct in the formation of a managerial process" (Schofield, 2002, p 665).

Figure 1.6: The Shoreditch NDC

The Shoreditch NDC, in the London Borough of Hackney, is a 10-year, £180 million regeneration programme that was initiated in February 2000. It is operated by the Shoreditch New Deal Trust Project Team and is designed to bring about the wholesale regeneration of the area. The programme "aims to bring lasting improvements to the community of Shoreditch by tackling worklessness and crime, improving education and health and housing conditions. Shoreditch New Deal Trust, a community led partnership, has been established to deliver the programme" (RENAISI, 2002, p 1).

The Shoreditch project was one of the first two NDC projects to be announced in February 2000 and represents a pioneering attempt to establish a community-led approach. However, the scheme has run into problems, particularly over the issue of housing provision. Local community activists, using surveys of tenants' views, have been calling for the development of social housing, so that local people are able to stay in the area and benefit from the regeneration. However, the government and the local authority "are concerned about the high concentrations of council housing in the area" and "want to see more homes for key workers and more houses for sale" (Weaver, 2001b, p 1).

A local activist claimed that the shift to owner-occupied housing represented an attempt to push local residents out of the area. He said, "many of us believe the ... plan is a crude attempt by the authorities to push working class people out of Shoreditch replacing us with middle income key workers and solving the social problems of poverty and deprivation. But we don't want to go" (Butler, 2001, p 1). The consequential dispute came to a head in October 2001 when the local community rejected the regeneration plan to transfer their council-run homes to a housing association. In response, local and central government withheld £20 million that was due to be spent in the area.

This episode exemplifies the structured nature of community involvement in urban regeneration. If community policy agendas differ, or run counter to what central and local government believe is the 'right' thing to do, then various disciplinary technologies and financial systems may be used to restrict the resources available. Conversely, giving responsibilities to communities to make decisions may encourage parochial politics in which local objectives are privileged over the 'broader needs' of other social groups.

Source: Weaver (2001a)

This is also evident in the NDC, in which projects have been slow to get going and have been dominated by central government directives over what the form and character of local community-based regeneration programmes should be (Diamond, 2001; Audit Commission, 2002). Weaver (2002b) suggests that the NDC projects have failed to spend two thirds of the £360 million allocated to them due to central interference. His research found that "money has often gone unspent because the government has rejected many of the proposals put forward by communities [so that] the New Deal is only community-led if the community comes up with the right answers" (Weaver, 2002b, p 2). This underspending is also a consequence of idealised notions of community in which local partnerships are required to develop a consensus view of local community needs and involvement, something that in many places has been impossible to achieve.

In part, this is because policy assumes that latent communities exist which can be identified, targeted and incorporated into government policy. However, as Amin (2002a) suggests, neighbourhoods are based on diverse attachments to place, and are open, culturally heterogeneous and socially variegated. Such spaces are not easily amenable to the Labour government's view that dialogical and cohesive communities, based on common values and trust, can be brought together to establish consensus-based programmes of action. For instance, following the riots in Oldham, Bradford and Burnley in 2001, the government responded by arguing that it was a lack of mixing between different ethnic communities that was a significant element in causing the riots. Yet, for Amin, the riots highlight "the problematic nature of attempts to build community and local consensus, and the limitations of seeing 'difficult' areas as places of fixed identities and social relations" (2002a, p 976). Community can also be used as a vehicle for the articulation of reactionary, protective agendas on different scales. Policy responses have "made too much of the demons of segregation" (Amin, 2002a, p 963).

Others concur in noting that Labour's emphasis on consensus and dialogical processes as the basis for creating harmonious and cohesive communities may well be misplaced. In commenting on the dialogical approach to regeneration in London, Ball notes:

> [A]nyone who lives in Waterloo – with its battles between landowners, residents, service providers, and local and central government – will know this is a nonsense. There is no single truth. There is inherent conflict. (Ball, 2002, p 1)

This has been a recurrent view of commentators on urban policy, as indicated by Benington's reflections on the experiences of the CDPs in the 1970s:

> We came to feel that the dialogue model embodied an inadequate analysis of the distribution of power within the class structure.... It did not deliver the goods for residents.... Our existence as a mediating agency actually served to

obscure some of the issues and to cushion out some of the conflict between
residents and the authorities. (Benington, 1972, p 4)

However, and perhaps most importantly, the political narrative of community
and individual responsibility is one that deliberately deflects attention from the
causes of poverty. As Hutton argues, "New Labour is reluctant to argue that
social deprivation or educational disadvantage are linked to poverty; rather,
they are linked to weak work incentives or badly run schools" (Hutton, 2000,
p 21). Likewise, Diamond suggests that "debate about wealth distribution has
been shifted to the margins of regeneration by a fixation on operational issues"
(2001, p 277). Thus, the Policy Action Team report on community self-help
reinforces the view that "self help has an enormous contribution to make,
particularly for disadvantaged communities – precisely because they lack other
forms of support" (Home Office, 1999, p 11). But it is precisely because
disadvantaged people lack 'other forms of support' that self-help, in and of
itself, is likely to fail or be marginal in overturning disadvantage in deprived
neighbourhoods.

Broader reforms to the welfare state are also impacting upon the wellbeing
of urban communities and, at times, are contradicting the objectives of urban
policy. As Figure 1.7 shows, core public services such as healthcare and transport
are increasingly being controlled and operated by private sector companies
intent on maximising their returns, often at the expense of poorer communities
that lack the consumer or market power to safeguard existing levels of service.
At the same time, poorer communities are often isolated from circuits of
consumption because providers of core private sector services such as banking
and food retailing have, with the assistance of planning policies, deserted poorer
locations in the search for profits elsewhere (Rose, 2000c). Arguably, such
trends have impacted upon the everyday lives of urban residents and communities
to a far greater extent than the various urban policy initiatives that have been
designed to assist them.

Labour's policy design for urban renaissance does not permit a critical
questioning of the market, because the operations of unfettered markets are the
fulcrum upon which urban policy is supported. Likewise, it is not surprising
to see little or no critical enquiry of the role of corporate or business interests
in contributing to the urban renaissance. Rather, the Labour government
socially constructs the actions of the business community to be pivotal to the
renaissance of cities. This, though, ignores much evidence that business behaviour
is often unstable, short-term, and not necessarily congruent with a core objective
of the programme for urban revitalisation, the creation of sustainable urban
communities (Lovering, 1995). As Schneider and Ingram suggest, (degenerate)
policy design will often select advantaged groups, such as some corporate firms,
as proximate targets to receive benefits (such as public contracts, subsidies, and
so on) even though there may not be any "logical connection between them
and the presumed public interest goals" (1997, p 4).

Figure 1.7: Bus privatisation in Sunderland

Sunderland has experienced the privatisation of its public transport infrastructure over the 1980s and 1990s, as have other cities in the UK. The local bus network is operated by Stagecoach, one of Britain's biggest private sector bus operators. The company has consistently sought to reduce the costs of its unprofitable (often community-oriented) services across the city and, in June 2002, it axed services 18, 19, and 6 running after 6.30pm, and reduced the frequency of several others. Such measures were justified by a Stagecoach spokesperson, who said that "we can't keep running services at a loss, so we had no choice but to stop these services".

These changes have had an adverse impact on city centre social clubs and commercial centres, and the social networks and community interactions that depended on the bus services. Research by Crosby (2002) demonstrates that one social club has been losing £2,000 per week since the cuts. A local community centre has suffered since fewer people are able to attend evening activities as existing social networks have begun to fall apart. One local resident, who attended the community centre regularly, reported how she feels increasingly trapped in her home. She said: "It affects you terribly, because you are stuck in the house. I still go to the community centre during the day but if there's anything on at night, like the bingo, I can't go because there's no bus to get home".

Such examples, while relatively small-scale, can be multiplied across Britain's cities. Public services such as healthcare, transport and housing are increasingly being provided by private sector operators intent on maximising profits over and above the quality of local service provision and the needs of local communities (see Monbiot, 2001). Far from tackling the indifference of the private sector, in responding to social needs that do not necessarily generate profit, the Labour government is enthusiastically expanding the role of the private sector. By 2002, over £25 billion worth of public projects has involved private investment (Sherman, 2002).

Source: Crosby (2002)

In this sense, we agree with the Audit Commission, which notes that Labour's urban policy programmes are not a radical departure from previous policy and "at the local level it appears to mean more of the same" (2002, p 10). Other commentators concur and argue that Labour's policies represent a 'pragmatic evolution rather than radical change' (Tiesdell and Allmendinger, 2001). Likewise, Schoon has characterised Labour's approach to the cities as just "another layer of plasters and bandages atop of all the others applied during previous attempts at regeneration" (2001, p 338). For others, Labour's recourse to urban renaissance, through the context of community, seems to signify no more than procedural change and the rescaling of government in ways that do not effectively reduce the powers of the central state (Jones and Ward, 2002).

74940

Overview of this volume

The objective of this volume is to explore and explain the ways in which particular conceptions of community have underpinned urban policy and are, in particular, a feature of New Labour's policy programmes for the cities. The various contributions provide a description and evaluation of urban policy's turn towards a community focus. Collectively, the chapters assess the emergence and practice of contemporary urban policy discourses of community, and evaluate the possibilities, problems and paradoxes of community involvement, empowerment and democratisation. In doing so, they each explore four interconnected themes:

- *Community: reality or social contract?* In what sense(s) have communities been important in the construction and implementation of urban policy? What are the contrasting discourses (and definitions) of community that underpin urban policy? How and why have they changed and with what implications for the form and content of urban policy?
- *New Labour's communities: do they exist and are they working?* What are the contrasting forms of community involvement in contemporary urban policy? How are communities (of interest) defined and drawn into policy networks and with what implications for the form and content of policy processes? What are the intellectual and practical possibilities and limitations of Labour's emerging urban policy frameworks?
- *Empowerment: can communities govern themselves successfully?* What are some of the experiences of community-led urban regeneration policies and programmes? Do communities possess the necessary capacities to take on greater roles and responsibilities in the development of urban policy and its delivery? How effective are community-led regeneration programmes? What does the evidence reveal about concepts such as 'social capital' and 'empowerment'?
- *The future of urban policy: are communities* really *involved?* What are the prospects for community involvement in urban policy in the 21st century? How will communities define themselves and to what extent will these definitions be reflected in, and reproduced by, urban policy agendas? In what senses is community involvement a necessary ingredient for an effective urban policy?

The volume has been divided into three parts. Part One, entitled 'New Labour and the turn to community regeneration', is concerned with exploring foundational principles and conceptual concerns in debates over the role of community in urban policy. Ade Kearns (Chapter Two) examines the concept of social capital, and assesses the ways in which it has been rediscovered by social scientists, politicians and social policy proponents. With its stress upon interpersonal relations and active citizenship, the discourse of social capital has chimed with Labour's urban policy agendas and has subsequently been adopted and promoted by government ministers, 'think tanks', and policy advisers. By deconstructing social capital into its component domains, and using examples from research into community-based activities, Kearns shows how social capital can be developed within neighbourhoods through regeneration programmes and projects. However, Kearns also acknowledges the limits to a renewal strategy founded upon social capital, and asks whether 'developing stocks of social capital' is the same thing as 'empowering communities'.

Loretta Lees (Chapter Three) considers the discursive construction of Labour's urban renaissance in relation to community regeneration. As Lees argues, government policy statements such as the Urban Task Force report and the White Paper interweave urban regeneration policy with gentrification practices and environmentalism. Thus, the (discursively invisible) process of gentrification is seen by policy makers to be the saviour of troubled British inner cities and it feeds into the language of community, citizenship and rights that they use. However, despite gentrification becoming established urban policy in Britain, the term itself is not used in these policy documents. Instead, terms like 'urban renaissance', 'urban regeneration' and 'urban sustainability' are used in its place. These neutered terms politely avoid the class constitution of the processes involved. Issues of social exclusion are also subtly ignored, as is the work of the SEU. The end result is a city for the few, not the many (Amin et al, 2000).

Part Two, 'Community involvement in urban policy', explores and evaluates the diverse ways in which discourses of community are influencing the content of contemporary urban policy programmes through the evaluation of specific examples of community-led urban policy. Annette Hastings (Chapter Four) analyses government policy documents and statements about urban regeneration, and seeks to evaluate how far discourses about community signify a new approach to the renaissance of cities. As Hastings suggests, the tone of urban policy documents seems to suggest that urban renaissance will only come about through the context of multilevel partnerships operating across spatial scales. The days of area-based initiatives, seeking to respond to local problems by recourse to local solutions, are apparently over. However, Hastings urges caution on this, and suggests that some of Labour's approach to the regeneration of cities is not wholly divested of pathological conceptions of people and place. Rather, the new multilevel approach remains surprisingly disengaged with wider structural issues.

Rob Atkinson (Chapter Five) draws on evidence from Plymouth to demonstrate how government agendas have sought to shift responsibility for addressing problems from state agencies to often ill-equipped and underresourced local communities. Atkinson notes that communities can find themselves in the position of being allocated key roles and responsibilities with regard to urban regeneration and social exclusion, but without the capacities, powers or resources to address key causal factors. The chapter seeks to evaluate how far communities, as the new terrain of governance, are able to exploit gaps in the programmes and technologies of government to their own advantage and develop forms of governance and action that reflect their needs. As he suggests, in order to gain access to limited resources, communities are expected to internalise a series of policy narratives, demonstrate adherence to particular programmes of government and develop technologies appropriate to them. This requires communities to restructure themselves internally and demonstrate that they are capable of self-government, both collectively and individually, in ways that reflect government's wider demands.

Peter North and Zoë Morrison (Chapters Six and Seven, respectively) document the discourses and practices of community involvement through specific case studies of South East London and Oxford. Their studies show the significance of local and contextual social relations in shaping the character of local strategies. In particular, North examines how far communities are able to use partnership structures as tools to wrestle control from partners more powerful than themselves, or at least to fend off unwelcome developments like gentrification, offices or malls, or what has become known in South London as 'social cleansing'. Chapter Six contests the conception of partnerships as necessarily mechanisms of 'incorporation and the management of decline'. With reference to specific London examples, North's evidence suggests that partnerships can, in some instances, be conceived of as 'spaces of engagement' in which gains for community organisations can be made.

Chapter Seven examines a 'social exclusion' policy in practice, and illustrates how it has the potential to enforce the cultural stigmatisation of communities. Despite Labour's rhetoric of inclusion, 'partnership' and community 'leadership', local people must acquire expert knowledge and adopt political discourses to participate powerfully in the project. This limits significant participation to all but a local elite. The excluded community is also subsequently denigrated when it fails to become either interested or involved in the project, or when its leadership of the policy fails. Morrison argues that a redistribution of funds through social exclusion policy must be coupled with a genuine redistribution of respect and recognition for the communities involved. Successful and empowering project spin-offs occur when local awareness is raised about community concerns, when local diversity is recognised, and when local people are able to run and profit from programmes run on local community terms.

Claire Edwards (Chapter Eight) draws on a study of the role of disabled communities and individuals in the government's SRB programme. Labour's buzz terms, such as 'community' and 'social exclusion', hide a multitude of groups and individuals with very different needs and access to the networks of regeneration. They can make invisible those people who are at the very margins of society. Disabled people have been excluded from society in a multitude of ways, be it socially, economically, or politically. In terms of urban policy, historically they have not been targeted as a 'disadvantaged group'. The chapter explores how disability and the needs of disabled people are defined, if at all, in Labour's partnership-based urban policy. Edwards' analysis suggests that that there is a hierarchy inherent in the perceived relevance and importance attached to different partners in SRB projects. This hierarchy also operates in the policy-making process itself, which creates closures for certain groups. As Edwards argues, disability groups can find themselves excluded from urban policy-making processes, as central government dictates the 'rules of the game'.

Bill Edwards, Mark Goodwin and Michael Woods (Chapter Nine) draw attention to the ways in which urban policy addresses community development and participation in Britain's small towns. As they suggest, small towns have been neglected in the urban studies literature. However, smaller towns are now key centres of population and employment growth, and are also seen by government as critical sites for regeneration strategies that serve surrounding areas. They are also viewed, if only implicitly, as sites of community engagement and involvement. The notion is that the smaller the place, the higher the sense of community, and hence participation. By referring to original empirical research, the chapter examines such issues by looking at community involvement and participation in a range of small-town regeneration schemes. This empirical work calls the extent of community participation into question, and leads the chapter's authors to examine issues concerning the scale at which such participation works best. The chapter also raises concerns about the linkage between participation and those agencies and institutions charged with undertaking urban regeneration.

Stuart Wilks-Heeg (Chapter Ten) examines the growing significance of urban policy evaluation in shaping the form and character of community engagement in urban policy making. Wilks-Heeg describes recent attempts to foster direct community involvement in the evaluation process, noting that the commitment to community-led regeneration does not yet appear to extend as far as allowing communities to take the lead in the contested politics of policy evaluation. The underlying inequalities of power in urban policy have not been sufficiently recognised by New Labour, the chapter argues, with the consequence that evaluation studies frequently serve to alienate local communities, and fail to capture forms of local knowledge that would provide more telling indications of change. The failure to engage communities in the evaluation process represents a significant Achilles heel for contemporary urban policy in that it seems to contradict the apparent New Labour objective of promoting community leadership.

Part Three of the book, 'The future of community in urban policy', consists of two chapters that comment on the broadcloth of New Labour's policy programmes for the renaissance of the British cities. Allan Cochrane (Chapter Eleven) develops the argument that urban policy is best understood as the sum of the initiatives that have been given an urban label, rather than being a continuing and coherent strand of social policy. The wider policy diagnosis has shifted between the identification of market failure, community failure and state failure. It is possible to talk about a new urban policy that has supplanted the old discourse that assumed a direct causal route from economic development to urban renewal. Rather, for Cochrane, the new urban policy is characterised by a discourse that highlights the interconnection of the different aspects of urban development – community, partnership, private sector stakeholders. In developing this point, the chapter highlights some of the potential of the new urban policy in seeking to realise the democratic credentials of communities (as well as its inherent paradoxes).

In the final chapter of the book, Mike Raco synthesises the volume's themes and provides a broader commentary on the changing nature of urban policy since New Labour came to power. While much of the rhetoric of urban policy promises to enhance community capacity and empowerment, Raco suggests that the reality is one whereby communities as the objects and subjects of government policy are part of a broader governmental agenda to restructure the nature of the welfare state. The chapter also discusses some of the broader processes impacting on community formation, and argues that using community as a vehicle for more inclusive forms of governance is inherently limited – that is to say, communities are always exclusive by means of their inclusiveness. The definition, identification and mobilisation of community is therefore always a selective process, something that is being exacerbated by the drive towards a 'new localism' in New Labour's discourses and policies. The chapter highlights the work of Amin and Thrift (2002) and others in critiquing this fragmentation of the welfare state, and the calls for an expansion of universal political rights and systems of welfare provision.

Note

[1] Not much had changed during Labour's first term in office. As Rahman et al (2000) note, nine million citizens had very low incomes in 1998-99 – 500,000 more than in 1996-97.

Further reading

In terms of pre-1999 urban policy, Oatley (1998a) and Imrie and Thomas (1999) offer excellent coverage. Hughes and Mooney (1998) provide a very good overview and introduction to debates about community. More detailed analysis of these debates and the controversies surrounding them are still best conveyed by Plant (1974). Tiesdell and Allmendinger (2001) provide a useful summary of New Labour's urban policies. David Blunkett's recent book (2001) provides the most succinct account of New Labour thinking. Government departments on the World Wide Web are an important and primary source of information on urban policy initiatives, especially www.odpm.gov.uk, www.homeoffice.co.uk and www.socialexclusionunit.gov.uk

TWO

Social capital, regeneration and urban policy

Ade Kearns

Introduction

From social exclusion to social capital

According to the Prime Minister's Special Adviser Geoff Mulgan when New Labour came to power in 1997, discussion among policy makers and policy commentators was dominated by the language of social exclusion (Mulgan, 1998b). An observer noted that:

> The term social exclusion has great appeal to many people because it provides
> a broad category that many people can identify their policy concern with.
> (Halpern 1998, p 269)

The government set up a Social Exclusion Unit (SEU), one of whose first priorities concerned regeneration – namely, to narrow the gap between the 'worst estates' and the rest of the country. For the SEU, the problem was that:

> over the past 20 years, poverty has become more concentrated in individual
> neighbourhoods and estates than before, and the social exclusion of these
> neighbourhoods has become more marked. (SEU, 2000, p 7)

Two principles that guided the work of the SEU were that "this is about more than poverty" (2000, p 7) and that "a joined up problem has never been addressed in a joined up way" (SEU, 1998, p 9). Through a review of Tony Blair's pronouncements on social exclusion and poor neighbourhoods, and the broader literature on the subject (see Room, 1995; Jordan, 1996), we can identify some of the key characteristics of the term social exclusion (Figure 2.1).

In contrast to poverty, social exclusion is said to be a *dynamic* rather than a static concept, implying that people move in and out of exclusion, not necessarily in accord with the incidence of poverty, and that something can be done about it. Unlike poverty or deprivation, the assumption is that the negative state of

Figure 2.1: Characteristics of social exclusion

Social exclusion: the elements

Dynamics – movement in and out of poverty

Disconnections from the mainstream

Lack of **opportunities** and low expectations

Processes of exclusion – individual and institutional

Exercising **rights** and recognising **responsibilities**

Quality of **relationships** of individuals and communities

Skills and **cultures** of individuals, families and communities

Barriers to advancement: eg status, power and self-esteem

exclusion is not simply transmitted in a fatalistic way across the generations. Social exclusion is also about *disconnection* from mainstream society in terms of distance, experience and aspiration. In Mulgan's words, "it defines better than poverty a situation in which large sections of the population are, in effect, cut off from qualifications, jobs and safe environments" (1998a, p 260). Thus, social exclusion highlights a lack of *opportunities* or prospects for the future. As Oppenheim says, social exclusion "is about the *processes* which lead people to being marginalised from the mainstream" (1998, p 13).

Social exclusion is *relational* in a number of ways. It highlights the importance of an area's relations with other areas and with organisations and institutions. For Atkinson, social exclusion can be more about groups and communities than individuals, for "people become excluded because of events elsewhere in society" (1998a, p 7). In Klemman's terms, "If someone is excluded, there is someone else – an individual, a group of people, an institution or a market – who does the excluding" (1998, p 9). Part of the analysis and policy attention then focuses upon institutional processes and how individuals, communities and places are treated by others.

While social exclusion has been the fulcrum upon which policies for tackling inequality and poor areas have been supported, it also neatly shifts the focus away from poverty, the economy and jobs towards 'softer' issues. Individuals and communities come to the fore in two ways. First, the earlier poverty lens "makes [problems] ... appear primarily material when they are often as much about skills and cultures" (Mulgan, 1998a, p 260). Second, Oppenheim (1998) suggests that the impacts of exclusion are often psychological, including loss of status, power, self-esteem and expectations. This perspective on exclusion implies that, among other things, the government can help people to help themselves through social, educational and training programmes.

Thus, observers have noted that social exclusion (perhaps especially area-based exclusion) opens up a wide agenda for government (Levitas, 1998). If social exclusion is the problem, the aim in tackling it is the achievement of social inclusion. This 'social exclusion to social inclusion' agenda has two distinct advantages for the government. It provides a potential route to achieving coherence across government programmes, so that all parties can see that their efforts are contributing to an overriding objective. Furthermore, by defining social inclusion broadly to embrace the economic, social and political, the modernisation of local government and public services that New Labour wishes to pursue becomes necessary to the achievement of social inclusion with a strong element of participation in political processes.

After several years of problem analysis, we have moved into the era of delivery, most notably after Labour's second successive electoral victory. Once policies for the regeneration of deprived communities and neighbourhoods began to be set out in detail, the dialogue seemed to shift away from social exclusion and economic development towards social capital. Kleinman, for example, argued for a shift from 'hard' to 'soft' goals in urban regeneration:

> It is now becoming clear that in obtaining [economic] outcomes, 'social' factors such as family structure and individual self-esteem, and personal characteristics such as punctuality, reliability and attitude are of equal or greater importance than 'economic' factors .... In other words, 'social capital' is as important to economic development as economic capital'. (Kleinman, 1998, p 13)

While not necessarily agreeing with Kleinman (that the social focus of regeneration has eclipsed the employment and economic instruments and goals), his reflection on the rise of the 'soft' goals agenda is certainly confirmed by others (see, for example, Hall and Hickman, 2002). Tiesdell and Allmendinger argue that New Labour's 'Third Way' approach to neighbourhood regeneration includes:

> greater recognition of the concept of 'social capital', in the form of local partnerships and bottom-up approaches and more generally in strategies, policies, and initiatives that integrate the 'people and communities' with a 'bricks and mortar' dimension. (Tiesdell and Allmendinger, 2001, p 921)

Social capital, then, has arisen as a means to the end of social inclusion and as a way of tackling social exclusion. The next section of this chapter considers social capital as a multidimensional phenomenon that operates at different levels. Social capital is seen to have downsides as well as upsides, and our knowledge of how it operates leaves a lot to be desired. Despite the level of ignorance and complexity surrounding it, the third section of this chapter shows how the concept of social capital has emerged as a key element of both regeneration and urban policy, allied to agendas of community self-help and social cohesion, and to goals of reducing crime and antisocial behaviour, improving services and stabilising communities. The reasons why the government is so attracted to the concept of social capital is then explored, highlighting its fit with New Labour's 'Third Way' political philosophy and the attractive prospect of achieving multiple outcomes from social capital ranging from better health to a healthier democracy. The chapter concludes with a consideration of some of the dangers posed by such a strong reliance on social capital in public policy.

Social capital: of bonds and bridges

Is social capital "a sack of analytical potatoes" (Fine, 2001, p 190)? Fine certainly thinks so:

> What is striking about social capital is not only the extent of its influence, and the speed with which this has been achieved, but also its ready acceptance as both analytical, empirical and policy panacea.... Social capital is the 'missing link' that can explain any aspect of social, cultural or economic (under)performance, across time and place. (Fine, 2001, pp 198-190)

In 1999, Francis Fukuyama published a book on how to reconstruct social order and recover from the 'great disruption' of rising crime, declining families and decreasing trust that had been setting in since the 1960s. In his view, modern post-industrial societies will have an increasing demand for social capital, but should nonetheless be able to meet the demand through the actions of private markets and governments. In 2000, Robert Putnam published a book on the decline of civic America entitled *Bowling alone*. Again, over a period of some 25 years, he sought to demonstrate that associational behaviours have declined in the US, with adverse effects upon a range of socioeconomic outcomes.

Most academic commentators locate the antecedents of these publications in the earlier works of Pierre Bourdieu and James Coleman (see Schuller et al, 2000). For Bourdieu (1991), social capital was one of several guises of capital (the others being economic, cultural and symbolic capital) that serve to constitute the social position of a person. In this schema, capital can be seen as comprising power and resources. For Coleman (1994), social capital was a set of resources within family relationships and community social organisation that complemented human capital and supported educational achievement. Although the concept of social capital has generated much debate and criticism, Schuller et al (2000) conclude that it has much promise and heuristic value. Its two key merits, they say, are that "it shifts the focus of analysis from the behaviour of individual agents to the pattern of relations between agents, social units and institutions" (Schuller et al, 2000, p 35) and that it acts as a link between micro-, meso- and macro-levels of analysis, or between the actions of individuals and groups and social structural events. This is similar to the criticism made of area-based regeneration initiatives to combat social exclusion, namely that there needs to be greater policy integration at local and national levels, and vertical linkages from neighbourhood renewal programmes to regional economic strategies and national mainstream programmes (Parkinson, 1998).

Figure 2.2 presents examples some of the most recent definitions of social capital. Evidently, there is confusion among them:

- What *is* social capital?
- What is it *used for*?
- What is the *outcome* of this use?

Figure 2.2: Recent definitions of 'social capital'

Social capital is

"features of social life – networks, norms and trust – that enable participants to act together more effectively to pursue shared objectives.... Social capital, in short, refers to social connections and the attendant norms and trust" (Putnam, 1995)

"features of social organisation, such as civic participation, norms of reciprocity and trust in others, that facilitate cooperation for mutual benefit" (Kawachi et al, 1997)

"defined simply as a set of informal values or norms shared among members of a group that permits cooperation among them. If members of the group come to expect that others will behave reliably and honestly, then they will come to trust one another. Trust is like a lubricant that makes the running of any group or organisation more efficient" (Fukuyama, 1999)

"the networks, norms and relationships that help communities and organisations work more effectively" (MacGillivray, 2002)

"the institutions, relationships and norms that shape the quality and quantity of a society's social interactions" (World Bank website, www.worldbank.org)

Figure 2.3 attempts to make sense of the various definitions by distinguishing between:

- the three core elements of social capital;
- the intermediate outcomes or manifestations of social capital;
- the different scales at which social capital may operate.

Figure 2.3: Social capital: components, outcomes and operation

Components	Intermediate outcomes	Scales of operation
Social networks	Quality and quantity of social interaction	Bonding capital
Social norms	Shared objectives	Bridging capital
Levels of trust	Cooperative action	Linking capital
	Reciprocity	
	Civic engagement	
	Access to resources and opportunities	

Components and types of social capital

Social capital is something useful that exists between people, and we may be interested in the social capital that is available to individuals, or in the levels of social capital that exist at an aggregate scale within communities. The three components of social capital most often referred to are:

- the social networks used by people;
- the social norms adhered to in people's behaviour, and in particular whether or not these norms are widely shared;
- the levels of trust people have either in their neighbours, in people in general, or in the institutions of government.

The relationship between the three main components of social capital is unclear, and the role of trust especially difficult to understand. For instance, do networks generate trust or do you need trust to begin to participate in networks? Are norms observable and therefore able to foster a sense of trust? Can norms develop through networks that do not involve face-to-face interaction? Putnam (1995) talks of 'vicious spirals' and 'virtuous circles' between trust and civic participation, since our expectations of others' trustworthiness will affect our own trustworthiness and behaviour. Schuller et al argue that Putnam has shifted his interest away from trust towards reciprocity, though they also summarise his view as follows:

> But overall, trustworthiness 'lubricates social life'. It promotes the kinds of interaction which reinforce norms of generalised reciprocity. This generalised reciprocity is the touchstone of social capital. (Schuller et al, 2000, p 11)

Social capital can be examined in terms of individuals or groups. De Souza Briggs (1998) sees social capital as individual utility, and he distinguishes two forms:

- *Social support* (or coping capital) enables one to 'get by' and is especially important to the poor and may be emotional or material (for example, getting a loan or getting a lift).
- *Social leverage* helps one 'get ahead' through access to influence or opportunity.

Commentators have observed that poor communities have more 'coping' than 'levering' social capital. Lang and Hornburg (1998) illustrate the group perspective on social capital. For them, *social glue* refers to the extent to which people take part in group activities, with a recursive relationship between this participation and trust: trust influences joining a group, while participation in the group builds trust. *Social bridges* are the vital links between groups that connect them and give them access to wider chains of affiliation.

These two perspectives on social capital – the individual and the group – bring us to the third column of Figure 2.3, which shows the three scales at which (and the modus operandi through which) social capital may operate:

• *Bonding capital* is akin to strong social ties between like individuals (for example, family members or an ethnic grouping), often located in the same neighbourhood, which enable people to 'get by'.
• *Bridging capital*, on the other hand, consists of weaker, less dense, cross-cutting social ties between heterogeneous individuals such as friends from different groups, friends of friends and business associates, which enable people to 'get on' (see Granovetter, 1973; Henning and Leiberg, 1996). Aldridge et al (2002) distinguish these two forms of social capital as *social glue* and *social oil*, respectively.
• *Linking capital*, attributed by Aldridge et al (2002) to Woolcock (2001), refers to vertical rather than horizontal connections, such as relations between the powerful and the less powerful, the political elite and the public, or between social classes.

Community capital

Within a regeneration context, the social capital that deprived communities need in order to attain a better future also comprises that between local community organisations and partnerships (see Hibbitt et al, 2001):

• organisational networks among a plethora of groups and bodies;
• norms of working practice;
• crucially, trust in each other, given that they are pursuing related but different objectives.

There is a need to focus upon the 'institutional infrastructure' (Temkin and Rohe, 1998) within local neighbourhoods and to assess the level and quality of relations between formal organisations in the neighbourhood and the actual ability of these groups to act on behalf of residents, or the extent to which cooperation is institutionalised (Boix and Posner, 1998). For Temkin and Rohe (1998), neighbourhood organisations provide an important bridge between residents and policy makers: their networks and linkages in wider arenas – *community capital* – have to be studied alongside an examination of social relations between individuals in order to fully explore a community's social capital. The relevance of community capital to the social capital and regeneration agenda is set out in Figure 2.4.

The Audit Commission makes the point that an area's past experience and its regeneration inheritance will influence how well placed the area is to tackle the issues of today, and that a key element of this inheritance is having "a well-established 'local institutional infrastructure' [which] ensures effective

Figure 2.4: The advantages of community capital

- An individual member of a community group may broker a link to another organisation. Furthermore, an organisation with diverse membership may be disproportionately network-rich in this way.

- Organisational networks may help connect people on an individual basis.

- An individual's power within wider decision-making arenas is enhanced if s/he represents a community group within representative politics.

- Community organisations have access to resources that can be deployed to support collective actions and social activities to generate social capital.

- In the context of regeneration partnership working, community organisations offer access to institutional networks.

communication and co-operation" (2002, p 19). It goes on to say, however, that in situations where past regeneration has produced conflict and disappointment, local groups and institutions will need time to build *trust* and mutual understanding.

Social capital and power

DeFilippis (2001) makes a particularly strong point when he says that social capital is about power relations, comprising a variety of realms and social interactions, as Bourdieu (1985) had previously put it. For Bourdieu, capital is almost synonymous with power:

> Bourdieu's notion of capital ... entails the capacity to exercise control over one's own future and that of others. As such it is a form of power. (Postone, 1993, p 4)

The reality is that democracy depends upon struggle and conflict more than on the comfortable 'civic-ness' expounded by the proponents of social capital (Foweraker and Landman, 1997). Civil society is characterised by unequal power relations and oligarchic forms (Alexander, 1998, quoted in Taylor, 2000a).

While social capital exists in the relationships between *individuals* (Routledge and Amsberg, 1996), social capital is also defined as the ability of people to work together as groups and *organisations* (Fukuyama, 1995). DeFilippis (2001) observes that it is *groups of people* who wield power and maintain control, and he has provided examples of how communities that have managed to alter their access to power have all involved local community organisations, rather than more informally connected individuals.

Putnam comes in for some criticism from DeFilippis, for in Putnam's work:

> social capital becomes divorced from capital (in the literal economic sense), stripped of power relations, and imbued with the assumption that social networks are win-win relationships and that individual gains, interests and

profits are synonymous with group gains, interests and profits. (DeFilippis, 2001, p 800)

DeFilippis argues that social networks are often confused with the ability to generate and control capital. Inner-city neighbourhoods possess social networks and community organisations but lack power, and they are unlikely to get that power from community development programmes that simply concentrate on voluntary associations as win-win relationships with no interest in conflict, but only in 'civic virtue'.

Social capital and context

Social capital is dependent upon context. Fine (2001) states that both the meaning and the distribution of social capital have been said to be context-specific, while Foley and Edwards (1999) point out that *how* social capital is produced, its 'use value' and 'liquidity' or 'portability', all depend upon the specifics of context. They argue that the potential for utilising social capital as a means of securing more effective policy delivery may be more severely limited in some contexts than others, and that there is little evidence to suggest that general trust explains the quality and effectiveness of policy delivery.

Clearly, the political context is very important. Networks have to be analysed within the context of underlying collective action problems and the prevailing political and institutional arrangements of which they are a part (Pennington and Rydin, 2000). Political structures and institutions shape the context of associational activity, in which the governance of an area is affected by social capital, and are mutually constituted (Maloney et al, 1999).

Local governance, through a city's political opportunity structure (see Eisinger, 1973; Tarrow, 1994), affects the distribution of social capital, for such a structure provides incentives, expectations and openings for people to undertake collective action within the political system.

The downside of social capital

For some observers, social capital is too 'cosy' a concept (see Taylor, 2002a), since in reality 'inclusion' also involves its obverse, namely 'exclusion'. In other words, without a 'them', there is no 'us'. Strong communities can breed what Giddens (2000a) refers to as 'identity politics' and operate on the basis of distinguishing between 'insiders' and 'outsiders'. The many disadvantages and misuses of social capital are set out in Figure 2.5.

First, economic performance can be undermined by associational memberships pursuing sectional interests (such as trade unions and chambers of commerce) that are inefficient. Second, the 'old-boy' networks of the middle classes help to maintain social class barriers and inhibit social inclusion across groups. The inherent advantages of the more extensive and diverse social

Figure 2.5: The downsides of social capital[a]

- Sectional interests undermine economic performance.
- 'Old-boy' networks inhibit social mobility.
- Strongly bonded social groups may exacerbate community conflicts.
- Strongly bonded and spatially concentrated groups can become insular.
- Social capital can be used to promote damaging behaviour.
- Strong communities can be oppressive and comformist.

[a] For a discussion of these polarities, see especially Portes and Landolt (1996) and Aldridge et al (2002).

networks of advantaged social groups can exacerbate inequality – this is social capital as a 'club good' rather than as a 'public good', as is often assumed.

Conversely, the strong bonding social capital of poorer groups can have its own disadvantages that limit advancement. In some places and societies, *bonding* social capital within groups far exceeds *bridging* social capital between groups, and is put to use for tribal purposes that often and inevitably lead to conflict. Some groups that have strong bonding social capital and are also geographically concentrated (such as the ethnic minorities of many cities) may become insular and disconnected both by desire and by default. Similarly, strong communities can be oppressive and seek conformity among their members, restricting routes out of poverty and exclusion. Last, social capital, through networks and norms, can be used to promote negative behaviours such as crime, truancy and drug addiction, thus damaging community welfare, health and education.

The great unknown

Social capital, then, has its upsides and its downsides. It can be viewed far more for its positive elements than its negative elements. However, despite the tremendous interest that the concept has generated in recent years, even its strongest supporters admit that there is much that we still do not know about it. For example, Putnam suggests that we need to know:

> more about how social capital works at a micro-level, for example in relation to education and health; to be able to better distinguish different forms of social capital and their associated benefits; to know how social capital operates across different cultural settings; and to understand the processes by which social capital is created, with the observable outcome that the social–capital-rich get richer and the poor get poorer because social capital runs in virtuous circles and vicious cycles. (Putnam, 1998, p vii)

Notwithstanding both the downsides of social capital and our limited understanding of it, the Labour government has firmly nailed its flag to the social capital mast in the battle against social exclusion. How, then, has social capital featured in recent regeneration and urban policy?

Social capital, regeneration and urban policy

Neighbourhood renewal

The SEU produced its first report on neighbourhood renewal in September 1998, constituting an interim statement in the process of producing a national strategy for neighbourhood renewal. The main themes outlined in relation to poor communities were:

- improving the skills base and overcoming barriers to employment;
- improving housing and neighbourhood management;
- improving access to public and private services;
- giving better opportunities and motivation to young people.

References to the 'community' were in relation to community involvement in the regeneration process (SEU, 1998, p 40), with an acknowledgement that maximising the community's contribution would entail "capacity building" (1998, p 57). The report made no explicit reference to social capital.

By the time the SEU's consultation paper on neighbourhood renewal was published, the concept of social capital was much more prominent. In his introduction to the document, the Prime Minister states that one of four imperatives is "to revive and empower the community" (SEU, 2000, p 5). This is later expounded to include two dimensions, namely removing local threats to the community (such as anti-social behaviour), and then "to build community confidence and encourage residents to help themselves" (SEU, 2000, p 10). The document argues that reduced social capital, due to increased fear of crime and rapid population turnover in deprived neighbourhoods, is "a key factor in decline" and that "social stability and a community's ability to help itself" are built upon the "vital resources of social capital" (SEU, 2000, p 24).

The 'reviving communities' theme that follows in the SEU document is very close to a social capital agenda. As well as requiring resident consultation and a local management presence, well-functioning communities also involve:

- a broad social mix;
- an agreed set of rules among residents that are consistently applied;
- places and facilities where people can interact, with particular mention of the role of shops and community venues.

Linked to the aim of rebuilding social capital is strong advocacy for volunteering, since:

> it often brings people into contact with those outside their normal circle, broadening horizons and raising expectations, and can link people into informal networks through which work is more easily found. (SEU, 2000, p 53)

A closely related theme is the promotion of self-help in deprived areas. The steps that flow from this aim are to build skills and confidence (capacity building) and to provide funding for voluntary and community groups so that residents "take independent action to improve things" and have "opportunities for more direct involvement in influencing or running core public services" (SEU, 2000, p 60). Social capital, then, is a means to this end: getting people to do more for themselves, particularly improving and filling gaps in services.

Social capital features less directly in the much shorter *National strategy action plan* (SEU, 2001), but many of the earlier community-related themes remain. In the summary of comments provided in the earlier consultation exercise, two important points are noted. First, not enough attention was being paid to the influence of the physical environment upon crime, and community disintegration. Second, community development ought to be more central to the strategy, involving community empowerment, control, ownership and support for local networks.

Social capital is now at the forefront of regeneration policy in Scotland, with similar aims to that in England (see Chapter Four of this volume). The Scottish Executive's *Community Regeneration Statement* identifies two pillars of the strategy to turn around disadvantaged communities in Scotland: first, making core public services as effective as possible in deprived areas, and second:

> making sure that individuals and communities have the social capital – the skills, confidence, support networks and resources – to take advantage of and increase the opportunities open to them. (Scottish Executive, 2002a, p 3)

The Scottish Executive have termed the means to achieve some of this as 'community learning and development' (part of the community development component missing from the draft strategy in England). This comprises "informal learning programmes and community action based on real issues in people's day to day lives" (Scottish Executive, 2002a, p 9), so that individuals and communities improve their confidence, motivation and sense of power and influence. The social capital – related goals of skills, resources and networks – may boost confidence and thus help address the problems of failure, inferiority, low self-esteem and powerlessness in poor communities that also manifest themselves within the individuals as apathy, withdrawal, depression and aggression (Wilkinson, 1994).

However, as Wood (2000) points out, this social capital agenda is not in itself enough to both overcome exclusion and empower communities as the government wishes. The latter also involves challenging the power relationships between professionals and residents, with cultural changes required in regeneration agencies, local authorities and bodies that fund regeneration (Duncan and Thomas, 2000; Taylor, 2000a; Wood, 2000). Wood (2000) argues that local people need to have knowledge and skills and to be in the position to understand their own problems, develop programmes they deem necessary, and take as much control as they wish in the regeneration process. This model appears to go further than the social capital and community involvement approach advocated by the government in England and the Scottish Executive. It is also entirely possible that some of the more intangible and tricky aspects of social capital such as norms, trust (beyond reducing fear of crime) and social interaction could disappear from regeneration action plans in favour of the more tangible aspects such as funding for voluntary groups.

Community cohesion

Within urban policy more generally, social capital has recently featured in discussions of community cohesion. This issue came to the fore after urban riots took place in three northern English towns in spring and summer 2001 (Oldham, Burnley and Bradford) that arose from tension between whites and Asians and conflict between Asian youths and the police. The riots took place in or around deprived areas inhabited predominantly by Pakistani and Bangladeshi communities. In response, the government set up an independent Community Cohesion Review Team, which adopted a framework for understanding cohesion. This framework was built upon five pillars, one of which was 'social networks and social capital' (see Figure 2.6).

The Community Cohesion Review Team was struck by the extent of physical, residential, separation of ethnic groupings, compounded by further polarisation in respect of education, employment, voluntary organisations and social and cultural networks (Home Office, 2001b, p 9). The parallel Ministerial Group on Public Order and Community Cohesion highlighted further social capital-related issues in these towns, including:

- a lack of shared social values between diverse communities;
- an increasingly territorial mentality among young people;
- an inability to broker relations between key interests;
- an erosion of trust in civic institutions (Home Office, 2001c).

The team recommended that a local community cohesion plan should include the promotion of cross-cultural contact between black and ethnic minority and white communities to foster understanding and respect and break down barriers. The team's report cites the importance of social capital, based on Putnam (2000), as being relevant to problems of community cohesion for a number of reasons (set out in Figure 2.7).

Figure 2.6: Domains of social cohesion

Domain	Description
Common values and a civic culture	Common aims and objectives
	Common moral principles and codes of behaviour
	Support for political institutions
	Participation in politics
Social order and social control	Absence of general conflict
	Absence of incivility
	Effective informal social control
	Tolerance; respect for difference
	Inter-group cooperation
Social solidarity and reductions in wealth disparities	Harmonious economic and social development
	Redistribution of public finances and of opportunities
	Equal access to services and welfare benefits
	Ready acknowledgement of social obligations and willingness to assist others
Social networks and social capital	High degree of social interaction within communities and families
	Civic engagement and associational activity
	Easy resolution of collective action problems
Place attachment and identity	Strong attachment to place
	Intertwining of personal and place identity

Source: Forrest and Kearns (2001)

Figure 2.7: The contribution of social capital to community cohesion

- Social capital allows people to resolve collective problems more easily.
- Business and social transactions work better and are less costly if people trust one another and repeatedly interact with one another.
- Social capital widens people's awareness of the ways in which their fates are linked to each other's.
- Networks serve as conduits for flows of information that facilitate the achievement of common goals.

Source: Home Office (2001c)

The Community Cohesion Review Team summed up its approach as follows:

> Community cohesion is about helping micro-communities to gel or mesh into an integrated whole. These divided communities would need to develop common goals and a shared vision. This would seem to imply that such groups should occupy a common sense of place as well. The high levels of residential segregation found in many English towns would make it difficult to achieve community cohesion. (Home Office, 2001b, p 70)

The report then urges the adoption of creative strategies to produce more mixed housing areas. The subsequent draft guidance to local authorities on community cohesion specified that strong and positive relations should be developed between people from different backgrounds in three key locations: the workplace, schools and within neighbourhoods (Local Government Association, 2002).

However, not everybody is convinced by the government's approach. Amin (2002b) in particular is sceptical as to whether the government's agenda can be realised. He has two key reservations. First, he is pessimistic that public spaces in general or housing estates in particular can generate intercultural or inter-ethnic dialogue and understanding. He argues in this case that marginalised and prejudiced people tend to stay away, and that habitual contact does not necessarily require the dropping of fixed identities and relations and the adoption of cultural displacement and transgression. Second, he argues more for what he terms an 'agonistic politics' from which new attitudes and identities can arise, rather than "the naïve pursuit of a unitary sense of place" (Amin, 2002b, p 14). In his view:

> Mixed ethnic neighbourhoods are communities without community .... Policy interventions need to work with the reality of mixed neighbourhoods as spatially open, culturally heterogeneous, and socially variegated spaces, not imagine them as future integrated communities. There are limits to how far community cohesion – rooted in common values, a shared sense of place and local networks of trust – can become the basis of living with difference in such neighbourhoods. (Amin, 2002, p 14)

Nonetheless, the government sees the National Strategy for Neighbourhood Renewal as a means of pursuing the community cohesion agenda in deprived and divided communities. The Ministerial Group on Public Order and Community Cohesion charged the Neighbourhood Renewal Unit with the task of making "community cohesion a central objective of all its programmes" and to "use all available opportunities to promote cross-community and cross-cultural experience" (Home Office 2001a, p 32). Among other things, this will involve building community networks to help resolve community conflicts and to include excluded groups. Thus, by this means, social capital and social cohesion serve as an important link between regeneration and urban policy.

Government interest in social capital

Why does social capital frequently occur in the government's regeneration and urban policies? Why has the government hit upon social capital as an important element of the solution to Britain's urban problems? There are a number of reasons, some of them ideological and others more utilitarian.

Treading an independent path

There are two senses in which the centrality of social capital to urban and regeneration policies enables the government to tread an independent path to social progress. The first is to avoid the alleged destiny that has befallen the US: the decline of associational activity and social capital as first reported by Putnam (1995). Indeed, the British desire to save British society from the social divisions and problems evident in US cities is a driving force of contemporary policy initiatives. Thus, if the US is suffering a loss of social capital, then we, the British, shall do all we can to shore up social capital, especially in our poorest neighbourhoods. In line with the view of the US that 'they've got all the money, but we've got the brains', the government would claim that it saw the social capital problem coming and was clever enough to head it off at the pass.

The government may actually be fortunate in having this window of opportunity, since Hall's review of levels of social capital in Britain, using aggregate measures of associational membership and generalised trust, concluded:

> The balance of the evidence seems to indicate, however, that aggregate levels of social capital have not declined to an appreciable extent in Britain over the post-war years. (Hall, 1999, p 457)

Hall makes two qualifications to this conclusion. First, levels of generalised trust do seem to have fallen, especially among the young. And second, the character of organisational involvement may have changed, even if the levels of activity have not, so that involvement is decreasingly intense and face to face, and less geared to public interest organisations.

The second way in which the social capital agenda serves to highlight the government's particular approach to urban policy is in its contrast with the years of Conservative rule during the 1980s and 1990s. More than anything else, social capital's place within regeneration policy signals that New Labour's approach to development differs from Margaret Thatcher's view that 'there is no such thing as society' and from the Conservative Party's property-led regeneration policies (see Oatley, 1998a). Although there is a strong element of tackling worklessness within national programmes for labour market inclusion, New Labour's policies also have a softer, community-centred focus edge and a bottom-up rather than a top-down rhetoric to them (although, see the arguments in Chapter One on the similarities between Conservative and New Labour policies).

Third Way politics

The crucial role attributed to social capital in the regeneration of deprived areas and in the building of community cohesion in British cities fits nicely with New Labour's so-called 'Third Way' politics. According to Giddens (2000a), this is about steering a middle course between highly statist policies and neoliberal free-market policies. It seeks to combine the state and the market while minimising their disadvantages and opening up new territory for intervention (Taylor, 2002b, p 108). Thus, rather than leaving neighbourhoods to the operations and effects of property and labour markets, or intervening as a nanny state to shore up failing enterprises in depressed regions, the Third Way supports the notion that self-help activities undertaken within existing market and governmental structures is the way forward for disadvantaged groups and communities. The government's role is to remove the barriers to self-help, be they lack of skills or fear of crime.

Of course, this approach avoids the issues of structural inequalities and redistribution of power and resources, since the ethos is to 'help others to help themselves' (see Chapter One of this volume). The approach implies that each individual possesses the capability and means to be creative and to achieve success, given the opportunity. Those who object to the authoritarian overtones of the communitarian approach to Third Way policies nevertheless offer a creative and optimistic alternative. This alternative strongly advocates that markets and communities (that is, financial and social capital) "should be harnessed [to] make us better off, put us more in charge of our lives and make us better able to look after ourselves" (Leadbeater, 1999, p 16) through creating, advancing and spreading knowledge. In other words, the government should help communities to 'harness' social capital resources, but need not (re)distribute resources.

This path is important to any government that wishes to occupy the middle ground in politics. For as Hirst points out, associationalism – the freedom and necessity for individuals to associate in order to achieve their needs and aspirations – that might sound collectivist "is justified on essentially individualistic terms, that it both enhances the freedom and the individuation of the individual" (1994, p 50), and is achieved more effectively by cooperative action. New Labour can claim that its social capital agenda is concerned with both individual and collective freedom, as well as with social solidarity. In short, it has both right-wing and left-wing dimensions to it.

Richards and Smith (2002) argue that the Third Way allows New Labour to move away from the postwar Keynesian welfare state and retain some of the mechanisms of intervention introduced by the Conservatives (such as deregulation, privatisation and the creation of public agencies). Rather than rely upon state intervention, the Third Way involves greater use of the private, voluntary and community sectors in the delivery of services and the creation of partnerships and networks based on trust between the state, businesses, and the voluntary and public sectors. Not only does the role of the state change, but so too does the role of the citizen. There is a much stronger emphasis in Third Way or stakeholder politics upon the "responsible and responsive individual – the notion of the developmental self, and the idea that through help and education people can improve" (Richards and Smith, 2002, p 237).

It is clear how the language of social capital chimes with the philosophy of Third Way politics. What is more, since social capital is a resource and social inclusion policy aims to foster individual, family and community assets (financial, psychological, social and cultural), the government can be seen to have a positive impact, giving communities a 'leg up' simply by enabling them to realise their social capital resources (Oppenheim, 1998). Having made the error of referring to disadvantaged areas as Britain's 'worst estates', the government now wishes to be positive about all neighbourhoods and communities since they can all be said to have potential in the form of unrealised social capital resources (SEU, 1998). The language of 'realising social capital assets' is much more in tune with New Labour's spin on deprivation than its earlier 'combating social exclusion' agenda. Furthermore, compared with eradicating social exclusion, social capital is a more nebulous target that is even harder to measure, thereby making it more difficult for critics to hold the government to account for inadequate progress.

Joined-up policy

One of the major aims of the Blair government has been to reform central government, in particular so that broad government strategy can be achieved (rather than thwarted) by departmentalism. State reform has been in the form of 'joined-up government', or, as the title of Labour's White Paper (DETR, 1998a) put it, 'modernising government'. Reforms were put in place to deliver a coordinated policy programme, including the creation of new coordinating units at the centre of government, such as the SEU. The components of joined-up government include the creation of joined-up delivery units, new cross-departmental budgets, cross-cutting reviews of policy and a greater focus on outcomes (Richards and Smith, 2002, p 241).

Social capital contributes to the joined-up policy agenda in two main ways. First, it provides central government with a cross-departmental outcome measure that can be thought of as both strategic and holistic. Social capital is not the property or goal of one single government department but is an archetypal cross-cutting goal. Of course, social capital is an interim goal, a means to the end of empowerment and so on. But these end goals can easily be ignored if progress on the interim goal – social capital – can be demonstrated. A neat trick for government! Second, social capital is a phenomenon that individual government departments can adopt as an objective. Consequently, different officials and ministers 'sing from the same hymn sheet'. It overcomes the pre-existing problem that certain actions, often preventative ones, are avoided because the benefits accrue to different departments (Mulgan, 2001, cited in Richards and Smith, 2002). If departments share a social capital goal, then the reverse becomes true: different departments can claim the credit for each other's activities or, better still, ascribe the benefits to the holistic action of all programmes.

Multiple outcomes from social capital

A major attraction of social capital to the government and policy makers is that it promises multiple social outcomes (Figure 2.8). Social theory and research indicate that social capital may result in positive outcomes in the fields of crime, health, employment, education and democracy. We shall briefly consider these in turn, drawing on the summaries provided by Kawachi and Berkman (2000) and Aldridge et al (2002).

Figure 2.8: The outcomes of social capital

Area of impact	Social capital mechanisms
Reduced crime	Improved socialisation processes
	Stronger local norms and sanctions
Improved health	Adoption of healthy behaviours
	Better provision of health services
	Higher self-esteem and less social isolation
Better labour market outcomes	Weak ties that offer information and opportunities
	Higher employment expectations
	Acquisition of soft skills through social networks
Higher educational attainment	Lower levels of truancy
	Parents more effective as educators
	Better home environment for learning
More effective democracy	Community more effective at expressing its needs
	Voluntary associations train future politicians
	Citizens more likely to engage and vote in politics
	Civic-minded citizens make policy implementation easier

Crime

In relation to crime, theories of informal social control (Shaw and Mackay, 1942) and 'collective efficacy' (Sampson et al, 1997) view communities as social organisations with complex social networks and socialisation processes that influence their ability to control youth and criminal activities. Perceptions of neighbourhood cohesion, trust and expectations that neighbours would exercise informal control over others have been related to levels of violent crime and property crime both within particular cities (Sampson et al, 1997) and across states (Kennedy et al, 1998; Kawachi et al, 1999). Social capital is interpreted as a community resource that is associated with better socialisation and collective norms (for example, lower self-interest), the supervision of leisure and youth activities, a willingness to intervene to prevent truancy and antisocial behaviour, and more effective community sanctions against transgressors, such as shaming.

Health

Health is another area where social capital analysts have been very active. Studies have shown relationships between various social capital measures (such as density of civic associational membership, levels of distrust and perceptions of generalised reciprocity) and health outcomes (including age-adjusted mortality and self-rated health; Kawachi et al, 1997; 1999). Three sets of links between social capital and health have been posited (Kawachi and Berkman, 2000):

1. Social capital may influence health behaviours, either by spreading health information quickly through a community, increasing the adoption of healthy norms, or acting as a break on health-damaging behaviours (for example, smoking, drug taking, crime). Of course, one could also argue that social capital may fuel health-damaging behaviours.
2. Communities with strong social capital may obtain better access to health services and other local amenities due to collective lobbying behaviour for services and better tactics to avoid any reductions in local services.
3. Social capital, especially in the form of bonding relationships, may impact upon psychosocial processes in a number of ways that have health benefits:
   - as a source of self-esteem and mutual respect (Wilkinson, 1996);
   - boosting feelings of safety and a trusting environment;
   - providing social support and care, which in turn produces a sense of wellbeing and belonging;
   - reducing social isolation and its effects upon ill health;
   - improving the functioning of the human immune system through emotional support;
   - confiding opportunities (Kennedy et al, 1990).

Health is an area where mainstream policies dovetail neatly with the concerns of regeneration policy (see Russell and Killoran, 2000). This ought not to be surprising, given that a recent review concluded that:

> neighbourhood conditions do appear to matter ... across a broad range of outcomes. We find the strongest evidence for the independent effect of neighbourhood on overall mortality. There is also reasonably sound evidence that neighbourhoods ... shape health-related behaviours and mental health. (Gould-Ellen et al, 2001, p 404)

The government has adopted a social model of health that explicitly acknowledges the influences of lifestyles and the social environment upon health outcomes (Department of Health, 1998). Indeed, reminiscent of the language of social exclusion is the government's report on health inequalities, which talks of 'upstream policies' consisting of non-health interventions and having a wide range of benefits including benefits to health (Acheson, 1998). Subsequently, the Health Development Agency commenced a programme of research into the links between social capital and health in order to see how social capital could be used "to support participatory approaches to health improvement in practice" (Swann and Morgan, 2002, p 5). The link to regeneration is very close, and one of the government's Health Action Zones has produced a guide to health impact assessment that views regeneration as something aiming "to change the resources at people's disposal and the conditions in which people live" (Cave and Curtis, 2001, p 11). It identifies social capital as one of four key aspects of regeneration programmes that influence health.

Employment

Social capital turns the focus from financial poverty to 'network poverty'. That is, areas of concentrated poverty are said to lack the network of weak ties that provide access to information and opportunities about jobs (Six, 1997). The thesis is that the labour market works as much through informal networks as through formal institutions, and that relying solely on the latter is insufficient. The government's Performance and Innovation Unit (Aldridge et al, 2002) cites research to show that, in the US, racial differences in employment outcomes depend largely on the fact that white communities – much more so than black communities – use their social capital in the form of personal networks to find out about employment opportunities (Petersen et al, 2000). In the UK, meanwhile, ethnic minority groups cite a lack of social 'connectedness' as a barrier to career advancement. While quantitative research based on British longitudinal data has found that individuals' employment expectations, the probability of someone starting a job, and the chances of leaving poverty are all lower in deprived areas, after controlling for the individual's characteristics, the area effects upon employment are modest (Buck, 2001). Moreover, the research does not identify social capital as the area characteristic that most influences outcomes.

Education

It is clear that the government believes that educational attainment depends upon factors beyond the skills of teachers, especially the ethos of the school and the attitudes of parents. Social capital is a way of linking these two factors, since a lot depends upon aspirations that in turn are communicated through social networks (Aldridge et al, 2002). In the field of education, the links between social capital and relevant outcomes are more nebulous and less clearly specified, though the connection between social capital and human capital was once the main concern of Coleman (1988), one of the most prominent writers on social capital.

By considering those factors that have been identified in educational research as impacting upon educational outcomes (see Sparkes and Glennerster, 2002), we can identify the role that social capital might play in relation to performance at school and adult outcomes. Social capital, through its norms and role in informal social control, may help reduce truancy levels, which have been shown to be related to lower-status jobs, less stable careers, unemployment, marital breakdown and heavy smoking in adult life. Labour market success is also related to the acquisition of soft skills, many of which may be acquired through social networks such as friendliness, teamwork, spoken communication and enthusiasm.

Social capital and the role of parents are also crucial to school performance. High levels of trust and contact between parents and the school are associated with better outcomes, and of course it may be the case that trust in the school is linked to general trust in institutions. The parents' role as educators has been shown to be important to outcomes in the early stages of schooling, yet a lack of confidence, knowledge and guidance inhibits parents taking part in learning activities with their children. This barrier could be overcome through social networks with capable parents who then disseminate information about their own approaches to home learning. Lastly, the home environment is important to pupils becoming good learners, in particular in terms of its organisational dimensions and levels of encouragement. Peer pressures and social capital that emphasises home learning may boost the perceived role of the home in this regard.

The functioning of democracy

The social capital agenda is part and parcel of New Labour's aim to achieve 'democratic renewal', creating a symbiotic relationship between effective government and interested, self-supporting and law abiding citizens. Putnam advanced this line of argument in his study of regional government in Italy, where he stated that 'the more civic the context, the better the government' (1993, p 182), with government performance measured in terms of effectiveness, efficiency and levels of citizen satisfaction. He ended his book with the line:

> Building social capital will not be easy, but it is the key to making democracy work. (Putnam, 1993, p 185)

More recently, the democratic renewal agenda in the UK has broadened to include voter turnout as well as government effectiveness. Falling participation rates in local and national elections undermine the government's legitimacy, and thus evidence that civic trust and group membership rates are related to voter turnout strengthens the government's interest in social capital (Kawachi and Berkman, 2000).

Thus, the New Labour government believes that social capital is the key to effective democracy, and we can identify a number of mechanisms by which this is held to be so. First, as stated above, local levels of trust and group involvement seem to influence turnout in national elections, so that developing social capital may have spin-offs for civic engagement and government legitimacy. Second, citizens with social capital resources are better organised, better informed about how government works, and more able to convey their needs to government, so that public services better meet their needs and they can put pressure on governments to allocate resources to them. Third, citizens are more civic-minded, more cooperative and more law-abiding if they possess social capital, with the result that government finds it easier to implement policies in this context. Last, civic engagement at the local level and involvement in voluntary associations can act as a recruiting and training ground for local and national politics, enhancing political interest and the capability of politicians.

Conclusions

We have seen that social capital features prominently in New Labour's approach to regeneration and urban policy. This is for a number of reasons, both practical and ideological. Most important is its role in unifying government policy and making a link between the urban/regeneration policy field and the government's wider agenda to modernise the way government works and renew British democracy. In this sense, social capital can be viewed as a good thing, demonstrating more creativity on the part of policy makers and integrating urban/regeneration policy with other policy areas. This begs the question: has social capital influenced urban and regeneration practice as well as policy?

However, there are dangers in the social capital approach. First, the government ought to be wary of being seduced by its own policy and linguistic creativity. The emphasis upon 'soft goals' such as social capital and self-esteem may not be enough to satisfy the electorate, who still want greater financial security and better public service performance, which social capital is still at some remove from delivering.

Second, there are drawbacks in the prominent role given to citizen responsibility and self-help as part and parcel of the social capital agenda. If better outcomes are not secured for poor communities, it may be possible for the government to lay the blame partly (or largely) at the door of the communities themselves, on the grounds that the conditions for greater cooperative behaviour, networking and so on were put in place but that these were not taken advantage of. Furthermore, a crucial weakness is the assumed correspondence between 'community empowerment' and 'individual empowerment; that is, the correspondence between the realisation of social capital resources, and the bigger issue of one's control over one's own destiny and influence over others. The social capital approach to neighbourhood renewal risks failing to make the connection between deprived areas and the operation of wider governance structures within urban regions. An analysis of power relations would have to entail scrutiny of the political opportunity structures in place within districts and regions, and the context-specific nature of trust in governance.

Third, while social capital has contributed to some deeper thinking about the nature of community cohesion within urban Britain, notably following ethnic tensions in medium-sized towns, it is also clear that some of the proposals that have emerged from this consideration are underexplored. The prescription that community cohesion should entail a unified, shared sense of place, a set of common values and a reduction in segregation of residence and institutions between ethnic groups, may not necessarily be essential. The extent to which this social reformulation is required, or the degree to which tolerant communities can be constructed without them, is open to question. But this is a set of issues that requires further consideration of the nature of identity and of the role of the public sphere in contemporary British society. Unfortunately, these issues tend to become hidden behind the social capital's nostalgic 'civicness'.

Last, social capital may be somewhat disabling as a central element of government policy because it is so amenable to New Labour spin. In the face of some overarching success in boosting measured levels of social capital, it is possible that policy makers may convince themselves that social conditions have improved when in fact society may not be quite as civic, harmonious, tolerant and collaborative as social capital indicators would have us believe. A reliance upon aggregate, cross-sectional measures of social capital (such as contained in the General Household Survey) is insufficiently informative about the nature of social processes and the quality of social relations at different spatial scales.

The New Labour government must remember that social capital, like other forms of capital, is only beneficial if it can be put to good use. Social capital is not an end in itself; rather, it is a resource that individuals and communities must have the opportunity to use. Thus, the political, economic and spatial structures of cities remain as important as ever, and any evaluation of policy should consider what communities have managed to achieve as a result of higher levels of social capital and how citizens' quality of life has been improved through social capital.

Acknowledgement

I would like to thank two of my colleagues, Caroline Hoy and Alison Parkes, for providing extensive comments on an earlier draft of this chapter.

Further reading

The SEU produces a wide range of policy statements and reports, and the key material can be accessed on its website (www.socialexclusionunit.gov.uk). For a good discussion of the philosophy of social exclusion underpinning New Labour policy agendas, see Mulgan (1998a) and Oppenheim (1998). The best critical review is that of Levitas (1998).

THREE

Visions of 'urban renaissance': the Urban Task Force report and the Urban White Paper

Loretta Lees

Introduction

> The production of images and of discourses is an important facet of activity
> that has to be analysed as part and parcel of the reproduction and
> transformation of any symbolic order. (Harvey, 1989a, p 355)

Recent government urban policy statements have invoked a discourse of 'urban
renaissance' that interweaves calls for urban sustainability with a prescription
of concepts and ways of living that are closely tied to gentrification practices.
The government's Urban Task Force (UTF) report, *Towards an urban renaissance*
(DETR, 1999a), and the recent Urban White Paper (UWP) on urban policy,
Our towns and cities – The future: Delivering an urban renaissance (DETR, 2000e),
both call for a move 'back to the city'. Their 'new vision for urban living' in
England is remarkably similar to visions of gentrification. However, the term
'gentrification' itself is never used in these policy documents. Instead, 'urban
renaissance', 'urban regeneration', and 'urban sustainability' are used in its place.
These neutered terms politely avoid the class constitution of the processes
involved. It is difficult to find favour with gentrification, but who would
oppose urban renaissance, regeneration and sustainability?

This chapter examines the discursive contexts within which urban policy is
being developed in the UK. It devotes considerable time to a critique of the
language used in these documents[1]. The discursively invisible process of
gentrification is promoted by policy makers as the saviour in troubled English
inner cities, and this vision of a continental-style café culture feeds into this
language of sustainability, diversity and community (and thus citizenship and
rights). My critique of the language used in both the UTF report and the
UWP is quite pointed. In their favour, each of these reports takes a long, hard
look at the problems of English towns and cities and goes some way towards
developing constructive solutions in the face of very complex issues. They

should be applauded for moving British urban policy (at least in principle) towards a more long-term and holistic set of prescriptions that balance West European models of urban regeneration with US models of the same. And thanks to the work of the UTF and the UWP, the most disadvantaged groups have been returned to the policy arena, as have long-neglected neighbourhoods and new models of public participation.

This chapter begins, then, by situating itself within a broader critique of the discourse of contemporary British urban policy. It then scrutinises the relevant policy documents and locates them within British postwar urban policy. The substantive part of the chapter shows contemporary urban policy to be a form of state-led gentrification. Here, I focus on three key concepts of these documents – sustainability, diversity and community. Each of these stands for the 'liveable city' in gentrification literature and practices. The chapter concludes by saying the government's urban renaissance initiatives can be read as gentrification initiatives, and thus are likely to come unstuck due to the mismatch between their inevitably class-dividing effects and the socially just, mixed and inclusive city that is the government's ostensible objective. This mismatch between rhetoric and lived reality demonstrates the importance of a discursive approach to urban policy, as well as the need for greater care within the policy community for a cultural politics of genuine representation that goes beyond a superficial focus on spin and immediate presentation.

Deconstructing contemporary British urban policy[2]

My particular interest in the UTF report and the UWP stems from my past work on discourses of planning (Lees and Demeritt, 1998) and gentrification (Lees, 1996). This discursive turn in urban studies (Hastings, 1999a) and urban geography (Imrie et al, 1996; Lees, 2002) attends closely to the language and rhetoric by which policy goals and mechanisms are framed. It originates in the belief that the cultural politics of representation and meaning are inseparable from the formal politics of governance and decision making. In this way, researchers seek to integrate the study of culture and language into a wider political and economic approach focused on "substantive concerns and empirical questions such as the nature of citizenship and citizen participation, urban governance and planning, policy processes and power" (Hastings, 1999b, p 7).

In what follows, text and language are approached as forms of discourse that help to create and reproduce social meaning. My focus is on the use of language and strategies of argument – that is, *rhetoric*. Rhetorical strategies include the use of metaphors, tropes, myths, associations, and so on. In exploring the active role of language in the policy process, I loosely follow Fairclough's (1992) three-dimensional framework of analysis – text analysis, discursive practice and social practice. For textual analysis, the vocabulary, grammar and text structure of the UTF report and the UWP will be scrutinised. In terms of discursive practice, I consider the context in which their policy statements are made and how they are linked to other debates and literatures. And in terms of social practice, finally, I am concerned with conceptualising the more general ideological context within which the discourses have taken place, for

> there is a dialectical relationship between the discursive and the non-discursive such that one cannot exist (or be thought) without the other. (Atkinson, 2000b, p 212)

The analytical advantage of a discursive approach is that it focuses attention on specifically historical and geographical pillars of institutionalised knowledge, power and practice, which advocate particular regeneration initiatives as the solution to urban ills (Hastings, 1998; Atkinson, 1999a, 2000a).

The Urban Task Force report and the Urban White Paper

In 1998, the architect Richard Rogers (now Lord Rogers of Riverside) was asked by the Deputy Prime Minister John Prescott to head the UTF[3]. Rogers was to coordinate a group of experts from both the public and private sectors, as well as a large number of working group members. The aim of this UTF was to identify the causes of urban decline in England and to "recommend practical solutions to bring people back into our cities, towns and urban neighbourhoods" (DETR, 1999a, p 1). As its mission statement explained:

> The Urban Task Force will identify causes of urban decline in England and recommend practical solutions to bring people back into our cities, towns and urban neighbourhoods. It will establish a new vision for urban regeneration founded on the principles of design excellence, social well-being and environmental responsibility within a viable economic and legislative framework. (DETR, 1999a, p 1)

As part of its research, the UTF visited not only English cities, but also cities in Europe and the US. The UTF's final report (DETR, 1999a) set out its urban vision for England. This is an explicitly pro-urban document that contains a plethora of exciting ideas about how to make cities in England better places. Its recommendations are presented under five headings:

• The sustainable city
• Making towns and cities work
• Making the most of our urban assets
• Making the investment
• Sustaining the renaissance.

One year later the government published the UWP (DETR, 2000a), its formal response to the UTF report. This is the first White Paper on urban policy since Peter Shore's *Policy for the inner cities* (DoE, 1977), which led to the Urban Areas Act (1978), and it stands as a statement of the centrality of cities in contemporary national life. The scope of the UWP is more comprehensive than the UTF report. In addition to the UTF report, the UWP draws on the work of the Social Exclusion Unit (SEU), and on work such as *The state of the English cities* (DETR, 2000f). At the heart of the UWP is 'a new vision of urban living':

> Our vision is of towns, cities and suburbs which offer a high quality of life and opportunity for all, not just the few. We want to see:
>
> - people shaping the future of their community, supported by strong and truly representative local leaders;
> - people living in attractive, well kept towns and cities which use space and buildings well;
> - good design and planning which makes it practical to live in a more environmentally sustainable way, with less noise, pollution and traffic congestion;
> - towns and cities able to create and share prosperity, investing to help all their citizens reach their full potential; and
> - good quality services – health, education, housing, transport, finance, shopping, leisure and protection from crime – that meet the needs of people and businesses wherever they are.
>
> This urban renaissance will benefit everyone, making towns and cities vibrant and successful, and protecting the countryside from development pressure. (DETR, 2000e, p 7)

Both the UTF report and the UWP are set to influence urban policy for the foreseeable future by providing a discursive framework for future policy initiatives. Both separately and together they seek to set the course for an 'urban renaissance' in England and the UK.

A policy document's formal 'Introduction' orientates the reader and sets the scene for the document's arguments and narrative (Hastings, 1998, pp 198-9). Its argumentative function is to guide the reader's interpretation of subsequent aspects of the text and lead the audience to a particular course of action. Following Stone (1989), Hastings argues that two dominant story lines are used for constructing arguments in policy making: first, the 'story of decline', and second, the 'story of control and helplessness' (which argues that decline is caused by human agents). Both of these story lines are apparent in the introduction to Lord Rogers' UTF report (DETR, 1999a). Rogers argues that:

> Since the industrial revolution *we* have lost ownership of our towns and cities, allowing them to become spoilt by poor design, economic dispersal and social polarisation. (DETR, 1999a, p 8, emphasis in original)

The story, then, is about the loss of control of our towns and cities. This is later elaborated in the section 'Urban legacy' (DETR, 1999a, pp 26-7), in which the industrial age is blamed for the severance of people and place in towns and cities and for the departure from a 'continental attitude' towards urban life.

For Rogers, a 'continental attitude' is one in which a person has "confidence in the ability of the city to provide a framework for humane civic life" (DETR, 1999a, p 26). The pollution and slums of the British industrial city, he argues, destroyed such an attitude in Britain and led to negative feelings towards urban life. In the introduction, Rogers also states:

> To stem a long period of decline and decay, pessimism and under-investment, we must bring about a change in urban attitudes so that towns and cities once again become attractive places in which to live, work and socialise. (DETR, 1999a, p 7)

The UTF report, then, is the story of urban decline and how *we* should respond to it. This story is addressed to us, to an undifferentiated 'we'. This serves two purposes: to universalise the problem (urban decline affects us all in the same way), and to diffuse specific responsibility for causing and alleviating urban problems. It is a classic example of the liberal rhetoric of moral responsibility.

There is no similar introduction to the UWP; they are not included in White Papers' specific formats. However, there is a preface written by Deputy Prime Minister John Prescott. Here, Prescott repeats the stories of decline and of loss of control and helplessness:

> In the twenty years since the last Urban White Paper, many of our towns and cities have suffered from neglect, poor management, inadequate public services, lack of investment and a culture of short-termism. (DETR, 2000e, p 5)

The solution, Prescott argues, is to let people have their say in shaping urban areas; so, too, argued Rogers in the UTF report. Indeed, human agency is the focus of both reports, and it is tied explicitly to notions of citizenship and democracy. Both the UTF report and the UWP state that "People make cities but cities make citizens". This offers an interesting contrast to Rousseau's classic statement, that "Houses make a town, but citizens make a city" (see Mumford, 1961, p 93), and to other urbanist scholarship that argues that citizens make a city, albeit one of disorder/spontaneity (see for example, Jacobs, 1961; Merrifield, 2000). The UTF report argues that 'we' have lost control/ownership of our towns and cities – could the argument that 'cities make citizens' be a latent attempt by the government to regain control over 'us'? It is certainly about 'ordering' cities (for a related discussion on this, see Lees, 2003: forthcoming).

'Urban renaissance': key words in British urban policy, 1945-2000

Since 1945, British urban policy and planning has been punctuated by a series of key words with a common prefix (Furbey, 1999). In the postwar years, it was 'reconstruction'; in the 1960s and 1970s 'renewal' and 'redevelopment'; in the 1980s 'regeneration', and in the 1990s 'renaissance'. Of all these, 'urban renaissance' goes the furthest. Urban renewal was public sector-driven and primarily concerned with the large-scale (and often highly zoned) redevelopment of 'overcrowded' inner-city slum areas. By contrast, urban regeneration focused on economic growth and used public funds to lever in largely undirected market investment, as exemplified by London's Docklands (see Brownill, 1990; Ogden, 1992). Current urban renaissance prescriptions seek to drive forward and coordinate a range of programmes (both public and private), with the aim of reinvigorating urban areas to make them both desirable places to live and at the same time more environmentally sustainable (DETR, 2000c; see also Carmona, 2001). Given the current government's continued reliance on private sector partnership and informal, unelected mechanisms of urban governance pioneered during the Thatcher years, this environmental awareness represents the biggest substantive difference between contemporary urban renaissance and the urban regeneration initiatives of past Conservative governments.

In contemporary British urban policy, then, the urban regeneration metaphor is being replaced by the urban renaissance metaphor. Both, however, have similar meanings: rebirth, revival, reconstitution. Critically reflecting on the urban regeneration metaphor, Furbey (1999) has explored the roots of the word 'regeneration' in religion, social theory and medicine. He reveals how more conservative meanings came to dominate use of the term in urban and social policy in the 1980s. In the Christian tradition, 'regeneration' is a word infused with religious hope, but also encompasses diverse and conflicting understandings. For example, some Christians see it as strongly social and ecological, requiring commitment to social justice and liberation, while for others it refers to the 'born again' Christian individual. Allied to this evangelical reading, 'regeneration' became a key word in urban policy statements in the 1980s, associated as it was with Thatcherite appeals to individualism. Regeneration also resonates with the organic social vision of classical one-nation Toryism. In particular, it expresses anxiety about social *degeneration*. Furbey also argues that, in terms of socio-medical interventionism, regeneration became a kind of urban medicine that could be applied to urban problems.

Urban policy's new key word – renaissance – defies a simple definition. In contrast to the previous Conservative government's urban regeneration, New Labour's urban renaissance has tended to ally itself to the social and the ecological, and to commit itself to social justice and liberation. Their concept of urban renaissance goes beyond physical environmental objectives to include concerns for social inclusion, wealth creation, sustainable development, urban governance, health and welfare, crime prevention, educational opportunity and freedom of movement, as well as of environmental quality and good design. Where regeneration was the medicine for social degeneration, renaissance is the medicine for urban malaise (see Figure 3.1)[4].

This new urban medicine is not intended to be a quick fix, but rather a long-term and sustainable one. Indeed, in documents such as the UTF report and the UWP, 'urban renaissance' is used interchangeably with 'urban sustainability': renaissance encompasses calls for urban intensification or densification and the need to develop more housing on brownfield sites, so as to create a compact or ecological city (see Breheny, 1992; Jenks et al, 1996). In large measure, the prominence of urban sustainability in urban policy discourse is related to debates over where to locate the projected increase in the number of households. In 1992, central government forecast the need for houses for 4.4 million new households, most of them in the already overcrowded south-east of England. Many commentators felt that locating new housing developments on greenfield sites was environmentally destructive, both exacerbating local problems of congestion, air pollution and habitat loss, and, through dependence on the private motor car, increasing national fossil fuel dependence and gas emissions (Carmona, 2001, p 170). It is interesting to note that, in this specific instance, discursive coalitions are seemingly forming between suburban Tory supporters of the Greenbelt environmentalists, and inner-city 'gentrifiers'.

Urban sustainability as a metaphor arrived on the policy scene in the 1990s. It acted as an elastic band, stretching to encompass both the urban regeneration and urban renaissance metaphors. As Healey (1997) notes, it has widened the spatial focus of regeneration/renaissance prescriptions from localities to cities and regions. Temporally, it argues that regeneration must be a long-term organic process (and not a quick fix), and substantively, it makes connections between the natural or physical and socioeconomic health of cities. The metaphor of urban sustainability has, perhaps for the first time, stretched British urban policy so that the urban and the rural – the city and the countryside – are ecologically interconnected. Indeed, in parliamentary discussions the UWP was introduced and debated simultaneously with the Rural White Paper. In the introduction to the debate it was noted that:

> On both urban and rural policy, the Government can influence matters so far, but beyond that it is essential that people adapt and change their behaviour. (House of Commons Hansard Debates, 2001)[5]

The metaphor of urban sustainability, like that of urban renaissance, is often used to promote solutions to English urban problems that could be conceived of as state-led gentrification.

Figure 3.1: Signs of urban renaissance or urban malaise

Dimensions	Signs of urban renaissance	Signs of urban malaise
Design excellence	A high-quality, well-connected and equitable public realm	Poor-quality, uncared-for and disconnected public realm
	High-quality, locally distinctive urban landscape and architectural design	'Anywhere' urban landscape and architectural design
	Individual design interventions that also contribute to a larger coherent whole	Isolated, individual and uncoordinated urban interventions
	A general valuing of high-quality design in both public and private sectors	Design given a low priority in both public and private sectors
	A high percentage of planning applications submitted by architects	Few planning applications submitted by architects
	Safe, pedestrian-oriented streets	Unsafe, traffic-dominated streets
	Investment in public art	Little public art
	Availability of dedicated public sector resources to reinforce long-term private investment	Lack of public sector resources and unfocused, short-term investment mentality
	Evidence of a café culture	No café culture
	High retail and commercial occupancy rates	Retail and commercial vacancy problems
	Animated streets – day and evening	Depressed daytime and evening economy
	Variety in urban housing market and mixing of tenure	Social housing ghettos and gated communities
	Innovation in local business activity	Stagnating local business economy
	High employment rates	High unemployment rates
	A viable urban retail sector	A declining urban retail sector
Environmental responsibility	Short home-to-work travel distances	Long-distance commuting, often by car
	Housing built at higher densities (terraces and town houses)	Low density housing (detached and semi-detached)
	Readily available public transport	Lack or absence of public transport
	Good pedestrian and cycle mobility	Reliance on car borne travel
	High rates of brownfield land reuse and reduced urban sprawl	Urban sprawl and continued greenfield allocation
	Reduced residential and business parking standards	High parking standards
	Concentrated employment activity	Dispersed employment activities
	Uses mixed and well integrated	Zoned development and single use residential areas
	Key built and natural assets conserved	Declining built and natural environment
	Low levels of pollution	Increasing energy use and pollution
	Well-integrated natural and built environment	Poorly integrated natural and built environment

Figure 3.1: continued

Social wellbeing	Availability of high-quality social and health facilities	Lack of social and health facilities
	Availability of good-quality schooling and training	Poor-quality schooling, low exam results and unskilled population
	Well-developed cultural sector and activities	Little cultural investment or activity
	A tolerant, socially and ethnically mixed population	Segregated and gated communities, and racial intolerance
	Good access to urban leisure activities	Limited choice of urban leisure activities
	High participation in public life and well-developed voluntary sector	Disenfranchised population and low public involvement
	Low crime rates and fear of crime	High crime rates and fear of crime
	Positive perceptions about (and more) urban living	Strong desire to escape from urban environments
	A sense of civic duty	No sense of civic duty
	Low levels of social deprivation	High levels of social deprivation
Good governance	Clean, efficient and well-used modes of public transport	Dirty, unreliable and poorly used modes of transport
	An enfranchised and active local population	A disenfranchised local population
	A shared vision – public/private/and community	No shared vision or no vision at all
	A clean, well-maintained and managed public realm	Litter and vandalism and little sign of urban management
	A responsive public sector	A detached and unresponsive public sector
	Readily available and skilled public sector advice and action	A deskilled public sector
	Evidence of public–private partnership	No public–private partnership
	Inter-agency coordination and cooperation	Ad hoc, uncoordinated public action
	Design award schemes in operation	No promotion of good design

Sources: DETR (2000c); Carmona (2001, pp 174-5)

Textbook gentrification

British urban policy's affair with gentrification is nothing new. It began almost as soon as the process of gentrification was realised in British cities. Hamnett (1973; see also Lees, 1994), for example, found that the availability of government improvement grants for private sector rehabilitation caused gentrification. During this period of first-wave gentrification:

> governments were aggressive in helping gentrification because the prospect of inner-city investment (without state insurance of some form) was still

very risky. While state involvement was often justified through the discourse of ameliorating urban decline, the effect was of course highly class specific. Conditions generally worsened for the urban working class as a result of such intervention. (Hackworth and Smith, 2001, p 466)

After years of laissez-faire gentrification, the British state, like the US (see Hackworth and Smith, 2001; Wyly and Hammel, 1999), is now assisting third-wave (that is, contemporary) gentrification much more assertively. Smith (2002) argues that a new revanchist urbanism has replaced the liberal urban policy of cities in the advanced capitalist world. He also argues that gentrification is now a thoroughly generalised urban strategy that has taken over from liberal urban policy, and that its incidence is now global.

As Butler and Robson (2001) note, the UTF report and the UWP read like a 'gentrifiers' charter'. (I have also heard it called 'the cappuccino cave-in'.) However, at first glance it is much easier to uncover the hidden face of gentrification in the UTF report than in the UWP[6]. Partly this is due to the very different styles of each document – the UTF report is more detailed and descriptive than the necessarily staccato-style policy statements of the UWP. Moreover, the import of the government's SEU is quite noticeable in the UWP, where it appears to have mediated some of the 'middle-class' excesses of the UTF report by making the policy prescriptions more inclusive of all sectors of society. Nevertheless, both documents would, if put into practice, facilitate gentrification (albeit at different scales).

Lord Rogers and the UTF, it seems, would have us all be 'gentrifiers':

> We must bring about a change in urban attitudes so that towns and cities once again become attractive places in which to live, work and socialise. (DETR, 1999a, p 7)

Gentrifiers, as we know, also hold particularly positive attitudes towards the urban (see Ley, 1996). Indeed, the UTF seeks to build on the gentrification that has already occurred:

> In England we are starting to see people move back into city centres, drawn by a lifestyle where home, work and leisure are interwoven within a single neighbourhood. These achievements are small but they can be built upon. (DETR, 1999a, p 27)

The UTF advocates practices that are commonly regarded as the preserve of gentrification:

> The presumption throughout should be to preserve and adapt historic buildings to accommodate new uses and provide a focus for urban communities. (DETR, 1999a, p 42)

Even the UTF's examples of good urban practice are taken directly out of gentrification catalogues. For example, the UTF singles out the property development company Urban Splash as a model for the refurbishment of underused buildings (DETR, 1999a, p 252). Urban Splash has redeveloped a number of warehouses around the UK into ultra-chic loft apartments. The UWP also lauds Urban Splash as a model example of how to bring empty property back into use (DETR, 2000e, p 56). But such warehouse redevelopment is expensive and for the most part, because of the limited space, high cost and lack of facilities for children, it is only attractive to wealthy professional singles or couples without children. The UTF promotes the kinds of gentrified enclaves familiar from US rust-belt cities such as New York, Boston and Baltimore. One of the UK examples that it praises is the Calls and Riverside district of Leeds, an enclave "filled with entertainment, media and creative businesses, hotels, housing, shops and visitor attractions" (DETR, 1999a, p 65). Based on an economy of conspicuous consumption, such enclaves are designed for and attract the middle classes – that is, the consuming and spending classes. They are not designed for, nor do they welcome, lower-income groups without the disposable income and cultural capital to participate in that kind of high-end living.

In fact, the UTF report assumes that we are all middle class. The 'general population' referred to throughout the report is always a middle-class one:

> As lifespans lengthen, and working and parenting are taking up smaller proportions of people's lives, the amount of time to devote to leisure, culture and education is increasing. On the one hand this points to a more mobile population. (DETR, 1999a, p 29)

But where in this image of the general population are to be found the single parents, the unemployed, the immobile poor or those on low incomes? And what is this 'culture' that we are devoting more time to? Reading between the lines, it is high-brow culture – the arts, for example, often unaffordable and indeed unattractive to those outside a particular middle- and upper-class cohort (see Bridge, 2001). The UTF report is littered with lazy assumptions that we all have new mobility and new lifestyle choices. For example:

> Fuelled by labour mobility and increasing personal wealth, many households will have growing choice as to where they live. (DETR, 1999a, p 35)

How many, exactly? The UTF sees such features to be the drivers of 21st-century change, but certainly not for the population of England as whole. The UTF want specifically to attract and retain the middle classes:

> In the 21st century, it is the skilled worker, as well as the global company, who will be footloose. Cities must work hard to attract and retain both. (DETR, 1999a, p 42)

If the tenets of the UTF were to be followed to the letter, the end result would be 'cities for the few, not the many'. Adopting a rather tongue-in-cheek style of critique, Amin et al elaborate on this:

> What are the industries cities should attract? Why finance and media and information technology (plus biotechnology if someone could make a profit from it)? How should cities be set up? So that they will attract workers in these industries – especially younger managers and professionals who will give a city the buzz. In turn, working-class people will find a niche – servicing middle-class people, acting as evidence of multicultural cosmopolitanism or exemplifying the problem communities. What they will not be is central to urban regeneration. They will only be allowed to cheer from the sidelines as the niceness squeeze of this gentrification continues. (Amin et al, 2000, pp 22-3)

While the UWP does take on board many of the ideas encapsulated in the UTF report, its middle-class excesses are tempered by the import of the government's SEU. Indeed, on its first reading the UWP appears to advocate cities for "all, not just the few", as indeed it states (DETR, 2000e, p 7). It argues that:

> everybody should be included. This is both a mark of a decent society and plain good sense as a society which allows some to be excluded loses the benefit of their contribution. (DETR, 2000e, p 8)

Yet even here the government's prescription for urban renaissance slots neatly into the gentrification textbook. The desire for social mixing and celebration of difference are hallmarks of liberal gentrifiers (Ley, 1980; Caulfield, 1989, 1994; Butler, 1997). As Ley (1994, 1996) demonstrates, the left-liberal politics of the 'cultural new class' is distinctly pro-social mixing, pro-public development, and so on. Gentrifiers also promote urban 'livability' of the kind that the UWP advocates under 'sustainability'. Given the origins and orientation of the New Labour government, it is hardly surprising that its urban policy should embody so much that is dear to the 'new' middle classes.

But the problem with the UWP is not that the new middle classes also use the same rhetoric, but that, despite all the talk of social inclusion and sustainability, the UWP does not actually back it up with any substantial plans to do anything about them. What the New Labour government will deliver is very modest (indeed, Lord Rogers is disappointed that the government has not taken his ideas on board more fully). To realise its vision of gentrification for all, the UTF report called for substantial state intervention, such as taxes on vacant urban land and the strengthening of local authority powers of foreclosure and enforced sale of abandoned and dilapidated sites or buildings (DETR, 1999a, p 225-6). In addition to substantially more public spending:

as much public expenditure as possible must work hard towards securing an urban renaissance .... Public capital investment must increase if we are to deliver 60% or more of new homes on recycled land .... This investment should be matched by increased revenue support to ensure higher quality local services in urban neighbourhoods. (DETR, 1999a, pp 279-99)

Although the UWP adopts most of the policy reforms advocated by the UTF, it systematically rejects proposals to increase public expenditure or interfere substantially with the workings of the free market. Instead, the fiscal measures proposed by the UWP amount to tinkering around the edges: the exemption from Stamp Duty for property transactions in disadvantaged areas; the accelerated payable Tax Credits for cleaning up contaminated land; the 100% capital allowances for creating 'flats over shops' for letting; VAT reforms to encourage additional conversions of properties for residential use (see DETR, 1999a, p 9). Rather than 'firming up' urban policy and bringing decision making closer to affected communities, this confusing plethora of complicated initiatives continues a wider pattern of neoliberal governmentality (all too familiar to academic survivors of the RAE, TQA, QAA, and so on). In addition to being drip-fed from the Treasury, this governmentality – combined with exacting auditing procedures – disciplines governmental subjects and cements the control of Treasury mandarins in Whitehall.

Reading between the lines and between budgets, the government intends to spend very little on urban renaissance. Nor is it prepared to intervene in any meaningful way in the market. The UWP specifically rejects UTF proposals to legislate in order to compel private sector organisations to release redundant land for regeneration; to introduce a scheme for taxing vacant land; and to require local authorities to bring empty homes back into use (DETR, 2000e, pp 147-50). Moreover the government lacks the will to implement a transit policy that disfavours the private motorist – policy that is key to the UTF's sustainability prescriptions. Friends of the Earth (2000) has claimed that, in its view, the UWP is "full of carrots but with few sticks". Its transport campaigner complains that without "radical measures" to promote brownfield development and public transit, "our cities will still be cities for cars and not cities for people". The increased expenditure on roads, the government cave-in on a petrol tax and the increasing costs of rail travel all stand in the face of calls for urban sustainability.

The government's education policy has not succeeded in preventing the middle classes from leaving the cities once they have children. Recent pledges of more money and specialist schools will have limited impact. The UTF has recognised that:

the crunch comes with having children. An urban environment, previously perceived as diverse and stimulating, starts to appear unsafe. Schools and health services become more important. While it is therefore accepted that, at this stage in their life cycle, many people will continue to move to more suburban or small town environments, we must look to persuade more families to stay. (DETR, 1999a, p 35)

Here, paradoxically, the influence of the SEU should be at its greatest. The paradox is that education, as Robson and Butler (2001, pp 80-4) note, is so key to middle-class reproduction, that middle-class cosmopolitans are much more active 'choosers' of their children's schools in the education market than working-class locals. Without some strategic engagement with such markets, the government is not going to attract – let alone keep – higher numbers of middle-class families in British inner cities. As such they will not achieve the social mixing they desire.

As a result of this failure to address the 'market failures' of our urban system through spending and regulation, the UWP is unlikely to live up to its rhetoric about social exclusion and inclusion and social mixing. Instead, the result of these modest reforms is likely to be 'business as usual'. Without more government intervention, investment and regulation, the only places that will get regenerated in the ways that the UTF would like to see are those that get gentrified through private/market forces, further exacerbating the problems of displacement, social exclusion and polarisation long familiar to gentrification researchers. Whereas the UTF wants to use government regulation and spending to transform entire cities into upmarket gentrified spaces of 'café chic', the UWP refuses to intervene in the market at all. By benignly leaving cities to the market, the result of the UWP is likely to be a few gentrified islands of prosperity amid a sea of inner-city decay and suburban sprawl. This is in contrast to the UTF's vision, in which islands of decay are flooded by seas of urban (and suburban) renewal.

My point here is not that all gentrification practices are 'bad', as has tended to be the case in the most dominant academic discussions of the process (for example, Smith, 1996). Rather, I am concerned that policy statements that prioritise a 'back to the city' move by the middle classes do so at the expense of other social groups. As the gentrification literature teaches us, gentrification inevitably leads to displacement and social polarisation. It does not in the long run lead to social mixing (see Lyons, 1996; Atkinson, 2000a; for a detailed analysis, see Robson and Butler, 2001). Indeed as Atkinson's recent review concludes, "the research evidence on gentrification largely relates to negative neighbourhood impacts" (Atkinson, 2002, p 18)[7]. It seems that state-led gentrification has crept *back* into the urban policy arena, and Britain is not alone in this. In Australia, Badcock (2001) reveals how both state and federal governments have been instrumental in enticing private reinvestment into the disinvested inner-western suburbs of Adelaide, ensuring that it is solidly gentrified. Likewise, Wyly and Hammel (1999) show that gentrification has exerted such a significant influence on urban and public policy in the US that Berry's (1985) 'islands of renewal in seas of decay' observation has metamorphosed into 'islands of decay in seas of renewal'.

The continued discrimination in mortgage lending and the transformation of low-income housing policy in the US (a public–private alliance) has allowed gentrification to become more rigorous and widespread in the US than is perhaps the current situation in Britain. In response to van Weesep's (1994) call 'to put the gentrification debate into policy perspective', Wyly and Hammel found that gentrification in the US has come to mediate the design and implementation of public housing policy so as to create "a simultaneous expansion of affordable homeownership and accelerated class turnover" (2001, p 264) that contributes to gentrification. To date, the impact of gentrification on urban policy, and of urban policy on gentrification, has not been a research priority – this must change.

Key words within the urban renaissance: *sustainability*, *diversity* and *community*

In their construction of urban renaissance, both the UTF report and the UWP argue that urban policy in England must embrace 'sustainability', 'diversity' and 'community' in the face of forces that are destroying the physical environment, causing social exclusion, fracturing communities and disrupting our sense of place. These key words are pivotal to both documents. In what follows, I consider each one in turn and explore the links between them. Then, using examples drawn from my ongoing reading and research, I point out some of the problems that these prescriptions might face in practice.

Sustainability

By 'sustainability', the UTF report and the UWP refer largely to environmental sustainability. That usage cuts against the grain of debates within the sustainable development literature, which have sought to expand the notion of sustainability more holistically to encompass social and economic issues (Redclift, 1987). Within these urban policy discourses, questions about social and economic exclusion are more typically addressed in terms of community and competitiveness. That said, the government's prescription of an environmentally sustainable urban renaissance is intended to provide auxiliary social and economic benefits of the kind imagined by the more holistic vision of mainstream sustainable development discourse. In both cases, the foundation for urban renaissance and sustainability is the densification of the urban form. Densification of the urban form has become a magic cure-all for a variety of environmental *and* social ills. The compact urban form will reduce traffic congestion and pollution, reduce pressure on open space, habitat and agricultural land in the greenbelt, and reduce global warming.

These environmental benefits are based on comparisons of the energy use and ecological footprints of US and European cities (see DETR, 1999a, pp 59-64). Compared with sprawling US cities, denser European ones consume fewer resources. By containing suburban sprawl and focusing growth and economic expansion back on the inner city, British urban policy makers hope that urban densification policy will counter the US doughnut effect of a declining inner city surrounded by affluent and ever-expanding suburbs. In both environmental and social terms, this compact city is modelled on the kind of continental-style, 'face-to-face', café-culture city that the UTF and the government would like to see replicated in English cities. Relatively compact cities such as Amsterdam and Barcelona are cited as good examples in both reports. The compact city is a liveable city:

> The compact urban form highlights the value placed upon proximity and ease of contact between people. It gives priority to the provision of public areas for people to meet and interact, to learn from one another and to join in the diversity of urban life. (DETR, 1999a, p 41)

Both the UTF and the government must be applauded for promoting such an urban form. However, in their proposals for urban sustainability they do not address some significant behavioural issues that complicate the agenda. One of the first issues is how to attract the English to dense urban living in the face of evidence that, despite their strong (and paradoxical) desire to protect greenfield sites, they have strong anti-urban sentiments and rural (or suburban) aspirations (see Champion et al, 1998; Popular Housing Forum, 1998, p 58; URBED et al, 1999, pp 4-6). A second issue is how the government will persuade the British public to give up using their cars so much. Indeed, the recent petrol crisis attests to the central place in British life enjoyed by the private car. The UTF and the UWP have ignored questions of individual perception and behaviour, and focused instead on large-scale relationships between urban form, energy use and emissions (Owens, 1986; Jenks et al, 1996; Burton, 2000).

This focus on aggregate statistical relationships follows from the scientific and policy concerns over global–ecological relations that are the driving force of much of the discussion of urban sustainability (Lees and Demeritt, 1998). However, recent research has found that individuals do not readily identify with such seemingly abstract problems, feel powerless to do anything about them and, when asked to change behaviours such as car use, often feel unwilling or unable to do so (Hinchcliffe, 1996; Burgess et al, 1998; Dowling, 2000). The government's plans for urban sustainability (DETR, 2000a) are predicated on the assumption that people will embrace green transport alternatives and other consumption activities when available, cost-effective and convenient. A number of academic critics charge that this vision of an economically rational and calculating agent is faulty. Furthermore, policies based upon it are doomed to failure, they argue, because they discount the degree to which individual choice is constrained by economic structures, cultural traditions, feelings of powerlessness and mistrust of authority (Macnaughten and Urry, 1998). Others suggest that appeals for behavioural change will only appeal in fact to specific social groups (see, for example, Brechin, 1999).

Diversity

The UTF and the UWP both argue that urban revitalisation initiatives must embrace 'diversity' (they also use the term 'mixing'). Gentrification has also long been associated with similar appeals to diversity and difference. As Caulfield (1994), Ley (1996) and Butler (1997) argue, the city promises gentrifiers 'difference'; that is, a diversity of people and of uses that make the hetero-zoned inner city attractive (perhaps even erotic and emancipatory) to gentrifiers. In the gentrification literature, this inner-city diversity and difference is constituted as the opposite of the stultifying and sterile suburbs (see Lees, 1996, 2000) and the modernist mono-zoned city. These latter models are exemplified by the Chicago School and Ebenezer Howard's Garden City, where work and home spaces and different populations were strictly segregated. A similar vision of diversity figures prominently in government plans for urban renaissance (see DETR, 1999a, figure 2.8). The UTF report, for example, trumpets the functional and spatial diversity of the city:

> Neighbourhoods need to comprise a mix of uses which work together to encourage formal and informal transactions, sustaining activity throughout the day. The mixing of different activities within an area should serve to strengthen social integration and civic life. (DETR, 1999a, p 40)

Cultural and economic diversity are also celebrated:

> This diversity of cultures attracts many people to city living.... In the future, we must develop on the basis of a mix of tenures and income groups. (DETR, 1999a, p 45)

This "diversity of different diversities is often under-theorised as are the benefits of (and relationships among) social and cultural diversity, economic diversification, mixed-use and multipurpose zoning, political pluralism, and democratic public space" (Lees, 2003: forthcoming). The function and value of 'diversity' in the UTF report and the UWP is simply taken for granted. It is the medicine for the centripetal forces of commercialised homogeneity, the centrifugal forces of suburban sprawl, and the exclusionary forces of housing segregation, both social and spatial. As the Deputy Prime Minister testified to parliament:

> The division between areas exclusively of owner occupation and exclusively of renting, which was very much a creation of the 20th Century, has not been a happy one in our view and it has led to social polarisation and social exclusion. (Select Committee on Environment, Transport and Regional Affairs, 2001, p 2)

In their research on Barnsbury, a mature, gentrified neighbourhood in London, Butler and Robson (2001) show that gentrifiers and low-income groups do not mix even when living on one another's doorstep. Indeed, in Barnsbury they reside in separate economies – one local and down-at-heel, the other global, part of the 'new economy' that the UTF and the government are pushing. Needless to say, any kind of social interaction is severely limited! Their discussion of gentrification in Brixton reveals very similar fractures:

> "There appears, in short, to be something of a gulf between a widely circulated rhetorical preference for multicultural experience and people's actual social networks and connections .... The model of social cohesion in Brixton, where physical interaction with an extraordinarily heterogeneous social landscape is an unavoidable feature of everyday life, might be characterised as 'tectonic'. That is to say, broadly, that relations between different social and ethnic groups in the area are of a parallel rather than integrative nature: people keep, by and large, to themselves". (Butler and Robson, 2001, p 77)

The focus of the UTF report and the UWP on diversity/mixing as a source of economic renewal and cultural vitality poses new challenges for city governments. Achieving the full potential of urban diversities requires more than just a celebration of abstract diversity. It also requires a commitment to broader concepts of toleration and justice (see Lees, 2003: forthcoming). Functional mixing too is problematic. London's Soho is in the frontline of Britain's 24-hour, continental-style city. Here, housing association flats, yuppie apartments, restaurants, dance clubs, bars and sex shops are mixed together in a dense urban neighbourhood. The result has been a massive increase in residents' complaints, which range from noise to litter to pedestrian behaviour. As a place to live, Soho has become intolerable for some:

> If Soho cannot balance city-centre living and late-night pleasure, then perhaps this mixing will ultimately fail elsewhere in Britain too. (Beckett, 2000)

Community

Since the 1980s, 'community' has had its own renaissance, not only because of its "seeming importance as a local counter to the socially erosive effects of globalisation, and its ideological handmaiden, neo-liberalism" but also because of its "common appeal to politicians and policy-makers" (Paddison, 2001, p 194). New Labour's ideal of community (see Levitas, 2000), which has many similarities to Putnam's (2000) thesis on the collapse and revival of American community, is to be found in both the UTF Report and the UWP[8]. 'Community', as perceived by these documents, is to be created 'naturally' through the sustainable compact urban form that will densify people together cheek by jowl. The vision of community is one of a harmonious, socially and culturally mixed community (see Chapter Seven of this volume). Geographically,

---

this community is place-based; it is located in the urban neighbourhood and in public spaces such as the street:

> The traditional street plays a key role in the formation of community. It is where people of all ages come together and interact .... The continuous presence of passers-by as well as informal surveillance combine to create the blend of urban vitality and safety that is characteristic of many successful urban areas. (DETR, 1999a, p 57)

However, the renaissance of 'community' has been at a time when social scientists are increasingly sceptical of the concept of community (see Chapter Seven of this volume). There is concern about the way 'community' is used as a totalising construct. For example, Young (1990) claims that the ideal of community privileges unity over difference, that it generates social exclusions and segregations, and that it is an unrealistic vision:

> The ideal of community privileges unity over difference, immediacy over mediation, sympathy over recognition of the limits of one's understanding of others from their point of view. Community is an understandable dream, expressing a desire for selves that are transparent to one another, relationships of mutual identification, social closeness and comfort. The dream is understandable, but politically problematic, I argue, because those motivated by it will tend to suppress their differences among themselves or implicitly to exclude from their political group persons with whom they do not identify. (Young, 1990, p 300)

Such critiques focus on the oppressive nature of community and lead into discussions that celebrate (as ironically the UTF report and the UWP also do) the emancipatory diversity offered by urban spaces (North and DeFilippis, 2003: forthcoming). In these terms, the conception of community found in the UTF report and the UWP may contradict their visions of diversity, difference and social inclusion. The vision of 'community' in both documents is very much a moral communitarian vision mobilised by a desire for social justice (see Chapters One and Twelve of this volume). Their concept of community is of balance, of social and cultural mixing, and of increased social participation and democracy.

> Moving towards more mixed and sustainable communities is important to many of our plans for improving the quality of urban life. (DETR, 2000a, p 8)

However, as Amin et al argue, it is a vision of harmony and order that is "unattainable in practice" and actually "undemocratic in intent" (2000, p 10). It is a 'designer community', devoid of the realities of conflict, aggression and alienation. The key role accorded to the street (and public space more generally) in the formation of community ignores the fact that "streets are the terrain of social encounters and political protest, sites of domination and resistance, places of pleasure and anxiety" (Fyfe, 1998, p 1). As I argued with regard to diversity, community sometimes causes more problems than it solves (see also Lees, 2003: forthcoming).

The UTF report and the UWP take little account of different purposes of community and the contrasting ways in which it can be mobilised as an agent of social change. Community is used, more especially in the UWP, as a way of *us* gaining control over *our* cities again and as a way of resocialising and remoralising certain 'citizens' in society. In short, it is about (re)building social capital. However, community can be a dangerous construct if "it hides *the process of making* individuals and groups behind the façade of its inclusionary rhetoric" (Paddison, 2001, p 202, emphasis added). We ought not to forget that the individuals and groups that the UTF and the UWP want to attract or make are middle-class ones. Part of the problem lies in the mismatch between the language and ideas of an urban renaissance and the practice of an urban renaissance.

Conclusions

When I came to write this chapter, I was struck by the startling lack of dialogue between academic researchers on gentrification and a government that is promoting gentrification in the guise of urban renaissance. Indeed, both the UTF report and the UWP show great ignorance of, or have deliberately turned a blind eye to, the very critical literature that exists on gentrification (and, in addition, sustainability, diversity and community). However, blame needs to be fairly apportioned: gentrification researchers have also made little effort, until now perhaps, to connect with urban policy agendas in the UK. Therefore, there is an urgent need for communication that would be valuable to both sides. What is the point of a substantial and vigorous academic literature on gentrification if we do not disseminate our findings to the appropriate people? And similarly, what is the point of our UTF if it does not draw on the work of academic experts who have spent years researching gentrification? I agree with Atkinson when he wrote that:

> [it would] be cynical to suggest that the Government agenda aims to produce displacement from gentrification but also naïve to think that the full impacts of a return to the city have been fully thought through. (Atkinson, 2002, p 20)

Acknowledgement

This chapter has grown out of the commentary that I delivered as an invited discussant at 'The New Urban Frontier', Institute of British Geographers Conference (2001), organised by Gordon McCleod, Mike Raco and Kevin Ward. Many thanks to Tom Slater and David Demeritt for their comments on an earlier draft of this chapter.

Notes

[1] Although the discourse of urban renaissance is a feature of urban policy throughout the UK as a whole, these specific reports (DETR, 1999a, 2000e) apply only to English cities.

[2] An emerging body of literature has begun the critical task of deconstructing the discourse of contemporary British urban policy. For examples, see especially Amin et al (2000) and Atkinson (1999a, 2000a).

[3] Undoubtedly, Rogers' selection warrants scrutiny, especially in ideological terms. Much of what is outlined in the UTF report can also be found in Rogers and Gumuchdjian (1997).

[4] Where urban degeneration appears metaphorically connected to disease and a dissent into some lower order, urban malaise is a more non-specific feeling of uneasiness and discomfort.

[5] This 'change in behaviour' is a core theme in contemporary urban policy, and one that is discussed later in the chapter.

[6] Although the UTF report does not use the term gentrification, the concept is put forward quite blatantly as a prescriptive remedy for British cities.

[7] I should mention here, however, that there are some dissenting souls who argue that gentrification is not necessarily negative and does not necessarily lead to displacement. For the UK, these include Hamnett (2002), and, for the US, Freeman and Braconi (2002).

[8] Prime Minister Tony Blair has met with Putnam on numerous occasions. The renaissance of 'community' in British public policy is paralleled in the US.

Further reading

Amin et al (2000) is a key text that discusses alternative urban futures. Atkinson's discussion (2002) is a useful summary of key debates. Another helpful summary is provided by Hackworth and Smith (2001). Alternatively, see Lees (2000) and Smith (2002).

Part Two
Community involvement in urban policy

Strategic, multilevel neighbourhood regeneration: an outward-looking approach at last?

Annette Hastings

Introduction

New Labour has lost faith in the capacity of standalone, special initiatives to address urban poverty and disadvantage (Stewart, 2002a). Of all its breaks with the neighbourhood regeneration policy of previous administrations, this is one of the most significant. Since the late 1960s, programmes of specially funded, short-life initiatives have been deployed in successive waves in residential neighbourhoods across Britain's cities. These spatially targeted or area-based initiatives (ABIs) have been charged with reversing the fortunes of declining and disadvantaged localities. Initially focused on single issues, ABIs have attempted, since the late 1980s, an integrated approach. They have done this by trying to identify and address the connections between problems such as environmental decline, unemployment and poor health for example, and through harnessing the resources of a range of public institutions, working in 'partnership' with community bodies and private sector representatives (Robson et al, 1994). By the late 1990s, the number of ABIs had mushroomed. As a result, the governance of neighbourhood regeneration came to be characterised by a kaleidoscope of interlinked and spatially overlapping partnerships (Dean et al, 1999).

However, New Labour's neighbourhood renewal policy (see SEU, 2001; Scottish Executive, 2002a) seems to provide for a different approach. The reliance on short-life, special initiatives and projects appears to have been replaced by a more 'strategic' approach that emphasises the role of mainstream government and public sector activity in determining the trajectory of neighbourhoods. Rather than depend largely on initiatives at the neighbourhood level, the new policy advocates a 'multilevel' approach, in which the importance is recognised of governance arrangements operating at a range of spatial scales. The central level or tier of the new strategic, multilevel approach is to be local authority-led, multi-agency partnerships of public service providers, private sector institutions and lay community representatives: Local Strategic Partnerships (LSPs) in England and Community Planning Partnerships (CPPs) in Scotland. However, rather than working at neighbourhood level, LSPs and CPPs will be responsible for coordinating efforts to achieve neighbourhood renewal at the local authority spatial scale.

Thus, LSPs are to devise a strategic neighbourhood renewal strategy that will identify and prioritise problem neighbourhoods, as well as develop appropriate solutions. The solutions developed may or may not be ABIs (SEU, 2000). In Scotland, the indications are even stronger that ABIs will have a residual role, although some targeted activity is still anticipated (Scottish Executive, 2002a). Thus, the multilevel approach seems likely to rationalise neighbourhood-level programmes and projects and to place them within a broader territorial and governance context. Indeed, in addition to LSPs and CPPs, the multilevel approach incorporates the Westminster government and the Scottish Executive – and, in England, regional bodies such as Government Offices and Regional Development Agencies (RDAs) – explicitly into the framework (see Morgan, 2002). In England, for example, the capacity for LSPs to deliver is to be enhanced by a range of activities at central government level. These include Public Service Agreements between local and central government, which will set floor targets for service outcomes in poor neighbourhoods, and the extension of the 'consumer champions' initiative in which board-level consumer representatives are inserted into key central government services (SEU, 2000). Although there was less detail at the time of writing on how the Scottish Executive would be involved in neighbourhood renewal, it had at the very least identified the need "to join up national, regional and local priorities better" (Scottish Executive, 2002a, p 6).

A range of concerns about the ABI approach appears to have provided the impetus for the break with the orthodoxy of the past. First, evidence that ABIs were enjoying only very limited success in addressing neighbourhood disadvantage began to emerge (Hall, 1997; Carley, 2002; Stewart, 2002). As Dabinett et al argued, local schemes and projects may have helped *some* people gain jobs, for example, but they "did not appear fundamentally to change the overall prospects of client groups or areas" (2001, p 13). Second, a number of concerns emerged that isolated initiatives were doomed to fail as they "may simply redistribute problems rather than resolve them" (Scottish Office, 1995, p 2; see also McGregor, 1992; Robson et al, 1994). The desire to avoid displacement seemed to imply the need to manage neighbourhood renewal at a spatial scale above the neighbourhood level. Third, as indicated earlier, the resilience of neighbourhood problems led to a proliferation of ABIs, as new schemes were devised to address the deficiencies of old programmes. Thus, 'partnership fatigue' became a pressing problem of the late 1990s (Dean et al, 1999). And fourth, the burgeoning of ABIs seemed to create a new set of difficulties for deprived neighbourhoods. Special initiatives made big demands on hard-pressed agencies, arguably deflecting them from their mainstream business (Stewart, 2002). And, crucially, it became clear that ABIs were masking significant problems with the quality and appropriateness of public sector provision in disadvantaged neighbourhoods (SEU, 2001).

In addition, and picking up on some of these themes, academic commentary on neighbourhood renewal began to argue that the ABI approach was overly inward looking. That is, it represented "a limited and unbalanced approach to regeneration [which] failed to tackle the root causes of decline" (Hall, 1997, p 885). Thus, it was argued that ABIs focused on internal characteristics to the detriment of external processes. This is an important hypothesis about why the ABI model has been unable fundamentally to challenge neighbourhood trajectories. The focus of this chapter, therefore, is on exploring whether New Labour's new strategic, multilevel approach is less inward looking than the previous ABI model. Before the main analysis is presented here, however, the next section explicates the various criticisms of ABIs as inward looking – 'the inward-looking critique' – as the basis for analysing the new approach.

Area Based Initiatives, the 'inward-looking critique' and the promise of the multilevel approach

The basis of the argument that the ABI model is inward looking is that it can develop solutions to local problems that ignore the impact of macro-economic structures in promoting socio-spatial polarisation and segregation (Hall, 1997). Thus, the model may fail to take account of the skill demands of the wider economy in its development of local training and employment initiatives, or of the fact that projects may not address structural barriers to employment such as physical peripherality from employment opportunities, or poor transport links (Webster, 1994; Hall, 1997). Crucially, ABIs are said to promote a 'bootstraps approach' to neighbourhood economic development: they focus on employment creation *in* the neighbourhood, and their emphasis is on the social economy and community self-help (Eisenschitz and Gough, 1993).

Related to the proposition that ABIs can ignore the effects of structural processes on patterns of social and economic segregation, a second strand to the 'inward-looking critique' is that it focuses attention on the characteristics of localities and, in particular, on the deficiencies of residents. This can encourage pathological explanations of social exclusion that argue that poor people are different from the mainstream by virtue of their lifestyle or aspirations, for example (Watt and Jacobs, 2000; Newman, 2001). While pathological explanations of the causes of poverty can be traced back more than a century (Rubington and Weinberg, 1995), they achieved a certain cogency within the regeneration policy of the Conservative administrations of the 1980s and 1990s (Hastings, 1998). The import of this moral underclass thesis is that it locates the blame for disadvantage with the disadvantaged themselves. Arguably, the inward focus of the ABI model has meant that it has tended to emphasise local cultural explanations of this kind.

The third element of the critique relates to the strong focus that ABIs have had, at least since the late 1980s, on community participation, consultation and self-help. More recently, ABIs have also sought explicitly to foster better social relations – or social capital – at the neighbourhood level in order to support sustainable renewal (Nash, 2002). The emphasis placed by ABIs on community participation can be argued to be inward looking in some important ways. First, it can lead to an insular approach, promoting, for example, the needs of existing residents rather than emphasising social heterogeneity and the long-term trajectory of the neighbourhood (Hall, 1997). Or it can provoke solutions located *in* the neighbourhood rather than explore the need to connect poor neighbourhoods and their residents into the mainstream urban fabric (Forest and Kearns, 1999; Dean and Hastings, 2000).

At another level, the diagnosis that neighbourhood decline is associated with low stocks of social capital is challenged by a number of writers (for example, Hastings et al, 1996; Forest and Kearns, 1999). Taylor (2002a), for example, argues that poor neighbourhoods do not routinely suffer from a deficit of neighbourliness or self-help. However, she does suggest that what such neighbourhoods often lack is 'outward-looking' social capital that can link people across residential and social space by, for instance, enabling people to access employment opportunities. Indeed, the focus of many ABIs on promoting internal social cohesion and participation can have a profoundly 'inward-looking' effect, binding residents more to their neighbourhood and possibly limiting the opportunities for change.

The final way in which ABIs are held to be inward looking relates to the ramifications of institutionalising action at the local level. Crucially, this appears to have provided for the de-coupling of special initiatives from the mainstream activities of public agencies. For Stewart (2002b), this is partly a problem of the constrained territorial focus of ABIs. This has reduced their influence over mainstream agencies and departments and therefore their capacity to provoke changes in the degree of resource prioritisation attached to disadvantaged neighbourhoods, for example. In addition, it is also argued to have led to an overemphasis on issues such as local management (Hall, 1997), or has channelled energies into debating the relative merits of small projects or the disbursement of relatively small pots of special resources at the expense of larger, more strategic, issues (Dean et al, 1999).

The development of the strategic, multilevel approach, however, appears to engage with a number of the criticisms that the ABI model is inward looking. Thus, the designation of city-wide partnerships may indicate a 'scaling up' of an understanding of the appropriate territorial scales at which to diagnose the causes of neighbourhood problems as well as to devise appropriate solutions. The emphasis on involving lay community bodies at spatial scales above the neighbourhood may shift the emphasis of community participation away from inward-looking conceptions of social capital. And finally, the emphasis on mainstream services and their operation beyond the neighbourhood level may counter the propensity for neighbourhood regeneration initiatives to become isolated from strategic governance.

However, the immaturity of the policy framework (at the time of writing the English LSPs were just in the process of being established and plans for the Scottish CPPs had only just been announced) means that this chapter's analysis focuses on the policy documents that propose the approach, rather than on an examination of the approach itself. The new neighbourhood regeneration policy is encrypted in a large number of documents, including consultation documents, action plans, good practice guidance, and so on. Through an exploration of the discursive construction of the multilevel approach in such documents, it is possible to gain a rich insight into the implications of the policy, although more detailed research as the new arrangements unfold will also be essential. My discussion is based, therefore, on detailed textual analysis of how language is deployed in the documents, particularly in explaining the nature of the neighbourhood problem and in constructing an 'appropriate' set of solutions. It is underpinned by an understanding of the significant role of language in the policy process as the medium through which policy issues and processes are shaped and, ultimately, social reality constructed (see Hastings, 1998).

The analysis draws on the main documents that relate to the new neighbourhood policy. In England, the key statement of policy is the SEU's *A new commitment to neighbourhood renewal: National strategy action plan* (SEU, 2001). This document (hereafter referred to as the Strategy) is a detailed document of some 127 pages, and incorporates sections explaining what it sees as the nature and causes of neighbourhood problems, sets out plans for new interventions and resources, and offers examples of good practice. Equally useful for understanding the rationale and aims of the new neighbourhood policy is a document published the previous year, the *National strategy for neighbourhood renewal: A framework for consultation* (SEU, 2000) and the government guidance summary issued on establishing LSPs (DETR, 2001).

By contrast, Scottish regeneration policy has generated considerably fewer documents thus far. The main statement of policy is *Better communities in Scotland: Closing the gap* (Scottish Executive, 2002a; hereafter referred to as the Statement). At only 28 pages long, this document is considerably shorter than its English equivalent. Furthermore, it lacks detail in a number of areas including targets, time-scales and resources. The other useful document in relation to the Scottish approach is *Local Government in Scotland Bill* (Scottish Executive, 2002b).

The multilevel approach to regeneration: reviving communities or reviving economies?

One way in which 'inward' and 'outward' approaches to neighbourhood regeneration can be identified is in the relative balance within each approach between addressing either the deficiencies of communities or deficiencies in the economy. This first part of my analysis explores the ways in which the core policy documents apportion blame between community pathologies and economic problems in their account of neighbourhood decline.

An initial reading of the Strategy could suggest that New Labour's regeneration policy is more outward looking than some earlier neighbourhood approaches (see also Watt and Jacobs, 2000). Thus, neighbourhood decline is placed within the context of "a sharp fall in economic activity" (SEU, 2000, p 23). For example, the Strategy notes the impact of urban industrial restructuring during the 1980s, the loss of urban jobs, particularly in manual and unskilled occupations, and the uneven distribution of these losses across geographical and industrial sectors. Indeed, in a chapter entitled 'Why does it happen?', which sets out the government's explicit understanding of the causes of neighbourhood problems, economic problems are given causal primacy in the account of neighbourhood decline:

> The cycle of decline for a neighbourhood almost always starts with a lack of work. This generates other social problems – crime, drugs, low educational attainment and poor health – all of which reinforce each other and speed local decline. The 'social capital' of local communities is undermined. All of this makes it harder for essential public services to cope. (SEU, 2000, p 23)

Importantly, this is not just a description of the cycle of decline but a hypothesis about how that vicious circle comes into being. It is a causal framework in which worklessness 'feeds' other social problems and undermines the capacity for local self-help and initiative. It seems to locate the explanation for local problems in processes that are external rather than internal to declining neighbourhoods, and can therefore be thought of as outward looking. Indeed, the nature and structure of the housing market, with its propensity to concentrate the most "vulnerable, workless people in the same place" (SEU, 2000, p 24), is another external process highlighted. One possible reading of the document, therefore, is that economic change is given explanatory power in relation to social and cultural problems at the neighbourhood level.

Despite this, there is evidence in the document of a substantial attachment to inward-looking, cultural explanations for neighbourhood decline. The language of the document is strongly inflected with references to the cultural characteristics of poor neighbourhoods. Newman, for example, argues that English neighbourhood policy in particular constructs the people who live in disadvantaged neighbourhoods as different from the mainstream – as having "a surfeit of troubling characteristics" (2001, p 154; see also Watt and Jacobs, 2000; Hoban and Beresford, 2001; Tiesdell and Allmendinger, 2001).

Thus, and in direct contradiction to the hypothesis described above that economic problems cause social problems, there is also a counter-argument in the document; that is, social problems cause worklessness. Thus, the cultural deficiencies of these communities means that members are often not equipped to take up new economic opportunities when they arise. In other words, worklessness can be explained by social rather than economic factors. For example, "family breakdown ... has often created circumstances which make it difficult for people to take work" (SEU, 2000, p 23). The emphasis here on family breakdown (rather than on the lack of affordable childcare, for example) arguably draws attention to cultural and moral reasons for worklessness.

The kinds of social problems that are emphasised and the degree to which they are highlighted is also indicative of pathological frameworks. Thus, while low educational achievement and poor health are mentioned in the document, there is considerably more emphasis on criminality, drugs misuse and antisocial behaviour. And, arguably, whereas educational and health disparities can be more readily explained as effects of resource distribution, antisocial activities are more commonly explained as having behavioural origins. Indeed, the document hints towards notions of cycles of deprivation and even essentialist accounts of the underclass (Murray, 1990) by raising the "fundamental question of whether the most disadvantaged people can ever change" (SEU, 2000, p 90).

There is also a strong emphasis in the Strategy on how the nature of 'community' explains the functioning of neighbourhoods. This seems to suggest a strong attachment to the 'inward-looking' hypothesis; that is, the quality of local social relations, or social capital, correlates with the spatial patterning of social exclusion (see Nash, 2002; Perri 6, 2002). Thus, the document explains the problem of poor neighbourhoods at least in part as a deficiency of social capital. Crime in particular is argued to undermine a community's capacity to help itself:

> Trust or community spirit are undermined .... It is on this foundation that social stability and a community's ability to help itself are usually built – and its absence is a key factor in decline. (SEU, 2000, p 24)

There are also various references to a number of deficiencies associated with low stocks of social capital:

- a lack of informal networks;
- insularity and narrow horizons;
- a lack of positive role models;
- low expectations (for example, SEU, 2000, p 53).

(And, as will be seen shortly, there is an even stronger emphasis in the Scottish Statement on social capital as key to neighbourhood renewal.)

The Strategy therefore explains neighbourhood decline in terms of both inward- and outward-looking discourses. Thus, the initial hypothesis about the importance of structural economic change is accompanied by a strong cultural discourse. Only a simplistic account of neighbourhood decline would argue that the two are necessarily mutually exclusive[1]. However, in order to assess whether New Labour's neighbourhood policy is inward or outward looking, it is important to come to some conclusion about the relative weight attached to the two frameworks. This is not immediately apparent as equal weight is seemingly signalled by the fact that the themes 'reviving economies' and 'reviving communities' are each the focus of a separate chapter.

However, the chapter on economic problems and solutions is actually titled 'Reviving *Local* Economies' (emphasis added) and its focus is largely on supply-side rather than demand-related measures to facilitate economic development, such as supporting employability initiatives and developing local entrepreneurial behaviour. Furthermore, whereas ABIs are criticised elsewhere in the document for promoting an insular approach to neighbourhood problems (SEU, 2000, p 28), the strengths of ABIs in relation to economic regeneration are emphasised (SEU, 2000, p 82). Thus, it is evident that neighbourhood economic problems are not conceived of in structural terms, but rather as local micro-issues capable of resolution through special initiatives and programmes.

The Scottish Statement contains considerably less explicit analysis of the causes of neighbourhood problems than the English Strategy. Despite this, it is possible to detect a more inward-looking perspective than the perspective of its English counterpart. Thus, whereas there is an acknowledgement that "the quality of life for people can be very different in different areas" (Scottish Executive, 2002a, p 8), there is no analysis of the wider context that conditions such disparities. Interestingly, a document published by the Scottish Executive on the same day as the Statement (Carley, 2002) and intended "to support the development of the Scottish Executive's community regeneration statement" (Carley, 2002, p v) adopts a more outward-looking perspective in its recognition of the interaction between macro-economic forces and neighbourhood trajectories:

> Neighbourhood renewal is dependent in part on the achievement of economic regeneration at higher spatial levels, that is, on the achievement of economic regeneration at the level of the local authority or the travel-to-work region. (Carley, 2002, p vii)

However, it is difficult to see how this analysis affected the *Community Regeneration Statement* (Bailey, 2002). Rather, the Statement proposes an even stronger relationship between the quality of social capital and the spatial incidence of social exclusion than the English documents. Thus, poor communities have not been able to take advantage of "the opportunities open to them" because they lack "skills, confidence, support networks and resources ... to do more for themselves and to ask for the services they need" (Scottish Executive, 2002a, p 9). Furthermore, lack of social capital is perceived to be related, therefore, to a lack of basic skills among individuals:

> People in deprived communities are less likely to have access to the resources they need when things go wrong. Increasing individual skills – particularly literacy and numeracy – and building the resources and networks within a community can help people find ways of tackling problems locally. (Scottish Executive, 2002a, p 10)

Indeed, this paragraph discusses individual basic skills, network poverty and material disadvantage as if they were all the same kind of thing and capable of common resolution. Thus, network deficiencies affording access to employment are cast as insularity and low expectations. The implied low propensity to engage in local associational behaviour is explained in terms of deficiencies that exclude individuals from the mainstream; that is, literacy and numeracy. A relationship is therefore set up between literacy and numeracy and associational behaviour. This point is amplified by the fact that the new regeneration agency in Scotland – Communities Scotland – has responsibility for improving literacy and numeracy as well as investing in neighbourhood renewal.

Arguably, the excerpt from the Scottish Executive Statement (see page 92) betrays an inward-looking pathological framework in two main ways. First, it does so in its elision of poor basic skills and poor community networks, and the implied explanation of the latter by the former. Second, there is silence here (and elsewhere) in the document on the long tradition of local self-help as well as community and political activism and organisation which characterises many of Scotland's poor neighbourhoods (Hastings, 1999a)[2]. Thus, the Statement's aggregate account of the skills, experience and capacities of residents of such neighbourhoods, and in particular its failure to acknowledge the substantial experience of self-help and community activism in many neighbourhoods, and its framing of neighbourhood deprivation in the internal dynamics and networks of neighbourhood residents, amounts to a pathological conception of the causes of neighbourhood decline. As such, it amounts to an inward-looking focus on the deficiencies of communities with little explicit acknowledgement about how these are structured by external processes.

In summary, the English and Scottish documents evince a considerable attachment to inward-looking approaches and display a strong continuity with previous pathological frameworks, especially in the case of Scotland. Neighbourhood deprivation is framed as a problem pertaining largely to the internal characteristics and dynamics of neighbourhood residents. However, as already highlighted, a key aspect of New Labour's neighbourhood policy is the development of a strategic, multilevel approach to the governance of regeneration. Superficially at least, the 'scaling up' of the institutional arrangements for neighbourhood renewal signals a more 'outward' approach.

Reviving local governance or reviving local government?

The deficiencies of the ABI model with respect to neighbourhood renewal, as well as the ineffectiveness of local governance processes more generally, are routinely highlighted in the policy documents. The English Strategy, for example, argues that there has been confusion among special initiatives and mainstream services as to where responsibility lies for addressing neighbourhood problems. Moreover, the activities of ABIs have "masked the problems of core public services" (SEU, 2000, p 28). In relation to local governance more generally, the "lack of joining up at local level has been one of the key reasons for the lack of progress in tackling neighbourhood deprivation" (SEU, 2001, p 44). In many cases, the ineffectiveness of partnership has become "part of the problem" (SEU, 2000). In the Scottish Statement, there is a recognition of the difficulties involved in making a reality of partnership working and a general exhortation that mainstream services need "to work together better" (Scottish Executive, 2002a, p 9).

There is certainly an 'inward-looking' perspective on local governance failure in the documents. Thus, the lack of coordination of services at neighbourhood level is identified as a problem. The proposed key solution is neighbourhood management – that is, the designation of clear local management and accountability structures for public services at the level of the neighbourhood – along with other locally orientated initiatives, such as neighbourhood wardens. However, we might expect the overall thrust of the multilevel approach to be outward looking. The extent to which this is the case can be explored by examining the role and anticipated impact of community participation in the strategic LSPs and CPPs.

In terms of the role envisaged for community participation in the strategic elements of neighbourhood renewal, it is clear that community representatives are expected to play a central role within LSPs. It is not only that the community should be "equal players" (SEU, 2001, p 45) but that:

> Effective engagement with the community is one of the most important aspects of the LSP's work and they will have failed if they do not deliver on this. (SEU, 2001, p 51)

The prominent role afforded in England to the community at the strategic level appears to be replicated in Scotland. Indeed, in the Scottish case, the exhortation is not just that the community should be an equal partner, but rather it should be central to, or at the heart of, community planning:

> Community Planning Partnerships must involve the community as the main partner in the process. (Scottish Executive, 2002a, p 13)

In the English case at least, the significant role given to community involvement has been widely interpreted as indicative of a more outward-looking 'empowerment' model of community participation. Thus, participation is a means by which poor people living in disadvantaged neighbourhoods can access power and influence and even begin to challenge material inequalities (Foley and Martin, 2000; Taylor, 2001). Evidence of an 'empowerment' model of community participation is argued to be present in various aspects of neighbourhood renewal policy. Among these aspects are the targeting of resources on facilitating community involvement, as well as the development of modes of government which make the facilitation of effective community involvement a condition of neighbourhood regeneration funding, for example (Foley and Martin, 2000; Hastings, 2002). For some, "there is much to celebrate"

(Foley, 1999) as English neighbourhood renewal policy is seen as a genuine attempt to make community influenced regeneration a real possibility. As Taylor argues, the view from regeneration practitioners is that the government shows a real commitment to making a reality of community empowerment, and they feel that, for the first time, "there is permission to do things differently" (quoted in Foley and Martin, 2000, p 484).

It is worth highlighting the contrasting tenor of some of the initial commentary on the model of community participation offered in the Scottish Statement. Indeed, it has been noted that the term 'empowerment' does not feature in the document at all. Rather, there is a rather nebulous aspiration to achieve 'community involvement' (Bailey, 2002). Furthermore, there is no mention of financial support for community engagement in CPPs and, again in contrast to the English model, no provision for redress when participation is not supported (Bailey, 2002). The details of the Scottish policy framework had yet to be elucidated fully at the time of writing. However, the Statement is clear that one of the 'two fronts' on which action needs to be taken in order to bring about neighbourhood renewal is to address what it portrays as a deficit of social capital (Scottish Executive, 2002a, p 9). There is, however, a tension between simultaneously constructing the neighbourhood 'problem' as an absence of social capital and arguing that such deficient communities should be at the heart of community planning.

This lack of congruence between inward-looking pathologies and outward-looking promises of empowerment is also a feature of the English documents. The incongruity is further revealed when we examine how the impact of community engagement at the strategic level is conceived. For instance, the excerpt below from the government guidance on LSPs suggests that lay participants in LSPs will have a major influence on the strategic governance of regeneration:

> Involving local people and communities is vital for the successful development and implementation of community strategies and local neighbourhood renewal strategies, and key to achieving lasting improvements. There is a wealth of resources and activity within communities which are not available to the statutory sector. Individuals, groups and communities provide an untapped pool of ideas, knowledge, skills, experience, energy and enthusiasm which, if tapped, can be a real force for change. (DETR, 2001, para 1.19)

The second part of this excerpt is particularly interesting. It suggests that the ideas and energies of lay people will be the motors of change, particularly within public agencies. It has been argued (particularly in Chapters One and Five of this volume) that community participation at the neighbourhood level is conceived of as means of reviving or transforming poor communities into active agents of self-help. At the strategic level, in contrast, participation is conceived of as a mechanism for reviving or transforming local governance processes. This implies a rather different conception of the characteristics of poor communities depending on the spatial scale under focus. Arguably, at the neighbourhood scale the defining characteristic of poor communities is a 'surfeit of troubling characteristics' (Newman, 2001). At the local authority scale it is a 'wealth of resources and activity'. It also implies a rather different construction of the problem. At the neighbourhood level, on the one hand, there is a need to invigorate the initiative, skills and networks of residents. At the authority level, on the other hand, the same residents' reservoirs of energy, experience and creativity are 'untapped' by other participants, and need to be drawn in to effect change.

Thus, there would appear to be a tension in the government's analysis. It is difficult to reconcile the need to revive the social capital of poor communities with the view that their peculiar energies and attributes are instrumental in reviving local governance. Clearly, place-based communities are not homogenous, and many neighbourhoods (whether disadvantaged or not) will be home both to defective and blameworthy individuals as well as to visionary community leaders. But there is no recognition of this possibility in the policy documents. Arguably, a reader of the documents requires prior knowledge of the resilience of community bodies and leaders in poor neighbourhoods in order to make sense of the suggestion that 'community participation' is the answer to transforming local governance.

There is, then, an incongruity in how notions of community and community participation are used by the government in relation to the different spatial levels of its neighbourhood regeneration policy. Some of the difficulty may relate to the fact that the instruments of the new neighbourhood policy are part of a broader agenda. The multilevel configuration of neighbourhood renewal is not simply a mechanism to make neighbourhood renewal more effective, but rather is also conceived as a means to bring about the 'modernisation' of local government. In particular, public participation is a key part of the process by which public services are to be modernised. Thus, public agencies are expected to facilitate public participation as a condition of receiving special funding or status from the government (Newman et al, 2002, p 4).

Indeed, the documents are apparently silent in relation to an important aspect of this agenda. This silence relates to attaching the blame specifically to local government for the intransigence of neighbourhood problems. While the new neighbourhood policy emphasises the importance of improving mainstream services, it is notable that the documents do not explicitly blame service providers for these deficiencies. In the Scottish Statement for example, the blame for service failure is located in a variety of spheres (although the local government sphere is conspicuous by its absence). The first sphere relates to the failure of *central* government to provide the incentives needed to modify budgets and programmes that are required to support disadvantaged neighbourhoods. Thus, the framework provided by the government has not created the conditions necessary to persuade mainstream services to adjust their practices in order to cater for needs in poor neighbourhoods, or to afford them the necessary degree of positive discrimination. The second sphere relates to the failure of local *governance* to work effectively; that is, the lack of responsiveness and coordination mentioned earlier in this chapter. The third argues that the lack of social capital in poor neighbourhoods helps to explain why they receive poor services: service failure can be blamed on the deficiencies of communities. Thus,

> building the resources and networks within a community can help people find ways of tackling problems locally and can also stop these services failing in the first place. (Scottish Executive, 2002a, p 10)

However, blame is not explicitly attached to the service providers themselves. The English Strategy is explicit on the need for cultural change within *central* government (for example, SEU, 2001, p 59) but silent on the same issue in respect of *local* government.

So there is a silence in the policy documents with regard to blaming local government for the resilience of neighbourhood problems. However, New Labour's antagonism to local municipalism is well known, and its determination to transform local government (and public services more generally) is a keystone of the government's project (Newman, 2001). The policy documents that accompany the development of LSPs (DETR, 2000a, 2001) provide some clues as to how this transformative process could take place. Again, scrutiny of the anticipated role in LSPs for community members as well as local councillors is helpful here.

Exploring the role of community representatives first, it is perhaps significant that the LSP guidance (DETR, 2001) does not envisage that community members will have a representative or advocacy role on LSPs. Their input will be mainly related to their "knowledge of the impact of service provision on local people", which will allow them to "bring their knowledge and experience" to bear on the overall assessment by all the public service partners in deprived neighbourhoods (DETR, 2001, p 70). Contrary to expectations about an empowerment model of community engagement, it seems rather that their role has been conceived of as influential, well-resourced 'expert advisers'. Thus, the guidance suggests that community representatives should not be considered to be representative or "the sole voice of local people" (DETR, 2001, p 70). It warns against a "systematic feed-up of representatives" from neighbourhood partnerships into the strategic partnerships. Rather there should be a "credible selection" of neighbourhood reps whose interests should also be balanced by individuals representing interest communities, especially hard-to-reach groups (such as minority ethnic groups), people with disabilities, and so on. Thus, it is likely that there will be some priority neighbourhoods that are not represented directly by community members on LSPs.

None of the English or Scottish documents goes into significant detail on the role of local councillors. There are only short paragraphs in the LSP guidance and the Scottish Local Government Bill (Scottish Executive, 2000b). From these, however, it is clear that elected members, like community members, should not be seen simply as representative of a territorial community. Thus, although the former document notes "the democratic legitimacy which elected councillors can bring to the decision making process" (DETR, 2001, p 68), it is also clear that this is not the basis on which they are expected participate in LSPs. The LSP guidance suggests that two types of councillor may be suitable to participate in LSPs:

- senior councillors with a strategic overview or involvement in scrutiny committees;
- ward councillors "who can provide a voice for their local communities *alongside other methods of engaging local people*" (DETR, 2001, p 68, emphasis added).

Elected members are therefore to be considered as only one of the community's many voices. An equivalency is set up between the voice of elected members and other community voices. There is no one-to-one correlation hypothesised between elected members and the interests and views of their electoral constituency.

That the basis of LSPs does not rest in its relationship with representative forms of governance is made clear elsewhere in the LSP guidance:

> LSPs are collaborative partnerships where each member is an equal partner. Each partner will have a different contribution to make, and their worth needs to be acknowledged. Resources, responsibilities and duties may differ, but the value to the LSP of each partner has to be recognised. (DETR, 2001, p 15)

Arguably, the mode of decision making suggested here is closer to a deliberative or participatory mode than the traditional, representative mode that characterises local government. As Newman et al (2002) characterise it, participants do not derive their legitimacy in deliberative forums from their representative status. Rather, they are constituted 'as "free and equal citizens whose experience and views can contribute to the shaping of more effective policy decisions or better service design" (Newman et al, 2002, p 6). Thus, participants are held to be capable of divesting themselves of their sectional interests, engaging in unfettered dialogue and thus transforming themselves. We can therefore see that LSPs and CPPs are not just about addressing neighbourhood problems at a higher spatial scale, but are part of a project to bring about a more collaborative and less authoritarian mode of governance. Crucially, local government, and elected members in particular, is just one set of actors in this new arrangement. Arguably, whereas community participation at the neighbourhood level is conceived of as a means to refresh the relationships *within* civil society, community participation at the strategic level is a means to renew and refresh the relationships *between* civil society and the local state.

However, there is still tension in the new neighbourhood regeneration policy between inward and outward-looking perspectives. On the one hand, the government's emphasis on community involvement and building social capital at the neighbourhood level is based on the inward-looking proposition that poor communities require to be 'revived' through resort to self-help, education and capacity building. Community involvement at the neighbourhood level is therefore part of the bargain to be made with poor communities, which must take on a specific set of responsibilities in order to benefit from investment. On the other hand, an outward-looking perspective is embodied in the 'scaling up' of the mechanisms for intervention to the level of local governance. Further, these same defective communities are afforded an agentive, transformative role in relation to the transformation of local governance, an agenda that seems profoundly outward. What follows in my conclusion attempts to account for this paradox and to assess the extent to which we can read the new strategic, multilevel approach to regeneration as an outward approach.

Conclusions

Much can be learned about what is at stake in New Labour's approach to neighbourhood renewal by examining how the notions of community and community participation are used in the policy documents. It has been shown that the new approach seems to embody two quite different propositions about the communities that reside in poor neighbourhoods: they are flawed, but also agents of change in relation to the flaws of local government. In order to understand how this can be the case, we need to return to Putnam's conception of social capital (see Chapter Two of this volume). While the policy documents appear to conceive of social capital as an internal issue for community health and neighbourhood wellbeing, Putnam (1993) argues that building social capital at the local level is a means to enhance local democracy through making communities more demanding of their politicians, for example. Thinking about social capital in this way helps us to see the link between the inward- and outward-looking perspectives on community participation.

The silence on the wider ramifications of building social capital perhaps highlights the political sensitivities that the New Labour government has felt with regard to overtly blaming the (Labour) municipalities for the extent and depth of neighbourhood decline. Whereas there is a willingness in the documents to say that poor people or central government are part of the problem, there is a reluctance to overtly blame local government in the same way. Thus, the insertion of community representatives into LSPs and CPPs could be viewed as part of a strategy to facilitate a self-regulating 'responsibilised' local governance (see Raco and Imrie, 2000), with community representatives charged with bringing about a kind of transformation by stealth.

Therefore, the strategic, multilevel approach incorporates both inward and outward perspectives on how to achieve neighbourhood regeneration. The policy retains the strong attachment of the ABI model to inward-looking perspectives on neighbourhood decline. However, there are important indications that a need for a more outward-looking perspective has also been recognised: the emphasis on mainstream services; the scaling up of governance arrangements to the local authority level; the need for a stronger role for central government. Interestingly, whereas there are strong similarities between the English and Scottish policies, Scotland's neighbourhood renewal policy appears to emphasise community failings to a greater degree than its English equivalent. This is rather surprising, perhaps, given the well-established tradition of resident engagement in a wide variety of community-based regeneration activity. Indeed, it will be very interesting to follow the development and implementation of the new neighbourhood renewal policy in Scotland. It is possible, for example, that there will be strong resistance to pathological explanations of disadvantage in many regeneration areas and equally strong demands for a firmer commitment to an empowerment agenda.

In summary, whereas the multilevel approach seems, at least in part, to signal a shift away from a simple focus on the internal problems of deprived neighbourhoods, it remains surprisingly disengaged from wider structural issues, such as the management of the regional economy. Thus, the new multilevel approach looks beyond the neighbourhood for the governance of renewal, yet achieves only a limited outward perspective in relation to the broader societal and structural processes that shape neighbourhoods.

Notes

[1] For insight into the connections between structural and cultural explanations of neighbourhood problems in the context of US cities, see Wilson (1987).

[2] See Bailey (2002) for the response of community activists to this aspect of the regeneration statement.

Further reading

For reviews of the evidence on the effectiveness of regeneration approaches prior to the multilevel approach, the following are particularly useful: Hall (1997); Dabinett et al (2001); Carley (2002).

FIVE

Addressing urban social exclusion through community involvement in urban regeneration

Rob Atkinson

Introduction

This chapter examines one of the ways in which urban regeneration under New Labour has sought to address social exclusion and facilitate social inclusion through the involvement of local communities in regeneration partnerships[1]. 'Community', and associated notions such as social cohesion and social capital, has played a central role in the discourses structuring urban policy under New Labour (see Part One of this volume). Among the questions that are raised by bringing together notions of community and social exclusion are:

• How will these concerns be translated into the practice of urban regeneration at a local level?
• And what impact has New Labour's obsession with 'joined-up government and action' had on practice at local level?

There are also wider issues at stake here as development in urban policy is closely related to New Labour's wider agenda to modernise local government (DETR, 1998a) and reform key aspects of the welfare state.

There is a danger that the 'solutions' to the problems faced by socially excluded communities are largely reduced to a 'technical exercise'. In this exercise, developing the 'right' structures of governance and forms of social capital within excluded communities is expected somehow to reverse years of decline caused by wider structural forces beyond the control of local areas. In a sense, responsibility for these problems has been assigned to those experiencing the effects of decline. Indeed, New Labour initially appeared to accept the general diagnosis of urban problems offered by its Conservative Party predecessors when it argued that areas of multiple deprivation in cities had been "largely by-passed by national economic success" (DETR, 1997, section 2.2). Subsequent pronouncements do seem to have accepted that, at least in part, the causes of decline lie outside of run-down areas, although even here much of the blame appears to have been placed on the shortcomings of local government and, to a lesser extent, central government. Nevertheless, there is a strong undercurrent within New Labour's policies towards urban areas, and 'excluded spaces' in particular, that those living there bear some of the responsibility for their situation. On the one hand, communities have been assigned a key role in urban regeneration and by extension responsibility for the success or failure of policy. On the other hand, it is questionable whether communities have the powers and resources necessary to address the factors that have created, and perpetuated, urban decline.

This chapter first sets out a theoretically informed approach to analysing and making sense of recent 'community-led' initiatives designed to address urban social exclusion. The latter will then be illustrated through a discussion of developments within a single English city – Plymouth – that has been the recipient of many of the key initiatives launched by Conservative governments and New Labour since 1997. In essence, the chapter argues that urban policy since the early 1990s, and particularly so since 1997, has attempted to restructure the terrain of governance by seeking to change the ways in which communities govern themselves. Access to regeneration funding requires communities to internalise a series of policy discourses/narratives, rules and targets that have been defined by the centre and to govern themselves accordingly. Following on from this, they are required to develop technologies of government (for example, organisational forms such as multi-sector partnerships) that will actualise these centrally defined 'rules of the game' at a local level. These developments in turn reflect the disaggregate of the way in which the socio-spatial governance of the UK operates.

The UK is no longer conceived of as a single governable space; rather, community is increasingly becoming the new terrain of governance. However, communities are not simply passive objects to be manipulated. Many have engaged in forms of resistance that have sought to adapt this new form of governance, exploit gaps in the programmes and technologies of government to their own advantage, and develop forms of governance and action that reflect their needs. Nevertheless, questions remain about the powers and resources necessary for communities to achieve the objectives that they have signed up to as part of the process of winning regeneration funding. The danger is that, having signed up to achieve the unachievable, they will end up being condemned as the authors of their own 'failure'. The outcome for failing communities could be either one of abandonment by national government or a new round of more intrusive forms of intervention by the centre.

Governance, governmentality and urban regeneration

The development of new and more effective modes of governance is central to New Labour's urban policy (see Chapter One of this volume). But how are we to make sense of the new forms of governance that are emerging so that the objectives of urban policy are achieved? To begin with, it is important to recognise that these developments are not restricted to urban areas. They may be most acutely expressed in such areas, but they are representative of wider developments. Thus, we must turn to wider theoretical approaches to make sense of recent developments. Here I propose to draw largely, although not exclusively, on Foucault's (1979) notion of governmentality and discourse/ narrative analysis of urban policy, which I have developed elsewhere (Atkinson, 1998b, 1999c, 2000b, 2001; see also Raco and Imrie, 2000).

Governance – a general overview

It is important to recall that what constitutes governance and how we understand it is the subject of considerable uncertainty and debate (see Stoker, 1998). Broadly speaking, one can argue that governance refers to the processes in increasingly complex and fragmented societies where the state no longer has the ability to govern successfully on its own, whereby some degree of societal order is achieved, goals decided upon, policies elaborated and services delivered (following Kooiman, 1993; Rhodes, 1995, 1997). The mode whereby governance is achieved involves an unpredictable combination of markets, hierarchies and networks in association with the use of formal and informal negotiations. Successful governance requires the existence of a substantial degree of inter-subjective agreement and the marginalisation (or exclusion) of potentially disruptive interests and groups, or else, such interests and groups have to be persuaded, by material benefits, symbolism or the 'art of rhetoric' (Thompson, 1993), to accept the boundaries and objectives of governance as established by powerful groups. This last issue points to the question of power and the opportunities that governance provides for the powerful to pursue their goals to the detriment of the less powerful with little likelihood of being held to account or subject to democratic scrutiny.

Urban government appears to lack both the resources and authority/ legitimacy to govern effectively (see Lefèbvre, 1998). In this context, attention has been focused on the fundamental need for cities to achieve economic growth (Peterson, 1981), downgrade social expenditures, and engage in what Harvey (1989b) terms 'urban entrepreneurialism'. However, during the 1990s this emphasis on enhancing the competitiveness of cities has increasingly been forced to embrace an agenda that, at least rhetorically, assigns considerable importance to addressing social exclusion and cohesion (Boddy, 2002). The task, then, is how to understand these developments in relation to contemporary urban policy and practice.

Foucault, governmentality, urban governance and urban policy

Foucault's notion of governmentality was marginal to, and underdeveloped in relation to, his work as a whole (see McNay, 1994)[2]. For him, governmentality was:

the ensemble formed by the institutions, procedures, analyses and reflections, the calculations and tactics that allow the exercise of this very specific albeit complex form of power, which has as its target population, as its principle form of knowledge political economy and as its essential technical means apparatuses of security. (Foucault, 1979, p 20)

The process of governmentalisation involves the development of specific apparatuses of intervention and the construction of a field of knowledge through which the objects of government are constituted, thought and acted upon. Government of the population, however, is not necessarily (or even mainly) directly exercised by the state. Forms of power outside the state apparatus "often sustain the state more effectively than its own institutions, enlarging and maximising its effectiveness" (Foucault, 1980, p 73). This is what Miller and Rose (1990) term 'action at a distance'. Action requires the development of political rationalities that:

conceptualises and justifies goals as well as the means to achieve them, thus defining the proper parameters of political action and the institutional framework appropriate to those limits. They do so through discourses that make it seem as if techniques are addressing a common problem through shared logic and principles. (Simons, 1995, p 38)

Political rationalities require the development of programmes of government. Such programmes express the hopes and intentions of government, and attempt to translate political rationalities into action in a particular space to address specific 'problems'. Programmes involve constituting a domain in a particular way, to 'understand' it and its internal relations, thereby making a domain amenable to action and open to 'diagnosis' and, therefore, open to a 'cure' (see Rose and Miller, 1992).

Programmes require the development of technologies of government that seek to translate thought into action through the development of mechanisms of intervention. These in turn necessitate the construction of alliances between agents and/or organisations. Such alliances may in part derive from resource dependency but also from the 'art of rhetoric', whereby:

one actor comes to convince another that their problems or goals are intrinsically linked, that their interests are consonant, that each can solve their difficulties or achieve their ends by joining forces or working along the same lines. (Miller and Rose, 1990, p 10)

The multi-sectoral regeneration partnerships that have become the defining characteristic and means of intervention in contemporary urban policy clearly incorporate many of these elements (see Atkinson 1998a, 1998b, 1999b, 2000a, 2001).

Moreover, Rose (1996a) has argued that the way in which we have conceived and constituted the 'social' for the past century or so is currently undergoing a profound change. What is in fact happening is that the language of the social is giving way to the language of community. For Rose, the community is currently being constituted as:

> a new territory for the administration of individual and collective existence, a new place or surface upon which micro-moral relations among people are conceptualised and administered. (Rose, 1996a, p 331)

That is, in other words, government through community. Communities and individuals are classified and problematised on the basis of their 'cultures' (as responsible active citizens, entrepreneurial, independent or as pathological, dependent, inflexible), and the boundaries of inclusion and exclusion are drawn and redrawn accordingly. Government is no longer government of a national territory as a unified whole, but rather, government of discrete areas (towns, regions, for example).

> [The] economic fates of citizens within a national territory are uncoupled from one another, and are now understood and governed as a function of their own particular levels of enterprise, skill, inventiveness and flexibility. (Rose, 1996a, p 339)

On the basis of my argument so far, it would be very easy to slip into a pessimistic and deterministic view of Foucault's conception of 'reality', one that understands it as an 'iron cage'. However, power always engenders resistance, and domination is only ever partial. Moreover, the programmes of government and their associated technologies are rarely realised as they were intended. The agents of liaison and localised hubs of power central to government have their own agendas and interests that frequently lead policies and their associated instruments to unfold in ways contrary to the intentions of central government. Policies collide with and contradict one another; quite frequently the 'solutions' entailed in one policy are the problems of another. Moreover, the means to actualise policies – that is, the activities required to put a particular diagnosis into practice – are rarely self-evident. New means are often required, and these frequently run into problems when they interact with existing organisations and institutions (as regeneration partnerships have all too often discovered). Although political discourse constitutes its own objects, knowledge of those objects and 'truth', reality remains resolutely unprogrammable, and constantly eludes the grasp of discourse and frustrates its objectives.

It is possible, then, to see a number of overlaps between general notions of governance and Foucault's work. At a general level, there is a common recognition of the difficulties of control and coordination, the need to develop strategies and construct alliances, the importance of tactics, networks and the use of resources to create interdependencies and steer action in certain directions.

One important difference is that governmentality recognises that government has always been complex and has involved a multiplicity of non-state bodies. Theories of governance, however, suggest that this is a relatively recent phenomenon.

Foucault's work emphasises *power to* – that is, the importance of the exercise of power and its relational nature. But it also highlights the key role of the mechanisms of power and the need to coordinate complementary capacities and projects, and stresses the significance of the relatively mundane in the exercise of power. Moreover, the use of discourse and narrative analysis, in my view (Atkinson, 1999a, 2000b), allows us to begin to understand how reality is constituted and known in particular ways that entail the production of certain 'truths' and representations of reality.

Implications for urban regeneration

From a governmentality perspective, urban regeneration's turn to the community represents at least in part an attempt to reconstitute socially excluded communities, the spaces within which they live, and how they live their lives. It does this by restructuring how they are governed and how they govern themselves.

> Such projects are forms of arms-length governance in that communities are encouraged to provide for themselves in recognition that many services will be 'unattractive to the private sector locally' and that state intervention will take only limited forms. Far from propagating agendas of social 'inclusion', SRB [that is, the Single Regeneration Budget] is underpinned by discourses of public and private sector abandonment in which the only response for communities in deprived areas is to develop their own capacities and services. (Raco and Imrie, 2000, p 195)

The point is equally applicable to the New Deal for Communities (NDC) and current urban policy more generally. However, we need to bear in mind that this is not a simple top-down, one-way process. As previously intimated, inscribed within the process of community participation are opportunities for resistance. Communities are not passive recipients of these initiatives, and, although the balance of forces is weighted against them, there are possibilities to contest they ways in which initiatives are actualised at local level within particular spaces; that is, to pervert and bend the technologies of government in ways that the authors of particular programmes did not intend. For instance, while government may claim that, by winning Single Regeneration Budget (SRB) and NDC funds, communities must assume certain responsibilities, equally those same programmes entail claims by communities on government to ensure that it acts, through its regional and local arms, in ways which develop particular programmes and technologies of government that support community-led initiatives. Theoretically at least, this places an onus on government, in all its forms and at all levels, to ensure that its actions support and complement the programmes developed by communities. This then provides a space for communities to demand that the government reform itself in ways that match the rhetoric contained in documents such as the Urban White Paper (see Chapter Three of this volume). Moreover, it also opens up the space for communities to develop forms of governance in the areas targeted by these programmes that reflect their needs and enables them to make further demands on government at all levels.

In terms of NDC, the clear intention of the programme is that government should provide additional resources through mainstream programmes at all levels to support and reinforce the activities of each NDC. In particular, this legitimises the demands of each NDC on local and regional government to ensure that it bends mainstream programmes in ways that complement its own activities. Furthermore, local and regional government is expected to learn and internalise lessons regarding how NDCs deliver services in ways that better meet the needs of socially excluded individuals and communities. Such agencies are expected to internalise discourses of community-led regeneration and reorganise their own internal and external relations. This in turn requires them to examine their own internal conduct and how they govern themselves and their relations with the external world and develop technologies of government that are appropriate to particular interventions in that world.

Of course, there are dangers inherent in this process. For instance, it compels cities and local authorities to compete with one another nationally for resources, and then it forces communities within successful cities to compete with one another for those resources (Edwards, 1997). This final aspect of the process can create considerable tensions between areas within cities, and then again within the successful community over the distribution and use of resources. Not only does it fragment relations between cities, local authorities and communities, and promote competition between them, it also requires them to demonstrate that they have internalised the particular discourses of competition promoted by government and restructured (or modernised) their internal structures accordingly. This in turn requires the development of technologies and programmes appropriate to delivering projects and achieving results. If there is a failure to do this, the risk is run of being identified as 'failed' authorities, cities or communities. And what happens next, of course, is that central government agencies are sent in to run services such as education, or else funding is withdrawn for specific projects such as NDC. More generally, there is a danger that NDCs will act in isolation from one another, leaving government free to deal with each one on a bilateral basis, thereby preventing the emergence of any collective representation of issues and problems by NDCs themselves. There is some evidence, however, that NDCs are aware of this danger and are organising to ensure that they have a collective voice.

Urban regeneration, governance and community in practice

Plymouth – the context

This section draws upon the ideas outlined above in order to make sense of governance and urban regeneration in one particular local context, the city of Plymouth in south-west England. My main focus will be on a Round Two NDC, established in an area of the city known as Devonport (see Figure 5.1). However, the NDC first needs to be set in its wider context. The south-west of England is an overwhelmingly rural region; the city of Devonport, then, is something of an anomaly. This has engendered a sense of difference from the rest of the region and a feeling of being out on a limb with regard to the rest of (urban) England. It has, then, created a sense of social and spatial isolation. Internally, perhaps, the important fact to be aware of is that Plymouth traditionally has been a city dominated by its naval dockyard. For example, in 1965, 24,000 people were employed in the dockyard. However, by 1981 this had declined to 15,000, and by 1997 to 3,500. The decline continues to the present day. Even though Plymouth made significant attempts to attract new investment and create new jobs over the 10 years up to 1996, the city still lost a net 4,000 jobs. Despite recent improvements in its economic performance the city has continued to perform less well than either the south-west region as a whole or the UK average.

While Plymouth (and the strategic partnership Plymouth 2020 in particular) has often been described as an exemplar of partnership working, there is a view within the city that this has largely been concerned in the past with the private sector. As a result, partnership working within the public sector, and between the public sector and the voluntary and community sectors, is underdeveloped. As Plymouth 2020 makes the transition to Local Strategic Partnership (LSP) status, this will necessitate more of a focus on how the public sector operates and greater engagement with a wider range of organisations, particularly in the voluntary and community sectors. In addition, more thought will need to be given to how strategy is implemented and the possibility that this will require additional powers and an increase in resources. In turn, this will require service delivery organisations (from the public, private, voluntary and community sectors and area-based initiatives [ABIs]) to take a more strategic view and coordinate their activities more effectively, so that 'everyone is singing from the same hymn sheet'.

This process was begun in the late 1990s when the city submitted its *Pathfinder strategy and action plan* to the Local Government Association's Pathfinder New Commitment to Regeneration (Plymouth 2020, 1999). This was a long-term, 20-year strategy for the city that "expected to lift partnership working in Plymouth onto a new plane" and intended to provide "a holistic, corporate approach that is firmly underpinned by a strong belief in the participative and consultative process expected in modern Britain" (Plymouth, 2020, p 1). Its clear intention is to ensure that the £1 billion of public sector funding the city

Figure 5.1: Street scenes in Devonport

receives is used in a coordinated and flexible manner so that economic performance is improved and the city's social problems targeted. The document contains evidence of the scale of the city's problems, showing that the city, or at least parts of it, display many of the symptoms associated with social exclusion. It pointed out:

> Plymouth is very much a tale of two cities. In November 1998 unemployment in the affluent suburb of Plympton stood at 1.7%, at the same date unemployment in the inner city waterfront community of St Peters stood at 17.6%. Unemployment is linked to a variety of other key indicators of social malaise within the city. In 7 wards 25% of the community lives in poverty and there is a 700% variation in coronary heart disease across the city. Four wards ... are among the worst 10% in England (according to the [1998] Index of Deprivation) and on the basis of the worst three wards, Plymouth is the 31st most deprived district in England. Some 30% of residents within the city have below average basic literacy and numeracy skills while a low proportion of residents have higher level qualifications. (Plymouth, 2020, 1999, pp 10-11)

Constructing neighbourhoods

In 2000, Plymouth 2020 and the city council initiated a consultation process to update the local plan that involved carrying out Community Planning Studies in all 20 of the city's wards. The overall aim of the process was to develop the vision for an urban renaissance of the city, but also included:

> visions for particular parts of the city. These are derived from the views of local people and describe how residents might see their ward looking in the future. (Plymouth 2020, 2000, p 1)

As part of this process, it was decided, building upon the Social Exclusion Unit's (SEU) work on neighbourhood renewal, to "try and work with a unit which most people regard as their 'Natural Neighbourhood'" (Plymouth City Council, 2002, section 3.3). While acknowledging that "this is not a perfect science", the consultative document, following SEU guidelines that each neighbourhood should have between 4,000 and 6,000 people, identified 42 'Natural Neighbourhoods' in the city (Plymouth City Council, 2002, section 3.4).

The criteria for constructing these 42 areas draw upon a range of factors: census area boundaries; political boundaries; existing ABIs; natural boundaries (such as the sea); artificial boundaries (such as roads or walls); local community groups' own definitions; type of housing; isolation from the rest of the city; who lives there; and so on. Often these factors are used in combination, and doubtless some are more natural than others. However, what is interesting to note is that one of these natural neighbourhoods – Devonport – is widely recognised as being composed of at least two quite distinct communities. Furthermore, one regeneration initiative in the area – The Urban Village (discussed later in this chapter) – has further subdivided it into 10 neighbourhoods.

This is not intended to criticise Plymouth's attempts at creating natural neighbourhoods. Rather, it is to point to the difficulties inherent in constructing such administrative areas. There is inevitably an element of artificiality involved in this process and, depending upon the purposes and the scale of operation that one is working at it, is quite possible to produce very different and even contradictory results. Moreover, given that this process is intended to create areas that reflect and capture people's everyday life worlds, there is immense room for dissension and the construction of alternatively imagined neighbourhoods. But why are these neighbourhoods being constructed and what will they be used for? Drawing on the governmentality arguments developed earlier in the chapter, I would suggest that these natural neighbourhoods are intended in part to be sites of government intervention, in some cases individually and in others collectively.

Attempts by governing agencies will be made to identify what people in these areas regard as their needs and priorities, in part through the drawing up of community strategies, but also through existing ABIs and other established consultation mechanisms. However, these will have to be aggregated to create an overall strategy for the city and/or local authority and, given that there is unlikely to be sufficient resources to meet all the desires and needs identified by each neighbourhood, some form of prioritisation and rationalisation is inevitable. It is not difficult to imagine that this will lead to conflict between neighbourhoods, or that those neighbourhoods that most effectively learn and internalise the rules governing the process will benefit the most. In this sense, neighbourhoods, or groups of neighbourhoods, will need to demonstrate that they have internalised the appropriate diagnosis of problems and are able to govern their own conduct in a manner that corresponds with the discourses, programmes and technologies underlying the particular central government programmes they are seeking to access.

On the one hand, this may simply reflect effective and symbolic 'game playing' by some neighbourhoods as they seek to attract resources by demonstrating that they have internalised the relevant political rationality and the associated problem diagnosis, and have developed appropriate delivery technologies and associated notions such as 'value for money'. On the other hand, however, they will be expected to produce results – that is, achieve targets – that are consonant with these rules. This will require a capacity to engage with the process of resource distribution and tread a fine line between meeting the guidelines, targets, criteria and outcomes governing the allocation of funds. Simultaneously, those funds will need to be utilised creatively in ways that are of benefit to an area without subverting them too openly.

What this represents is a contest, whereby the relatively powerless are able to exploit gaps and contradictions in the interstices of government and its projects. Yet at the same time it still represents part of the wider process of government through community (Rose, 1996a), in which neighbourhoods and even whole cities become separated from a 'national community' and are expected to demonstrate that they are governing themselves in a manner congruent with dominant national governing discourses. In this sense, government may be able to achieve its objective of restructuring, reclassifying and reordering such communities without directly intervening in them – a form of action at a distance.

The New Deal for Communities

Clearly the city has widespread economic and social problems that are associated with social exclusion. When it was invited to bid for a Round Two NDC, Plymouth City Council asked the most deprived areas in the city to present a case for why they should be an NDC. This procedure drew on Bristol's Round One experience of selecting an area. In this instance, Bristol, through its independent regeneration organisation, Bristol Regeneration Partnership, brought together people from around the city to engage in a deliberative process in order to decide which neighbourhood should bid for NDC status. The outcome was largely consensual. In Plymouth, however, the council led the process and a more competitive system developed, including a 'scoring system' for each bid's assessment. For many involved in the process, the council's leading role meant it lacked independence. Furthermore, the scoring system was questioned and its basis not widely understood. There was certainly a feeling of confusion on the part of some participants and neighbourhoods felt that they had been forced to compete against one another for scarce resources. Nevertheless, Devonport was selected and submitted its Phase One bid in April 2000 and the final version in early 2001 (Devonport NDC, 2001).

Devonport NDC mainly lies within the city's St Peters ward (a small section also lies in the adjoining Keyham ward) and has the characteristics of an area and population experiencing social exclusion. According to the Index of Multiple Deprivation 2000, it is the 249th most deprived ward in England. Devonport NDC is dominated by The South Yard of the naval dockyard that divides the north and south of the area into two quite distinct and 'isolated' places. These places comprise three different communities, Mount Wise, Granby Island and Pottery Quay. The area's geography is dominated by large areas of high-density postwar social housing that makes up 80% of the housing stock, with only 20% owner-occupation (this is almost the mirror image of Plymouth's tenure structure). The area had already been the subject of several previous regeneration initiatives, including a variety of postwar urban renewal schemes, Estate Action Programme, SRB and a Housing Partnership Scheme. Apart from the Estate Action Programme, the different programmes were locally perceived to have had only a minor impact on the area and had left a legacy of cynicism and disbelief.

It ought to be borne in mind that Devonport NDC is part of the NDC's Round Two, which only began in April 2001. Indeed, Devonport was given permission to delay its formal launch until July 2001, although preparation did begin in April 2000. Thus, this is the early part of the initiative and the focus is very much on developing the strategy and constructing systems to put the delivery plan into practice. It is arguable that it would have been wise to give many of the NDCs more time to prepare before formally setting them up. This would have allowed more space for community involvement, and more time to put organisational structures in place and develop relations with major public service providers in the surrounding area. The point is particularly important as government has increasingly stressed that urban policy on its own cannot deal with the problems faced in socially excluded areas.

This view has been most cogently expressed by the Treasury in a document entitled *Government interventions in deprived areas* (HM Treasury, 2000). This document argued that the primary responsibility for tackling (urban) deprivation should lie with main programmes and that this requires a refocusing of those programmes. The report argues that:

> Targeted initiatives, including holistic regeneration programmes, have a role
> to play. But they should be part of a clear framework for tackling deprivation,
> rather than the main tool for doing so. (HM Treasury, 2000, p 2)

At one level, this supports the importance of a 'joined-up' approach to urban problems; but it also recognises the need for mainstream policies (such as social security, health, education, employment and economic policy) to play the main role. The NDC is intended to internalise this approach and places considerable emphasis on the role of mainstream public service providers at local level. It assumes they will bend their programmes to benefit NDC areas as well as learning lessons from NDCs about new ways to deliver services so that the needs of users are met more effectively. This requires NDCs to establish close and reciprocal relationships with major public service providers and other ABIs delivering services in their area.

Devonport NDC secured the signatures of a wide range of organisations to its delivery plan, but the problem, as with all such documents, is achieving engagement by signatories. While the city council's commitment covers all of its service departments, direct engagement with several of those departments has developed rather slowly. On the other hand, there has been growing evidence during 2002 of closer links developing with senior managers in mainstream agencies and a greater degree of reciprocal understanding. Much depends, however, upon the overall financial position of these agencies and the extent to which they feel able to bend mainstream funds in ways that support the NDC's activities. Agencies will point out that they have responsibilities to other, often seriously deprived, neighbourhoods and the rest of the city or region, and that they cannot simply take resources from one area to benefit another.

As one might expect, council officers from the Regeneration Unit have been, and continue to be, closely involved in the development of the NDC, while the three city councillors on the Shadow Board act as the formal link between the council and the NDC. However, it is debatable whether the council's service departments have fully recognised as yet the significance of the establishment of an NDC. (However, the NDC has engaged in discussions, facilitated by Plymouth 2020, to convey the need for more active engagement by service delivery agencies.) Nor have close relationships been established with other ABIs whose area of activity either cover all or part of the NDC area. To date, there has been little substantive evidence of a joined-up approach developing, thereby replicating the experience of earlier 'action zones' (see Painter and Clarence, 2001).

The NDC's plans for the Devonport area are ambitious. A central element is the development of the Urban Village, sponsored by Plymouth City Council, the South West Regional Development Agency and the Prince's Foundation. Planning for this commenced in 1998. In order to ensure that the coverage of the two initiatives was identical, the NDC was given permission to extend its area. The Urban Village will have a 10- to 15-year life span and is intended to change the tenure mix of the area, act as a motor of economic development by attracting new private investment, create new employment opportunities for local people, and to be a high-quality urban environment. This will occur through an integrated approach that combines the refurbishment and/or demolition of council housing, the building of a range of new housing for owner-occupation and by new registered social landlords and the release of sites for new private sector development. The NDC views the Urban Village as an essential element in the development of its plans and the key vehicle in its forward strategy. It is intended that the two initiatives be brought together under the umbrella of the Devonport Regeneration Company (DRC)[3].

In its first year, the NDC spent considerable time laying the foundations for the DRC. This has not been an easy process, as all the participants do not view the role of the Urban Village in the same light. The NDC is determined to ensure that the development of the Urban Village is of direct benefit to people who live in Devonport. Others are concerned that the regeneration of Devonport should result in successful economic development that will benefit people in the area. Partly resulting from these arguments, but also reflecting the relatively low, quantitative, level of local involvement, there have been delays in deciding the nature and form of community representation on the board of the DRC (such as what form any elections should take and their area basis). Elections to the board were held in July 2002 with a 29% turnout.

More generally, the NDC, and particularly key members of the local community on its board, has sought, by attempting to engage with local people, to ensure that the interests of the local community constantly structure its actions. Only time will tell whether or not this has been successful. More specifically, these people have not been willing simply to accept central government directives on how the NDC runs its affairs. Following complaints that the 30-page project appraisal form, which the DETR imposed on all NDCs, was far too complex and deterred individuals and groups from applying for funding, Devonport was given temporary permission to develop its own, much simpler, procedure. However, one could argue that central government can afford to make such small concessions on the understanding that on the bigger questions of strategy the actions of NDCs reflect its views about the causes of an area's decline and how to address them.

The NDC has two key aspects of strategy. Engagement with the community through capacity building is central to creating a 'community-led' programme that benefits the people of Devonport. Community engagement is also central to the second dimension of the strategy – 'breaking the poverty cycle' – which aims to get people back into work by changing the culture of 'worklessness' and welfare dependency that, combined with informal work, is seen to characterise the area. This involves not merely traditional forms of labour market interventions (such as skills training) but also an attempt significantly to improve the levels of educational achievement of all those living in the area, thereby increasing the range of opportunities available in the labour market.

Such an approach strongly resonates with the problem definition and policy narrative developed by New Labour at the national level to describe the causes of social exclusion and urban decline and the perpetuation of these problems in areas such as Devonport (Atkinson, 2000b). However, it is worth bearing in mind Wilson's (1987) analysis of the underclass and its associated culture in the US. Wilson argued that the structural forces underlying industrial restructuring and long-term unemployment created a situation in which new cultural attitudes began to emerge and were expressed and materialised in a distinct 'ghetto culture' as part of everyday survival strategies. Devonport NDC's strategy, reflecting that of the government, assumes a similar process has taken place in its area. But does it possess the powers and resources necessary to reverse the factors underlying that decline?

In reality this seems highly unlikely. In effect, and in order to obtain NDC status, it has internalised the government's problem definition, diagnosis and policy prognosis about how to 'solve' the area's problems. But by doing this, it has taken responsibility for tackling a problem that it cannot resolve and has allowed government to effectively retreat from direct engagement and absolve itself of responsibility – action at a distance. Those living in the area will be required to change how they behave; the NDC will need to develop forms of governance that encourage that change and reward those who change. Community groups and individuals that demonstrate, through their applications for NDC funding, that they have internalised these principles of action will be rewarded – those that do not will lose out. Thus, there is a real danger of creating, or perhaps recreating, a degenerate policy culture based on a division within the socially excluded between the 'deserving' and 'undeserving' (see Chapter One of this volume).

Moreover, the issue of how the DRC will bring together and deliver both the NDC's strategy and that of the Urban Village is likely to be contentious.

Some of those involved in the partnership would prefer to see the NDC section of the DRC focus on delivering the 'social side' of the strategy, while the physical regeneration and much of the economic development is left in the hands of professional property and economic developers. This is indicative of wider tensions inherent within current (and past) regeneration policy between achieving competitiveness through a primary focus on economic and physical regeneration and ensuring that local communities both decide upon and benefit from these developments. Those involved in the NDC are determined to ensure that the development of the Urban Village is done in such a way that the primary beneficiaries are the current residents of Devonport.

However, given the Urban Village's plans significantly to change the area's tenure structure by reducing the amount of council housing and by building large numbers of dwellings for owner-occupation, and given the low level of income in Devonport, it seems inevitable that there will have to be a significant influx of more affluent households into the area. If this strategy is successful, it is likely to alter significantly Devonport's social mix and lead to some degree of gentrification that may well impact upon how the NDC's strategy is viewed by local residents. This might then lead to calls for immediate changes. Ironically, if the NDC fails to change the area's tenure structure, many will deem it to have failed.

What is occurring here is a contest that is rooted in wider discourses. For instance, property and economic developers believe that only they have the skills necessary to carry forward effectively the area's physical and economic reconstruction. Community involvement is viewed as a threat to their autonomy and hence likely to undermine their effectiveness. Equally significant is that the Urban Village's strategy has internalised the assumption that, by bringing middle-class households into the area, its fortunes will somehow be turned around. There is an underlying assumption that these new groups will bring with them new forms of social capital that will magically create new social networks both within the area and be linked into the wider locality. It is assumed that the attitudes and values of these newcomers will somehow 'rub off' on longer standing residents and that they will change their behaviour in ways that allow them to be reinserted into mainstream society. Even if such households are attracted to the area there is little evidence to suggest that this will happen. Indeed, if successful, it is more likely to produce demands for greater change within the area as the middle-class inhabitants seek to protect their property values. One unintended result could be increased social polarisation within the area.

What we can see taking place here is a struggle by different groups over the construction of problems and the development of a political rationality that will allow the partnership to develop a 'common logic', enabling it to think about and address those problems. To date, while the NDC has internalised elements of New Labour's wider policy narrative, there has been an unwillingness to concede ground to the logic of particular professionals and experts. This has been maintained through an insistence, particularly by local community activists on the DRC board, on the prioritisation of the needs of the area's current residents. However, as I have pointed out, the long-term plans for the area imply a change in its social mix. If this is successful, there will inevitably be some displacement of the socially excluded groups currently living within the area.

Who knows what the future holds? If, as I have suggested, the NDC necessarily lacks the ability to address the fundamental causes of the problems in the area, then there is little likelihood of it being able to reverse the social and spatial exclusion that Devonport has experienced over the past 20 years. Such a failure could invite more central intervention or a strategy of abandonment on a national scale, whereby areas such as Devonport are simply left to survive as best they can. Much will depend on the political salience of the issue to a future government. Perhaps more importantly, such a failure would simply reinforce the existing scepticism within the area's population, although having already developed its own survival strategies it will continue to manipulate the existing welfare system in ways that allows it to get by.

Conclusions

The concept of governmentality, rather like that of governance, provides us with a way of looking at, analysing and understanding contemporary arrangements and structures developed to govern society. Unlike other approaches to government and governance, it emphasises that 'government' has always been complex and should not simply be restricted to traditional notions of government. Indeed, it points us towards the notion that individuals and communities have a key role to play in their own 'government'. In part, this reflects government at a distance, as they internalise ways of behaving (in other words, governing their own conduct) through particular policy discourses and narratives by participating in particular programmes of government and developing associated technologies.

Nevertheless, there is always the possibility of resistance: both individuals and communities have the *potential* to develop ways of governing themselves that, while meeting the requirements of central government, can better meet their own needs. Governmentality, therefore, provides us with a means to understand both the mechanism through which government governs and the ways in which individuals and communities can 'undermine' these mechanisms. However, governmentality remains somewhat underdeveloped: theoretically, it is quite sophisticated, but much remains to be done in terms of its empirical development as a concept of analysis and empirical methodology. Like any theoretical approach, it will not provide all the answers and needs to be developed in relation to existing analyses (for example, governance) to learn from their strengths and overcome their weaknesses.

Turning to contemporary urban policy and ABIs such as NDC, I have argued that they have developed as part of a series of changes that have sought to recast the governance of the UK as a whole. These changes began before New Labour came to power, but New Labour has sought to accentuate particular aspects of them, most notably through the 'turn to community' as a new site of disaggregate governance. Within this wider context, particular communities in excluded spaces are being asked to take responsibility for their own future and wellbeing. This appears to be an attractive offer, congruent with a modernised and more participative system of governance that gives local people greater control over their lives.

However, as I have suggested, there are serious obstacles to local people exercising this control. Most notably they lack the power and resources necessary to address the wider structural forces that have caused decline in their areas. Moreover, in order to gain access to limited resources, communities in 'excluded spaces' are expected to internalise a series of policy discourses and narratives, demonstrate adherence to particular programmes of government and develop technologies appropriate to them. This requires that communities restructure themselves internally and demonstrate that they are capable of governing themselves, both collectively and individually, in ways that reflect these wider demands. Any failure will be their failure. The great irony is that, for programmes such as NDC to be a success, there need to be major changes in the way that the government itself operates. Yet it is clear that the government has failed at national, regional and local levels to reorder the ways in which it governs itself and its relations with the external world. Such failures further limit the possibilities for excluded communities to successfully address the deep-rooted problems they face.

Nevertheless, initiatives such as NDC do offer genuine possibilities for communities such as those in Devonport to exploit the rhetoric of community-led regeneration and develop community-based forms of governance that reflect the needs of a particular area. The problem is that in order to gain access to resources, they are forced to engage in competition with other deprived areas and to restructure the way in which they behave and govern themselves in a manner that is at least superficially in harmony with dominant political and policy discourses. In the case of Devonport, a particularly ambitious project has been developed, which, if successful, will fundamentally restructure the social and political structure of the area. The problem is that, if it were to be successful, there is a real likelihood that many of the socially excluded individuals currently living there could be displaced into other areas. In a sense, this is, and has been, the reality of urban policy for the past two decades.

What communities such as Devonport are trying to do is to negotiate a tightrope. They have to buy into dominant views on what regeneration should aim for, and how it should be achieved, which entails quite fundamental changes in the area, although without the resources to bring about that change. At the same time, they have to address the everyday needs of people currently living in the area and ensure that they are the primary beneficiaries of action. This dilemma is not new, but the terms in which it has been recast in recent years do appear to imply that excluded communities will be expected to bear the responsibility for any failure. This will allow government either to disengage from these areas or intervene in new and more intrusive ways.

Acknowledgement

I would like to thank the editors of this volume, Rob Imrie and Mike Raco, for their valuable comments on earlier versions of this chapter.

Notes

[1] The debates on social exclusion and community have been extensively covered, and it is not my intention to restate them here. On social exclusion see Silver (1994); Room (1995); Levitas (1996); Atkinson (2000a); Kearns and Forrest (2000). For debates concerning 'community', see Part One of this volume, and also Crow (1997); Taylor (2000a); Forrest and Kearns (2001); Howarth (2001).

[2] This concept, however, has recently attracted the attention of a number of researchers. See, for example, Miller and Rose (1990); Rose and Miller (1992); Rose (1993, 1996a); McNay (1994); Dean (1999).

[3] At the time of writing the DRC Board had not been formally constituted and existed as a Shadow Board. It will be formally constituted as a company limited by guarantee in March 2003.

Further reading

Since 1999, a number of important documents have been published, not least the Urban Policy White Paper (DETR, 2000e). Also the SEU has published numerous relevant reports that are available at www.cabinet-office.gov.uk/seu. Similarly, the Neighbourhood Renewal Unit provides information and guidance to the 88 areas eligible for the Neighbourhood Renewal Fund, available at www.neighbourhood.gov.uk. The Office of the Deputy Prime Minister is now the 'lead' urban department at central government level, and its statements are worth reading at www.odpm.gov.uk. For an overview of recent developments, see Atkinson (2003: forthcoming).

SIX

Communities at the heart? Community action and urban policy in the UK

Peter North

A recipe for violence: Promise a lot: deliver a little. Lead people to believe they will be much better off, but let there be no dramatic improvement. Try a variety of small programmes, each interesting but marginal in impact and severely under-financed. Avoid any attempted solution remotely comparable in size to the dimensions of the problem that you are trying to solve .... Get some poor people involved in local decision-making, only to discover that there is not enough at stake to be worth bothering about. Feel guilty about what has happened to black people: tell them you are surprised that they have not revolted before: express shock and dismay when they follow your advice. Go in for a little force, just enough to anger, not enough to discourage. Feel guilty again: say that you are surprised that worse has not happened. Alternate with a little suppression. Mix well, apply a match, and run. (Wildavsky, quoted in Moynihan, 1969, p ii)

Introduction

As the chapters of this volume show, many commentators have welcomed a new willingness to listen to and involve local people in area-based regeneration policy in the UK (Atkinson, 1999a; North, 2000; Purdue et al, 2000)[1]. To take one example: the Single Regeneration Budget Round Five (SRB5), 1999. Among the plethora of funding regimes, SRB has a particularly poor reputation as a bureaucratic, inflexible process that emphasises number crunching rather than 'real' results or innovation (see Chapter Eight of this volume). Many of its processes are opaque to those who have not cracked the mysteries of its specialist language and style! Its management and reporting requirements assume that participating organisations have the administrative structures to handle the voluminous paperwork involved. Funding is normally paid in arrears, which again assumes that participating organisations have extensive financial back-up. There is little support to involve small community groups in developing schemes. As a result, few voluntary organisations have been successful at winning these funds, despite encouragement from Government Offices.

Single Regeneration Budget Round Five was the first round held under rules written by New Labour. It was supposed to be different; it claimed to have learned from criticisms. Certainly, its guidance includes commitments:

- to use SRB monies *actively* to foster social inclusion and fairness;
- to support and develop genuine partnership working in which the voluntary sector and local people have a real voice;
- to take practical steps to secure the wholehearted support of the community, with partnerships being urged to include in their bids proposals for community involvement;
- explicitly to invite bidders to submit free-standing, skills-enhancing, capacity-building projects;
- to encourage bids that stress a 'slow burn' process via an introductory 'Year Zero';
- to encourage the full involvement of ethnic minority communities and the ethnic minority voluntary sector.

Significantly, the SRB5 guidance did not stand alone. It formed part of a pattern, including publications from the Department of the Environment, Transport and the Regions (DETR) and the Social Exclusion Unit (SEU) (DETR, 1998a, 1998b, 1999a; SEU, 1998; PLCRC, 1999). Another aspect of SRB5 included the idea of 'Year Zero', a slow, phased build-up to regeneration. During this start-up phase, no project spending would occur. Instead, the focus would be on establishing new partnerships, and ensuring that management and appraisal arrangements were in position, and that local community and voluntary organisations were fully involved. It had been recognised, therefore, that those organisations, not being well versed in the regeneration game, might need some time to develop their capacity to work with these bureaucratic requirements. In 1999, New Labour was moving in ways that seemed to facilitate community involvement in regeneration.

There are also long-held concerns that funding allocated to partnerships is inadequate in the face of the scale of the urban problems they are expected to address, while local initiatives have proliferated, they are characterised by the incorporation of communities into the management of urban and economic decline and/or the creeping privatisation of local services[2]. Worse, it is argued that community groups are effectively disarmed and then silenced through a rhetoric of partnership that regards disruption, objection, raised voices and organisation as illegitimate forms of action; that is, outside the inclusive ethos of partnership.

> The partnership approach has the effect of reducing conflict, forcing the different sectors to engage in consensus politics. For example, while ... community interests are not in most cases happy with their status within the

partnership, few are prepared to oppose the process or boycott it, for the simple reason that they do not want to miss the opportunity to secure at least some benefits for their area. (Colenutt and Cutten, 1994, p 239)

While friendly disagreement over ways forward within an overall framework of agreement about a certain regeneration strategy is permissible, fundamental critics are not seen as 'good partners'. They are told to take their views elsewhere, and not prevent those who are signed up to a common agenda from doing their work. If they engage in partnerships, then, community organisations will be structured into collaborative endeavours in which they connive in the decimation and/or privatisation of services (Giddens, 1984). While the rhetoric of contemporary urban policy is that of community involvement, to what extent can community-based groups set the local agenda? Can they take the lead or be involved in participation on terms set by others?

This chapter looks at the extent to which the cosy, inclusive rhetoric of 'community' deals with harder, sharper concepts such as 'struggle', 'opposition' and 'resistance'. It is not the place of this chapter to look at whether there is such a thing as 'community'; whether or not communities are ever unitary agents (obviously they are fractured); or whether or not those agents who ascribe the name 'community' to themselves are right to do so. Rather, the argument is to look at the effectiveness or otherwise of two resident-based organisations that claimed to represent local people and also used confrontational tactics. This chapter asks whether these organisations were able, using these tactics, to advance the arguments they made, and whether they could have advanced them more effectively within or outside the partnership. I work from the understanding that to attempt to adjudicate between competing claims for authentic 'community' is akin to attempting to 'tame' or even disarm these agents, and that a far more fruitful line of enquiry is to examine their effectiveness (Routledge and Simmons, 1995). The focus of this chapter, then, is on the reality of rhetoric of community involvement in partnership working – and not the authenticity or otherwise of claims for community by those groups that joined with partnerships.

Consequently, the chapter also focuses on how community actors are involved when their discourses are constructed *against* the main thrust of local or central government policy. If so, what of partnership? Are our conceptions of urban governance, resting as they do on networks, coalitions and partnerships, able to handle conflict, come through it, and develop agendas that meet fundamental criticisms without either excluding these fundamental critics or imposing the consensus of the dead? What are the implications for partnerships of struggle? Do we need to rethink social capital and empowerment to better understand resistant networks within our cities that become visible through regeneration partnerships? Or should opponents take their arguments elsewhere, and not disrupt the work of those who wish to work in more inclusive ways? If the latter is the case, do we need to move away from more democratic conceptions of partnership that stress the centrality of community involvement (what you might call regeneration by local people), and foreground coordination, effectiveness and management (or regeneration of places)?

I want to argue in this chapter that early regeneration policy under Tony Blair's first term as Prime Minister (SRB5, SRB6, and the New Deal for Communities [NDC]) was characterised as an uncritical and poorly conceptualised idea of community. Local people – whoever they were, for it is never spelt out – were placed front and centre in partnerships. In many regeneration partnerships, levels of community involvement stayed at fairly low levels on Arnstein's (1969) scale. Communities were informed, consulted, and often subject to what Arnstein called 'therapy' in which they would be made to feel central to policy development, while in reality decisions were made elsewhere. In the two case studies presented here, community groups aimed for real involvement if not leadership of regeneration, a claim that in one case was challenged and in another was seen to be hollow. Both case studies show the problems of uncritically placing communities at the heart of regeneration while not making community ownership real.

Elephant Links community forum

Elephant Links is a regeneration programme centred on the Elephant and Castle in south-east central London (see Figures 6.1 and 6.2). The Challenge Process, whereby regeneration funding was allocated in the late 1990s, encouraged applicants to demonstrate need through pointing out why their proposed regeneration area simultaneously combined great deprivation,

Figure 6.1: Map of London: Elephant and Castle, and Vauxhall

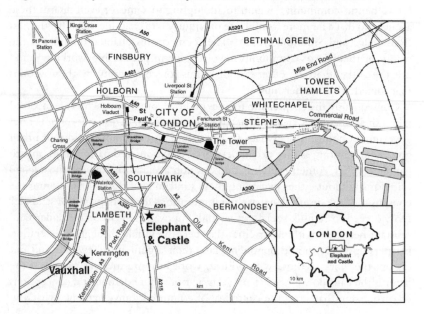

Figure 6.2: Street scenes from Elephant and Castle, London

exclusion and need with unmissable opportunities for change (Oatley, 1998a). As it happened, the Elephant fitted the criteria perfectly. It is the as yet undiscovered fourth quarter of central London alongside Westminster, the West End and the City, and ready to capitalise on the revitalisation of the South Bank with its Tate Modern, Millennium Bridge and London Eye. It has a locally popular yet run-down shopping centre, which was also the UK's first covered centre and a prime resource for redevelopment.

Next to it is a modernist planning disaster – the Heygate Estate – replete with monolithic deck access blocks, 13 storeys high, sitting on prime development land (Collins, 2001). The Elephant is a major transport artery and suffers from high levels of traffic congestion. Yet the road and transport interchanges could be remodelled to recreate the Elephant of the 1930s, when it was the terminus for trams. A new plaza could be created – a Piccadilly Circus for South London! Finally, the Elephant is home to gangsters (McDonald, 2000), gay activists (Tatchell, 1982), MPs, architects, journalists, and some of the highest levels of social exclusion in the city (LEPU and PPCR, 2001). The Elephant, then, has it all: opportunity and need. Surely it fits the bill perfectly for regeneration?

Southwark Council decided that the core elements of the regeneration infrastructure at the Elephant would be a public–private partnership to redevelop the site of the shopping centre and the Heygate, and a £25-million, seven-year SRB application to run parallel to the physical redevelopment. This application would focus on environmental improvements to facilitate land assembly and on tackling social exclusion. In particular, the SRB would develop two major programmes: first, a community advocacy project to ensure that local people were helped into work through customised support for personal advisers modelled on the New Deal or Employment Zones; and second, a community information project that would see the Elephant wired up for internet access to enable residents to get access to information more easily. This was described by the London Borough of Southwark as "a demonstration project of government thinking on social exclusion". The bid was successfully won in August 1999, while Southwark Land Regeneration was selected as a development partner in 2000 (London Borough of Southwark, 1999; Birch, 2000).

To what extent were local residents involved in the development of this vision for the Elephant? As is so often the case, residents had little say in the design of the regeneration of the Elephant and Castle. A Residents' Regeneration Group (RRG) had met for some 18 months before consultations about SRB began, arguing that the needs of local people were in housing and environmental improvements and new community facilities. The RRG was not opposed to redevelopment but felt that plans should fully replace any lost council housing, avoid high-rise development, and provide gardens and open spaces. The consultation process for the SRB included working groups and a Stakeholders' Forum, to which key local public, voluntary sector and private sector partners were invited. The RRG joined these discussions somewhat late, having had to fight its way in by threatening not to agree the bid.

As it became clear that the council's plans for a bid involved meeting government rather than local priorities, the Stakeholders' Forum became a battleground. The main themes of the bid were worked up by council officers and were presented to the Stakeholders' Forum somewhat late in the day, without first going through the working groups. Consequently, they appeared as a fait accompli, to the obvious annoyance of those who had been working on the subgroups in what was looking like a therapeutic consultation exercise while the real decisions were taken elsewhere. Bottom-up, community-focused projects, council officers argued, would not win the challenge contest and would not be appropriate for a strategic programme, which, in effect, aimed to ensure that residents understood and benefited from the changes happening to them. They argued that a community-led programme would be limited by the Government Office for London to £2-3 million, whereas a strategic programme could generate as much as £25 million. However, significant voices in the community initially refused to sign the bid:

> Then they rang me up the day before and said, "Come and sign the bid", and I said "No". I wouldn't sign something I had nothing to do with and didn't understand …. Which is quite a big thing when the Heygate is not signed up to it and it's the key. (Community representative)

Once the bid had been approved and the partnership established, community representatives were more successful at winning resources. The partnership included a Community Forum to act as a voice for local tenants and residents, eventually growing into a federation of 63 local tenants' and residents' groups, faith groups, black and minority ethnic groups, and small community-based groups such as allotments. It is on this federative structure that the forum based its claim to legitimacy. The forum would elect five of the 16 Partnership Board members (one of whom went on to chair the partnership). Very quickly, however, the forum felt that it would need to battle to get adequate logistical support if a real local voice was to be heard alongside the better-resourced private and public sectors. Conflict arose over the speed at which this would be provided, with officers feeling that a slower, organic process would be best to help the organisation find its feet. In contrast, the forum felt that it had already missed out on the opportunity to shape the SRB programme, and would not make the same mistake for the physical development, in which community interests were central. The impasse was broken only when the activists wrote their own 'guerrilla' bid for funds for a community office and three staff for three years, at suitably high grades. A community office was opened in the shopping centre, which became a focus for community organising.

The forum used its new-found strength and independence to ensure that the partnership understood the importance of housing to residents. It did this by influencing the criteria through which a development partner would be selected, by ensuring that one criterion would be a 100% reprovision of social housing. It further argued that social housing meant council housing – not housing association (HA) housing. It felt that the leaseholds offered by HAs gave tenants fewer rights, less security of tenure, and higher rentals in many significant ways. This latter point became an ongoing bone of contention as the council insisted that the social housing would be managed by Registered Social Landlords (RSLs). Again, then, while residents argued for their conception of housing, the council promoted government agendas for a reduction of council housing. Interestingly, the forum did not waver from its view.

Significantly, residents were able to influence the selection of the developer. The forum argued that the SRB programme and the physical development should be interconnected, while the council saw the two processes as separate but linked. The council argued that it alone would make the decision as to with whom it wished to enter into a public–private partnership, whereas the forum argued that the Partnership Board should manage the development process. In a compromise, a Development Working Group was established to connect the SRB and physical elements through which local people could influence the selection of the developer, with the final decision being taken by the council. Yet again, however, this process was seen by some in the forum as problematic. The concern was that, while there was a creditable amount of consultation and information sharing, this was not shared power and decision making. The council consulted, but made the final decision, and more importantly managed information flows between the developer and the community. The community side did not have access to its own technical support, in what were becoming crucial decisions about the fundamental redevelopment of the area by property interests. So the forum successfully argued for a more robust tripartite structure including the Board, the council, and the developer, and for significant levels of independent technical support from SRB.

Consequently, there were trade-offs. The forum was less successful in its communication than it was in its organisation. The council argued that this was an attempt at a community 'take-over' of the process, perhaps to prevent regeneration happening. It portrayed the community as being too dominant, and of taking too many seats on the tripartite structure. It argued that it was unrealistic to expect new organisation such as the Elephant Links Board to manage a complex redevelopment. It also refuted the suggestion that the developer would take advantage of the community's inexperience, and added that it had responsibilities as the landowner. Other partners agreed, and the perception of a community take-over stuck. Conflict became embedded in board meetings. The Community Forum took up considerable time in Partnership Board meetings arguing its case, and walked out when progress was not made to its satisfaction, testing the patience of its partners. Community action led to paralysis within the partnership as the council tried to head off what it saw as unreasonable demands, while the community's strident defence of its action meant that other partners felt that the community was being over-dominant.

The community, then, won a significant role in decision making. Other partners, however, perceived this as an illegitimate voice, won through effective organising and caucusing before meetings, rather than through negotiating and taking partners with it. It was seen as a group that held the partnership to ransom, that made its demands, and would walk out if it did not get them. Eventually, this burned representatives out. They began to fall out with one another, as radical and more conciliatory voices clashed. The key Heygate estate left the Community Forum, feeling that its issues were not raised adequately in an organisation that had, as a consequence of the need to fulfil SRB outputs, significantly widened its membership such that it was no longer dominated by housing interests. Conflict meant that progress on the development, both of the masterplan for the physical development of the area and of major SRB projects, was delayed.

Conflict also had a human cost. It involved hundreds of hours of community activism, not all of it directed at the most effective target. Issues were fought over that need not have been brought up at that particular moment. What can be said is that the community had the power to clog up the workings of the partnership if it was not listened to – a power it was ready to use. It won resources and influence through using this power, but Community Forum members also wondered if they would be able to stay the course. The partnerships entered a 'dual power' situation in which neither side could impose its will on the other. The forum was accused of going for control in what should be a partnership. It was, in effect, accused of being an over-mighty subject.

The outcome was perhaps predictable. The council organised against these 'unruly subjects', and gained control over what had become, for it, an unmanageable process. The Community Forum chair was deposed by a local business person, who began to take a much stronger line against the forum. The chair attempted to reduce forum representation now the Heygate had left. The Community Forum successfully resisted these attempts to reduce its influence, and made defensive counter-claims such that, as the Community Forum had grown, local residents should form a *majority* of Elephant Links. Neither the new chair nor the forum backed down. The result was all-out war at board meetings, culminating in a near riot.

The council then came for the Community Forum's resources. It accused the forum of being a failing project as it was not involving the number of residents as volunteers at volumes and in timescales that SRB could count, even though the forum had grown significantly in numbers of affiliated bodies. Pressure was put on it to justify its funding. Southwark Council's Department of Environment and Transport (DET) voted to move from the forum office to the site Heygate estate, under council line management. The council then asked the forum to pass all the DET papers to the new team. The forum refused to do this, arguing it was a community resource and included sensitive information on the community's negotiating position in the development. The council then refused to pay the forum's grant, and the staff were issued with redundancy notices.

The development was then called off. The council's ratification committee voted in April 2002 to terminate the agreement with the selected developers, and to seek partners for a smaller programme involving one partner for the shopping centre, and a new housing-based development on the Heygate involving a consortium of RSLs. At this point, it became clear that the council had gone around the Community Forum's earlier victory in winning full replacement of council housing in the new development, and had for some time been negotiating separately with HAs on proposals for the Heygate site.

The Community Forum attempted to challenge this decision at the board. After the chair attempted to rule the resolution out of order, a near riot erupted as forum representatives vented their collective spleen at what they saw as the combined and multiple injustices of the chair's autocratic behaviour. And it did not end there: they were infuriated by the chair's attempts to limit their influence at board meetings and to use evaluation to close the forum down, the removal of the DET project that they had fought long and hard for against constant council opposition, and the coup de grace, the council's decision unilaterally to cancel the development. The council then moved quickly. It went to court and gained an injunction requiring the forum to hand over all the DET documents, a requirement the forum eventually complied with.

Project Vauxhall

The second case study also comes from London's South Bank, this time one mile from the Elephant and Castle in the neighbouring borough of Lambeth (see Figure 6.3). In 1996, Lambeth Council began to explore proposals for the redevelopment of the borough's northern border, on the south bank of the Thames between Vauxhall Bridge and Waterloo. The council's aim was to deal with the considerable social problems it faced through maximisation of Challenge moneys and a proactive asset disposal programme, the assets in question being council homes and the land they sat on. Lambeth would work with a private sector partner to use the high land values in an area that was, as one developer put it, "within the limits of the division bell", and carry out redevelopment of what was felt to be underutilised land. New and improved council housing and a range of other social and environmental programmes were to be provided. Redevelopment would change the mix of the area, introducing more diverse tenure and what was seen as a more sustainable community mix. While major changes were envisaged, the plans also included a commitment both to the development of a consensus for redevelopment among residents of the proposed areas, and to making sure that tenants would benefit.

This approach, or 'Project Vauxhall' as it was called, was discussed with constituents of two estates in north Lambeth, Vauxhall Gardens and the Ethelred. Vauxhall Gardens declined to take part. Following an earlier decision by the Government Office for London to turn down a programme for housing renewal for the Ethelred from SRB1 and a decision against exploring stock transfer,

Figure 6.3: A view across Vauxhall, London

Lambeth felt that the best way forward would be to seek a private sector partner for the Ethelred. Support for this approach was gained at a meeting held on the estate in February 1997.

During 1997, Lambeth held a series of meetings with 11 potential development partners. A brief was developed for a competition to select a partner and a scheme that would include the demolition of the Ethelred deck access blocks and some or all of the tower blocks, and the provision of 300 new council homes on a cleared site – if tenants agreed. In November 1997, four submissions were shortlisted, and a year later Wimpey was appointed as preferred developer with a plan that included the provision of 2,223 new flats. However, Wimpey quickly felt that it would not be able to take the development forward alone. It therefore entered into a Joint Venture Company (JVC) consortium with another developer, St George, which had come second in the competition. A Project Board was appointed including representatives from the two estates, head teachers and governors from local schools, and London Borough of Lambeth officers. Councillors attended as observers. Lambeth decided that the best way to ensure that communities were at the heart of these plans would be for council officers to *support* community representatives in negotiations with developers, rather than take Southwark's approach where the council would see its role as ensuring community benefit.

This Project Board negotiated with the Wimpey/St George consortium during 1999 and into 2000. A further round of consultations was held, including newsletters, a public forum (the residents' subgroup), and a second round of exhibitions and open days. Tenant's Friend supported residents, while Lambeth opened a project office. The programme changed as residents' views were taken on board, and in particular the amount of social housing was gradually increased to 109 housing association and 510 council properties. However, as negotiations continued, those opposed to Project Vauxhall organised themselves, and a number of campaigns emerged to oppose the plans. Save Ethelred Homes argued that the Project Board was being taken advantage of by both the council (which wanted to demolish the estate and create homes for high-income newcomers) and the developers. The Project Board tried to get as much community benefit as it could, and the developers argued that they had met as many community demands as was possible. The result of protracted negotiations was a programme that the Project Board felt was the best likely to emerge, but not one it was actively prepared to support. It felt that residents should be given the chance to vote on it, one way or the other. In August and September 2000 a ballot was held. The 'No' campaigns were active, attending public meetings and providing weekly leaflets that covered the full range of arguments they deployed against the programme. In this, they were supported by Defend Council Housing (DCH; www.defendcouncilhousing.org.uk), the national campaigning organisation that opposes stock transfer and housing privatisation.

The 'No' campaigners successful took apart the rationale for Project Vauxhall. They convinced residents that Project Vauxhall meant not the regeneration of the Ethelred, but its destruction. The proposals would benefit developers, the council and those who bought the new flats rather than local people, and the demolition was unnecessary. In effect, they claimed, the residents were being asked to vote for their own demise (North and Winter, 2002). They argued that the 15-year timeframe envisaged for comprehensive redevelopment would mean too much disruption, and that there was insecurity about where tenants would be transferred during redevelopment and no guarantee that they would be able to return, as insufficient council housing was being rebuilt. This destroyed trust in the council and the developers. Finally, they argued that government would provide Lambeth with the resources it needed if a campaign was mounted. All sides agreed that the 'No' campaign successfully outmanoeuvred the council, the developers and those residents who were in favour of development. Nobody ever mounted a campaign in favour. The result of the vote was 60/40 against the proposals. The result meant that Project Vauxhall did not go ahead, and the board met for the last time on October 2000 (North and Winter, 2002).

There are a number of differences between the Project Vauxhall and Elephant Links case studies. Key community activists were inside the process at the Elephant, and attempted to change it from within. In Project Vauxhall, community representatives were involved, but the 'awkward squad' was successfully excluded from discussions. They organised successfully from the outside, and, as a result of Lambeth's admirable (if suicidal) commitment to gain residents' support for the proposals, the development did not go ahead once residents voted against them. Those inside the process did not argue for the level of independent technical advice agreed in the Elephant, and despite the council's perception that their role was to support residents, they saw their role as making sure that the council got the best deal. Consequently, there was none of the community–council antagonism that characterised the Elephant case study. But neither, it must be said, was the council and the developer pushed to deliver a project that would meet the objections of opponents through, for example, the 100% reprovision of council homes that activists successfully argued for in the Elephant. With a more robust community voice, and attendant (perhaps uncomfortable) conflict, these problems could have been uncovered earlier.

For its part, the council took a radically different approach to the development from that of Southwark. Southwark Council was very clear that it would lead the development, and that it would make the decision on whether to go ahead or not, after consultations of course. Lambeth's view was that its role was to facilitate interaction between the developers and local residents who would vote on whether they wanted the programme to go ahead. This they did: residents were empowered, and made a decision. The problem was that the council was then accused by both developers and local residents of a failure of leadership, while the 'No' campaigners successfully characterised Project Vauxhall as a council-led project (North and Winter, 2002).

Given that the council instigated Project Vauxhall, there is some justification in this claim. When Project Vauxhall was conceived in 1996, a public–private partnership such as was proposed was 'state of the art' in regeneration policy. For an inner London authority with multiple and extensive social problems and local authority stock in poor repair, limited resources and the then existing funding arrangements, seeking a public–private partnership was the only viable alternative. Lambeth tried to raise the necessary finance from SRB, but the proposed housing programmes were rejected. Lambeth was also operating within a wider and unfavourable housing finance environment. Given restrictions on public borrowing, housing associations have access to private finance that is denied to local authorities. Further, the political environment was one in which local authorities, rightly or wrongly, were not perceived by successive administrations as effective managers of social housing, and the thrust of successive waves of housing policy from the mid-1980s onwards was against local authority ownership and management of housing. It can, for example, be contrasted with the environment of the 1950s, when local authorities would vie with each other for the honour of having built the *most* council housing per year. The national housing agenda was moving towards less local authority ownership in favour of housing associations. Lambeth, it was felt, must move in this direction if it was to have any chance of addressing the deep-seated social problems the borough faced. As the Ethelred did not wish to explore stock transfer, a public–private partnership was the only possible alternative. Given this wider policy environment, Lambeth showed a commendable commitment to taking residents with it.

However, a number of issues arise that point to fundamental problems with the design and vision for Project Vauxhall. From the beginning, tenants' satisfaction levels with the Ethelred suggested that, while they wanted improvements, the extent to which the problem was at an intensity to require wholesale demolition was questionable. Incremental improvements were never seriously examined. The development consortia were not encouraged to come up with a range of less comprehensive approaches involving different levels of social housing provision, including the replacement of council housing. It is not clear at all that when residents said that they were in favour of 'improvement', even if this involved demolition of all or part of the estate, that they understood that Lambeth envisaged a project on the scale that emerged. In other words, they thought they were discussing the renovation of their estate, not its destruction.

While residents were involved from the beginning and had the final say in whether it would go ahead, Project Vauxhall was clearly a programme engaged primarily in the regeneration of *place* (that part of north Lambeth) rather the regeneration of *people* (the residents of the Ethelred estate). A significant change in the demographics of the area was envisaged. This was not spelt out to people when Project Vauxhall was being developed. When they realised the scale of changes envisaged, they reacted against them. As regeneration was focused on place rather than people, inadequate attention was paid to the development of a bottom-up vision for the area by existing residents. The approach focused on bricks and mortar, rather than how the people of the Ethelred lived their lives and what their needs were. Consequently, the vision developed was not able to meet people's needs, and residents did not feel that they had ownership of the suggested scheme.

Despite Lambeth's claims that it is agnostic about housing management and that there was no hidden stock transfer agenda, the small number of council homes requested of developers in briefs seems to suggest that securing new council homes was not a high priority. Ethelred residents had previously decided not to pursue stock transfer. Given this, claims made by the 'No' campaigners that an underlying commitment to tenure transfer still drove Project Vauxhall, seem to have some justification. Lambeth, at best, failed to manage changing agendas, and, at worst, was being disingenuous in claiming otherwise.

Project Vauxhall failed because the goal posts changed. The Labour government changed conceptions of effective regeneration with a greater emphasis on community ownership and social inclusion, and the election of Ken Livingstone as Mayor of London in 2000 raised expectations even higher, putting a greater emphasis on affordability in central London. A public–private partnership, involving a significant reduction in social housing, was no longer seen as acceptable. Consequently, the arguments of those with a fundamental opposition to privatisation began to have an audience. Public opinion, in short, moved to the left, and urban policy was slow to move with it. The result has been a number of high-profile defeats for stock transfer (Aylesbury Estate, Southwark and Birmingham being prime examples). While Project Vauxhall involved prior demolition and the rebuilding of new stock, the majority of which would be RSL-managed rather than council housing, it was portrayed by the 'No' campaign, and experienced by residents, as a de facto stock transfer.

Thus, Project Vauxhall was an early example of what later became a more widespread trend.

Conclusions – community involvement within partnership

In both of the case studies, partnership processes were characterised by considerable conflict. To a large degree, this comes down to a mismatch between rhetoric that puts communities at the heart of regeneration, and a reality that regeneration was carried out as a technical fix that aimed to change a place. One conception might be that neither of them 'worked', in that the proposed development did not happen. Elephant Links SRB was behind projected spend, residents were not seriously involved in the development of the plans, and Elephant Links was a partnership of organisations focused *on* the community that delivered programmes that would benefit local people. In short, it was not a partnership led *by* community representatives. Local people put considerable time and effort into fighting their corner within the partnership, only to be ejected and to see the development called off by the council. Was the Elephant little more than, as *Estates Gazette* put it in a leader article, an example of "Council stupidity and greed, plus developer over-optimism"?

> The council's stupidity was over-ambition: to think that 35 acres of South London could be wrapped up in one package and delivered to this generation of ill-housed tenants; tenants who will now suffer once more as their small-minded representatives again play God with the Lego set ... no other developer should touch the scheme as it now stands. Southwark should wave goodbye to what was never going to be there: then break the plans down to manageable chunks and start again. And the tenants? Oh, they can just wait. (*Estates Gazette*, 2002, p 1)

Project Vauxhall followed an agenda developed by the council, but which left so much say in the hands of local residents that it was accused of a failure of leadership. However, those local residents that were fundamentally opposed to the plans were kept out, and they successfully outmanoeuvred the development consortium, the council, and residents in favour of the proposals.

Could it have been different? There are two scenarios. First, both partnerships could have become more sophisticated in dealing with partners with fundamental objections by taking their arguments more seriously, working with them to meet their objections, and treating them as partners. This would have involved some fundamental changes in policy towards housing tenure, policy changes directly at odds with government policy. Elephant Links could have reassigned those of its SRB funds previously set aside for land assembly and environmental changes associated with the development to meet community-identified priorities. No such attempts were made.

The Habermasian communicative rationality approach associated with the work of Healey (1997) and Forester (1999) is insightful here. Better communication, more honesty, authenticity and the avoidance of strategic behaviour could have improved both partnerships. Community activists suffered from a lack of brokers, sympathetic voices in the 'enemy' camp that could help develop mutual understanding, change minds and find allies. In both case studies, there was an observable lack of good, clear and honest reasons for choosing actions from both sides. Community activists at the Elephant used their strength in numbers, their ability to caucus and develop an agreed line that they stuck to, their effective veto, and their ability to disrupt effectively. However, they explained the reasons for their actions much less so. The council systematically undermined the legitimacy of community representatives, supposedly at the heart of regeneration. At Vauxhall, community activists opposed to development systematically undercut the legitimacy and trustworthiness of the council, the development consortium, and local residents in favour to such an extent that the 'No' campaign emerged. The development was left to sell itself, and residents decided that they did not like what was on offer. The council argued that this was fine: tenants had the information and made their choices, and the council would respect this. Project Vauxhall, Lambeth said, was:

> tenant power in action: Residents took a full and active part in progressing this project and should be praised for the vigour they have shown in assessing and considering the issues. Project Vauxhall has been tenant led, and it is appropriate that local people should be in charge of their won destiny .... They had an exciting choice placed before them, and now they have made their decision which Lambeth will respect. (Lambeth Council Press Release, 2000, p 1)

But the case studies also show the limitations of the communicative approach. When homes and power imbalances are on the line, is it realistic and reasonable to expect residents to be able to engage in technical discussions with those who feel that they know how regeneration should be undertaken? And furthermore, Southwark Council argues that there is a difference between the community being involved and those best able to gain benefit on behalf of the community doing all the running. Do we hear examples of local residents trying to get the most for themselves from the high-value land they live on at the expense of the wider needs of the communities of the two boroughs? Or are they quite reasonably defending their interests against the incoming development growth machines by being legitimately 'unreasonable' (Ferman, 1996; Clavel and Kraushaar, 1998; Jonas and Wilson, 2000)?

Just because arguments are made, there is no guarantee that material and economic interests, which seek profit and a changed built form rather than justice and empowerment, will accept them. In both these cases, decisions that went against this economic rationality were made not by argumentation leading to consensus, but by organisation, either at community level or through the courts. Who else decides? Certainly, in both cases planning professionals were out of their depth in a wider politicised environment. These case studies would reinforce the view of those who find the Habermassian approach too optimistic (Tewdwr-Jones and Allmendinger, 1998). More perhaps can be learned from the defence of the value of disruption, riot and robust demonstration in winning demands for working class groups (Piven and Cloward, 1977).

Literature on partnership and urban management suggests that too much conflict within regeneration partnerships leads to inertia in the short term, and that in the long term the partnership will fail or lead to the destruction of the weaker partners. For Mayo (1997), this usually means the community. However, both case studies here show that well-organised and politically sophisticated activists can survive to fight another day. In both the Elephant and Vauxhall cases, the weaker partners turned out to be the council and the developers. This is important now that the balance of the rationale for partnership working is arguably moving away from democratic to managerial conceptions of regeneration in which priorities are put on developing strategies that work for communities, rather than necessarily empowering communities to run their own affairs in whatever way they feel appropriate (Atkinson, 1999a; Stewart, 2002b).

This new emphasis away from community-led to community-focused policy means that the space for the development of community-led strategies for urban revitalisation is closing. The Regional Development Agency Single Pot, which replaces SRB, focuses on 'hard' economic outputs, rather the social and environmental programmes often developed from the bottom up. Resources are going into community organisations through the Community Empowerment Fund, but this focuses on helping communities to act as equal partners within Local Strategic Partnerships where the focus will be on commenting on and working towards the achievement of other people's agendas, and not developing community ownership.

Notes

[1] This research was undertaken while I was Research Fellow in Community Economic Development at the Local Economy Policy Unit (LEPU), South Bank University, London. It draws on my own involvement in Elephant Links Community Forum and Defend Council Housing campaigns, and on evaluations of Elephant Links and Project Vauxhall funded by the SRB and the London Borough of Lambeth, respectively. The views expressed in the paper are my own entirely, and do not express the views of either LEPU, the London Borough of Southwark, or the London Borough of Lambeth.

[2] See Taylor (1995); Mayo (1997); Craig (1998); Oatley (1998a, 1998b); Byrne (1999); Colenutt and Cutten (1994); Peck and Tickell (1994); Bailey et al (1995); Nevin and Shiner (1995); Stewart and Taylor (1995); Hastings et al (1996); Anastacio et al (2000).

Further reading

The past 20 years has seen the publication of a great many books on urban policy but, until this volume, very little has been published with regard to the New Labour era. For reviews of partnership working in the context of competitive cities, see Oatley (1998b) and Bailey et al (1995). More up to date is Roberts and Sykes (2000). For urban social movements, the classic is still Castells (1977).

SEVEN

Cultural justice and addressing 'social exclusion': a case study of a Single Regeneration Budget project in Blackbird Leys, Oxford

Zoë Morrison

Introduction

How do we address the social injustices of deprivation and social polarisation? These are issues the New Labour government is currently addressing through the concept of 'social exclusion', and through social exclusion policies such as the Single Regeneration Budget (SRB). In this chapter, I want to assess how successful this concept and these policies may be. In particular, I am interested in whether or not New Labour's social exclusion policy successfully addresses cultural aspects of injustice and social exclusion.

Cultural injustice refers to a lack of respect and recognition of certain people and groups in society (Fraser, 1995). It can be distinguished from economic injustice, which, by contrast, involves the unfair distribution of economic resources (such as money) among people and groups. These are important concepts to define, because I assume in this chapter that addressing injustices of poverty and social polarisation, and thereby addressing social exclusion, involves dealing with both cultural and economic aspects of social justice. If 'social inclusion' is to be achieved, both economic and cultural aspects of injustice must be taken into account. In this chapter, then, I argue that while 'social exclusion' itself is a multidimensional concept, promising to encompass both economic and cultural aspects of injustice and exclusion, its use in current British social exclusion discourse and policy can in fact be seen to perpetuate and reproduce, rather than successfully address, cultural aspects of injustice.

First, the chapter examines the concept of social exclusion, and its political use in discourse by government in contemporary Britain. It also critically evaluates the British social exclusion discourse, and argues that it fails to take into account issues of cultural justice. The chapter then looks at how this translates to policies in place, through a case study of a social exclusion policy project in Blackbird Leys, Oxford. Through a detailed, qualitative study of the processes of a 'community capacity building' project there, funded through Round Five of the SRB, I find that cultural justice is, again, not sufficiently taken into account. Indeed, I find that harmful stereotypes about Blackbird Leys are even reproduced by this policy, and local people are disrespected within, and excluded from, the very processes of a policy that is aiming to achieve social inclusion.

Overall, the chapter calls for a greater realisation of issues of cultural justice within British social exclusion discourse and policy. It points out that, while these are also clearly connected to economic aspects of injustice, it is crucial that the cultural is taken into account along with the economic when attempting to address social exclusion and injustice in general.

Social exclusion – a multidimensional concept of injustice?

In this section, I start by giving a more detailed description of what I mean by cultural aspects of social injustice and exclusion. Then, with this theoretical backdrop, I go on to look at the concept of social exclusion itself, as a contemporary way of conceptualising deprivation and social polarisation. The feminist political and cultural theorist, Nancy Fraser, perceives cultural justice as "rooted in social patterns of representation, interpretation and communication" (1995, p 71). She states that it is:

> *cultural domination* (being subjected to patterns of interpretation and communication that are associated with another culture and are alien and/ or hostile to one's own); *nonrecognition* (being rendered invisible via the authoritative representational, communication, and interpretative practices of one's own culture) and *disrespect* (being routinely maligned or disparaged in stereotype public cultural representations and or/in everyday life interactions). (Fraser, 1995, p 71)

In contrast, she defines socioeconomic injustice (or 'economic injustice') as "rooted in the political–economic structure of society with examples including exploitation, economic marginalisation, and deprivation" (Fraser, 1995, p 70). Giving a more detailed description of cultural injustice, Fraser focuses on the key concept of recognition, defining misrecognition as social subordination; that is, being prevented from participating as a peer in social life:

> To be misrecognised ... is to be denied the status of a full partner in social interaction, as a consequences of institutionalised patterns of cultural value that constitute one as comparatively unworthy of respect or esteem. (Fraser, 2000, pp 113-14)

Fraser argues that to address misrecognition requires politics aimed at establishing the misrecognised person or group as a full member of society, capable of participation on a par with the rest. She says that such politics should seek to overcome status subordination by "changing the values that regulate interaction" and "entrenching new value patterns that will promote parity of participation in social life" (Fraser, 2000, p 116). These are the sorts of things that a policy seeking to achieve social inclusion should be aiming for.

Fraser's specific political concern is that struggles for cultural justice are supplanting struggles for economic justice. By contrast, I argue in this chapter that, in the context of contemporary British urban and social exclusion policy, issues of cultural justice are not receiving enough attention. And more, they are sometimes displaced by a greater emphasis on economic aspects of injustice and exclusion, with cultural aspects of exclusion in fact perpetuated and reproduced, rather than successfully addressed.

This is perhaps surprising, giving the multidimensional potential of the concept – social exclusion – that I want to briefly examine here. Social exclusion is the latest and most dominant definition and conceptualisation in Britain and parts of Europe of problems of deprivation and social inequality. As Edwards states, "while the problem of social divisions is not new, it is in a process of constant definition" (2001, p 267). Social exclusion is the latest form of definition of these problems, and its multidimensionality means that it seeks to go beyond a definition of these problems that focuses on the economic dimensions alone. In this way, the concept has the potential to pay due attention to cultural aspects of injustice, which is the focus of this chapter.

In Britain, social exclusion entered political discourse in the lead-up to the General Election of 1997, when a Labour government was elected for the first time in 18 years. Tony Blair, the Prime Minister, stated that "if the next Labour government has not raised the standards of the poorest by the end of its time in office, it will have failed". Social exclusion was the concept used in relation to addressing these living standards of the poorest people, and "tackling social exclusion" was stated in the first term of the New Labour government to be "one of the government's highest priorities". A Social Exclusion Unit (SEU) was set up "by the Prime Minister" in December 1997. Reporting "directly to the Prime Minister", its task was to "help improve Government action to reduce social exclusion by producing *joined up solutions to joined up problems*" (SEU website, www.socialexclusionunit.gov.uk, my emphasis). The SEU continues to exist in Labour's second term of office, and has expanded since it first began, although it is now the domain of the Deputy Prime Minister.

The rhetoric of 'joined-up' problems, solutions and government is central to understanding the approach of the political concept of social exclusion in Britain. 'Joined up' is said to mean that the concept looks upon the (old) problems of poverty, inequality, and so on in a 'new' way, by targeting other societal problems that are perceived as 'joined up' to poverty. Thus, in this way the concept in Britain ideally represents a "multidimensional" (Edwards, 2001, p 267) and "multi-faceted" (Benn, 2002, p 311) approach to addressing deprivation and inequality. So, for example, the SEU defines social exclusion as:

a shorthand term for what can happen when people or areas suffer from a combination of linked problems such as unemployment, poor skills, low incomes, poor housing, high crime environments, bad health and family breakdown. (SEU website, www.socialexclusionunit.gov.uk)

It is also explicitly states that "this is a deliberately flexible definition and the problems listed are only examples". This explanation continues:

Many other dimensions of social exclusion could be added. The most important characteristic of social exclusion is that these problems *are linked and mutually reinforcing,* and can combine to create a complex and fast moving vicious cycle. (Emphasis added)

Edwards (2001) also states that the term 'socially excluded' can have multiple meanings, so that addressing social exclusion may take into account exclusions suffered on the basis of physical or mental impairments, race or gender; that is, personal characteristics of identity, rather than income or socioeconomic class. Rather than just focusing on poverty and low income, it is also said to be broader and addresses some of the wider causes and consequences of poverty. The European Commission, for instance, has "linked the notion of social exclusion more closely with the idea of inadequate realisation of social rights" (Cousins, in Edwards, 2001, p 267). Thus, as Edwards notes, through the concept of social exclusion, debates about social divisions have moved away from ideas of a purely economic nature to identify exclusion as a phenomenon that is relational. So through this conceptualisation, for example,

Marginalisation is as much about 'inadequate social participation, lack of social integration and lack of power' (Room, 1995, p 10) as it is about access to resources. (Edwards, 2001, p 267)

Therefore, social exclusion is understood to look beyond only the economic, redistributional nature of inclusion and social justice, to also include social and cultural issues such as social participation and access to power. However, as well as considering the theory and rhetoric behind this concept, it is also important to consider how it is used in actual political practice. My findings about the current use of the concept of social exclusion within Britain suggest that cultural justice issues are still not being given adequate attention, despite the use of this potentially multidimensional concept. I want to examine this by looking more closely at British political social exclusion discourse.

Re-examining the multidimensional nature of the British political concept of social exclusion

Despite the potentially multidimensional nature of social exclusion as a concept, a textual analysis of British government social exclusion discourse indicates a prioritisation of 'economic' dimensions of social exclusion over forms of cultural exclusion. Employment in the labour market is usually portrayed as the only reliable route to social inclusion (Radcliffe, 1999, p 4; Levitas, 1998; Stepney et al, 1999). Concurrent with this emphasis on only economic forms of exclusion, this discourse can also be seen to reproduce the cultural injustice of stigmatisation and disrespect, thus perpetuating social divisions.

For instance, social exclusion discourse can be seen to reduce cultural difference by constructing society as a binary of two seemingly homogenous groups, an included 'majority' and an excluded 'minority' (Levitas, 1998, p 7). The implications of this could be that the excluded individual needs to cross some sort of dividing line to become an insider in society. However, through this conception, structural inequalities within society appear to remain largely unaddressed, so that it is the excluded that must change, not the society that excludes them:

> Whether in relation to education, housing, community or work, on closer scrutiny many of the underlying positions require a great deal more of the powerless than of the powerful. (Benn 2002, p 310)

This is directly related to cultural injustice because, through this use of social exclusion, those labelled 'excluded' are socially subordinated (see the definitions of cultural injustice given earlier in this chapter), constructed as the problem to be fixed, with remedies focused on them, rather than on the inequitable society within which they exist. For instance, the definition of social exclusion itself, given by the SEU and quoted above, could alternatively be seen as simultaneously devaluing other aspects of their lives:

- the places 'the excluded' live in, their neighbourhoods and homes (which are only portrayed as 'poor' and situated in 'high-crime environments');
- their families (which are all said to be 'broken');
- their abilities (they are said to have 'poor skills');
- even their bodies (which are all said to be in 'poor health').

Also, devaluing 'excluded' people through a binary construction of excluded/included can be seen as a way of implicitly valuing those qualities apparently possessed by 'the included', such as being in an intact nuclear family, and participating in full-time paid work, completing the process of social subordination. Within such a discourse, individuals who are sole parents and/or unemployed, for example, are implicitly constructed as problematically transgressing supposed positive societal norms, apparently represented by a homogenous majority. So, in this way, social exclusion discourse can be seen as expressing the sort of people, activities and relationships that are valued, recognised and respected by society cultural justice – and those that are not.

Furthermore, this discourse is specifically gendered. For example, in the social exclusion policy the New Deal for Lone Parents, 'lone' parenthood is constructed as a problem within itself. For example, Smith (1999, p 316) shows that in characterisations of 'deprived areas', sole parenthood itself has come to be defined as a social problem, regardless of its association with incidences of poverty. Also, the remedy in this social exclusion policy for sole parents is economic, based on sole parents 'getting a job'. Yet this seems to ignore or disrespect the work such people already perform, implying that even if they are full-time unpaid carers, such work is subordinate and insubstantial, compared with the 'real' jobs of paid employment. Thus, while attempting to address the deprivation many sole parents experience, this discourse and policy could in fact be said to reproduce a lack of recognition and encourage disrespect (aspects of cultural injustice) of many sole parents, 95% of which in Britain are women (Rake, 2000, pers. comm.).

Social exclusion discourse and policy also particularly emphasise the role spaces and place play in exclusion, and Lee (1999, p 483) argues that the concentration of poor people and particular social groups within a place ensures that neighbourhoods, 'communities' and estates become convenient tools, and often powerful metaphors, within this discourse. In a report entitled *Bringing Britain together: A national strategy for neighbourhood renewal*, the opening sentence belongs to the Prime Minister: "We all know the problems of our poorest neighbourhoods" (SEU, 1998, p 1). But just in case 'we' do not, the reader is reminded about "decaying housing, unemployment, street crime and drugs", so that "people who can, move out. Nightmare neighbours move in". The reader is told that "the gap between these 'worst estates' and the rest of society has grown", which has left 'us' with a situation "no civilised society should tolerate". Not only is this said to "shame us as a nation", it "wastes lives" and "we all have to pay for the costs".

This is powerful language that may indeed convey a genuine awareness and concern for the results of inequality. Yet its evocation of place, its 'us' and 'them' typology, could also be seen as further constructing and perpetuating cultural aspects of injustice and exclusion in society. It is worth noting that 'the excluded' are even constructed outside this discourse. The 'we' and 'us' referred to clearly excludes those people whose homes are on the 'worst' estates, who are considered 'nightmares', whose lives are a 'waste', and who are implicitly viewed as uncivilised and therefore not part of 'civilised society'. Thus, 'the excluded' are who 'we' are not. In this discourse they are constructed outside this portrayal of knowledge about them, which is not written for them anyway.

In an interview with a government official of the SEU, I asked about the use of such evocative language. He replied that such language is used to make social exclusion an issue that "everyone cares about": there is a "political imperative" to "keep an alliance between the poor and the middle class", by showing how interdependent they are. Demonstrating interdependence undoubtedly has much merit, but the way this is gone about is perhaps more questionable. For instance, crime stereotypes in documents, particularly the kind of – "they'll nick your car!", was said to be "the one that's played up most – because it's the one that resonates most". Such tactics suggest a strategy whereby in portraying 'the socially excluded' as a threat, the middle class does not mind the government spending taxes on addressing their deprivation – and therefore what threatens them. Yet, by stressing only economic solutions in this way, this surely disregards the cultural harm that such stereotypes engender. And these stereotypes have very real consequences, such as the physical avoidance of estates by people who do not live in them, contributing to the spatial isolation, stigmatisation and exclusion of the residents who do.

It can be argued, therefore, that current British government political 'social exclusion' discourse, despite its potentially multidimensional conceptualisation of disadvantage, does not adequately take into account cultural aspects of injustice. What I want to look at now is how this translates to policy 'on the ground', and to do this, I look at a case study of a policy – the Single Regeneration Budget (SRB) – that aims to address exclusion in a local place.

Reproducing cultural justice in localities: the Single Regeneration Budget political process and practice in Blackbird Leys, Oxford

Background to the case study – the policy, research methods and field site

The SRB was inherited by the current New Labour government from the former Conservative government, and since 1994 it is said to have been "one of the British government's main tools in tackling inequality in Britain's cities" (Edwards, 2001, p 267). The SRB focuses on deprivation and social exclusion at a local level, and it works on the basis of a competitive bidding process whereby local 'partnerships' have to bid to receive funding in competition with other localities.

A central tenet of the SRB has been its encouragement of local response to local needs through giving local people more influence over spending priorities. This could signal evidence of cultural justice – a true respect and recognition for people labelled 'excluded', and a practical way of ensuring equal social participation rather than subordination within society. Under the Conservative government, however, commentators found that the policy failed to effectively 'devolve power in a way that met local needs and priorities', and this prompted a litany of sustained complaint (see Ward, 1997a). For example, research by Hall (2000) found that the community and voluntary sectors were in fact the least represented of major sectoral interests in Round Three of the SRB. Instead, the dominant players were local authorities, leading 60% of bids. Indeed, there were even claims at this point that the SRB signalled an increased centralisation of power, involving communities less rather than more. Thus greater social participation, respect, recognition and social inclusion in general of those labelled 'the excluded' was not only not achieved by this policy, but also worsened by it.

Despite these problems – and despite attacking the SRB when in opposition (Hall, 2000, p 2) – the Labour government opted to keep it as part of its social exclusion and regeneration strategy. Under New Labour, the strategy has undergone little change. Certainly, Labour adapted the policy to its own priorities, especially its objective to address 'social exclusion' (Hall, 2000, p 11). The government also recognised that the SRB it inherited did not in practice produce the local involvement aimed for, due to "the differential capacity of local organisations to become involved in regeneration" (DETR, in Hall, 2000, p 11). Labour's revised version of the SRB incorporated a new emphasis on 'capacity building', with the involvement of communities a prerequisite for the receipt of funding (Hall, 2000, p 12). Indeed, as a government official explained to me in an interview, "every aspect of government philosophy is now based on the bottom-up approach". This was particularly so in Round Five of the SRB, which required that most bids should have capacity building as a key objective. In the bidding guidance, for example, it is stated that:

> the Government believes it is crucial to ensure the active participation of local communities in the regeneration of their areas and that they should be directly involved, both in the preparation and implementation of bids. (OPDM, 1998, para 3.6)

This emphasis on the involvement of local people is potentially the key to achieving cultural aspects of social inclusion. An equal, respectful recognition and involvement of local people within the policy process and outcomes could begin reversing a crucial factor of cultural injustice, the denial of people labelled 'excluded' from "the status of a full partner in social interaction" (Fraser, 2000, p 113). How successful, then, has the policy been?

The SRB case study examined here is based in Blackbird Leys in Oxford. Blackbird Leys' bid for Round Five SRB funding embraced Labour's emphasis on community involvement (see Figure 7.1). The bid was directly focused on 'community capacity building', and the impetus for the bid came from voluntary and housing sector representatives on the estate, rather than the local authority. A local community development partnership, comprised mainly of resident professionals and volunteers, was the bid's 'lead partner'.

So, we have then Labour's 'new' emphasis on the multidimensional nature of deprivation and community involvement, which suggests more attention to cultural aspects of social injustice, and the reflection of this emphasis in Blackbird Leys' bid for funding. My research, however, found that notions of cultural aspects of social inclusion, such as the truly equal status of local participants, and evidence of respect and recognition were often experienced more as rhetoric than reality. The cause of this is a lack of attention to cultural justice issues within the policy, with the focus still more on issues of economic justice.

The small-scale case study that follows, which investigated one project in depth using qualitative methods, can in fact be seen to provide a relatively unique story of this policy. Other research on the SRB has mostly been either of a quantitative nature, or focused on a large scale[1]. Why, then, use qualitative methods in this context? Qualitative methods such as semi-structured interviews

Figure 7.1: Oxford City, showing the location of Blackbird Leys and Greater Leys

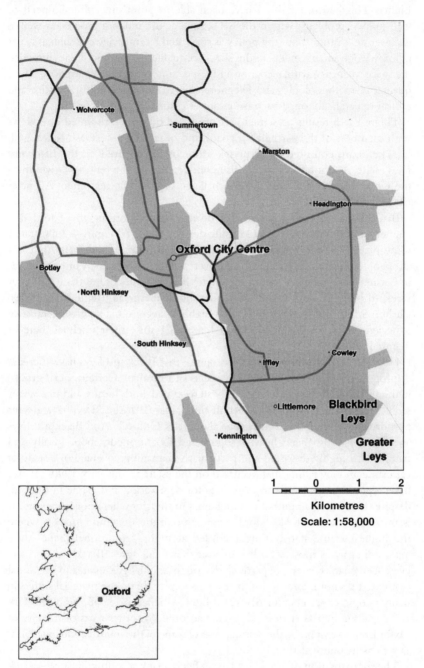

allowed me to investigate cultural justice issues through detailed and subjective data, seldom raised in any previous context of SRB policy (although see Chapter Eight). This has meant that I have been able to point out cultural aspects of well-known problems within the SRB, such as the bidding process, as well as discover new issues about the policy as suggested by interviewees, such as issues of knowledge and payment. In this way, also, qualitative methodologies provided the space to engage with, recognise and respect interviewees' experiences. Thus, qualitative methodologies also felt more akin to practising cultural justice and ethical research, although such issues are of course far from clear-cut.

The research results presented here are based on semi-structured interviews with members of the partnership board, and other key people associated with it. The board consisted of 12 people (four of whom lived on the Blackbird Leys estate), and interviews were also conducted with the representatives from the Government Office for the South East, Regional Development Agencies (RDAs) and the SEU[2].

Blackbird Leys itself is an area of diverse tenure housing in Oxford that contains a number of phases of housing development. As Figure 7.2 illustrates, some phases include a high percentage of social housing and many (but not all) people on the estate suffer from poverty. For instance, 27% of households in Greater Leys (a newer part of the estate) have incomes of less than £100 per week (this figure rises to 42% for households in socially rented properties; Carlton Smith and Darke, 1998). This highlights economic aspects of injustice experienced by people in Blackbird Leys, suggesting their unequal share of material resources.

However, it is also important to recognise that Blackbird Leys has suffered a disproportionate degree of cultural aspects of injustice. Certain social groups living in Blackbird Leys are negatively stereotyped, both locally and in a wider sense, such as single mothers and ethnic minorities (Blackbird Leys has a greater proportion of ethnic minorities than the rest of Oxford). And Blackbird Leys as a place has also been heavily stigmatised by the media, both locally and nationally, a highly distorted and particularly damaging coverage of a spate of car crime and joy riding that occurred on the estate in the early 1990s. It also has a reputation of being the worst area for deprivation and crime in Oxford, despite there being a number of other areas in the city where poverty exists. It is, in fact, in the centre of Oxford – right among the 'dreaming spires' – where the highest crime statistics are recorded at night. Additionally, and quite extraordinarily as those who live or visit there will agree, Blackbird Leys has even been characterised as a particularly 'rough' and dangerous area in a national context. I do not mention this in any way to play down the material suffering many people experience in Blackbird Leys, which is made all the more stark and appalling by the riches and respect accorded to other parts of the city of Oxford, but to emphasise the cultural basis of some of this injustice and exclusion, as well as its unjust nature.

The stigmatisation of Blackbird Leys reflects a lack of cultural justice – a lack of recognition of Blackbird Leys outside of common negative stereotypes about

Figure 7.2: Contrasting housing styles on the Blackbird Leys Estate, Oxford

housing estates, and a lack of respect for the people living there, in all their diversity. However, SRB policy processes often work against this, reproducing and perpetuating the negative stereotyping and stigmatisation of place. This is particularly evident if we take a closer look at the policy's competitive bidding process.

The competitive bidding process

The competitive bidding process of SRB has already been widely criticised (see Ward 1997a, 1997b; Hall, 2000; Fordham et al, 1999; Tewdwr-Jones and McNeill, 2000). In relation to cultural issues in particular, bidding is said to direct a narrow range of projects with easily quantifiable outcomes so that non-economic objectives receive 'limited priority' (Ward, 1997a; Fordham et al, 1999). Foley et al (1988) point out that the bidding system is designed to offer payment for 'performance measure', and not for valuable 'qualitative outcomes' like "giving people back a sense of confidence or pride". Bidding leads, therefore, to the structuring of a funding system that simply does not encompass cultural aspects of 'social exclusion'.

Also, other research has pointed out that SRB's bid objectives exclude particular groups within communities, viewing 'community' as a single and unitary group with unitary interests (Edwards, 2001, p 269). This has meant that issues of exclusion based on race have been hardly addressed at all by the SRB, with a stunning proportion of only 11 out of 900 (1.2%) successful SRB bids granted to black and ethnic minority projects up till 2001 (Loftman, 2001). Involvement in the SRB by disabled people has also been particularly limited (Edwards, 2001).

What I believe this research on cultural aspects of the bidding process has not yet pointed out, is that bidding may in fact contribute to the further stigmatisation and cultural harm of places and people already suffering from cultural injustice. When partnerships bid for funding, they need to demonstrate a sound strategy for using the funds. As the SRB bidding guidance notes state, it is

> for local partnerships to make the case for SRB support by marshalling available and relevant information about local need. (DETR, 1998b)

The competitive motivation of the funding process means that partnerships establish this need in a context where their community's need is compared with the need of another community. Essentially, this means that communities are bidding to be viewed as the 'worst off'.

In this way, the competitive bidding system can be seen to discourage positive discourse and imagery about a place. This appears to be clearly understood by professionals and residents (and resident professionals) involved in the bidding process. For example, a professional member of the partnership board, when asked what he thought would be the best way of conceptualising Blackbird

Leys in a way that was best for the people living there, replied "as an active, mature, safe, vital community". He then added, however, that to portray the place like this in a funding proposal would be a "disaster in terms of levering funding". In fact, he stated that bidding,

> "is encouraging you to focus on the negatives rather than focusing on the positives, so a lot of minds are kind of aimed that way."

Certainly, in many interviews it appeared to be common knowledge that a place has to be portrayed in a negative way in order to get funding. When asked, "So how do you think Blackbird Leys has to be portrayed to get government funding?", one resident replied:

> "As poor, down-trodden, drug-ridden, alcohol-ridden, crime-ridden, everything bad you can think of. That's the way you get money."

Another resident involved in community projects other than the SRB said:

> "Blackbird Leys is sort of portrayed as really downbeat, really rough. I mean I'm not going to turn around and say – no, it's perfect in Blackbird Leys …
> but they do kind of make out that Blackbird Leys is the dregs of the dregs.
> And I think they do exaggerate it when they're looking for funding."

In Blackbird Ley's successful bid for funding from Round Five of the SRB, the opening sections of the bid document firmly establish Blackbird Leys as spatially peripheral within Oxford, and particularly deprived. And the caption on the cover reads, 'This is Blackbird Leys'. A summary of various research findings about the estate reveal:

- high indicators of social disadvantage;
- low-income families;
- benefit dependency;
- high child density;
- households headed by lone parents;
- high unemployment;
- educational underachievement;
- low expectations (see, for example, Carlton Smith and Darke, 1998).

A version of the estate's development history and various deprivation and crime statistics were all cited to "confirm the picture of a vulnerable community with high indices of social exclusion", with "residents fear of crime, vandalism and threatening behaviour … the most important reason for disliking living on Blackbird Leys" (Community Development Initiative, 1999, pp 4-6). Thus, through highlighting and emphasising many possible negative aspects of the place, this text establishes Blackbird Leys as a deprived, vulnerable, dangerous place right from the start, with the clear implication that people do not like living there.

People themselves are also constructed in a negative way. And certain social groups suffer more than others. In particular, children and young people living in the area are only ever portrayed as threatening and potentially dangerous, rather than, say, sources of energy, and potential sources of creativity and joy in the community waiting to be tapped, particularly when adequate and appropriate resources are provided. For example, the bid states:

> By 2003, it is predicted that around 60% of the large number of children and young people in Greater Leys will be between 10 and 18 with serious implications for the need for increased youth provision and possibly problems for community safety. (Community Development Initiative, 1999, p 6)

This prediction of large numbers of young people in the area, with nothing to do, and thus posing a criminal threat, was not confined to the bid document. It is frequently cited in interviews with community leaders, workers and residents. Bidding procedures seem to ensure the reproduction of negative stereotypes and thus the cultural harm inflicted on the community. Indeed, while negative images in a bid document reach far fewer people than a media item, the people that they do reach are often precisely the people who have a direct influence on the place. For instance, one professional cited a conversation he had had with a 'very senior officer' in the branch of government he worked in, and what this officer said when hearing he had just been in Blackbird Leys:

> "his only response was, 'So were there wheels on your car when you came back?' So it's – I think if it's in the mindset of movers and shakers in the community that there's likely to be criminality around then it's likely to filter through."

In this way, we can see that while bidding can be a way of addressing economic injustice by bringing funds into a community (if the bid is successful), at the same time, it can also worsen cultural injustice by reproducing and enforcing harmful stereotypes. Clearly, issues of cultural justice have not been sufficiently taken into account here, with a policy that in fact encourages a perpetuation and reproduction of aspects of cultural injustice, rather than their abolition. Furthermore, this is something connected to issues of economic justice: remedying economic justice (bidding for funding) in this instance exacerbates cultural injustice (such as harmful stereotyping). This suggests that cultural issues need to be recognised, but not in isolation – economic justice issues also need to be considered in terms of how they influence the cultural and work in conjunction with rather than against them.

Issues of knowledge, information and communication

Government and professional SRB discourses are often exclusive, because they frequently require expertise to understand, and expert skills to participate in. These factors can all be exclusionary mechanisms within the policy's practice that contribute to a denial of local participants' equal status within the policy process. Furthermore, a hierarchy of knowledge can be seen to exist in the SRB policy process, with government and professional knowledge prioritised over local knowledge and language, which is correspondingly subordinated, directly impacting issues of cultural justice within the policy's outcomes as well as processes. It influences whose voices and priorities are heard, valued and acted upon, and whose are not[3].

Constructing a bid requires expertise; that is, a range of specialist skills that unpaid community representatives and local residents are unlikely to have had the opportunity to acquire. According to an interviewee who used to assess SRB bids, "professional bid writers" who are highly experienced and paid to write bids, produce "slick" documents that "push all the [right] buttons". In contrast:

> "where the local authority isn't the dominant partners and it's a community-based bid – they haven't got the experience of writing bids, so we have to take that on board."

In Blackbird Leys, the bid was composed by a professional from outside the estate who worked for a community organisation, and it was looked over and adjusted by senior members of the Trade and Enterprise Council. As one community worker put it:

> "you have to have certain expertise at speaking that language .... Little community groups coming off the street – they wouldn't get it [SRB funding]."

Professionals and officials also emphasised the importance of access to networks and 'insider' knowledge for funding success. Such access to 'insider' knowledge also entailed control of the policy at a local level. For example, information networks created through informal links between city and county councils in Oxford meant that officials not only knew more about the policy, but also knew about it before estate residents did, resulting in officials that did not live on the estate taking charge.

This leads to a subordinated status of local people right from the start of the policy's workings, indeed local people are more than aware of the disadvantages their lack of access to insider information entails. As the local resident 'lead partner' of the Blackbird Leys' SRB project stated when in the process of relinquishing the lead role:

"things weren't spelt out in guidelines, such as what the role of the lead partner entailed. Volunteers and residents were left wondering, 'Was it just assumed that people would know this?'."

Locally based workers also stated that information from local authorities was not passed on, leaving local organisations guessing and floundering. Indeed, it appeared that the sources and bearers of 'important' information, necessary for the policy to run successfully, were, in reality, often located off the estate. This indicates a lack of recognition and respect for knowledge within the estate, which seems to run counter to the aims of local leadership, equal involvement and, of course, social inclusion.

Moreover, forms of 'official' knowledge from government sources off the estate can be highly exclusive. Indeed, the essential bidding guidelines are intimidating documents. I heard little information from local residents on these issues (hence the lack of quotes presented here) because few were involved with the policy at this level, and simply had not received or read these official documents. For instance, one local resident who had actually received such material said she had read the first few pages but then gave up, finding them impenetrable. She relied on professionals to deal with it.

But even a professional member of the voluntary community, who had enough expertise to write a bid, looked to government officers for the interpretation of guidelines. Research (Foley et al, 1998) has shown that SRB managers often had to explain the rules of the policy to their civil servant counterparts. It is not surprising, therefore, that another resident community worker involved in bidding stated:

"Our main problem was getting our head around the guidelines .... You need an expert. And an expert is somebody again who can be paid to do nothing much else then go around to all the conferences and meetings and talk to all the people and get the jargon and get it very firmly in their head exactly what GOSE [the Government Office for the South East] mean by 'capacity building'."

And another professional worker who lives off the estate complained about components of the guidelines:

"All this rigmarole around, you know, 'outputs' and 'milestones' and 'targets' and 'quantifiable outputs' and all that crap – I don't understand it, and I've got a degree in geography! It's a real turn-off."

Furthermore, he felt that it is "designed to inhibit – to be a barrier to local people, to local residents being involved". This appears to be borne out by the evidence. No local volunteers were involved in the bidding process, or roles of leadership on the partnership board, and it was local volunteers who apparently attended board meetings least often.

Indeed, exclusive language was not limited to printed documents. The high degree of jargon involved in SRB and its day-to-day running is said to require a high degree of familiarity just to follow what happens in SRB meetings. One local arts community worker explained:

> "The first board meeting I went to, it completely lost me .... I thought, what is this? I stood up at the meeting and said 'I don't know what you are talking about' ... For a start, I had to have 'capacity building' explained to me, and they were going on about fulfilling certain criteria like job training hours and what that all meant .... There's 'milestones' – I think they ought to be called tombstones. Um, 'key indicators' – okay I understand most of that. But it was the way people are talking. It's a different language. It's a kind of governmentee-ism, and I'm not comfortable with that, because I don't speak that language and a lot of people don't."

Some local residents and professionals in the partnership who did attend meetings regularly found they came to grips with some of the language after a while. However, these exclusive policy mechanisms not only perpetuate exclusion within policy processes, but also in what the policy aims to achieve in the long term. For instance, 'SRB speak', and the policy process it is part of, can have the potential to dictate the content of meetings, and the nature of policy action. That is, this language can create aims and targets that are removed from real-world impacts. For instance, meetings were said often to deal with technical matters such as fulfilling bureaucratic requirements of 'strategic objectives' and 'quantifiable outputs'. Real concerns of residents, expressed in everyday language, were sometimes not heard, and not in reality viewed as an important part of the policy's agenda, and subsequently not acted upon. In this way, SRB policy processes created a dominant 'knowledge-culture' that has "its own rules as to what counts as legitimate knowledge" (Tsouvalis et al, 2000, p 912), which, despite rhetoric of local participation, in fact prioritises 'SRB speak' over local knowledge.

For example, I was told of a particularly frustrating experience of a local resident, who was the only non-professional and resident at an SRB subgroup, a community safety working group meeting. Domestic violence was raised at this group as a major focus for community safety. This particular resident felt that the provision of a bus that would pick up women and children at risk and take them to a safe place was a real need on the estate, and a practical way of beginning to address this community safety issue. Her request, however, did not fit into the committee's 'strategic objectives' nor its 'quantifiable outcomes'. Apparently, it appeared utterly foreign in this context and was subsequently disregarded. Yet this is in a context where 'community consultation' is sought and supposedly encouraged.

Significantly, in this 'community capacity-building project', a non-local professional chaired the partnership board meetings, which was said to be because of his 'expertise'. Indeed, within Blackbird Leys, it was professionals involved in housing associations or charities that acquired knowledge about the SRB, and the possibility of Blackbird Leys constructing a bid. This meant that the bid was initiated by professionals who lived both on and off the estate, rather than by local residents.

The use of exclusive language, and its implicit prioritisation over local knowledge, implies that local residents must learn to communicate like the professionals and government authorities from outside the estate to be part of the project, rather than the other way round. This infiltrates many aspects of SRB, so that in many practices of the policy, while there is a theoretical thirst for local input, there is often in practice an assumption of the superiority of the knowledge of outsiders, and the subordination of the knowledge of local people.

For instance, a strand of discourse that ran through many interviews was about the community being 'taught'. A professional described how "we'd train the community to run projects here". She described how the involvement of local volunteers had required a lot of 'hand-holding', almost as if they were children, needing the guidance of wiser parental figures from off the estate. There was also an emphasis on 'getting them' – that is, the local residents – to do things, conveying a sense of coercion, and that the professionals 'know best'. A professional from outside the estate said:

> "There's been a lot of time involved sort of guiding them [the local residents]
> along the right lines ... and it's a bit frustrating at times."

She went on to explain how the community and voluntary sector members of the bid just did not seem to understand government priorities like 'urgency'. This indicates an assumption that the community must conform to the government, which could in this way devalue the skills and priorities of the community.

Perhaps more worryingly, such attitudes sometimes filter through to local resident members of the partnership board, who also talked about the community being 'taught', and needing to 'improve itself'. But if a policy is supposed to be bottom-up and locally led, and if it is about local needs and local solutions, and is supposed to refute the notion that "Whitehall knows best" (DETR, 1997, in Hall, 2000, p 11) and truly achieve social inclusion rather than subordination, then, surely, what locals have to say should be prioritised. Would it not make more sense for the community to teach the professionals what needs and priorities exist in the estate, and what may be helpful ways for these to be addressed (which has happened in other community projects in Blackbird Leys)? These are issues of recognition and respect of the local community, issues of 'cultural justice', that are vital to the effective functioning of a policy that seeks to influence material inequality and 'social exclusion'.

Indeed, these elements of SRB can be seen as indicative of wider societal patterns of social subordination and cultural injustice – of whose knowledge is valued, and whose is not. For instance, it is crucial to point out the cultural and socioeconomic bias of SRB participation and the implications this has on the knowledge that informs the project. All professionals heavily involved in the SRB in Blackbird Leys were white men and women. The professional asked to chair the partnership board meeting was a white man. All paid residents involved in the project were white men, and all resident volunteers were white women. Only one black resident was involved with the policy, a professional woman, but she did not even have a major role on the partnership board. (In fact, some people were uncertain as to whether she was on it or not.) Given the ethnic composition of the estate, the absence of residents was conspicuous. No disabled people were in any way part of the SRB process. In this way, issues of exclusion on the basis of gender, 'race', disability and class intersect in determining whose knowledge is heard and whose is not, and which knowledge is valued, and which is subordinated. As one unemployed female resident on the estate involved in the policy vividly put it:

> "The system has for a long time put people like us down .... They've told us we're useless, we're worthless, we're liars, we're cheats, we're lay-abouts, we're lazy and this, that and the other. And then – you say that to somebody often enough and they believe it. To actually reverse that trend is really, really difficult. And that's what's happening now [through the SRB] .... We're trying to reverse that trend and we're trying to teach people that they do have value, they are worthwhile, and what they've got to say is really, really, really worth listening to. But getting that across to them is not easy."

Interestingly, the resident here puts herself in both camps – as both resident and professional. Indeed, she was one of the very few residents heavily involved in policy processes on the estate (breaking down the exclusive categories of 'resident' and 'professional'). She has both an acute understanding of the cultural injustices of being stigmatised, yet also speaks about 'getting this across to them' (that is, educating them) that 'they do have value' and so on. Perhaps she may herself have realised more of her own value through the SRB policy, hence her optimism about it? This would indeed be a wonderful outcome. Yet it is also interesting that she refers to 'us' being put down, but 'them' being valued – as if she still feels undervalued. Are discourses about valuing residents externalised rhetoric rather than internalised reality?

Attention to issues of knowledge, information and communication thus reveal a lack of cultural justice within the SRB, both within the policy process, and its longer-term outcomes in 'the community'. These issues indicate the need for attention to cultural justice issues within the policy. Yet it is also important to recognise that cultural justice issues of social subordination, respect and recognition (such as whose knowledge and participation is valued, and whose is not) are also enforced in this context, through economic issues of payment and labour force status. This is in contrast with what was found in the bidding process, where issues of economic and cultural justice worked counter to each other.

Issues of payment and labour force status

Payment for participation in the SRB is selective, mostly going to professionals who live off the estate. These salaries sometimes come out of the SRB money allocated to Blackbird Leys. Professionals already living and working on the estate are seldom paid extra for their participation, and local residents with no professional status are not paid for any of their involvement either in this or in other local representative roles. It is important to recognise and value the role of voluntary work within locally based projects. But for some volunteers on the Blackbird Leys project, their work was particularly time consuming, and its unpaid status began to feel exploitative – and thus an instance of economic injustice.

As an example, one resident on the estate who worked many unpaid hours a week for local organisations, including the SRB, said that despite getting much satisfaction from the voluntary work she did, she also sometimes felt 'used' and 'abused'. This resident was unemployed and lived in social housing but reported not even being reimbursed for telephone calls related to this work. This is not only exploitation, but indicates to me an utter lack of recognition and respect of her situation. She was asked at one stage to move and accept social housing in another Oxford estate in order to work on another SRB project there (in an unpaid capacity). When she refused, the job was advertised as a paid position. Not surprisingly, she stated, "I mean I feel I've got a job, but it just doesn't have a salary attached". This entailed regularly jumping through the various job-search hoops that claiming unemployment benefit involved. Yet if she did get a full-time paid job elsewhere, people in the area would suffer from the lack of her labour.

Local professionals agree that voluntary work by residents is a complex issue. One professional pointed out that while he can not even read these complex documents, the SRB policy's emphasis on community participation seems to expect "unpaid locals to read quite complex documents ... to expect people to do it for free, for love". Similarly, another local resident involved in community programmes (although not the SRB), and who previously worked for a company involved in 'development' work on the estate, explained:

> "I kind of feel used ... a lot of these things kind of make me feel used. I'm quite happy for Blackbird Leys to get funding for things that we really need ... but half the time they don't want to pay local people that are qualified to do that. They'd rather bring in someone from the outside who's white, middle class, doesn't have the same feeling about the area, and pay them loads of money to do these things. And you know, if you're in a position to sort of do that job, they don't give you an advancement. They won't promote you, 'cause you're of the community. They will keep you down – they keep you in low-paid positions, but [still] actually working for the company. But they won't pay someone that's ... qualified to do the job, but they live in the community or they're of the community, because they don't put money

into the community in that respect .... When people sort of come from outside – they're just basically getting loads of money – using the community to get loads of money and they don't give a damn."

These are clear examples of residents' economic exploitation through the SRB. Indeed, the economic benefits the policy provides could also be questioned on a wider scale, as it can be argued that the place itself actually receives little economic benefit from the policy. One professional community worker pointed out that most of the SRB 'match-funding' money was not 'real' money. For example, she observed that when it was said that part of the 'match funding' would be to provide a worker, a new job was not in fact created on the estate. Rather, 'provision of a worker' just meant that someone from the council was seconded to work in the area. And match funding through the provision of training places, "just means the [existing] training centre". Thus, while the SRB appears to be perpetuating cultural injustice, little economic benefit appears to be being received either.

The lack of payment of local residents fits again into wider cultural patterns of whose participation is valued and whose is not. All workers working on an unpaid basis were white working-class women. And as I have already noted, people from ethnic minorities – despite constituting 10% of the estate's population – played no part in the administration of this 'social exclusion' policy, whether paid or unpaid. A black woman, a resident who has lived on the estate all her life and had worked for another community development organisation on the estate but not the SRB, related in a conversation and then in an interview the many experiences of exploitation and denigration she and another black woman had had in this work environment.

"When you're working class or you're of the community, you don't – you're not in tune to how to get money. You tend not to be the ones to get the money. And if you tend to be the people who know how to sort of like twist and turn and get into all that sort of stuff ... they [professionals off the estate] know how to do it. So they're the ones who end up with the money ... and the area ends up with a small portion of that money. And that's so wrong. When we [local residents] do projects and we're able to get some money, most of that goes back into the community – because, you know, we're of the community, and whatever we do, the time and energy we put into the community is for our community and so ... but we don't get that kind of money, you know there's no way we get that kind of money because we just don't know how to manoeuvre ourselves to kind of get that sort of money. And I think that is really wrong, that's totally wrong."

We can see that as well as factors of cultural injustice being highlighted in the SRB, issues of economic injustice are apparent too. Furthermore, the two appear to be connected, with issues of knowledge and payment combining to create situations of exclusion of local residents within the processes and outcomes of this policy that aims for social inclusion.

At one level, this calls for a greater valuing of local residents within social exclusion policy. And crucially, it is vital that this is in both a cultural and economic sense. Local residents' knowledge must be more greatly respected within the policy process (at the level of policy practice rather than just rhetoric) to ensure that the policy does not perpetuate the cultural injustice of social subordination, but rather works towards achieving cultural aspects of social inclusion. And at the same time, in order to prevent the economic injustices of exploitation within the policy, the value of local residents' contribution must also be justly economically compensated, to prevent exploitation. Indeed, these suggestions would work together, with a greater recognition and respect for local residents' knowledge, for example, a likely catalyst for less economic exploitation of their work within the policy process.

At a more general level, this draws our attention to wider issues about achieving social justice through social exclusion policy process, practice and outcomes. This chapter has argued for greater attention to issues of cultural justice within social exclusion policy. Indeed, this has been shown to be vital to achieving social inclusion. However, the chapter has also shown how achieving cultural justice cannot be done in isolation, and that addressing economic injustice may have a positive or negative effect on achieving cultural justice, for example. Overall, this means that a call for greater attention to issues of cultural justice in no way implies less attention to issues of economic justice, but rather that the two must be considered, in a complementary way, when addressing issues of deprivation and social inequality.

Conclusions

This chapter has shown that current British government social exclusion discourse and policy does not pay enough attention to issues of cultural justice. While 'social exclusion' itself is a potentially multidimensional conceptualisation of social injustice that takes both cultural and economic aspects into account, the current usage of it within British government social exclusion discourse gives more attention to issues of economic justice than to those of cultural justice. Thus cultural justice is often displaced, and in fact aspects of cultural injustice such as disrespect, misrecognition and social subordination are even perpetuated within discourse and policy. Looking at this more closely through a detailed study of the practices of a specific social exclusion policy – the SRB in Blackbird Leys – it was found through examining the policy's bidding process that attention only to issues of economic justice could indeed worsen aspects of cultural injustice on the ground.

At the same time, however, examining issues of knowledge and payment within the policy also showed that aspects of cultural and economic injustice could also work to perpetuate – or potentially improve – each other. This means that, overall, greater attention to cultural justice issues would be most successfully achieved if attention were also paid to the ways economic and cultural remedies worked together. Specifically, I suggest that social exclusion policy should both culturally and economically revalue (rather than subordinate) those labelled 'socially excluded', in order to achieve social inclusion more effectively.

Notes

[1] For instance, Brennan et al (1999) used numerical data on SRB expenditure and the Index of Local Conditions to gauge an idea of the overall effectiveness of the policy. Foley et al (1998) interviewed the project managers of 16 different projects and officials from two Government Offices to gain an understanding of the project's procedures.

[2] This research formed part of a wider investigation of mine into issues of social exclusion and cultural justice in Oxford and Britain, which involved over 60 interviews, as well as participatory and archival research and textual analysis.

[3] See, for example, Tsouvalis et al (2000) for a study in the area of knowledge construction and power-knowledge relations in the area of expert and lay knowledge.

Further reading

A fascinating and far-reaching debate on the comparative merits and difficulties of addressing both cultural and economic aspects of social justice (and whether this is even, in fact, a suitable way of conceiving these issues at a theoretical level) can be found in the *New Left Review* – see Fraser (1995, 1997, 1998, 2000), Butler (1998) and Young (1997). See also the chapter by McDowell, entitled 'Economy, culture, difference and justice', in Cook et al (2000). For a more detailed examination of the specific issues raised above, see my forthcoming article (Morrison, 2003). For reading on the wider context of the New Labour's social exclusion policy, Levitas (1998) is a good place to begin.

EIGHT

Disability and the discourses of the Single Regeneration Budget

Claire Edwards

Introduction

Since the late 1960s, successive British governments have sought to tackle the 'urban problem' through a range of different policies. From the Community Development Projects to the Urban Development Corporations (UDCs), and most recently, Local Strategic Partnerships (LSPs) in neighbourhood renewal, the sheer number of different initiatives is reflective of the fact that no administration to date has been able to solve the problem of inequality within Britain's cities (Atkinson and Moon, 1994; Hambleton and Thomas, 1995; Wilks-Heeg, 1996). Criticisms of past initiatives have been well documented, the most recurring theme being the failure of regeneration processes to engage with those whom regeneration was intended to benefit (Colenutt and Cutten, 1994; Geddes, 1997).

New Labour claims to have learnt from the past mistakes of previous initiatives, with an emphasis on "the area aspects of social exclusion" and partnership-based approaches to regeneration (SEU, 2001, p 12). Core to its plan for tackling deprivation is the need to involve local communities and previously excluded groups in regeneration processes (DETR, 1998a; SEU, 2001). As the Social Exclusion Unit's (SEU) National Strategy Action Plan for neighbourhood renewal states:

> The Government is committed to ensuring that communities' needs and priorities are to the fore in neighbourhood renewal and that residents of poor neighbourhoods have the tools to get involved in whatever way they want. (SEU, 2001, p 51)

Yet such commitments need to be cautiously received. Terms such as 'community' and 'social exclusion' may hide a multitude of groups and individuals with very different needs and access to the networks of regeneration. They can make invisible those people who are at the very margins of society, and it is with one such group – disabled people – that this chapter is concerned.

Disabled people have been excluded from society in a multitude of ways, be it socially, economically, or politically (Oliver, 1990; Barnes, 1991). Historically, in terms of urban policy, they have not been targeted as a 'disadvantaged group' in the way that ethnic minorities have, for example (Atkinson and Moon, 1994; Brownill et al, 1996). Yet this neglects the fact that disabled people face barriers in accessing employment and the built environment, partly as a result of societal discrimination, and have some of the lowest levels of income of all groups in the country (Dalley, 1991; Imrie, 1996a; Imrie and Hall, 2001). In noting that ethnic minority groups and young people are overrepresented in deprived areas, the National Strategy Action Plan states:

> No comparable figures exist for disability in deprived areas, but the experience of NDC [New Deal for Communities] pathfinders is that disabled people are also over-represented. (SEU, 2001, p 14)

Given the goal of current neighbourhood renewal strategies to ensure that "no-one should be seriously disadvantaged by where they live" (SEU, 2001, p 8), it would seem imperative that disabled people have a stake in regeneration processes.

This chapter explores how disability and the needs of disabled people are defined, if at all, in Labour's partnership-based urban policy. In so doing, it draws on research conducted between 1997 and 2000, which examined disabled people's involvement in one particular regeneration initiative, the Single Regeneration Budget (SRB) (see also Edwards, 2001, 2002). Based primarily on in-depth interviews with disabled people, disability groups, regional and local government officers responsible for the SRB and others involved in SRB partnerships, the research sought to examine disabled people's involvement at different spatial scales of analysis; that is, from the national to the local level. This chapter is concerned with the SRB policy at the national scale.

This chapter takes, as its starting point, an analysis of SRB policy documents, to provide an understanding of how the SRB policy itself defines disability and disabled people's needs at a strategic level. Focusing on the SRB bidding guidance (which sets out the policy objectives and targets) and other related documents, it examines and situates disability within the broader *discourses* underpinning the policy. However, it also employs interview material to understand how those implementing the SRB at the national and regional level interpret and give material form to the policy. Interviews were conducted with five officers responsible for administering and monitoring the SRB in different government offices for the regions, as well as with representatives from four key national, and one regional, disability organisations:

- The Royal National Institute for the Blind (RNIB);
- The Royal National Institute for the Deaf (RNID);
- The Royal Association for Disability and Rehabiliation (RADAR);
- The National Centre for Independent Living (NCIL);

• The Greater London Action on Disability (GLAD), formerly the Greater London Association of Disabled People.

The disability organisations were selected as they lobby and have contact with the government at the national level, and the selection included organisations both *of* and *for* disabled people – defined as those run primarily by disabled people and able-bodied people respectively (the significance of this distinction is set out later in this chapter). It is my intention in this chapter to explore the organisations' awareness and understanding of regeneration initiatives, as well as how far they had been involved in the policy-making processes of the SRB. I also want to examine the extent to which they perceived disability to be relevant to regeneration. While not a primary focus, the chapter also draws on some material from three local disability organisations, which had received funding from the SRB and therefore had some experience of the policy.

It is, however, the discourses underpinning the SRB policy documents that form the basis for this chapter's discussion. Discourses and language are important in the policy process, not least because they play a central role in struggles over legitimacy, and such a recognition has come to inform many academic disciplines, including planning (Hillier, 1993) and urban studies (Atkinson, 1999a; Hastings, 1999b). Barnes and Duncan describe discourses as "frameworks that embrace particular combinations of narratives, concepts, ideologies and signifying practices, each relevant to a particular realm of social action" (1992, p 8). To some extent, discourses may be likened to types of rules (Harley, 1992). The SRB, for example, has its 'rules of the game': the bidding guidance contains its own glossary of terms and definitions, which might have other meanings in different contexts.

In the evaluation of a seemingly neutral piece of policy, examining discourses can help expose the silences of the "well-heeled image" (Eagleton, 1986, p 80), illuminating who is 'in' and who is 'out' of the policy process. Grant (1989) distinguishes between insider and outsider groups within policy processes, whose needs and interests may or may not become encapsulated in written policy documents:

> Insider groups are regarded as legitimate by government and are consulted
> on a regular basis. Outsider groups either do not wish to become enmeshed
> in a consultative relationship with officials or are unable to gain recognition.
> (Grant, 1989, pp 14-15)

For disabled people, gaining recognition as an 'insider' group can be difficult, as they have been perceived historically by the state as a dependent group for whom others speak on their behalf. However, such categories are not always clearly delimited. Many disability organisations have sought to challenge and reconstruct such paternalistic state discourses in recent years, rendering the boundary between 'insider' and 'outsider' less distinct in certain policy arenas.

Placing disabled people within the SRB, I argue, requires an examination of the notions of partnership and community that the SRB appears to champion, as well as an evaluation of how policy makers and administrators view those whom they believe the policy is intended to target. My analysis of the policy revolves around three sections. First, after introducing the SRB, I examine the place of disability and disabled people in relation to those whom the SRB states it seeks to target, namely the 'community'. Thus, I explore the language of community within the policy, and ask how disabled people fit into this, if at all. I also suggest that there is a tension between casting the people whom the policy impacts upon as 'disadvantaged', and potential 'outputs' of the scheme on the one hand, and as participants in regeneration processes on the other (also see Chapter Seven).

Second, I explore the SRB's discourse of partnership, and, in examining the place of disabled people within it, suggest that there is a hierarchy inherent in the perceived relevance and importance attached to different partners. This hierarchy also operates in the policy-making process itself, which creates closures for certain groups. Disability groups can find themselves excluded from policy-making processes, as central government dictates the 'rules of the game'. Finally, I examine the discourse of monitoring, measurement and outputs, which is as much a feature of the SRB as the language of partnership and collaboration, and has implications for disabled people's involvement in urban policy processes.

Evaluating the place of disability within the Single Regeneration Budget

The SRB Challenge Fund was introduced by the Conservative government in 1994, as an amalgamation of the multitude of previously existing urban initiatives. Past initiatives had been heavily criticised for their emphasis on physical and economic regeneration and failure to address the concerns of the local communities they were intended to benefit (Colenutt and Cutten, 1994; Nevin and Shiner, 1995). In seeking to address these criticisms, the SRB sought a partnership-based approach, bringing together the public, private, voluntary and community sectors to bid for money from the fund (Oatley, 1998a). Its objectives range from improving opportunities for the disadvantaged to enhancing the employment and educational prospects of local people. New Labour has promoted the Challenge Fund as an "important instrument in the Government's drive to tackle social exclusion" (DETR, 1998b, p 3).

There have been six rounds of bidding for the SRB, which, at the time this research was conducted, was administered by the Government Offices for the Regions. Responsibility has since transferred to the Regional Development Agencies (RDAs). In 2001, it was announced that the RDAs' existing programme funding streams (of which the SRB was one) would be brought together into a single budget, and that there would be no further national bidding rounds for the SRB. Schemes continue to bid for Rounds One to Six of the SRB, but the policy is in many ways being superseded by the National Strategy Action Plan for neighbourhood renewal, in which the Office of the Deputy Prime Minister will designate resources to the 88 most deprived local authority areas in England through an £800 million Neighbourhood Renewal Fund (SEU, 2001).

Yet while the policy environment is changing rapidly, the insights that can be gained about disabled people's place in regeneration policies from an exploration of the SRB are significant. In part, I would argue that this is because many of the cornerstones of the National Strategy Action Plan – including the commitments to partnership and community involvement – are a continuation of themes established in the SRB. It is also because still very little is known about the relationship between disability and regeneration or disabled people's place within urban policy, despite this supposed era of 'joined-up thinking' and the rhetoric of social inclusion under New Labour.

It is not yet clear what, if any, impact the National Strategy Action Plan will have on the involvement of disabled people in regeneration processes, but evidence from the SRB paints a somewhat negative picture. Indeed, disabled people's place within the language of SRB policy documents, as well as in the eyes of those who implement the SRB at the regional level (and who utilise these documents), is limited. Disabled people are mentioned as an output just once in the bidding guidance, and are not conceptualised as part of the local community that policy makers are intent on involving. Moreover, the discourse of partnership that dominates the bidding document would seem to be underpinned by hierarchies that exclude groups deemed irrelevant to the SRB. As a group, disabled people are something of a non-issue on the regeneration agenda, reflecting both the way in which regeneration is defined as an activity, and the perceptions of disability held by those within government who implement the policy. Clearly, this has consequences in terms of disabled people's ability to influence, and gain access to, the policy-making processes of the SRB.

Community, disadvantage and disability

Since the election of the Labour government in 1997, notions of stakeholders, social exclusion and community involvement have come to dominate the language of urban regeneration. The SRB itself is clear in stating that the 'local community' has a role to play in regeneration partnerships. As the Round Five bidding guidance stresses, partnerships will have to demonstrate:

> how local communities have been involved in the development of the bid; how the partnership will ensure the local community will have a say in decisions ... and what arrangements will be put in place to fund local community projects. (DETR, 1998b, p 5)

Examining the place and definition of disabled people in the SRB requires a broader understanding of *who* the policy defines as the 'community', and its target groups. For Young (1990), community may be an inherently exclusive term: it denotes boundaries. Interestingly, despite the fact that the SRB bidding guidance has a glossary of terms, 'community' is not one of them. For a definition, we have to consider a manual produced for regeneration practitioners by the former Department of the Environment (DoE) in conjunction with consultants, entitled *Involving communities in urban and rural regeneration* (DoE, 1995). This document provides a substantive guide on how and why to involve communities in regeneration partnerships. In defining the community, it suggests that "those people living or working within those target areas, are in general, the people intended to benefit from regeneration initiatives" (DoE, 1995, p 7). As it continues, "this definition embraces small business proprietors, such as shop keepers and traders who run businesses in the area" (DoE, 1995, p 7). Already, therefore, communities are delimited by geographical boundaries (also see Chapter Twelve of this volume). Moreover, there is a certain emphasis on including those with an economic stake in the area. The guide does go on to note that "any area will contain groups of people with divergent interests, backgrounds and experiences" (DoE, 1995, p 10). It thus recognises the heterogeneity of different localities. However, it is left to the partnerships themselves to discover these different groups, and decide which are relevant to the regeneration process.

The SRB bidding guidance takes a somewhat contradictory approach to defining the community. For on the one hand, it is left up to partnerships to decide who or what the community is. Yet on the other hand, the guidance does name certain groups it deems important to include. Ethnic minorities receive particular attention, for example, and separate monitoring figures have to be provided for outputs where this group is implicated. Within the Round Five bidding guidance, communities include the "faith-based voluntary sector, the wider voluntary sector ... ethnic minorities and local volunteers" (DETR, 1998b, p 5). Little mention is made of a whole host of other marginalised groups, including disabled people. An officer responsible for the SRB in the Government Office for London (GOL) suggested that the problem of naming those groups the SRB purports to target lies in trying to balance competing needs. As he said in interview:

> "The problem is in writing a framework. How far do you go in identifying all these various priorities? The more you enumerate them, the longer it becomes, and it becomes all things to all people ... there may be some which are slightly higher priority than others, but it's difficult getting the balance."

When asked whether the SRB put enough priority on disabled people, the officer with responsibility for the SRB in the Government Office for the North West responded:

> "Urban regeneration is wider than the disabled, and they're not drawn out in the guidance, so in that context, yes. You get down to helping specific groups, which is not what the SRB is supposed to do."

As we have seen, however, the guidance does mention certain groups. Given its importance in dictating what partnerships do, and who they target, those groups mentioned in the guidance will take higher priority than others (although whether or not this stated priority is translated into greater involvement on the ground is a different story). Other groups not mentioned in the guidance are subsumed under the terms 'community' and 'disadvantaged'. The danger of using such ill-defined categories, however, is that they include those whom partnerships *want* them to include. Disabled people, and other marginalised groups, may be ignored under the 'wider' remits of urban regeneration, whatever they may be. As an SRB officer in the Government Office for the East (GOE) said of disabled people:

> "We've got an opportunity to feed in their needs ... but if you don't get out and about ... there might be a big need in an area and if nobody picks it up, nothing's going to be done about it."

Where, then, do disabled people sit in relation to the SRB? How does the policy define them? The one mention of disability in the bidding guidance is within an output: "number from disadvantaged groups being targeted who obtain a job, *e.g.* disabled people" (DoE, 1997, p 28). As the extra notes for this output in the Round Five bidding guidance state, "including everyone in the target area as being disadvantaged is unlikely to be very helpful" (DETR, 1998b, p 34). However, it then goes on to suggest that "for this output, members of ethnic minority groups should only be included where they have some other disadvantage *e.g.* physical disability" (DETR, 1998b, p 35). What, and who, then, is disadvantaged? Defined by the SRB, not everyone in the target area can be disadvantaged. Disabled people apparently fit into this delimited category, yet they receive no recognition as being part of the community.

I would argue that there is a distinction embodied in the SRB that defines those the policy impacts upon either as communities (participants in the regeneration process) or as disadvantaged (socially excluded people the policy should be to provide for). Yet these are the same people. Therefore, the language of participation and exclusion do not sit easily together. As a group, disabled people are defined as disadvantaged in the SRB; beyond that, however, they are marginalised, both linguistically in the policy and in its outputs. The fact that SRB indicators place little, if no, emphasis on disability, means that disabled people, and other 'non-guidance' groups, create little value for partnerships in terms of outputs. When it comes to being seen as part of the community or as active participants, disabled people are marked by their absence.

That disabled people should be absent from the SRB is reflective of the more general way in which urban regeneration policy has defined what counts as regeneration, as well as the marginalisation and disempowerment that disabled people have historically experienced, and indeed still experience in society. At the time when urban policy was being born, for example, many disabled people were sequestered from society, behind the closed doors of large institutions

(Barnes, 1991; Imrie, 1996a). Like other 'deviant' populations, they were recognised as people who did not fit the collectivist public norm and, certainly in the initial postwar period, required charity (Clarke and Newman, 1997).

The first urban policies defined ethnic minority groups as 'deviants' of urban areas; indeed, it was concerns about immigration and race riots in the 1960s that put race firmly on the urban agenda (Atkinson and Moon, 1994; Brownill et al, 1996). Despite the perception that disability, like race, required state intervention, disabled people were never seen as part of the urban problem in the same way. In part, this was reflected in the way regeneration policy itself changed from being an activity concerned with social problems to one largely concerned, in the 1980s, with physical and economic development (Lawless, 1991; Hambleton and Thomas, 1995). However, it was also related to the definition of disability within state institutions. Disability has often been seen as an issue for the former Department of Social Security (now Department for Work and Pensions) and the medical profession. Dominant government perceptions of disabled people have focused on their unique, biological problems, which require professional medical and social care (Oliver, 1990).

Not surprisingly, therefore, the urban environment, and societal barriers more generally, were never perceived as a problem for disabled people. It was only with the formation of disability groups in the 1970s that the definition of disability started to be rearticulated. Groups such as Union of the Physically Impaired Against Segregation propagated the notion of a social model of disability, which recognised that barriers within society define the person's disability as much as their actual bodily impairment (Oliver, 1990; Barnes, 1991; Shakespeare, 1993). This became ever more obvious as the advance to move disabled people out of institutions and into the 'community' took place. Despite the agreement embodied in the 1990 Community Care Act that disabled people should be able to live as 'normal' a life as possible in their own homes, the 'community' presents many alienating barriers, ranging from discriminatory attitudes to the inaccessibility of the built environment.

Although attitudes differ across departments, the categorisation and medicalisation of disability by the institutions of the state still remains. In terms of central government departments today, disability is categorised into bounded issues for which different departments are responsible. For example, the Department for Work and Pensions deals with disability benefits and welfare to work, while the Department for Education and Skills deals with special educational needs and the Department of Transport deals with disabled people's transport and mobility. However, as a worker in the Joint Mobility Unit Access Partnership, a section of the national disability charity RNIB suggested, "there can be a problem in some departments not recognising disability as an issue at all".

Nowhere is this more apparent than with regeneration. Despite the recognition that disabled people are, in the SRB's terms, 'disadvantaged', at the time of conducting this research the Department of the Environment, Transport and the Regions (DETR) had no information on how many disabled people had been involved, or what the nature of their involvement had been. Nor did the Government Offices have any kind of working definition of disability. The officer in GOE suggested that this was the case because no one asked them for clarification:

> "There's only one output that actually relates to disabled people and it never causes a problem from partnerships. I think if the partnerships had queried us and said, 'What do we put under this output?', then perhaps we would have felt the need to describe what we mean. I think it's anyone who's disadvantaged."

Another officer suggested that, because disabled people were not a priority in the guidance, they had no need to utilise a definition of disability. Disabled people are therefore not high on the list of those the SRB seeks to involve or target, nor indeed perceived as particularly relevant. Perhaps this finding is not surprising, given the way in which the state has sought to classify and divide disabled people off as a group with 'special needs' (Oliver, 1990). However, it raises questions about how far 'joined-up thinking' and the rhetoric of partnership really has substance within regeneration as a policy realm.

The Single Regeneration Budget: partnership or hierarchy?

Partnership working, while not a new phenomenon, has perhaps been the 'trademark' of Labour's approach to urban policy. The rhetoric of "joining up locally" (SEU, 2001, p 10), and the creation of LSPs as part of the National Strategy Action Plan, bear witness to this continuing concern. Yet as a range of authors have demonstrated, partnerships do not necessarily draw in a wide range of networks. Rather, they may seek consensus based on a small elite (Cochrane, 1986; Raco, 2000). This is particularly the case where partnerships or 'grant coalitions' have come together in the race for government funding (Peck and Tickell, 1994; Cochrane et al, 1996; Jones and Ward, 1998). Collaboration, then, becomes a necessary part of succeeding in a competitive environment.

The SRB (and City Challenge before it) represented perhaps the first 'recycling' of the partnership approach after the market-led initiatives of the 1980s, and indeed, one look at the SRB bidding guidance shows that 'partnership' is the password to the SRB (Atkinson, 1999a). The guidance text is littered with terms such as 'true partnership', 'real involvement' and the definition of a policy where groups must 'share a view' of a scheme's importance (DoE, 1997, pp 4-5). "Effective partnerships", we are told, "depend on a balance of power and responsibility" (DETR, 1997, p 7) between partners. It suggests that partnerships work on the basis of equality, a common goal and an inclusive ethos. According to a discussion paper issued by DETR:

> partnerships should include all the relevant players (including central and local government, the private and voluntary sector and the local community itself). (DETR, 1997, p 7)

How the term 'relevant' is defined, and by whom, is crucial. The bidding guidance has no qualms in establishing who the 'relevant players' are. As it states:

> Given their role in local regeneration and development, local authorities and TECs [Training and Enterprise Councils] can be expected to play a central role. (DoE, 1997, p 4)

While it goes on to assert the importance of including other interests (such as the private sector), and, last in the list, the community, it depends again on their perceived relevance.

Underpinning the notion of shared responsibilities and collaboration, therefore, is a structured hierarchy (Atkinson, 1999a) that depends on the importance of an organisation as perceived by the eyes of those judging the schemes, a perception often constructed out of past experience. As the officer in GOL stated:

> "There can be different types of partnerships, but it basically means that we want all the key players that should be involved in any particular bid involved. A bid with a large component of training in it that doesn't involve the relevant TEC is not likely to succeed. And on the community side, quite clearly they start at a lower point on the learning curve."

Partnerships cannot, as the language of the bidding guidance would suggest, be equal. Among the rhetoric and good intentions, it is clear that disabled people gain little recognition as potential partners at a strategic level. Even considering the place of the 'community' within the language of partnership presents a bleak picture. The rules of the SRB, it would seem, are established prior to community involvement, initially by civil servants in central government. As Atkinson (1999a) notes in his analysis of the DoE manual (1995), the emphasis on those in strategic positions suggests that the structures of regeneration are already in place, and the community has to be absorbed into those. It suggests that the community is a coherent entity, somehow 'out there' and waiting to be tapped. This does not bode well for disabled people, who are linguistically excluded from the policy in the first place, and thus "rendered invisible" (Young, 1990, p 59).

If, as DETR suggest, regeneration partnerships should include central and local government, and if we are now in an era of 'joined-up' government, what does partnership mean between central government and those doing regeneration 'on the ground'? Moreover, does partnership operate in the policy-making process itself? Like the policies that were its product, the process of *making* urban policy has never been a coordinated one. The SRB's language of consensus is grounded in the history of a policy realm in which fragmentation and incoherence have been key themes (Rhodes, 1988; Bailey et al, 1995), with different departments taking responsibility for urban initiatives at different times. While attempts to increase collaboration horizontally across government departments at a regional level has taken place in the form of the Government Offices for the Regions and more recently, the RDAs, boundaries remain. As the officer in GOL stated of disability, for example:

> "Disability is really a DfES and DSS policy area, and in so far as we're informed of what's going on in that particular area, we get information from our colleagues in that part of the office."

Boundaries still prevail, keeping policy realms separate.

The government appears to be acutely aware of criticisms that urban policy has operated in a hierarchical way, for as the National Strategy Action Plan states:

> Everyone agrees that central Government will not help turn around deprived neighbourhoods if it is too 'top-down' or prescriptive in the way it works with local partners. (SEU, 2001, p 54)

Yet in the implementation of the SRB, central and regional government sit outside the rules of partnership they determine. Government offices monitor partnerships, rather than collaborate with them, and in this research saw their relationship with partnerships as a distanced one. As the SRB officer in the Government Office for the South East (GOSE) stated:

> "SRB is very 'hands-off' management. We want to know at the initial stages that schemes are good value for money, and then we delegate most of the running ... to partnerships."

Government Offices have the power to withdraw funding if the scheme is not meeting its targets, however, for as the same officer said: "If partnerships don't perform, we're expected to bring them into line". It therefore pays for an organisation to develop a good relationship with the local Government Office, as a housing association in London that had been involved in an SRB partnership aimed at providing training for people with learning difficulties stressed:

> "We worked very hard to chat up GOL and get good connections there. And GOL perceived us as being an efficient organisation that could generally do what it says it could do. It was wary of becoming involved in programmes where it wasn't achievable."

Not only is this indicative of the government's hierarchy of organisations it deems relevant and efficient in regeneration partnerships, it also bears witness to the need for organisations to get on the inside. This is problematic for disability groups wishing to put disability on the regeneration agenda or access the SRB at a strategic level. Contact between disability organisations and central government departments has tended to reflect the specific categorisation of disability issues – including impairment-specific issues – and has depended on the nature of the disability organisations themselves. Disability groups have not always operated as a homogenous 'movement', just as the experience of disability itself can be defined more by its diversity that by a singular, universal reference point. Many of the disability organisations that operate at the national level focus on issues affecting specific impairment groups (for example, the RNIB for people with visual impairments, or Mencap for people with learning disabilities). Moreover, distinctions are made between those groups *for* disabled people, run predominantly by able-bodied people, and those groups *of* disabled people (Oliver, 1990). Despite the obvious problems of such distinct categorisations, those groups *for* disabled people, such as the larger national disability charities, have traditionally received more funding, and had more sustained contact with central government.

As an established group, for example, Disability Alliance is represented in several high-profile fora, including the Disability Benefits Consortium and Social Security Consortium. They meet regularly with government ministers and civil servants, and along with another established disability organisation, RADAR, have presented evidence to House of Commons committees, including one examining the provision of medical services to the former Benefits Agency (Disability Alliance, 2000). As a representative from RADAR stated in interview:

> "I think in Westminster we're particularly known for providing good quality, impartial briefings which put the case for disabled people, but not hysterically."

Similarly, the Joint Mobility Unit Access Partnership of the RNIB has links with departments within DETR, over specific issues such as mobility and access in the built environment. There is a feeling however, that government departments only appreciate input where they feel they should be addressing disability an as issue. One worker at the Joint Mobility Unit Access Partnership stated:

> "Apart from the Mobility Unit, within DETR, there's more resistance to us and organisations like us giving advice, because they're not required to listen to us, but also because they don't have the internal driving force to do that .... There may be some consultations that we would like to respond to, but we don't get, so we actively seek those."

Yet none of the national disability organisations I spoke to had had any contact with the Regeneration Directorate within DETR.

For smaller, less well-funded disability organisations, and indeed, those perceived as confrontational by government in their approach, it is nothing less than a struggle to access Whitehall and even regional Government Offices, although some may not wish to engage in negotiations with the government (Barnes and Oliver, 1995). On the next rung down the regeneration ladder, for example, a local disability organisation providing training in south London, and actually part-funded by the SRB, stressed the difficulty of getting involved strategically with the GOL:

> "I think the problem is that much of the contact has to be through other agencies like the TECs and local authorities and the message that we wish to push gets diluted. It's very, very difficult to get into GOL at a strategic level to make points about the broader issues and how disability needs to be put on the agenda in a different way to the way it's currently considered. And that, I think, is virtually impossible to do."

A London-wide disability organisation, GLAD, had managed to access a regeneration meeting with GOL, but only through being a member of a pan-London voluntary regeneration network. Had it not been part of this network, their representative noted, it would not have been able to gain access to the Government Office. In terms of regeneration, therefore, links between central and regional government and disability organisations are minimal. They reflect the alienation of disability from the regeneration agenda, and the very specific nature in which disability is perceived. As the representative from GLAD said of consultation with disabled people:

> "People's attitudes towards disabled people can be patronising. They see that they want to talk to disabled people about one particular aspect of something, but not other things."

Disabled people are often perceived as only being interested in issues that affect them as service users, rather than more broadly as residents in a local area, or as citizens. In many ways, this would seem to describe the perception of disability in regeneration circles. However, in addressing inequalities within society, the SRB would seem like a prime opportunity to tackle some of the barriers that disabled people face living in urban areas.

Speaking to Government Office officials around the country and national disability organisations alike, there was a belief that disabled people want the same things out of regeneration as anybody else: they want 'choice' in the way they live their lives, as the officer in GOE said. This includes, as the representative of the London-wide organisation of disabled people said, "access to employment, decent affordable housing, good transport links". Yet the mechanisms and commitment to giving disabled people the 'same as everybody else' are less than satisfactory, and often downright exclusionary, while gaining access to the implementers of the SRB is limited.

Measuring the Single Regeneration Budget: the language of economy and efficiency

The SRB bidding guidance embodies a distinct set of rules about the way regeneration should operate, not only in terms of the composition of partnerships, but also in the plethora of measurements employed by the Government Offices to monitor the success of schemes, and check that partnerships are delivering what they say they will deliver. 'Outputs','milestones', 'key indicators' and 'value for money' are as much part of the language of the SRB as 'inclusion','shared' vision and 'partnership'. The SRB bidding document states:

> Rigorous appraisal is essential to secure regularity, propriety and value for money in delivering project outputs. (DETR, 1998a, p 13)

It is the role of the Government Offices to ensure that targets are met, and indeed, the ethos of output-driven value for money is as much an objective as tackling urban problems, it would seem. As the officer in GOSE said:

> "It's difficult when you have a grant regime that provides resources for such a wide range of activity to apply yardsticks. But nonetheless, when you've been running schemes for quite some time, you tend to build up a fair amount of expertise in what constitutes good value .... If you've got two bids that you're weighing up, you will probably go for the one that costs less, but it is saying it will produce more, providing you can be reasonably sure that those figures are fairly robust."

Another officer, this time in the Government Office for the South West, said: "we effectively buy outputs". That such a discourse should dominate the SRB is reflective of the more widespread managerialism encouraged by the Thatcher government in the 1980s as a means through which "more rigorous discipline could be introduced into the public sector to produce more effective services" (Clarke and Newman, 1997, p 34). Yet, the reliance on quantification within the SRB is also symptomatic of the perceived 'best method' to evaluate and measure policy. The SRB is reflective of a policy realm in which central government establishes seemingly objective ways of monitoring and evaluating schemes based on a positivistic approach that places priority on figures above the lives of those the policy is impacting upon (Turok, 1989). As Imrie (1996b, p 1447) notes, since the 1950s and 1960s there has been an "idealistic preoccupation" with the production of pure, neutral knowledge to be utilised by policy makers. The 'expert systems' of which policy makers and researchers are a part are distinguished from those who are researched or evaluated (Giddens, 1990, 1991). Thus, in the terms of the SRB, the 'disadvantaged' are objectified by the outputs; they are put into 'tick boxes' by civil servants, and categorised in a seemingly scientific way.

Outputs in the SRB range from number of jobs created to hectares of land increased. Many commentators have criticised the outputs for placing too heavy an emphasis on physical and infrastruactural development, and too little on social indicators (Robson, 1994). Others have suggested that they serve to exclude the community, for while some of the outputs focus on community initiatives, the quantitative approach that they embody is an inappropriate way of assessing community development (Colenutt and Cutten, 1994). As the first section of this chapter showed, outputs are central to defining disabled people's place in the SRB. Although they are defined in terms of their ability to work, the fact that they appear in only one output also renders them marginal, and less relevant as a group to be targeted. While job creation for disabled people is important, social inclusion cannot be reduced to economic inclusion. As the representative of GLAD stated:

> "Social inclusion is about more than employment. It's about valuing people's contributions in whatever way they can make them .... An awful lot of disabled people put a lot of time in on a voluntary basis and that's never recognised, or seen as contributing to society."

For Clarke and Newman (1997), performative frameworks are part of the managerialist imperative to divide activities into 'core' and 'non-core', or essential and non-essential business. For the SRB, counting the number of disadvantaged people who obtain jobs is 'core'; what they might need to do to get to this point is not so important. Disabled people's needs, or indeed the needs of any individual, cannot be neatly defined by SRB outputs. For example, the manager of a scheme to train people with learning difficulties to be gardeners, which had gained some money from the SRB for a pilot scheme, stated of the targets:

> "In many ways its difficult to class disabled people as outputs. This is where we come unstuck with Youth Training because you basically get passed on their dole money which you pass on to them as a training allowance, and then you get £1,000 per output which is for Wordpower or Numberpower. But for some of our trainees, that's like a degree, they come to us and can't read and write .... And it's the same with SRB targets and outputs – I can't say from this that so many people are going to end up as super-qualified gardeners."

The problems of meeting targets and outputs are difficult for community and voluntary organisations in general, but for disability organisations it may be even more of a struggle. The manager of an SRB project aimed at providing employment opportunities for people with learning difficulties noted how it had to drop the local TEC as one of its partners because of the rigid outputs it set as targets. He said:

> "We had to fulfil quotas which we couldn't do. You say 'come off benefits'to any of our carers, and they immediately get a bit uptight, because if you withdraw from benefits, it takes a hell of a long time to get back on them again. Our philosophy is that it takes as long as it takes for the client to do it, we don't really put time frames on it. It would put too many stresses on our clients and have a counter effect."

The notion that schemes, and their impact on people's lives, can be quantified in such a way is problematic, and particularly so for a group whose needs are potentially complex (Imrie, 1996b).

It is not the intention of this chapter to go into detail about individual projects, but such examples demonstrate the potentially exclusive nature of outputs. From the perspective of those who have tended to lead SRB partnerships – local authorities and TECs – the pressure of outputs may also mean neglecting certain groups, or allowing time for only minimal involvement from the community.

> It takes time to develop the trust and confidence needed for higher levels of community involvement. It may be therefore that at the outset of a programme, it is realistic only to seek to inform and consult. (DoE, 1995, p 18)

Community involvement in strategic decision-making processes is thus compromised: meeting targets and deadlines takes priority.

As Atkinson (1999a) notes, there is a rationale for involving the community in partnerships that does not relate solely to their rights as citizens to have a stake in the regeneration process. The DoE manual states that:

> It is important to ... recognise that involving the community has a range of benefits in terms of better decision-making and enhanced cost effectiveness. Involving the community can therefore be a means to ensure that regeneration programmes are more effective in achieving their objectives. (DoE, 1995, p 21)

Again, the discourse of efficiency, value for money and outputs rears its head. The rhetoric of stakeholders and communitarianism, which is such an important part of the Blair agenda, would suggest that every member of a local area has an equal right to participate in the process of regeneration. Yet participation is conducted on other people's terms. Community groups can only break into the regeneration circle if they employ the discourse of efficiency and effectiveness; that is, if they talk in outputs. Yet the distinction between monitors and the monitored serves to abstract those who are the recipients of the SRB from the policy process, not least because the language of outputs is alien to many people. In the SRB, 'correct' knowledge based on positivism takes precedence over, and subsumes, multiple and different knowledges that exist among urban communities and those trying for a stake in the regeneration game.

Conclusions

New Labour is keen to stress that its urban regeneration initiatives are underpinned by working partnerships, and the involvement and empowerment of local communities whom policies impact upon. Reflecting this, the SRB is underpinned by the discourse of partnership, with its language of consensus, shared vision, and an equal balance of power between partners. Deconstructing this term, however, suggests a hierarchy in which different interests and organisations compete for key roles, to the exclusion of others. Urban policy has never been integrated and coherent, either in the policy-making process or the initiatives themselves, and this is something that the government itself now acknowledges (Rhodes, 1988). As the National Strategy Action Plan states:

> Over several decades, the policies and actions of central and local government
> have not been good enough at tackling these issues; and sometimes they
> have been part of the problem. (SEU, 2001, p 17)

Indeed, as this chapter has demonstrated, both the hierarchical nature of partnership and the exclusivity of an outputs-based policy impact upon the involvement of those whom the SRB has sought to target. Recipients of the SRB are defined in the bidding guidance as 'disadvantaged' and the 'community', although the two do not sit easily together. For while disadvantage harks back to notions of state dependency, the idea of community propagated by the current government is one of active participants in policy processes (see Chapter One of this volume). Disabled people are linguistically defined as disadvantaged, and yet receive no mention as part of the community, or as active participants in the regeneration game. They are marked more by their absence, as a non-issue.

It is clear, then, that the government does not see disabled people as part of the urban problem, despite the exclusion they experience and their overrepresentation in deprived areas. In part, this reflects the traditional categorisation of disability into specific issues, such as welfare benefits and mobility and so precludes any responsibility for them by regeneration. More broadly, it raises questions about the objectives of urban policy more generally. Who should urban policy be targeting and seeking to involve, and should disabled people be part of this? Should it specify target groups at all? Urban policies, as Cochrane (1999) notes, have not been founded on the notion that different groups living in particular areas have rights to funding or services. Rather:

> Urban policy expenditure instead tends to flow through particular projects
> and programmes, following a process of selection based on a changing set of
> criteria, which are rarely specified. (Cochrane, 1999, p 247)

How far groups become the targets of urban policy depends in part on the type of activities that urban renewal engenders. Different administrations have had their own opinion about the roots of urban malaise, and what the appropriate solution should be. Cochrane (1999), too, notes that the demise of the UDCs has been marked by initiatives that take up contemporary social policy's emphasis on tackling dependency. In contemporary urban policy, he argues, "training, rather than local economic development has become the panacea of the 1990s" (Cochrane, 1999, p 257).

If this is the shape of future urban policy, then it may be the case that dependent or excluded groups – from the young unemployed to ex-offenders – become increasingly targeted through projects that seek to counter their dependency, and "transform their status, to make them active citizens capable ... of managing their own risk" (Dean, 1999, p 168).

Yet what does this offer to disabled people, and should they be a part of it? Disabled people should have as much access to schemes as anyone else – equality of opportunity. Perhaps more crucially, disabled people need to be identified within the SRB and other initiatives as vocal citizens. Groups may not have formal entitlements to urban policy, but certain ones are highlighted within the bidding guidance to be targeted. Being mentioned, as in the case of ethnic minorities, does not guarantee funding or involvement; to suggest so would be to negate the different ways in which partnerships prioritise activities at the local scale. Yet in a policy that purports to tackle social exclusion, disabled people have an equal right to recognition as a group that not only experiences disadvantage, but as citizens that can contribute to the policy-making process. Disabled people's discursive alienation from the SRB is a significant one, and serves only to perpetuate their invisibility in society.

Acknowledgements

I would like to thank the Economic and Social Research Council for funding this research, and the two anonymous referees for their helpful comments. It should be noted that any views expressed here are my own, and do not represent those of my employer, the Department for Work and Pensions.

Further reading

Perhaps unsurprisingly, little has been written on disability and urban regeneration, although some literature does exist on disabled people's access to policy-making processes. Of particular note, Imrie (1996a) and Imrie and Hall (2001) explore disabled people's exclusion in the built environment and the ways in which disabled people are seeking to challenge the policies and practices that give rise to inaccessible environments. These insightful books also set out key debates in disability theory regarding the relationship between disabled people and society. In terms of regeneration-focused work, Brownill and Darke (1998) helpfully discuss issues in seeking to involve marginalised groups in regeneration policies.

NINE

Citizenship, community and participation in small towns: a case study of regeneration partnerships

Bill Edwards, Mark Goodwin and Michael Woods

Introduction

Small towns, regeneration policy and the assumption of community

Small or market towns with populations of between 2,000 and 20,000 people are a neglected part of the urban studies literature, a point confirmed by a recent report by the Countryside Agency, which concluded that "data and knowledge about market towns is generally weak" (2002a, p 1). Indeed, in many ways, research on small towns has been hampered by an academic division of labour, which categorises objects of enquiry as either 'urban' or 'rural'. The disciplines of Geography and Sociology have both recognised sub-disciplines in Urban Geography, Rural Geography, Urban Sociology and Rural Sociology, complemented by interdisciplinary work in urban or rural studies. Specialised journals and research groups follow this pattern. Small towns fall uneasily between the two areas – not large enough to be readily admitted as 'urban', but too large to fall within the classic agricultural and village foci of rural studies. Urban policy work in particular has concentrated on larger urban areas and conurbations, and almost all empirical examples of urban policies in practice are drawn from cities such as London, Manchester, Liverpool, Leeds, Glasgow and Birmingham. This is not just a question of scale: empirical studies of urban policy in these conurbations often examine neighbourhood or estate-based schemes that target populations of less than 5,000. More precisely, then, it is a question of small towns as a category falling outside the lens of most urban-focused research.

This is particularly unfortunate at the present juncture, when small towns are viewed as critical sites for regeneration strategies that serve their own communities and those of surrounding areas, and when they are also seen as places where community engagement and involvement in such strategies can be easily fostered. A new policy focus on small towns was heralded by Labour's

Rural White Paper for England, *Our countryside: The future* (DETR and MAFF, 2000). For the first time in a rural White Paper, a chapter was dedicated to 'market towns'. In setting out a coherent strategy for small-town regeneration, the White Paper drew together a number of initiatives targeted at small towns that were already operated by the Countryside Agency and Regional Development Agencies (RDAs), as well as by the Welsh Development Agency. Having done this, the White Paper repositioned them more centrally within the wider scheme of rural development.

Moreover, the approach adopted by New Labour (as suggested by Chapter One of this volume), marks an evolution in 'the regime of practice' in small-town regeneration from previous Conservative emphases on entrepreneurship under Margaret Thatcher and active citizenship under John Major, to a regime of collective self-responsibility. This new approach has not altered the key tenets in small-town regeneration of partnership working and community engagement – both of which have been heavily promoted as requirements for EU funding – but has reconfigured the discourse and rhetoric of regeneration to reflect core New Labour political and ideological concerns.

Politically, New Labour's concern with small towns can be seen as part of an attempt to shift the balance of rural policy and politics from agricultural and property issues to Labour's traditionally stronger areas of health, education, housing and social exclusion (Woods, 2002). However, placing responsibility for regeneration with the communities of small towns also resonates with the emblematic New Labour themes of 'citizenship' and 'rights and responsibilities'. The New Labour discourse of citizenship differs from that of its Conservative predecessors in representing the practice of citizenship as a *collective* more than an individual act. Accordingly, a key difference between the 2000 Rural White Paper and its Conservative equivalent of 1995 was the substituting of an emphasis on active citizenship with an emphasis on active communities.

As such, small towns have emerged as prime candidates for the New Labour agenda of inclusive community involvement. In population terms, they appear to fit perfectly – large enough and compact enough to provide a critical mass for mobilisation, yet also fulfilling the notion (often held implicitly by policy makers) that the smaller the town, the higher the sense of community and hence participation. It is also easy to proceed with the assumption that regeneration in small towns will automatically embrace the whole community. In contrast to larger urban areas, where the rhetoric of inclusion and inclusiveness is often aimed at previously excluded groups, the policy discourse in small towns tends to assume the presence of a single 'integrated' community. Indeed, policy documents on small towns often elide notions of place and community – as if one neatly overlaps the other. It was in this manner that the South West of England Regional Development Agency (SWERDA) introduced its new Market and Coastal Towns Initiative:

> Market and Coastal Towns is run by a number of national and regional
> public bodies, to help people in towns in the south-west to revitalise their

own communities. Through the initiative, public funds will be injected into those communities to give initial impetus to locally conceived projects that will produce dramatic change. The result will be towns that are thriving and prosperous in both the short and the long term. (SWERDA, no date, p 2)

Here, notions of the town and the community are almost interchangeable. Indeed, one could substitute 'community' and 'town' for each other in this passage with no loss of meaning. It is this elision between the interests of a spatially defined geographical area ('the town') and the needs of all its residents ('the community') that makes small towns ideal for examining the delivery of an urban policy built on ideas of inclusiveness and community (see also Chapter One of this volume).

This chapter explores these assumptions by looking at community involvement and participation in a range of small-town regeneration schemes. In the first part, we examine the theory of small-town regeneration, reviewing and critiquing the assumptions that underlie contemporary policy. In the second part, we proceed to investigate small-town regeneration *in practice*, outlining recent initiatives and drawing on case studies from our own research in England and Wales to explore the nature and extent of community participation. This empirical work allows us to raise conceptual concerns around the themes of governance, empowerment and elite engagement that are addressed in our conclusions.

Imagining the small town: policy assumptions

The 'rediscovery' of small towns in government policy has been premised on a number of assumptions about the nature of small towns and their relationship with the wider countryside. It is through the scripting of these assumptions into policy documentation that small towns have been defined and described as an object of governance. By this means, the government justifies the identification of small towns as a discrete focal point of regeneration policy, and informs both the economic strategies promoted in regeneration initiatives and the mechanisms adopted for their delivery.

The first key assumption is that small towns, or, more specifically, market towns, are critical nodes in the rural economy, and therefore initiatives that target market towns can be a means of regenerating wider rural areas. The Rural White Paper mobilised this representation in establishing the justification for devoting an entire chapter to market towns, stating that, "market towns play a critical role in helping rural communities to thrive and in regenerating deprived areas" (DETR and MAFF, 2000, p 74). The White Paper proceeds to propose that market towns have "a crucial part to play in the future development of the rural economy" (DETR and MAFF, 2000, p 75), and identified a number of ways in which 'prosperous' market towns could help to regenerate surrounding rural areas. It states that market towns can be:

- a focus for economic development and regeneration, including markets for local food and other countryside products;
- centres that meet people's needs for access to a wide range of retail, professional and public services without destroying the character of the area;
- a focus for properly planned and coordinated public transport;
- distinctive places to live, often with a fine heritage and historic buildings and the potential to act as a centre of cultural activity (DETR and MAFF, 2000, p 75).

Closer reading of the White Paper's statements, however, reveals something of the complexity of small towns and their relation to the wider countryside, and indicates that the representation of market towns as focal points of the rural economy is not as straightforward as one might initially assume. First, it is striking that this description is positioned in the future tense, implying that market towns are not necessarily serving their surrounding area to the fullest potential at present and that connections between small towns and their hinterlands need to be reconstructed. For example, the potential role of small towns as markets for local food is not as obvious as one might think. The growth of the Farmers' Markets movement has highlighted how agricultural produce is routinely exported from the locality of production for processing and packaging and sale in national or international markets, often under contract to food processors or supermarkets. Breaking this trend and re-establishing a culture of buying locally produced food would require the intervention of special initiatives (Holloway and Kneafsey, 2000).

Certainly, there is considerable variation in the extent to which small towns are integrated with their local economies, both in terms of the sourcing of materials and in terms of the markets that they supply. As Courtney and Errington (2000) demonstrate, the local integration of a town can be mapped as its 'economic footprint', quantifying its relative economic linkages with the local, regional, national and international economy. The degree of a small town's integration with its local economy is dependent, they argue, on its existing economic structure and its proximity to metropolitan centres. Thus in their thesis, the small towns that are best placed to lead a revitalisation of their rural hinterland are those in peripheral regions with more agriculturally related economies and without the presence of successful export enterprises.

Alongside this, the specific identification of 'prosperous' market towns both displays a faith in 'trickle-down' (or, in this case, 'trickle-out') economics, and suggests that a small town's capacity to influence its locality is dependent on its economic health. This is significant, as in other paragraphs the White Paper acknowledged that many rural small towns have their foundations in manufacturing, textiles, mining and other industries, and have suffered from the economic decline of these sectors. On conventional indicators of deprivation such as unemployment and low incomes, there are many small towns that stand out as being significantly more deprived than their neighbouring rural wards. While this provides further justification for community-scaled regeneration programmes that can address pockets of deprivation overlooked by larger-scale initiatives, it also raises questions about the capacity of small-town regeneration to benefit wider rural areas, not least since the causal economic processes may have more in common with those that impact on larger urban centres than with those that shape the post-agrarian rural economy.

Finally, it is notable that the government's vision of the potential role of market towns goes beyond that of simply providing a focal point for the rural economy: it also has social and cultural dimensions. Indeed, small towns are already the centres of social investment in the countryside. For example, while rural districts are relatively more successful than urban areas in obtaining Lottery funding for community, arts, heritage and sports projects, both in terms of grants awarded and total funds received, closer examination shows that the majority of this investment in rural areas goes to projects in small towns within those districts (Edwards et al, 2002). The implication is that such facilities serve the population of the town's hinterland, as well as the town population itself. Thus, there is an implicit reworking of the imagined spatiality of rural communities, carrying forward an assumption that rural residents are integrated into social and cultural activities scaled on a 'community field' that is fixed on and around a local small town. However, no formal units of local government exist at this scale, raising problematic issues of governance. To construct coordinating bodies that represent both town and hinterland means the creation either of non-governmental organisations or of partnerships between town and parish councils. Consequently, a new politics of local territoriality has emerged as town councils and organisations seek to spread the costs of projects to other beneficiary communities and as outlying parishes contest their duty to contribute (see Edwards et al, 2001).

The second key assumption is that small towns have an identifiable unified 'community', which can be effectively engaged with and drawn into the regeneration process. For example, the Countryside Agency recently introduced a Market Town Health Check as a participatory tool aimed at engaging the 'entire community' in the process of identifying the strengths and weaknesses of small towns and their hinterlands, agreeing a 'vision', and establishing an action plan (Countryside Agency, 2002a). A successful 'health check', therefore "needs to embrace the concerns of the whole community". Implicit in this model is the additional assumption that the capacity for community participation is greater in small towns than in larger settlements. This assumption is informed by the 'community identification' (Hampton, 1970) and 'social interactionist' (Putnam et al, 1970) theories of participation. These theories held that political participation would be greater in smaller communities, but also reflects lay discourses of small-town life that emphasise community spirit, frequent interaction and civic tradition[1].

However, the evidence for high levels of participation in small towns is inconclusive. Small towns do tend to have greater opportunity for participation than either rural communities or (relative to population) larger towns and cities, but there is significant variation. Recent research, for instance, has identified 88 social and community organisations in the small town of Kington (Herefordshire), 71 in Winchcombe (Gloucestershire), 80 in Alresford (Hampshire) and 25 in Beaminster (Dorset) – that is, in terms of ratios, 1:25, 1:68, 1:96 and 1:110 organisations per head of population respectively[2]. Moreover, town councils tend not only to have more status and be engaged in a wider range of activities than parish councils of an equivalent size, but they are also more likely to have contested elections than either rural or suburban parish councils (Woods et al, 2003: forthcoming).

Yet these characteristics can be largely explained by structural factors. Small towns have a high preponderance of social organisations because there are many groups that tend to be established in every town and do not necessary divide into more branches with a larger population. Such groups would include Rotary Clubs and Round Tables, Inner Wheels and Soroptimists, Chambers of Commerce and a range of established voluntary groups representing national charity and caring organisations. Many of these groups draw their membership not just from the town itself but also from the town's hinterland. In terms of more formal routes to participation, elections to town councils are more likely to be contested because they tend to have a higher ratio of electors to councillors, so that competition is greater. Also, they are more likely to be fought on party political lines – often a legacy of a previous incarnation as a municipal borough or urban district council.

More significant, and yet less tangible, is the civic infrastructure that is both constituted through and reflected in the range of organisations active in a small town. Many small towns have long civic histories, having been granted status as boroughs or markets in the medieval period, and the legacy of this heritage is manifest in organisations such as town councils, chambers of trade, town trusts and local charities, and in annual civic events, ceremonies and rituals. The facilities remain in the shape of town halls, council offices and market places. Collectively, these provide focal points for participation at the scale of the town community. Moreover, they contribute to the existence of a civic culture in small towns, whereby the institutional portfolio and sense of continuity through heritage encourages residents to readily identify themselves as citizens of the town and to think of the town as the appropriate locus for public-sphere participation (Smith, 1999; Woods, 1999).

However, the visible presence of a civic infrastructure in small towns does not necessarily mean that the residents of small towns are participating in public life to greater extent than in rural or larger urban communities. Moyser and Parry (1989) criticised the association of participation with community size, arguing that there is no correlation between the strength of community identity and levels of participation. While individuals in strong social networks do participate more in politics, their levels of participation are consistent regardless of the size of community in which they live (see also Parry et al, 1992). More recently, the Local Voluntary Activity Surveys conducted by the Home Office revealed considerable variation in volunteering levels between the small towns included in their sample. Total volunteering recorded in the most active small town, Great Torrington in Devon (85,682 volunteer hours a year per 1,000 adults), was not that much greater than that for the most active urban area, Norwich (76,568 volunteer hours a year per 1,000 adults). Overall, an area's prosperity, the local government context and access to external funding sources were identified as more significant factors on the level and type of volunteering than community size (Marshall et al, 1997).

Furthermore, questions can be raised about the breadth of involvement in small-town civic life. Institutions such as town councils, chambers of trades, Rotary Clubs, and the like, tend to be dominated by white middle-class, middle- to late-aged men with a broadly conservative outlook. The continuing importance of elite networks to the functioning of small-town politics and governance further reinforces these biases. Those who do not fit this profile (most notably the town's young people, but increasingly also immigrants) either have to find ways of 'breaking into' these cliques, or challenge the existing civic leadership. More commonly, they set up their own organisations to participate in the public life of the town. In this way, civic events and ceremonies that routinely serve to reproduce community identity can become sites of contestation as different visions for the town come into conflict (Smith, 1993).

Small towns, therefore, are not unified communities, nor can they be engaged with as a single entity. Rather, they are spaces that multiple communities occupy, sometimes with very different perceptions about the town and ideas about its future. As these communities tend to participate in different organisations in the town, the ability of one group or body to represent 'the local community' has been undermined. This is implicitly recognised in the adoption of partnership working as the preferred means of delivering small-town regeneration initiatives. Hence, partnership in this context means both a partnership being forged between the state and local communities, and multiple partnerships being established between organisations within small towns as a prerequisite for funding. These issues raise an interesting set of questions about the power and politics of the process that seeks to encourage greater citizen participation and community involvement in market-town regeneration initiatives.

In the remainder of this chapter two themes are addressed. First, the recent policy context for small towns is presented, and this is followed by a consideration of the nature of citizen engagement in a market-town initiative that operated in Wales between 1996 and 1999. In both cases, policy addressing small towns and mobilising local citizen engagement at a community level precedes and overlaps with the current New Labour agenda. This allows some reflection on the challenges facing the current policy context in the light of the experience in comparable earlier initiatives. At the same time, this evidence raises critical issues regarding the aims of such strategic policy intervention and the instruments its employs; the rhetoric of citizen engagement and participatory development; and the established and emergent networks of power that are now being mobilised in a market-town context.

Small-town regeneration in practice

The academic neglect of small towns noted at the beginning of the chapter is all the more surprising given small towns' economic and social importance to almost a quarter of the country's population. They are home to some five million people, and act as economic and service centres for a further five million who live in surrounding rural areas (Action for Market Towns, 1999). In population terms, they have grown faster than any other type of area over much of the postwar period. Between 1961 and 1971, the population of towns in England and Wales of less than 50,000 people grew by 13%. Between 1971 and 1981, the growth was 5.5%. London and other metropolitan areas recorded massive population losses over the same period, while the population of larger towns and remaining rural areas grew far less rapidly (Coleman and Salt, 1992, p 104). These trends continued during the 1980s and 1990s (see Boyle and Halfacree, 1996). Between 1991 and 1997, an average of 90,000 people per year moved out of English conurbations to the countryside (Countryside Agency, 2001, p 26). Furthermore, between 1971 and 1996, the population of rural England grew by 24% compared with 6% across England as a whole (Cabinet Office, 2000, p 46), while rural Scotland witnessed a population gain of 3.5% between 1981 and 1991, although the Scottish population as a whole fell by 1.4% (Shucksmith, 2000, p 7).

However, in many ways the much-vaunted urban–rural shift in employment and people has actually amounted to a shift from metropolitan areas to small towns. Much of this population growth actually took place in and around small towns, where housing land was more plentiful, and planning permission more easily available, than in the surrounding countryside, and where services and retail opportunities were concentrated. Perhaps because of this growth and vibrancy, the academic neglect of small towns has been matched by policy neglect for much of the past 30 years. Regeneration initiatives in particular were either aimed at declining inner cities or at peripheral rural areas suffering from depopulation.

However, not all small towns participated in the population and employment boom. Indeed, the category of the 'small town' covers a wide variety of settlements, including traditional market towns, seaside resorts and fishing ports, as well as mining and manufacturing towns (Countryside Agency, 2002a, p 1). As might be expected, these towns have been subject to a plethora of social, cultural and economic changes, and many have suffered considerably from the decline of mining, agriculture, textiles and other industries. Recognition of this localised decline, in addition to an appreciation of the critical role of small towns in stimulating growth across a wider rural hinterland, has recently led to specific regeneration policies aimed at the small town. Critically, in the light of this volume, many of these initiatives place issues of community involvement and participation at their core.

Interestingly, Rural Challenge, one of the first schemes explicitly to require community involvement as part of the bidding process, was aimed at rural areas in general, yet small and market towns were the main beneficiaries. Rural Challenge was a regeneration initiative administered by the Rural Development Commission (RDC) between 1994 and 1998. The 31 County Rural Development Areas in England were split into two groups, which were then invited to bid in alternate annual rounds for six awards per year of up to £1million each. The 15 or 16 annual bids were submitted by partnerships in which, according to the bidding guidance, evidence of local consultation and involvement together with "the support of the local community is essential" (RDC, 1995, p 4). Each county selected its final bid from a number of shortlisted applicants, and the county winners were then submitted to a further competition to select the six annual winners. The scheme's emphasis on community involvement and competitive bidding thus mirrored the City Challenge initiative introduced to urban areas in 1991 by Michael Heseltine as Secretary of State for the Environment. Heseltine had purposefully decided on competitive bidding as the best means of translating John Major's notion of active citizenship into urban policy practice. As he put it, "men and women will compete with one another and give of their best" (Heseltine, cited in Atkinson and Moon, 1994, p 122).

The same principles underpinned the Rural Challenge scheme. However, far from giving equal opportunity to all rural areas, the winning projects that emerged from the two phases of competition were those that were largely centred in small and market towns (Jones and Little, 2000). Such towns could demonstrate the best chance of long-term success, having at least some concentration of private sector resources, a funding base for project continuation and a heritage of industrial infrastructure that was capable of physical redevelopment. What was trumpeted as a resource for all rural areas in effect became concentrated on a small number of market towns. The quality of their historic townscapes has meant that small towns have also benefited disproportionately from conservation-led regeneration schemes. English Heritage is spending some £18 million over four years from 1999, rescuing and reusing historic buildings, and the scheme is expected to lever in private funds of four or five times that amount.

As we noted in the introduction, contemporary policy on small-town regeneration was launched in the Rural White Paper (DETR and MAFF, 2000), and is jointly implemented through the RDAs' rural programme and the Countryside Agency's Market Towns Initiative (MTI). The MTI involves funding for a series of individual towns to undertake health checks allowing local people to identify the economic, environmental and social strengths and weaknesses of their town. The health check is designed to help people identify the impact of changing local circumstances and hence provide a sound basis for creating an action plan for economic and social revitalisation. Figure 9.1 sets out the claimed benefits of the health check, while Figure 9.2 summarises what can be achieved through community participation. As each of these shows, the emphasis has switched from the Conservative stress on the active citizen 'giving of their best' to compete with other places for scarce funds, to a

Figure 9.1: The benefits of Market Town Health Checks

Market Town Health Checks are:

- a way to bring residents of the town and the surrounding countryside together;
- an inclusive approach to regeneration that involves all ages and sections of the community;
- a tool for communities to understand their strengths and weaknesses, and devise a shared but achievable vision for regeneration and revitalisation;
- a way to set standards and learn from what is happening in other successful community development and regeneration projects;
- the use of practical action plans that direct resources and effort to achieving real improvements and projects;
- the use of robust action plans that have widespread community support are a key tool in securing funding and support from national, regional and local programmes for revitalising rural and urban communities;
- a properly researched action plan is influential in the decisions that public authorities have to make, for instance, in local plans, transport and health service investment programmes.

Source: Countryside Agency (2002b)

Figure 9.2 Community participation in Market Town Health Checks

What is it and what can be achieved?

- mutually supportive working links between different sections of the community, including businesses, service providers, voluntary groups, the public sector and the community at large;
- a shared vision of the future identity, function and quality of life in the town that meets the needs of its residents and the people it serves in the surrounding area;
- a means to unlock the ideas, resources and commitment that exist in all communities and to direct that to managing change and delivering that shared vision;
- a practical and democratic way to involve the community as widely as possible in the future of the town and its surrounding countryside;
- a means to devise and deliver an action plan and specific projects.

Source: Countryside Agency (2002b)

New Labour focus on inclusiveness, 'mutually supportive links' and 'shared visions'.

The Countryside Agency provides practical advice and support for those towns that wish to carry out a health check, and together with the RDAs provides funding to employ project officers. Support may be available to enable the implementation of the action plan. The focus of advice is on involving the community through a series of techniques (such as planning forums, community profiling, open house events and planning for real) that can be used by themselves or in combination to provide community consultation, participation and involvement that meets local circumstances. To participate in the scheme, towns needed to show that they have, or will have the potential to develop, the following characteristics:

- the ability to act as a focus for growth, relieving disadvantage and increasing economic opportunity;
- the ability to act as a service centre for a broad range of services, including public transport links to the surrounding rural areas;
- the ability of local partners to commit resources alongside the partnership programme;
- the capacity of the local community to form and sustain an effective partnership capable of delivering an action plan.

In addition to the health check scheme, some regions are using the RDAs to develop their own initiatives for small towns. For example, SWERDA has committed £30 million over five years to its Market and Coastal Towns Initiative. The initiative offers resources to local communities to:

- prepare or review a strategic 'Action Plan' covering social, economic, environmental and cultural themes in their towns;
- provide training and support to local people, organisations and agency partners to carry out this work;
- provide access to professional assistance at every stage;
- get projects in the plan to a 'funding ready' stage;
- fund 'early action' and 'priority' projects;
- identify and train local people as Community Agents to keep things moving;
- fund events that encourage networking and exchange skills.

In addition, the initiative promises to establish:

- local 'brokering tables' where agencies and other partners will coordinate their involvement;
- a Learning Network to fund supportive action/research projects, help networking and assist in the exchange of information and skills;
- a Management Group at a regional level to coordinate the involvement of agencies and maintain an overview across the region.

The most recent policy initiatives have two things in common: recognition of the economic and social importance of small towns, and a focus on community participation and engagement. Through them, small towns have been designated as key economic and social spaces for the mobilisation of the New Labour agenda on inclusive citizenship. It is too early to tell whether such designation will be successful, either politically or economically. However, this stress on community engagement in the small town is not entirely new, and the current proposals resonate strongly with the methodology adopted in rural Wales during the Market Town Initiative, which was first introduced in 1996. It is to this that we now turn, in order to examine some of the processes and mechanisms actually involved in establishing effective community participation. Through our empirical work on this scheme, we hope to shed some light on the political, social and cultural negotiations that lie behind the deceptively benign notion of inclusive community participation.

Participation and partnership working in 'market-town' regeneration in Wales

Policy in context

Given the failure of the central and local state to deliver adequate investment and development to all sections of society in all places, the past 10 years have seen a strong swing in both urban and rural settings towards encouraging local engagement of residents in the development process. The promotion of partnership working in rural policy has strongly emphasised the potential it offers as a mechanism for devolving decision making, assisting a transition from 'top-down' to 'bottom-up' planning in development and potentially 'governing through communities'.

As any historiography of participation in development practice is to a large extent both politically and place-specific, it is appropriate to position such practice in Wales prior to exploring our exemplars. From the late 1970s, through the 1980s and into the 1990s, regional investment and development in rural Wales focused primarily on rejuvenating market towns by means of:

- land accumulation and the development of new industrial sites;
- the encouragement of inward investment;
- the provision of business support with a strong emphasis on an assertive entrepreneurialism.

The impetus for these developments, encouraged by both the Development Board for Rural Wales and the Welsh Development Agency, built on traditional modernist assertions and subsequently reflected the conservative drive of the New Right.

Alongside these developments, the countryside at large saw the development of a strategy that adopted a principle of self-help and community action driven in the late 1980s and early 1990s by a growing emphasis on engagement by the 'active citizen'. Here, a neoliberal strategy encouraging the competitive engagement of committed individuals in self-help initiatives was further compounded by strong sentiments supporting a more egalitarian engagement in community activities and development. This trajectory for development received further support by the availability of European funding through two rounds of LEADER initiatives that not only prioritised involvement of citizens and community in the regeneration process, but also placed a key emphasis on the necessity to work in partnership with a range of other state, quango and third-sector bodies to deliver local outcomes. Consequently, what emerged in the countryside was a regeneration strategy with a community focus that integrated participatory engagement, social provision and economic regeneration through partnership working.

In a market-town context, such practices were less uniformly adopted. In the late 1980s and early 1990s, the Welsh Development Agency devised a series of experimental Rural Action Areas focused around specific market towns. The agency promoted in these the involvement of key local representatives in the regeneration process, but rarely extended such involvement to the wider community. In addition, one of the key strategic instruments in these areas driving the regeneration process was seen to be the promotion of partnership working. However, the extent to which such partnership working operated as an equal engagement between a representative range of partners is a moot point. Alongside these developments, the Development Board for Rural Wales was also increasingly using partnership rhetoric and beginning to argue for a more inclusive form of market-town development, other than through the top-down economic regeneration of such centres.

This brief historiography suggests that policy transfer between the centre, quango and local state, and their consequent emergent operational practice in rural and urban settings, was producing a climate and a policy emphasis that prefigured the New Labour agenda of the late 1990s, but was driven by different ideological presumptions. Initially, the shift towards both an individual and community emphasis might be evidenced as a 'rolling back of state engagement', alongside a shift of responsibility to locally active citizens. However, this was tightly controlled through sources of funding, strategic targeting of such funds, and the requirement of a partnership mode of working to produce checks and balances. But those citizens that were engaged in this process in an urban context from the late 1980s to mid-1990s were very much representatives of the traditional local governing elite – local politicians, businessmen, and established third-sector and voluntary leaders. Engagement with citizens was therefore selective and constituted a representative elite drawn from the multiple communities of interest present or at least those considered acceptable. Subsequently, post-1997, the relative success of these earlier strategies encouraged their continuation in the policies described above, but now founded around an ideology of inclusiveness and with a strong integrative community and implicitly communitarian focus.

The conjunction of this history of 'regimes of practice' in both rural and urban development settings, and in England as well as Wales, may do much to account for the production of a regeneration climate in which the transfer of strategies between rural and urban settings became more commonplace and which led in Wales to the Market Towns Initiative (MTI). The emergence of this strategy coincides with Rural Challenge in England and the formation of 'Action for Market Towns' and precedes the designation of market towns as key sites for the delivery of regeneration policy in the English Rural White Paper of November 2000. Consequently, the experience gained from an examination of this initiative can inform our understanding of the problems and potential inherent in the new Blairite agenda.

The adoption of a community focus and partnership mode of engagement was a key priority in the promotion of the market-town initiative across rural mid-Wales following the Rural White Paper, *A working countryside for Wales* (Welsh Office, 1996; see Figure 9.3). As the White Paper specified (Welsh Office, 1996, p 39), the initiative strategically selected market towns as key sites in order to reverse the decline of rural areas and stimulate regeneration. This strategy reflected past practices of both the Welsh Development Agency (with its town-focused Rural Action Areas) and that of the Development Board for Rural Wales, which had traditionally employed a graded hierarchy of market towns to deliver growth pole development across mid-Wales. At the same time, the policy ensured that regeneration would operate in partnership mode involving local communities, the development board, unitary authorities and local private interests to produce integrated local practice. Local engagement was required as community members were to be involved as members of the partnership boards, as well as in auditing local needs, in specifying the direction and intent of projects, and in developing action plans (Welsh Office, 1996, p 39), thus drawing on local social capital and self-determination to build and develop local capacities. The MTI offered a competitive partnership programme aimed at stimulating and supporting community development in small towns across rural Wales (see Figure 9.4). Grants of £90,000 of revenue funding over three years were awarded to 10 initiatives in two rounds of awards.

Figure 9.3: Publicity for the Development Board for Rural Wales' Market Town Initiative, emphasising the rural setting of small towns

Figure 9.4: Promoting small towns in rural mid-Wales

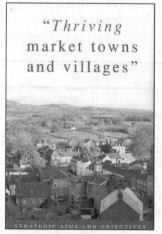

Source: Powys County Council promotional leaflet

Source: Development Board for Rural Wales (1995)

Figure 9.5 reveals the focus of partnership working that developed in the successful market towns in rural mid–Wales[3]. Considerable emphasis is given throughout the MTI to:

- the regeneration of the economy in general rather than specific terms (although tourism plays a central part);
- the promotion of place and the refurbishment of facilities;
- engaging by implication the *whole* community in this process.

The strategy was therefore both developmental and empowering, highlighting in the process the collective engagement and local specification of priorities by residents as central to the process.

Successful engagement with the community varied considerably from scheme to scheme. Any review of these early attempts to encourage the engagement of residents in market towns in their own development raises three key questions that are equally relevant to the more recent New Labour agenda:

1. To what extent is greater participatory involvement a strategic policy priority constructed through the instrument of partnership working with the aim of governing through communities (Rose, 1996a, 1996b; Murdoch, 1997)?

Figure 9.5: Aims of market-town regeneration partnerships in mid-Wales

In order that local development priorities are met, market-town partnership working needs

- to develop a year-round economy, recreational facilities for all and the restoration of the natural and built environment, and to *build a consensus in the community*;
- to market the town, develop an exhibition and undertake an environmental survey; to encourage community activity to achieve the overall aims of ... 2000 and to improve the economic, cultural and social structure of the town by *focusing community energy* through promotion and local development;
- to create a *stronger sense of community*; to establish what people want; to maximise local influence in the distribution of aid and funding; to work in partnership and to develop the results of consultation with a particular emphasis on development linked to the cultural identity of the area;
- to improve facilities and the quality of life in the area;
- to promote green/sustainable tourism and encourage low-impact economic development *through community effort* (such as heritage trails, game fishing, kite sanctuary and *youth groups*);
- to research and initiate projects aimed at regenerating the local economy (traffic and pedestrian management, business and commerce, tourism and amenity, civic pride and environmental improvement, *youth projects*); to renovate the medieval town core; to regenerate the local produce and livestock market);
- to encourage *local community development* through enhancing cultural and community spirit and promoting sustainable social and economic development (building refurbishment, street enhancements, *established a community and family resource centre and a youth centre* organised a local festival to promote river tourism).

Source: Documentation provided by MTI projects

2. When regeneration monies are available, do market towns successfully construct partnership bodies reflecting multiple communities of interest?
3. To what extent and through what means is the 'whole' place-based community drawn into the regeneration process?

We have recently undertaken work that provides important insights into each of these questions[4].

Partnership working as a policy priority

In the promotion and guidelines for the MTI, it is quite clear that greater participatory engagement together with the opportunity to re-establish a more socially inclusive approach was central to the project. This point was emphasised by the scheme's coordinators, the Development Board for Rural Wales. It saw the initiative as an opportunity to formalise once again its relationship with communities and localities after a period of Conservative rule, which had emphasised centralised economic strategy rather than a 'bottom-up' engagement with local regeneration. In addition, the guidelines for the bidding process identified the importance of a partnership mode of working as a strategic priority and the key instrument through which schemes must be delivered. As an interviewee said:

> "We were looking for partnership, and we were looking for a demonstration that the town council were involved, that the business sector were involved, that the Chamber of Commerce were involved, and that the voluntary sector were involved.... All of this obviously strengthened an application if the application was seen as a partnership effort." (MTI coordinator)

Indeed, certain bids were rejected in the first round of application because they came from single-interest groups within the towns. In addition, the demonstration of wider community involvement was critical to success:

> "We were ... looking for communities that could persuade us that they were working together and that their projects were achievable and realistic. We were also looking for communities that recognised the need of their community and whether they had undertaken an audit, or whether they had undertaken some kind of informal consultation." (MTI coordinator)

What is clear from both of these interviews is the strong emphasis placed by policy makers on partnership and community engagement as the mechanism and the process, respectively, through which citizen involvement is to be achieved. Here the emphasis on joined-up practice and local empowerment as necessary prerequisites for providing access to funding streams, together with the resultant audit trail that receipt of such funds requires, made this strategic partnership mode of development an appropriate technique of post-Thatcherite governmentality and one of the key instruments through which local engagement and citizen empowerment was to be achieved.

Constructing local partnerships and recruiting members

The rhetoric of governance makes much of the inclusiveness of the partnership mode of working. However, empirical evidence suggests this is not always recognised by participants (Edwards et al, 2001). The notion of 'community' itself is widely recognised as problematic, as is the claim that one unified community can be easily or adequately represented. Even more questions are raised when multiple communities of interest exist: who is enrolled? What constituencies are served? And who is empowered as a result of the partnership process – the 'whole' community or the established elite?

Such prioritisation of both the mode of partnership working and the emphasis on community participation reflects the contemporary regeneration climate. The literature of community development argues strongly for increased public participation in community development from the 'bottom up', so that the complete range of needs that occurs in such settings can be addressed (Community Development Foundation, 1995; Taylor, 1995, 1997, 2000b). Such involvement, it is argued, improves the definition of local needs, mobilises local initiatives and draws on local capacities to act that will compensate for the failure of the centre. From the process of participation and mobilisation comes ownership of initiatives, empowerment and a heightened 'capacity to act' for all groups, which in turn makes the regeneration process increasingly emancipating. However, it has to be added that the centre has all too often contrived the opening of this route, and specified parameters for local engagement, as is apparent in the MTI.

Much of this thinking is drawn from community development literature of the late 1960s. Around this time, Arnstein developed the 'ladder' of citizen participation, which involved a "redistribution of power that enables the have-not citizens, presently excluded from political and economic processes, to be deliberately included in the future" (Arnstein, 1969, p 216). Burns et al (1994) have subsequently refined Arnstein's ladder, arguing that citizens may enjoy different degrees of participation in different areas of social and community decision making. However, it is worth emphasising here that *partnership practice* is considered an advanced contribution in the facilitation of greater democracy and citizen empowerment. But, there is also a need at the local scale to address a number of key issues in understanding this process of empowerment (Atkinson and Cope, 1997), namely the constitution of the community, the weight attached to different views from the community, and the power relations between the state and its public in the process (Atkinson and Cope, 1997, p 207). At the local level, these sites of regeneration represent both a real and imaginary 'place-based' community. But they also contain within them a multitude of different interest groups and circumstances and hence diverse "communities of interest"

(Burns et al, 1994, p 227), not all of whom will be incorporated into the partnership process.

When one examines the successful MTI bids, a range of different strategies for constructing a body of stakeholders becomes apparent. On all such partnerships, the funding agency was represented and representatives were drawn from a selection of local organisations, together with elected representatives from town and community councils. However, how those representatives were recruited varied, and consequently the coalitions of interest constructed and the forms of community represented also varied quite considerably.

It is apparent from exploring the initiation and construction of both unsuccessful and successful bids that various strategies were mobilised to construct local partnerships (Edwards et al, 2000). In some cases, a genuine range of community organisations was recruited through local contacts and public meetings to ensure that a comprehensive group of stakeholders was included. In other cases, response to the MTI was led by the town council, which then sought selectively to enrol others. However, the enrolment of local councils and councillors as 'community representatives' on partnerships raises questions about who they actually represent. This is especially problematic in areas where there is a strong tradition of non-party local politics and where many councillors are elected unopposed. Furthermore, councillors may not always be willing participants in partnerships. A number of community-scale partnerships in the study region had experienced frosty relations with the local county councillor or the local town, parish or community council, because the councillors feared that their role or authority was being challenged by the new partnership.

Elsewhere, local organisations, on occasion mobilised in opposition to the local council, became the driving force. In some places, on the other hand, 'concerned and independent individuals' became the core group who led the discussion and bidding process. Depending on the route adopted, the coalitions of local people varied in the constituencies they represented and often had to wear many hats as a result of the breadth and depth of their participation in local activities. In most contexts, however, those who were mobilised were constituted from the established elite of 'active citizenry', rather than selected as elected or nominated representatives of community organisations.

What becomes apparent, however, is that the balance of the members and the extent to which different 'communities of interest' are represented, each with their own particular constituencies, raises critical questions about the inclusiveness of the partnerships that have been constructed. Often, participation by such stakeholders may only be for specific projects where particular expertise or organisation engagement is required. Such partial engagement, frequently through subgroups of the main committee, limits the numbers involved in collective ownership of the whole regeneration programme. In assessing these ventures into 'citizen empowerment' and 'collaborative working', the disentangling of internal community power relations (that is, who is represented and who has no voice) is essential to understanding community participation.

Understanding this may allow more reflection on the possibly exclusionary nature of partnership working. Our research indicates that the conflation of the partnership mode of governance with community participation and empowerment needs, therefore, to be more directly problematised.

This is well illustrated by one instance of a failed bid for MTI funding that was subsequently reconfigured and successful. Its success, however, was the result of a rather exclusive form of representation. Initially, a submission was made primarily from the relevant town council supported by a local chapel lobby. It was rejected, in part on the grounds of its lack of inclusiveness. After a subsequent public meeting, a wider, more representative partnership grouping was constructed that mobilised a range of local organisations, business and private interests together with principal and local councillors to join in the submission. As the chair of the meeting noted:

> "What we did was to invite people to sit on [the steering group] from various organisations. But rather than inviting the organisations to send somebody, we instead almost 'cherry-picked' from the organisations who we wanted in order to make sure that we could get people working together."

These elite actors included those with a whole range of specialist skills and established interest allegiances. Consequently, the partnership process was deliberately injected with profession expertise, rather than being allowed to engage a group of stakeholders typical of the residential, place-based community. Consequently, rather than opening doors to the community as a whole, it created opportunities for local and non-local experts to exert disproportionate influence.

Much of the rhetoric surrounding partnership development implies that this kind of thing does not happen. It suggests that these initiatives are seen as opportunities for residents spontaneously and willingly to engage with the regeneration process. It stresses the opportunity this strategy provides for drawing together different interest groups to address problems. In combination, it is argued, the blending of the public, private, voluntary and community sectors will produce more effective and representative policy, create synergy, and strengthen collective capacities to act. In building partnerships, it is further suggested that there should be appropriate representation by gender and social background. Consequently, surrounding partnerships is the presumption that they will be inclusive, incorporate all sectors and interest groups and blend such agents into an effective planning and delivery unit. Often, however, encouraging participation is problematic, and engaging the most effective partners involves a set of tactical decisions that coordinates the contribution that can be made by elite members at the expense of the contribution that community participation implies might come from local residents.

Engaging the community

Having noted what we have just said, once leadership was established, all of the MTI bids did involve as a formal requirement engagement with the broader community they were intended to serve. However, such engagement varied. At a limited level, we found that most partnerships were engaged in some form of *wider community consultation*, particularly on identifying needs (effectively undertaking a health check), finding solutions, and, to a lesser degree, reviewing partnership action (Figure 9.6). All small-town partnerships recognised identifying local needs as a key role of consultation, and most engaged the community in finding or identifying solutions and participating in projects. A lower priority was given to community consultation as feedback on partnership activity or to providing or exchanging information. Figure 9.7 indicates that local liaison often involved consultation with community representatives – local councillors, 'key individuals' or other community groups – rather than with the community at large. Small-town partnerships more commonly liaised with the local community through public meetings, although some partnerships employed newsletters, notice boards, or 'planning for real' and 'community appraisal' exercises, as well as publicity in the local media. Partnerships operating at this scale inevitably engage with the community rather more than other more territorial extensive partnerships, but the rank order of the relative engagement with each activity is highly comparable in both figures.

What our findings have shown, then, is that the employment of more direct

Figure 9.6: Priority given by market-town partnerships to community engagement (by task), compared with all other partnerships in mid-Wales (%)

	Very important		Reasonably important		Not important	
	Small-town partnerships	*All other partnerships*	*Small-town partnerships*	*All other partnerships*	*Small-town partnerships*	*All other partnerships*
Identification of local needs	100	76	0	20	0	4
Finding solutions to local needs	88	68	13	20	0	12
Involvement in projects	88	60	13	20	0	20
Feedback on partnership action	63	40	26	44	0	24
Provision and exchange of information	38	44	63	36	0	24

Source: 'Community action, partnerships and emergent forms of governance in rural Wales and the borders', Joseph Rowntree Foundation Project 1998-2000 (Bill Edwards, Mark Goodwin, Simon Pemberton and Michael Woods)

Figure 9.7: Methods adopted to liaise with the local community by small-town partnerships compared with all other partnerships (%)

	Small-town partnerships	All other partnerships
Public meetings	100	44
Liaison with local councillors	75	32
Liaison with other key individuals	75	64
Liaison with community groups	75	56
Through local media	75	4
Newsletter	38	4
Flyers	13	0
Noticeboard	13	0
Postal survey	13	0
'Planning for real' exercise	13	0
No liaison with local community	0	8

Source: 'Community action, partnerships and emergent forms of governance in rural Wales and the borders', Joseph Rowntree Foundation Project 1998-2000 (Bill Edwards, Mark Goodwin, Simon Pemberton and Michael Woods)

forms of community engagement does not necessarily mean that the views received will be any more representative of the population as a whole. The turnout at public meetings tends to be low, often attracting a relatively small group of people who are known to be active in the community:

"What you tend to find then of course is that it is the same faces that attend.... You see the same people who sometimes wear a different 'hat', but essentially there are the same people there. So there is a 'clique' – I suppose this is an unfair word – but there is a section of the community which is well geared up, and which is on everybody's invitation list." (Partner representative)

The true value of forms of direct community engagement (such as public meetings), therefore, may not be in the compilation of a 'community viewpoint', but rather in the identification and mobilisation of a core of active volunteers willing to work for partnership in a community. Proactive involvement in partnership activity by communities and community organisations does vary and is very dependent on the character of local residents and the resources, both individual and collective, they can mobilise. Previous experience of working in and with partnerships is also significant in raising the willingness and capacity of market towns to become engaged with new partnerships. Alongside this, two factors appear to restrict the extent of community engagement:

1. In most circumstances, the partnership process is seen as being too formal and bureaucratic – community groups seeking to form partnerships or apply for grants are put off by the paperwork involved.
2. Untrained community representatives invariably find it difficult to contribute equally with public sector representatives in partnership meetings. This inhibits full participation.

Certainly, effective community engagement can help to enhance the perceived legitimacy of partnerships. But what emerges from our evidence is that community participation and engagement are not always as emancipating as one might suppose. Indeed, the whole consultative process that is involved at this scale might work to exclude those with greatest need as they do not necessarily find it easy to participate in the process.

Conclusions

This chapter charted the growing importance of small towns as a tier in an urban hierarchy that is receiving increasing policy attention. Small market towns have seen considerable change within the past 30 years. Most have experienced significant recomposition during this period as a result of demographic forces. For some, this has involved considerable growth, while for others, marginalisation and decay. Opportunities for change have been encouraged through policies providing funding initiatives that are competitively structured, most recently through the local health checks that build on a culture of audit, and through the presumption that local stakeholders should engage in partnership working to produce joined-up strategies for future development. As we have set out, notions of participation and engagement at community level underpin these policies. As we have also noted, such engagement in practice is difficult to mobilise and tends to be limited, in the words of one of our respondents, to "the same people ... on everybody's invitation list". This raises several issues that take us beyond the sphere of the small town into broader concerns about power, engagement and the rhetoric of inclusiveness.

Our Welsh evidence suggests that mobilising communities to produce a health check and to identify local needs is relatively easily achieved. However, the marshalling of such local activity is frequently and all too strongly guided by the strategic framework that the centre lays down, and is carried out through mechanisms that are also centrally specified. Power to engage with such activities depends in part on existing capacities to act, which are driven all too often by established, elite members of communities. Such individuals are in possession of important social networks that allow existing social capital to be mobilised and directed to facilitate these activities. In certain other instances, local development workers do encourage and support the recognition that latent social capital is present, which can be mobilised through engaging non-elite participants, but this tends to occur less frequently. Ironically, the success of attracting and using regeneration monies in many market towns depends less the development workers and the local political elite. In this sense, the key role of particular elite agents in the regeneration process highlights the difficulty of generating a more collective engagement that is capable of involving the wider community and delivering the rhetoric of New Labour collective empowerment.

When we examine these concerns, it does not appear to be any easier to mobilise community participation at the scale of the small town than in larger urban counterparts. Indeed, it may well be more difficult to meet the challenges of genuine inclusiveness given the multiple communities that exist in most small towns, than it is in urban neighbourhoods of similar population size, where the social mix may be more homogeneous. In this sense, the label of the small town becomes a convenient mask for a range of social, economic and cultural divisions that act to prevent the participation of more than a small element of the 'entire community'. Indeed, our research has even uncovered divisions between those members of local elites who were normally involved in governing such towns, especially when locally elected representatives perceived appointed partnership members as a threat to their established authority. In this case, scale can work to prevent – rather than increase – inclusiveness.

This problem becomes compounded when we consider the twin issues of governance and territory. As we noted earlier in this chapter, small towns are now discursively constructed in policy realms as the nodal points for regeneration strategies that may be expected to embrace surrounding rural areas. Yet very few partnerships or other governance structures operate across this larger territorial area. This immediately raises a disjunction between economic strategy and political representation. The territorial form of governance does not match the anticipated spatial impact of the regeneration policies that threatens to lead to a 'democratic deficit' for some of those involved. These are all issues that are likely to remain the concern of the immediate future. Indeed, given the policy focus of both the Countryside Agency and the RDAs, which concentrate rural funding and regeneration strategies on small towns, they are likely to assume a greater importance, both for public policy and for academic work on community engagement and participation.

Notes

[1] These discourses are not particular to Britain, but also form a core element in the American small-town idyll. See Mattson (1997) and Woods (2003: forthcoming).

[2] The figures presented in this chapter, including those relating to Lottery funding and to town and parish council elections, are derived from the ESRC-funded project, 'Participation, power and rural community governance in England and Wales', which involved the work of Bill Edwards, Michael Woods, Jon Anderson, Graham Gardner and Eldin Fahmy (see Edwards et al, 2002).

[3] The MTI-funded projects in Abercraf, Blaenau Ffestiniog, Cardigan, Dolgellau, Hay-on-Wye, Llanfair Caereinion, Llanidloes, Penrhyndeudraeth, Rhayader and Tregaron.

[4] Our case study of the Development Board for Rural Wales MTI and other material on partnership working are derived from a project funded by the Joseph Rowntree Foundation entitled 'Community action, partnerships and emergent forms of governance in rural Wales and the borders'. This project was undertaken between 1998 and 2000 by Bill Edwards, Mark Goodwin, Simon Pemberton and Michael Woods.

Further reading

For an empirical study of community engagement in small towns prior to the New Labour phase of policy, see Edwards (1997). For further details on the empirical examples used in this chapter, see Edwards et al (2000). Jones and Little (2000) explore the development and introduction of the Rural Challenge initiative. For research that provides a broader context for an understanding of contemporary rural politics, see Woods (2003: forthcoming).

TEN

Economy, equity or empowerment? New Labour, communities and urban policy evaluation

Stuart Wilks-Heeg

Introduction

You would be forgiven, reader, for approaching a chapter on policy evaluation with feelings of intense indifference. Policy evaluation may well suggest a purely bureaucratic or technical exercise, of interest only to those obsessed with the minutiae of policy design, research methodology and data collection. Such perceptions are undoubtedly underpinned by much of the literature on evaluation, which has tended to focus largely on technical issues such as measuring the net impact of policy intervention and of demonstrating causal links between policy change and policy outcomes. At the same time, however, a growing number of authors have emphasised the deeply political nature of policy evaluation and, in the specific context of urban policy, have shown how evaluators play a central role in what is invariably a highly contested policy context (Turok, 1991; Townley and Wilks-Heeg, 1999). Here, it has been argued that evaluation provides a focal point for competing visions of urban policy and that it is inextricably bound up with wider ideologies of urban policy intervention. Far from acting as detached and objective observers, evaluators may implicitly reinforce, subtly redefine, or, much more rarely, explicitly challenge the key ideological assumptions on which urban policy initiatives are founded.

Seen in this way, evaluation constitutes a critical issue in relation to the emerging discourses of community involvement in urban policy. The stress that New Labour has placed on the need for community leadership at all stages of the urban policy process has increasingly prompted observers to raise fundamental questions about the character and role of evaluation (see NCVO, 2000; Slowey et al, 2001; Sullivan and Potter, 2001). Do conventional evaluation approaches alienate local communities, rather than promote their involvement? If so, how can evaluation methodologies promote community involvement in line with wider policy objectives? Should community ownership of urban policy extend to evaluation? In other words, contemporary evaluation practice constitutes a key test of the extent to which governments are committed to community leadership in urban policy. It is with this issue of the relationship between the politics of policy evaluation and the role of local communities in urban policy that this chapter is concerned.

The chapter is presented in four main sections. In order to place subsequent discussion of current evaluation practices in context, the first section briefly outlines and assesses conventional models of urban policy evaluation. It is argued that the assumptions that underpin these models are deeply flawed and that the character of evaluation studies is very much shaped by the prevailing political and ideological context. This was particularly evident during the 1980s, when urban policy evaluation tended to define economy as the key criterion of success and eschewed any consideration of community impact. However, it is also suggested, somewhat ironically, that the ineffectiveness of urban policy has had the indirect effect of enhancing the role of local communities in urban policy. The second section turns directly to consider urban policy evaluation under New Labour, focusing particularly on the extent to which evaluation approaches have embraced wider concerns to promote community leadership in urban policy. It critically examines recent attempts to foster direct community involvement in the evaluation process, noting that the commitment to community-led regeneration does not yet appear to extend as far as allowing communities to take the lead in the contested politics of policy evaluation.

The third section argues that this failure to engage communities in the evaluation process represents a significant Achilles heel for contemporary urban policy, and that current approaches flatly contradict the apparent objective of promoting community leadership. While pluralist evaluation approaches advocate that local community perspectives are considered alongside those of other agencies involved in the urban policy process, it is argued that they fail to consider prevailing inequalities of power. Rather than placing communities on a more equal footing, pluralist evaluation tend to operate as part of a wider attempt to co-opt communities to predetermined policy agendas and assumptions. Given these arguments, the final section briefly explores alternative evaluation philosophies that have emerged particularly in the US and considers the case for their adoption in the British urban policy context. It is suggested that, although notions of empowerment deployed by such approaches may superficially suggest potential to promote community leadership in urban policy evaluation, the tendency to work towards the generation of consensual outcomes acts as a form of closure, preventing the emergence of more radical, community-led assessment of policy.

Urban policy evaluation

The theory and practice of urban policy evaluation have received detailed attention in recent years (Turok, 1991; Hambleton and Thomas, 1995; Imrie,

1996b; Ho, 1999; Murtagh, 2001). While this literature is in part a reflection of the growing importance of evaluation in public policy generally, it is evident that evaluation plays a particularly critical role in urban policy. As Turok (1991) notes, there is unevenness in the extent to which public policies are evaluated, with urban and regional policies being subjected to much closer scrutiny than larger and more expensive programmes. Indeed, every major urban policy initiative since the mid-1980s has been the subject of a major national evaluation, with several initiatives being subject to multiple evaluations. These studies have included, inter alia:

- the evaluations of enterprise zones (PA Cambridge Economic Consultants, 1987, 1995);
- urban development grants (PSMRU, 1988);
- garden festivals (PA Cambridge Economic Consultants, 1990);
- inner-city task forces (PA Cambridge Economic Consultants, 1991);
- the Action for Cities programme (Robson et al, 1994);
- Urban Development Corporations (Roger Tym and Partners, 1998; Robson et al, 2000);
- the City Challenge (Russell et al, 1996; KPMG, 1998);
- the Single Regeneration Budget (Brennan et al, 1998).

In addition, independent local evaluation of urban policy programmes has been mandatory for initiatives such as City Challenge and New Deal for Communities (NDC). City Challenge alone led to the production of multiple evaluation reports for each of the 33 localities that received funding.

Conventional models portray such evaluation activity as part of a rational model of public policy making. In conventional models, the purpose of evaluation is to assess the success or failure of a policy against its original objectives and to "provide policy-makers with information which will enable them to improve on existing policies" (Doig, 1992, p 3). In order for evaluation to inform policy in this way, two key assumptions are made. First, evaluation is regarded as a technical exercise, concerned with establishing hard facts and therefore providing an objective assessment of policy, free from more narrowly political concerns. Unsurprisingly, this first assumption's evaluation methodology is strongly biased towards a preference for quantitative techniques. Second, evaluation is assumed to contribute to a wider process of informed policy making and to constitute "a discrete stage in a rational policy-making cycle" (Turok, 1991, p 1544). Typically, evaluation takes place after a policy has been implemented, and the results of the evaluation are used to inform subsequent reappraisal of policy options. As one British government report puts it, evaluation is "part of a cyclical process of appraisal, policy-making, implementation, monitoring, evaluation and re-appraisal" (Doig, 1992, p 3; HM Treasury, 1988).

However, these assumptions are rarely born out by actual experience of the role of evaluation in the policy process. Two key criticisms of the conventional model are generally advanced. First, the notion of evaluation as rational, objective and value-neutral bears little relationship to the real world of evaluation practice. In actual fact, evaluation studies tend to mirror the political character of the initiatives they are designed to assess. As Berk and Rossi (1990) suggest, the content of an evaluation is almost entirely determined by the prevailing 'policy space'. As a result, approaches to policy evaluation are critically shaped by the prevailing ideologies present in public policy discourses. In this regard, it is particularly important to note that the approaches to urban policy evaluation that first emerged in Britain during the 1980s drew heavily on the frameworks associated with the New Public Management (Sullivan and Potter, 2001). The influence of Monetarist economics and Public Choice theory on the policies of the Thatcher governments were not only reflected in policies aimed at achieving reductions in state expenditure and enhancing the 'productivity' of public service; they also significantly informed evaluation methodology. As a result, evaluation studies during this period were almost solely concerned with the three Es: economy, efficiency and effectiveness. In urban policy, this meant that most initiatives were assessed primarily in terms of the net costs of the outputs achieved. Indeed, as Deakin and Edwards (1993) note, in some instances cost-per-job figures provided the sole basis for determining the success or failure of urban policy. In other words, urban policy evaluation was narrowly "based on an ideology of value for money" (Ho, 1999, p 423). Given this context, analysis of the relationship between urban policy intervention and local communities was entirely absent from evaluation studies in the 1980s.

Second, despite the logical appeal of conventional models of the policy process, where evaluation findings feed directly into rational policy change, the relationship between policy and evaluation is, in reality, far more complex. Political and ideological considerations play a major role in determining the purpose to which evaluation is put. Policy makers respond selectively to evaluation findings and, when reappraising policy options, will have a predilection towards studies that are compatible with dominant policy discourses, while disregarding conclusions that challenge such thinking (Turok, 1991). In some cases, policy makers do not even wait for the results of an evaluation before embarking on policy change. As Ho (1999) has pointed out, the decisions to replace the Urban Programme with City Challenge in 1991 and City Challenge with the Single Regeneration Budget in 1994 were both made a full two years before the respective interim national evaluations of the outgoing initiatives were published. Policy change frequently appears to stem as much from short-term political considerations as it does from the systematic review of evaluation evidence.

Ironically, it is precisely because of the political issues at stake in urban policy evaluation that communities have been propelled to centre-stage in urban policy discourse. The stubborn persistence of concentrated urban deprivation has meant that urban policy has acquired a symbolic importance: governments must be seen to be addressing the problem, even though all evidence suggests that urban policies actually have very limited impact (Wilks-Heeg, 1996). This political context creates something of a conundrum for urban policy evaluation, which must recognise the limited success of policies when measured against their initial objectives while also providing a justification for the continuation of such initiatives. Since the mid-1990s, the favoured way of squaring this circle has been to argue that relative improvement has taken place, while arguing for a progressive strengthening of community involvement in urban policy.

The evaluation of the Action for Cities programme was pivotal in making this shift (Robson et al, 1994). Although based primarily upon conventional quantitative modelling of the relationship between urban policy spending and measurable outcomes, the Robson report augmented this statistical analysis with surveys of inner-city residents and local employers and interviews with policy practitioners. Among its detailed findings, which pointed overwhelmingly to the failure of urban policy, the report noted the loyalty of inner-city residents to their neighbourhoods, and argued that this loyalty constituted the basis for community involvement in urban policy. These points were reinforced by the report's concluding policy recommendations, which stressed that local communities should play a key role in reconfiguring urban policy around a longer-term partnership approach. Although these issues were not to feature significantly in the national debate that the Robson report triggered, hindsight enables us to see that the Action for Cities evaluation played a highly significant role in bringing the notion of community involvement to the heart of national urban policy discourse.

Indeed, the pivotal role of the Robson report in respect of community involvement in urban policy is underlined by the concern accorded to local communities in subsequent national evaluations. The interim national evaluation of City Challenge (Russell et al, 1996) highlighted the value of the initiative's emphasis on community involvement and stressed the need for ongoing capacity building to ensure that the benefits of active community participation were achieved. By the time of the final national evaluation of City Challenge, the virtues of community involvement were being defined as fundamental to the success of urban policy. Poor partnership performance in City Challenge was linked to the failure to engage local communities; KPMG (1998) re-emphasised the need to enhance the capacity of local residents to engage fully in the regeneration process. In each case, the evidence produced to support such conclusions was scant, but the recommendations were seized upon by the government in need of justification for continued small-area urban policy intervention. With evaluation studies defining community involvement as a necessary condition for policy success, a Department of the Environment report (DoE, 1997) concluded that engaging local communities in regeneration programmes encouraged better decision making, prompted more effective programme delivery, and served to sustain the benefits of regeneration activity. The ground had been laid for New Labour's turn to community in urban policy.

Urban policy evaluation and New Labour: empowering communities?

Since the election of the Labour government in 1997, the ideological assumptions underpinning urban policy have been more eclectic than under the Conservative Party, but have been no less significant in shaping both policy objectives and evaluation approaches (see also Chapter One of this volume). Of key importance is the emphasis on community leadership, capacity building and social capital in New Labour's urban policy, reflecting the influence of communitarian and 'self-help'. These ideas are nowhere better captured than in the Prime Minister's belief that success in urban policy "depends on communities themselves having the power and taking the responsibility to make things better" (Tony Blair, Foreword in SEU, 1998, p 7). It would seem, however, that the process of the state encouraging residents of deprived communities to improve their own lot also requires the state to take a tough stance against 'deviant' members of the very same communities. In particular, the stress that New Labour has placed upon tackling problems such as 'worklessness', vandalism and drug dealing underline the authoritarian role of the 'disciplinary state' in Blairite policy discourse (Jones and Novak, 1999). Nonetheless, with notions of community informing a range of new urban policy initiatives, it is apposite to ask what implications they have for urban policy evaluation. Is community-led regeneration under New Labour also giving rise to community-evaluated regeneration? Does the Prime Minister's belief that success in urban policy depends on communities having power and responsibility extend to local residents having the power to determine what is meant by success and the responsibility for assessing whether it is being achieved?

The extent to which evaluations engage with local communities is largely premised on the degree to which urban policies define community as a relevant concern. During the 1980s, local communities were, at best, included as an afterthought in the design of urban policy initiatives and were similarly absent from evaluation criteria. However, as a result of the 'turn to community' in urban policy, evaluators have been increasingly compelled to engage with community concerns. Consequently, evaluators have played a significant role – sometimes consciously, but more often unwittingly – in representing local communities. The growing emphasis on community involvement in urban policy, therefore, has significant theoretical and methodological implications for approaches to evaluation. As Sullivan and Potter argue, the new focus on community in urban policy "requires the adaptation of community capacity building programmes to incorporate an awareness and understanding of ways in which to evaluate regeneration activity" (2001, p 20).

However, despite the increased emphasis on community, the assumptions that underpinned the emergence of conventional evaluation approaches under the Conservative government have also strongly coloured New Labour policy discourse. In its approach to evaluation, the Labour administration places consistent emphasis on concepts such as 'evidence-based policy' and 'what matters is what works'. These principles permeate almost all New Labour discourse on policy evaluation and are flagged as a central justification for the national evaluation of the NDC. Thus, it is suggested that the NDC "offers a unique opportunity to learn lessons about what works (and what doesn't) in neighbourhood renewal", and that the national evaluation will serve to "put together a valuable evidence base to inform effective policies for neighbourhood renewal" (Neighbourhood Renewal Unit, 2002, p 16).

In line with the conventional model of evaluation discussed earlier in this chapter, these concepts clearly evoke the notion of policy evaluation providing objective evidence on the basis of which policy can be determined rationally. Moreover, the sheer scale of the evaluation, which is being undertaken by a team drawn from 17 universities and consultancies, working to a budget of £15+ million, indicates the degree of New Labour's investment in conventional, top-down evaluation models. Urban policy evaluation on this scale is unprecedented and, unsurprisingly, the national evaluation of NDC has attracted considerable criticism from local communities. The Bishop of Liverpool and chair of the Kensington NDC, the Right Reverend James Jones, reports that locally the initiative has been dubbed 'New Deal for Consultants' (Jones, 2001).

While conventional approaches continue to dominate, there has been a degree of departure from previous evaluation practice. Prior to New Labour coming to power, urban policy evaluations had rarely included any real consideration of community impact, or limited such consideration to the most easily quantifiable types of general social change, typically rates of unemployment in the locality. Since 1997, there has certainly been an increased emphasis on urban policy evaluation taking some account of community perspectives, reflecting New Labour's wider drive to encourage policy makers to consult local communities at all stages of the policy process. The character of this commitment to community consultation is again evident in the NDC evaluation. Thus, the evaluation is characterised as an action–research approach that "will engage fully with partnerships, communities and the government offices" (DETR, 2000a, p 15). The role of local evaluations in examining the dynamics of partnership working and assessing the extent to which the community is fully engaged in the regeneration process is also underlined in this same document. However, this apparent preference for more pluralist forms of evaluation in urban policy does not appear to have translated into any real departure from the key assumptions of conventional evaluation approaches. In particular, consulting local communities alongside other stakeholders remains a far cry from community involvement or leadership of evaluation.

It is important to ask, therefore, whether or not the case is being made for urban policy evaluations to become integral to the wider objective of community leadership in urban policy. There is certainly no indication within the government's NDC guidance that community leadership should extend to the community undertaking evaluation activity. Instead, the emphasis is placed on commissioning independent evaluations that are consistent with Treasury guidelines and that "explore key issues such as what changes have occurred, how far this is attributable to NDC activity ... and the overall cost effectiveness of projects and the scheme as a whole" (DETR, 2000a, p 14). A separate document for NDC partnerships, *New Deal for Communities: Gathering baseline information* (DETR, 2000c) goes no further than discussing the pros and cons of using local residents to undertake surveys, and concentrates overwhelmingly on explaining the basic techniques in drawing up a set of impact indicators. The list of suggested indicators supplied in the annex of the same document concentrates overwhelmingly on designing indicators using quantitative data drawn from official statistical sources. There is no discussion whatsoever of alternative, community-based forms of evaluation. The evaluation priorities outlined in these documents would appear to confirm the conclusion reached by Atkinson (1999a); that is, community involvement in urban policy has largely been promoted as a means of ensuring the effectiveness of regeneration initiatives, rather than as a democratic right of local communities to determine the nature of change in their locality.

Unsurprisingly, a number of commentators have highlighted the limited attention given to the role of local communities in the government's approach to urban policy evaluation. Dissatisfaction with such approaches is highlighted by the National Council for Voluntary Organisations (NCVO), which notes that "a number of NDC areas have recognised that the (evaluation) process ... can either be an empowering or alienating experience for the local community" (NCVO, 2000, p 25). Here, there is an explicit recognition that while evaluation can play a key role in supporting community-led regeneration, it must also be recognised that "it has the potential to reinforce existing 'top-down' approaches if attention is not paid to how to evaluate progress from local people's perspectives" (NCVO, 2000, p 25). Elsewhere, Slowey et al (2001) note in their response to the National Strategy for Neighbourhood Renewal that it has relatively little to say on the issue of evaluation, other than the proposal to use neighbourhood statistics to track progress. They advocate that "there should be a greater emphasis on monitoring and evaluating community and neighbourhood impact in a way that enables community participation in the process" (Slowey et al, 2001). Similarly, Sullivan and Potter argue that the government's emphasis on community participation and leadership suggests a need for "a reconsideration of the role of monitoring and evaluation in community based regeneration programmes with particular reference to local communities' 'ownership' of these aspects of regeneration" (2001, p 19). They go on to advocate an approach to urban policy evaluation that builds community capacity and that "represents a challenge" to conventional evaluation approaches.

The introduction of NDC and other community-based regeneration initiatives have clearly raised the prospect of community-based evaluation. Indeed, the NCVO (2000) reports that a number of NDC areas have begun to examine ways of designing evaluation frameworks that contribute to the wider objective of local residents playing a lead role in regeneration activity. Although highly conscious of the problems that some first-round NDC partnerships were experiencing with the practical arrangements for community-led evaluation, the NCVO's unambiguous recommendation is that "investment in such work will pay dividends in the long-term" (NCVO, 2000, p 26). Two years on from the NCVO review, there is no shortage of proposals for the use of community-led evaluation within NDC partnerships, though genuine examples remain thin on the ground. In some cases, there is advocacy of the use of community-led evaluation, but little or no notion as to how to take it forward. Devonport NDC in Plymouth advocates democratic evaluation whereby "those involved in delivering the programme or as a beneficiary should be most critical of its performance", yet it remains unclear as to how this will be utilised in practice (see Chapter Five of this volume).

Elsewhere, consultancy studies on community-led evaluation have been completed, but their proposals have yet to be implemented. In Liverpool, the Parks Partnership, which plays a lead role in Kensington NDC, commissioned a feasibility study in 1999 for a proposed Community Applied Research Project (CARP). This study proposed that CARP would operate as an Intermediate Labour Market, using the research and evaluation opportunities offered by NDC and other urban policy initiatives to provide local unemployed people with research training and experience, as well as routes into full-time employment. The Parks Partnership and Kensington NDC are yet to act on the feasibility study. The most fully developed conceptual model is Birmingham NDC's 'Framework for Community-Led Monitoring and Evaluation'. This model was commissioned by the Birmingham Voluntary Services Council (BVSC) with the specific intention that evaluation activity should contribute to community development (see Sullivan and Potter, 2001)[1].

However, despite the fact that BVSC acts as the accountable body for Birmingham NDC, concerns about the model's acceptance among public sector stakeholders have so far thwarted its introduction. In short, it seems that with central government apparently reluctant to embrace more radical directions in evaluation methodology, attempts to introduce more innovative, community-based approaches to evaluation at the local level have generally run into the sand. As Slowey et al (2001) note, while the new policy context offers opportunities for "the voluntary sector to redefine monitoring and evaluation and introduce a community perspective at its heart", any such redefinition of evaluation must also face the fact that "as it currently stands the national strategy seems to make no space for it".

In the absence of central government support for the development of new forms of community-led evaluation, it is indeed the voluntary sector that has taken the lead in generating more innovative, community-based evaluation methodologies. Evaluation techniques developed by Groundwork, an environmental regeneration charity in which local people are actively engaged in evaluating regeneration activity, have recently been assembled by the New Economics Foundation into a handbook to enable local people to evaluate the impact of neighbourhood renewal on their own communities (Walker et al, 2000). This work has been paralleled by the 'Evaluation for Real' approach devised by the Neighbourhood Initiatives Foundation, which builds on the interactive principles of its highly successful 'Planning for Real' techniques.

Elsewhere, the Community Development Foundation has developed the Achieving Better Community Development evaluation model, which facilitates the involvement of community groups in evaluation and has been applied in a variety of policy contexts (Barr et al, 2000; Chanan et al, 2000). Based on similar principles, Action on Smoking and Health in Scotland has produced a resource pack designed to enable community groups to undertake evaluation projects, particularly those involving the assessment of their own activities (McKie et al, 2002). The pack lays considerable stress on a range of qualitative methods, such as photographs, a video, diaries and creative writing, which can be used to elicit community perspectives on an initiative. Such developments indicate that there is no shortage of models available to promote community involvement in urban policy evaluation. Given the strength of the case for community-based evaluation, the lack of uptake of these approaches in contemporary urban policy is all the more surprising.

The policy paradox: local residents know best, outsiders know better

Although urban policy evaluation may no longer be blind to local communities, the continued dominance of conventional evaluation approaches raises important issues about how evaluation relates to contemporary policy objectives. The mismatch between an urban policy premised on community leadership and promoting capacity building among local communities on the one hand, and, on the other, an approach to evaluation dominated by top-down governmental criteria, is considerable. It creates a paradoxical situation, in which residents of deprived areas are held to know what is best for their own localities, but are then judged against standard criteria laid down by government, consultants and other expert 'outsiders'. This disjunction underlines the extent to which British urban policy evaluation generally fails to consider the role of evaluation in relation to the wider distribution and dynamics of power in the urban policy process. Despite the central role accorded to communities in urban policy discourse, the manner in which evaluation studies are commissioned and carried out tends to accord low priority to the role of local residents in the evaluation process. The continued emphasis on top-down evaluation approaches not only raises questions about the extent of the government's commitment to promoting community leadership in urban policy, but also renders evaluation findings deeply problematic.

The process of commissioning evaluation studies is fundamental to shaping the relationship of the evaluator to local communities. While notions of multi-agency and multi-sector partnership dominate urban policy discourse, evaluations are generally commissioned and controlled by a single, public sector body – typically a central government department, Regional Development Agency or local authority. The organisational priorities of these commissioning agencies will therefore be fundamental to determining the character of an evaluation initiative, since the criteria for evaluation and the methods used will be "influenced by who is asking whether policies are effective and why" (Turok, 1991, p 1549). Given that the organisations tendering to undertake evaluations depend on the income generated by such contracts, these assumptions about the focus of the evaluation are rarely questioned in the commissioning process or thereafter. Evaluators that are committed to a community-based, bottom-up approach to evaluation, therefore, will rarely seek to assert such models in the face of a commissioning agency that, even implicitly, expresses a preference for conventional models. Clearly, the commissioning process raises key questions about the extent to which an evaluator can claim to operate independently from the hierarchies present within prevailing organisational arrangements.

Once an evaluation study has been commissioned, the process of carrying it out raises subtler, though equally significant, issues of the power inequalities involved in urban policy evaluation. Even where the commissioning process results in avowedly pluralistic approaches to evaluation, in which the evaluator canvasses opinions from the full range of partners involved in an urban policy initiative, evaluators frequently fail to recognise that they are operating within the context of prevailing social divisions. This applies particularly to evaluation studies taking place in disadvantaged communities, where much research "is done *on* the relatively powerless *for* the relatively powerful" (Bell, 1978, p 25). Similarly, Packman (1998) argues that research on local communities frequently serves to exploit and deskill local residents, whom it sees as passive research subjects rather than active citizens. If local residents are engaged in the research process at all, it is generally not until the data collection phase. Survey questionnaires, the method most commonly used to obtain community views, are almost universally designed by professional evaluators who will impose their subjective definitions of key issues in determining which questions the survey should contain. Questionnaires rarely offer respondents the opportunity to recast research questions or oppose the value-laden assumptions on which they are based. In other words, there is a tendency to define the researcher/evaluator as the sole possessor of expertise, allowing him/her to use local people to gain knowledge (Hall and Hall, 1996). It is not surprising, then, that research and evaluation often alienate local communities, particularly if it does not contribute to an improvement in material conditions (Oliver, 1992).

The alienation of local communities represents a key weakness of contemporary urban policy evaluation (see also Imrie, 1996b). Even without the significant ethical issues that it raises, the contempt that communities frequently feel towards evaluation studies seriously undermines evaluation methodologies on both practical and epistemological levels. In practical terms, the understandable reluctance among local residents to fill out survey questionnaires or participate in focus groups, frequently described by evaluators as the problem of 'evaluation fatigue', may render findings statistically unrepresentative or even wholly insignificant. Indeed, Walker et al (2000) suggest that "the hostile reaction triggered by conventional evaluation approaches not only affects the scope to measure change, but may well diminish the impact of urban policy as a whole" (p 7). Evaluations of community projects that are done *to* the community, not *by* the community, can easily reduce the overall impact of the project. This may be due to questionnaire fatigue, suspicion of outsiders or lack of timely feedback. It is especially likely in deprived neighbourhoods that may well already have experienced such treatment.

From an epistemological perspective, the inability of an evaluator to work with a local community often means that evaluation approaches become heavily reliant on one particular type of knowledge. As Healey (1998) argues, public officials, researchers and evaluators rely almost universally on relatively narrow professional paradigms when seeking to understand localities. They routinely downplay the value of local knowledge present within a community that is "built up though their day to day experience of a place" (Healey, 1998, p 1540). Merridew (2001) suggests that consultants may be particularly prone to overlooking such forms of local knowledge, resulting in their short-circuiting of the process of organisational learning in urban policy. To overcome such shortcomings, Hall and Hall (1996) suggest that researchers should recognise their informants as experts in their own right, arguing that where the relationship between researcher and researched is based on collaboration rather than hierarchy, findings tend to be of a superior quality. Yet, the favoured approach in urban policy has instead been to adopt pluralist methodologies, in which the evaluator may adjudicate between competing perspectives, but continues to do so within a context of gross inequalities of power between the plurality of interests involved. As Atkinson (1999a) notes, advocacy of community involvement in urban policy has, in reality, occurred only at the stage where the rules of the game have largely been established. Pluralistic evaluation simply reinforces this pattern and can therefore be read as part of a wider attempt to co-opt communities to predetermined policy objectives.

The reluctance to adopt collaborative, community-based approaches to urban policy evaluation is also a reflection of the continued faith placed in positivist models of social research. Positivist models are largely derived from the natural sciences, which have traditionally emphasised the central importance of systematic empirical observation as a means of either testing or establishing hypotheses (Robson, 1993). There is an emphasis in such models on identifying regular patterns and statistical relationships between variables. Thus, positivist approaches to evaluation claim to offer objective assessments of policy and explicitly reject any method that is deemed to involve subjective or value-laden assumptions. It would be difficult to underestimate the influence of positivism on the theory and practice of policy evaluation, particularly during the formative years of the 1980s. Yet, positivist models of evaluation have been subjected to widespread criticism. With specific reference to urban policy evaluation, Turok (1991) argues that the emphasis in positivist approaches on quantitative measures, and the allied tendency towards highly mechanistic approaches to evaluation, not only perpetuate the myth of objective truths in evaluation, but also makes for inadequate analysis of impact. Thus, positivist methodologies do not offer objective and definitive assessment – they merely endow one particular form of analysis with a superior status. Their continued dominance in urban policy evaluation indicates the extent to which the role of community in urban policy remains highly circumscribed.

Beyond positivism in urban policy evaluation

In response to these concerns, a number of proposals for alternative approaches to policy evaluation have emerged in recent years. These reflect a wider interest in research methodologies that engage local communities as *active* participants in the research process. New paradigms emphasising collaborative approaches to evaluation and research have emerged from a variety of sources, including feminist and anti-racist critiques of conventional social science methodology (Humphries and Truman, 1994), critical community development perspectives (Dixon, 1995), and bottom-up approaches to international development programme appraisal (Fals-Borda, 1992). The experience of engaging grassroots communities in research in contexts as apparently diverse as international development and the British Community Development Projects (Atkinson and Moon, 1994) can be traced back to the late 1960s. However, it was not until the 1990s that these critical research perspectives began to inform new approaches to evaluation, with the most significant development arising in the context of evaluation debates in the US. Two closely related approaches have emerged in US evaluation practice in recent years, seeking to overcome the shortcomings of conventional evaluation methodologies: empowerment evaluation and participatory evaluation.

Empowerment evaluation is particularly associated with the work of David Fetterman (Fetterman, 1994, 2000; Fetterman et al, 1996). Defined as "the use of evaluation concepts, techniques, and findings to foster improvement and self-determination" (Fetterman, 2000, p 2), the approach has much in common with participant evaluation. It firmly rejects the possibility of value-free evaluation and instead advocates that evaluation projects should be designed around an open and democratic process. Instead of the evaluation being led by a single 'specialist', a selection of individuals with a stake in the policy (including clients or community representatives) form a group with collective responsibility for evaluation. The role of the evaluator becomes one of facilitation, reflecting an approach that stresses that "evaluation is conducted *with* the community not *on* the community" (Fetterman et al, 1996, p 130). Increasingly influential in US evaluation discourse, empowerment evaluation has been applied in a wide range of policy and organisational contexts, including evaluations of crime prevention programmes and substance-misuse prevention work.

Similarly, participatory evaluation stresses the central importance of full stakeholder participation in the design and implementation of evaluation studies. There is a strong emphasis in such approaches on sharing responsibility for the evaluation between a group of stakeholders and an external evaluator, with inequalities between participants being recognised and addressed within the evaluation process (Quintanilla and Packard, 2002). There is also a stress on evaluation methods that are designed to promote dialogue between stakeholders that will "bring to the surface the values, assumptions and assessments being made" (Folkman and Rai, 1997, p 456). Thus, a participatory evaluation of the Neighbourhood and Family Initiative (NFI) in Milwaukee (Wisconsin) involved the establishment of a 'Learning Community', a group of stakeholders that met regularly to enter into a dialogue "where deeply felt opinions of the project are open to inquiry" (Folkman and Rai, 1997, p 458). The authors, Folkman and Rai, highlight a number of difficulties that were experienced with this approach, not least the open criticisms of the national evaluators of NFI, who dismissed the findings as 'anecdotal', and the defensive stance taken by the NFI Collaborative (the public/private/community partnership heading the initiative). Nonetheless, they suggest that the approach was broadly vindicated by its commitment to ensuring that the evaluation recognised conflicting value judgements.

At first sight, both participatory and empowerment evaluation would seem to be tailor-made for the current UK context, where urban policy is being reconfigured around notions of community leadership. These approaches offer a clear alternative to positivist models, directly address the power inequalities evident in urban policy and offer the potential to overcome the contradiction between community-led policy and government-led evaluation. They might also provide a coherent intellectual basis for voluntary sector approaches to community-based evaluation that have emerged in recent years. Yet, there appears to be a danger that such approaches to policy evaluation will tend to work towards the generation of consensual outcomes. It would appear that the outcomes of participant evaluation are more likely to be regarded as successful, and be regarded as legitimate by policy makers, if competing value judgements converge around an agreed interpretation. Quintanilla and Packard (2002) report on a participatory evaluation of an inner-city science enrichment programme in San Diego (CA), designed and undertaken by a team of stakeholders – staff, students, parents, board members and funders. In this instance, the process of power sharing among the participants was found to operate in a more consensual fashion, leading to an unambiguous validation of the project's success. Yet, the apparent success of participatory evaluation in this case appears to have been contingent upon the lack of controversy about the design and operation programme being evaluated. This experience contrasts sharply with the resistance encountered among the wider policy community to the findings of the NFI evaluation in Milwaukee, where the participatory approach did little to alter the balance of power in the decision-making process.

Despite their immediate appeal, the prospect of importing these models into the British context raises a number of concerns. While New Labour continues to portray the role of local communities in urban policy as an issue of delivering effectiveness, it is likely that such approaches would only be adopted with a similarly narrow remit and be driven by a concern to produce consensus regarding evidence of 'good practice'. As such, there is a risk that empowerment and participatory evaluation would effectively amount to a form of closure, preventing the emergence of more radical, community-led assessment of urban policy, aimed at producing a diversity of perspectives and serving to reinvigorate and democratise local policy debate.

Conclusions

This chapter has argued that, while policy evaluation has been central to the process of bringing communities to the centre of urban policy discourse, evaluation also plays a key role in restricting the scope for genuine community leadership. In particular, the chapter has highlighted a number of limitations in the New Labour urban policy agenda. Despite powerful arguments in favour of community-based evaluation, it has shown that conventional, government-led approaches continue to dominate. This creates an evident paradox in urban policy – that is, new initiatives are founded on the assumption that local communities are best placed to determine what is needed to regenerate a locality; yet the knowledge of outside professionals is assumed to be the only legitimate means of evaluating the policy choices that arise from this bottom-up approach to regeneration. Evidently, the underlying inequalities of power in urban policy have not been sufficiently recognised by New Labour, with the consequence that evaluation studies frequently serve to alienate local communities and fail to capture forms of local knowledge that would provide more telling indications of change.

While examples are beginning to emerge in the UK of evaluation methodologies designed to engage and empower local residents directly, these have mainly been developed by the voluntary sector and currently have very little influence on mainstream urban policy debate. With community-based evaluation techniques remaining marginal to urban policy discourse, there is a case for examining the transferability of established US approaches, such as participant evaluation and empowerment evaluation. Yet, any attempt to draw such models directly into British urban policy would seem to carry the danger of further entrenching a discourse that defines community involvement as an issue of policy effectiveness rather than as a democratic right. Either way, current trends in evaluation would also appear to suggest that genuine community leadership in British urban policy is likely to be some time in coming.

Acknowledgments

I would like to thank the editors of this volume, Rob Imrie and Mike Raco, for their valuable comments on earlier versions of this chapter.

Note

[1] Birmingham NDC's framework was designed by staff from the Institute for Local Government Studies at the University of Birmingham, the Neighbourhood Initiatives Foundation and Social Economy Solutions.

Further reading

For an introduction to urban policy evaluation, see Hambleton and Thomas (1995). Turok (1991) provides a seminal critique of mainstream urban policy evaluation. Sullivan and Potter (2001) outline the model of community-based evaluation proposed to Birmingham NDC, while McKie et al (2002) is recommended as an example of emergent voluntary sector approaches to evaluation.

Part Three
The future of community in urban policy

The new urban policy: towards empowerment or incorporation? The practice of urban policy

Allan Cochrane

Introduction

If there is a core understanding that underpins the practice of urban policy in England it is, unfortunately, a rather banal one[1]. As the foreword to the White Paper, *Our towns and cities*, puts it: "How we live our lives is shaped by where we live our lives" (DETR, 2000e, para 3) – and most of us now live in urban areas. Urban policy, in other words, can be understood as the attempt to shape the places in which our lives are lived. The vision identified in the White Paper is "of towns, cities and suburbs which offer a high quality of life and opportunity for all, not just the few" (DETR, 2000e, para 3). Unlike other forms of social policy that are defined through the identification of problems faced by particular groups, urban policy is defined through the places in which those problems find their expression.

As this implies, there is no straightforward definition of urban policy as an explicitly specified and delimited area of social policy. Even the definition of the places to which the 'urban' label has been applied has varied over time – from community to neighbourhood, inner city to metropolitan area. Even the inner city has been a remarkably elastic concept, sometimes incorporating large areas of cities, sometimes being defined through small area initiatives. The object of urban policy is a "chaotic conception" (Atkinson and Moon, 1994, p 20), in the sense that there has been no widely shared conception of an urban problem around which policy might be defined and, since Castells (1977), there has been little serious attempt to find one. In principle, it appears at times as if almost any aspect of public policy could become part of urban policy[2].

Nevertheless, it is impossible to ignore the extent to which a (changing) cluster of initiatives has been brought together under the heading of urban policy. In practice, the existence of urban policy is taken for granted and there has been a significant growth of academic and policy literature as well as government statements concerned with it. The search for a coherent policy object may be frustrating, but there is rather more agreement around the need to tackle specific urban problems. Discussion of urban policy tends to be approached through the story of particular policy initiatives (Atkinson and Moon, 1994) or the clustering of particular problems deemed to be 'urban'. In seeking to identify his 'chosen city', for example, Schoon (2001) works his way through a series of such problems, the most significant of which seems to be the reluctance of the middle classes to live in densely populated areas.

Urban policy is unselfconsciously 'practical'. Its practitioners seek to identify 'best practice' in one place that is capable of being borrowed in order that it can work elsewhere. The professional and official literature is dominated by case studies of success, along similar lines to the approach adopted in many popular management texts. A menu is developed from which professionals are able to choose, even if the range of offerings on the menu is always rather limited, as each urban policy fashion is superseded by the next. So, for example, there was for some time an emphasis on waterfront development as a pathway to economic regeneration, and this was followed by an explosion of strategies aimed at mobilising 'culture' as a means of transforming older industrial areas. In other words, the lessons of Baltimore, Barcelona and Bilbao were to be learned well by Glasgow, Manchester, Newcastle and Huddersfield (Bianchini and Parkinson, 1993).

In this context, therefore, urban policy is best understood as the sum of the initiatives that have been given an 'urban' label, rather than being a continuing and coherent strand of social policy. In some respects, this also allows urban policy more easily to take on the features of each succeeding social policy fashion – from case work to community work; economic regeneration and land reclamation to workforce development; interagency and partnership working to single-purpose development agencies; slum clearance to urban renewal; multicultural community festivals to opera houses; celebration of the market to the search for democratic participation (Cochrane, 2000). The wider policy diagnosis has zigzagged between the identification of market failure, community failure and state failure.

The 'new' social policy

Edwards (1995, 1997) persuasively makes the point that the analysis of urban policy has all too often taken place without reference to debates within the field of social policy (see also Ginsburg, 1999). However, it is increasingly clear that contemporary urban policy can only be understood in the context of New Labour's wider programme of public service 'modernisation' and the set of understandings that underpins its approach to social policy.

The new social policy rejects the notion that people are simply victims of circumstance, yet acknowledges that there may be significant obstacles in the way of some people achieving their full potential. In the language of New Labour, they may be 'socially excluded'. The principal aim of social policy, therefore, is to find ways of enabling those people to overcome the obstacles or (where possible) to look for ways of removing them. And the obstacles are not simply to be defined in terms of economic inequality or levels of income. On the contrary – Giddens, for example, argues that the "freedom to achieve" is as significant as any lack of resources or income (Giddens, 2000a, p 88). Approaches suggesting that systemic or structural deficiencies are to blame for social problems are treated sceptically in New Labour's world view. Instead, the emphasis is on finding practical solutions to particular problems.

Instead of assuming that the role of public policy is to act as a safety net, catching those who are unable to fend for themselves, this approach emphasises the need to develop policies capable of enabling people to help themselves – providing, in New Labour's words, "a hand up, not a hand out" (see, for instance, Commission for Social Justice, 1994, p 224). Instead of just helping the poor to survive, this model suggests that it is the role of public agencies and their partners to look for ways of ensuring that they can be brought into a productive economic role, both for themselves and for society (or 'community'). As Hill notes, work – or rather paid employment – is perceived as a "passport to social and economic citizenship and the way out of social exclusion" (Hill, 2000, p 105). This is a model in which the citizens have obligations as well as rights; indeed, it is only a readiness to accept their obligations that gives them rights. They are expected to "take their responsibilities seriously, while recognising the rights of others" (Hill, 2000, p 102). The implication is that not accepting these obligations, or the opportunities offered by the state, will also imply that some of the 'rights' (to support, benefits, education or training) will be withdrawn.

The bringing together of social rights and responsibilities lies at the core of this approach, influenced by communitarianism (Hughes and Mooney, 1998; Levitas, 2000).

> [Community is] strongly linked to very particular notions of civic responsibility and citizenship, notions that informed Labour's attempt to overcome social exclusion and reform the welfare state. (Newman, 2001, p 148)

The notion of 'community' highlights the interdependence of people and the importance of their relationships with one another, while also emphasising the shared responsibilities of those who are members of 'communities'. Levitas notes that it provides "an alternative both to the untrammelled free market (of neo-liberalism) and the strong state (of social democracy)" (2000, p 191).

The revitalisation of 'community', in the sense of a shared understanding of rights and responsibilities, is an important element underpinning a wider vision of society capable of moving beyond what is seen to be the sterile and simplistic choice between state and market. It brings with it the possibility of a moral order based on this collective or shared identity. Prime Minister Tony Blair is explicit about this in his reflection on the 'Third Way': "strong communities depend on shared values and a recognition of the rights and duties of citizenship" (Blair, 1998b, p 12). This sense of 'community' has no direct territorial or urban implications, at least in principle. It is a particular view of society – and, indeed, a normative view of society, what it should be as much as what it actually is.

However, this appears to give licence for the term to be used to describe an extensive range of social, economic and political relationships at an equally wide range of spatial scales. Levitas highlights the "promiscuity" (2000, p 191) with which the term 'community' is used in the policy debates of New Labour. She identifies six uses:

> local communities or 'neighbourhoods'; the rather wider constituencies of local government (or the local state); a substitute for society which is not spatially defined; or the world community ... that complex of institutions, neither market nor state, which can otherwise be described as civil society. And ... imputed communities of interest – from ethnic minorities to the business community. (Levitas, 2000, p 192)

Levitas might have added that:

> For policy makers and street-level bureaucrats within the state the idea of community has been used as a form of shorthand for the socially excluded. (Hoggett, 1997, p 11)

Towards a 'new' urban policy

Its 'practical' orientation and emphasis on 'what works' may be precisely what makes urban policy fit so well with the new-model social policy being developed in the context of New Labour 'modernisation'. Instead of a commitment to the delivery of universal (or even targeted) services, the dominant approach emphasises the value of evidence-based policy, learning from successful practice without having fundamental preconceptions about what might 'work'. And alongside this orientation, urban policy in practice has also increasingly required a commitment to partnership, to working across the boundaries of state, private and voluntary sectors and community. The skills of successful professionals working in the field are those that are most highly valued within the rhetoric of 'joined-up' thinking and social entrepreneurialism.

Although they are no longer quite as explicit as they once were, tensions remain between the two main strands of contemporary urban policy. These are reflected in the different emphases of two key policy documents:

• the Urban Task Force (UTF) report, chaired by Lord Rogers, which called for an 'Urban Renaissance' (DETR, 1999a);

- the Social Exclusion Unit (SEU) report, which emphasised the importance of 'neighbourhood renewal' (SEU, 1998).

The UTF report explicitly argues that "Successful urban regeneration is design-led" (DETR, 1999a, p 49) and argues for the development of integrated spatial master plans (DETR, 1999a, pp 73-4). In contrast, the SEU report suggests that, in the past, "there has been too much emphasis on physical renewal instead of better opportunities for local people", and argues for "investing in people, not just buildings" (SEU, 1998). Admittedly, the Urban White Paper (DETR, 2000e) that followed from the UTF report called for a 'people-centred' approach, and emphasised the importance of community, while the SEU's Action Plan (2001) that followed from the consultation over neighbourhood renewal acknowledges the importance of the physical environment. Nevertheless, the tension is still apparent, if only in the division of labour between the White Paper (planning, housing and development) and the Action Plan (services, community leadership and the 'joining up' of government policies).

Despite this tension, there is also a much clearer attempt to integrate these different aspects of urban policy, or at least to view them together. This is what makes it possible to talk of the emergence of a 'new' urban policy (Cochrane, 2001). What is important is that it is becoming increasingly recognised that the different aspects complement or reinforce each other. Instead of a discourse that assumes a direct causal route from economic development to urban renewal, the new urban policy is characterised by a discourse that highlights the interconnection of the different aspects of urban development – community, partnership, private sector stakeholders. Instead of believing that growth will solve problems, the understanding is that the processes of social exclusion and community breakdown may themselves get in the way of growth. In this context, a key management role for those involved in urban regeneration is to reduce social exclusion (admittedly rather narrowly defined), not for its own sake, but as an essential component of wider regeneration and economic renewal.

Most of these understandings have a place in the development of urban policy, and sometimes do not work easily together. Each may be mobilised, as narratives of urban policy are developed in particular places, and approaches are constructed in which the different elements reinforce each other. Although the notion of 'community' has had a rather chequered history in the development of urban policy, it has always been an undercurrent within the local practice of urban policy. Once the potential of 'community' to deliver forms of self-help and self-management, and to enable the identification of collective rights and responsibilities, is added to the mix, then it might be argued that 'urban policy' is almost the perfect social policy for the present period.

Within urban policy, 'community' is generally used to mean one of two things – a territorially delimited neighbourhood, within which there is deemed to be some sort of shared identity or set of interests, or some identifiable ethnic group that is also often understood to have its own 'community' leaders. So, for example, a local community might also be seen as a site of shared social responsibility and a place within which a community of interest (particularly one associated with ethnicity) finds its expression. In other words, in this context the 'community' metaphor can be translated into the identification of particular groups of people and particular places, through which it becomes possible to deliver or enable a range of social and political approaches, beyond the state and the market. The power of the metaphor is powerfully reflected in the following extract:

> Even in the most deprived neighbourhoods, there are considerable social strengths on which policy could build. Social surveys consistently show that high proportions of residents in deprived areas speak warmly of the 'quality' of the people in their neighbourhoods and argue that the problems of crime, dereliction and social disruption are caused by a small minority of residents. This suggests that almost all deprived communities still retain elements of their traditionally strong community structures. Much of this is maintained by women, and particularly middle-aged and elderly women. (Robson et al, 2000, p 25)

Robson et al argue for "neighbourhood strategies that put local communities at the heart of decision-taking about neighbourhood management and change" (Robson et al, 2000, p 25).

> The concentration of problems within small neighbourhoods … reinforces the argument for the development of forms of neighbourhood management that may capitalise on some of the inherent community strengths within such areas and can encourage what might be called 'guided community-led' approaches to the revitalisation of such neighbourhoods. (Robson et al, 2000, pp 25-6)

Managing – or empowering – communities

It is widely acknowledged, however, that the notion of community is not only elusive, but also ideologically slippery. In the past, I have argued that it has often been used "as if it were an aerosol can, to be sprayed on to any social programme, giving it a more progressive and sympathetic cachet" (Cochrane, 1986, p 51). Levitas is equally critical of its current use:

> The role of community is to mop up the ill-effects of the market and to provide the conditions for its continued operation, while the costs of this are borne by individuals rather than the state. (Levitas, 2000, p 194)

While the renewed policy focus on community is often couched in terms of empowerment for those who have previously been excluded, the notion of shared responsibility remains central to an understanding of its role in public policy. Raco and Imrie (2000) highlight the extent to which the discourse of community implies a process of self-management. Instead of relying on the state (or even the market) as regulator of behaviour, the implications of highlighting the role of community are that self-discipline becomes equally important (see also Atkinson, 1999a). Rose (1996a) suggests that the rise of community as an object of policy also provides a means of redefining the subjects of intervention.

> Communities become vectors to be investigated, mapped, classified, documented, interpreted ... to be taken into account in numberless encounters between professionals and their clients, whose individual conduct is now to be made intelligible in terms of the beliefs and values of their community. (Rose 1996a, p 332)

In other words, as well as offering the prospect of self-management (either ideologically or discursively), the notion of community also offers new ways of management, through new managerial technologies and new professional styles.

Amin and Thrift helpfully point out that "the networks of control that snake their way through cities are necessarily oligoptic, not panoptic: they do not fit together" (2002, p 128). It is this that makes the effective management of communities so important within the new urban policy. Since urban change is not predictable, the state requires an approach to governance that is capable of drawing on the skills and understanding of those being managed.

> Nearly all systems of governance in effect acknowledge that they are dealing in part with the unknown and ungovernable; they do not just tell their inhabitants what to do, they learn from them. (Amin and Thrift, 2002, p 129)

And, in learning from them, they also offer ways in which the challenge of governance may be transferred from the urban managers to those being managed – or, rather, learning to manage themselves.

This helps to explain the new stress on the identification of 'champions', on social entrepreneurs and community leaders. Robson et al (2000) identify 'best practice' in neighbourhood management, which includes the need for:

- an action plan and a means of monitoring it;
- the oversight of a 'champion' leading a team;
- a community development fund for pump-priming;
- neighbourhood forums for local involvement (Robson et al, 2000, box 6).

Diamond links the search for 'social entrepreneurs' to a "strategy of co-option and inclusion" in which key professionals are empowered "to act as a local neighbourhood catalyst or 'supremo'" (Diamond, 2001, p 277).

In this policy model, the role of the state (particularly as universal provider) is questioned, although it is recognised that it still has a significant role to play. In the past, it was said that the state had failed to deliver adequate services and had treated those dependent on it with contempt. Partnership with private sector agencies is, it is believed, likely to deliver better services more efficiently while community and voluntary organisations are expected to offer a better means of enabling people to make progress in their own terms. The new arrangements are intended to encourage an active involvement of a range of people with local and expert knowledge, so that there is less reliance on the particular expertise of traditional (bureau) professionals (Clarke and Newman, 1997).

The position of voluntary and community groups within the new arrangements is ambiguous. They certainly appear to be given a more central role, and their value is explicitly and formally recognised. The Neighbourhood Renewal Unit (currently located within the Office of the Deputy Prime Minister) will be seeking to ensure that there is community involvement in the preparation of Community Strategies and within Local Strategic Partnerships (LSPs) (DETR, 2001; Chapter One of this volume). Nevertheless, there is some justifiable scepticism about the extent to which excluded groups really will be given significant influence or involvement in the new arrangements (Geddes, 1997; Brownill and Darke, 1998; Colenutt, 1999; Diamond, 2001). And there is also a concern that, by becoming involved (such as delivering services on behalf of the state), organisations and their leaders may simply be incorporated, gaining little for their constituencies, while losing the ability to challenge decisions. Taylor et al (2002) have reviewed the impact of the national and local compacts with voluntary and community organisations, and conclude that groups may be affected differently. They question simple models of incorporation, suggesting that some groups have been able to gain more, while others have found themselves sucked in, with extra work but little additional benefit. What matters is how the balance between the different agencies can be negotiated.

So perhaps a focus on the tensions between empowerment and incorporation misses the point. The management of 'communities', whether by themselves or through state professionals, is a complex and uncertain process. Instead, it may be more appropriate to see the process as one related to the manufacture of different forms of political and civic legitimacy. In the case of contemporary urban policy, the notion of community has a key role of providing a different sort of legitimacy, one that that is not based on elected local government or on the state professional responsible for delivering services. The traditional (delivery-focused) structures of local government are fundamentally challenged by the emergent arrangements, even if councils are often given formal responsibility for achieving change. Instead, the careful construction of LSPs and Community Strategies suggests the possibility of a partnership model within which both the state professionals and the community organisations accept the rules of a very different game, a game in which each is fundamentally dependent on the other, as part of a broader system of governance.

A democratic vision?

There may be wider (and potentially more exciting) possibilities underlying the new arrangements, however managerialist their intent. The notion of community that underpins the new urban policy is also one that promises a new vision of democracy. As it moves away from traditional forms of electoral representation, it suggests a shift towards increased participation by those who have previously had little involvement in the workings of urban governance. The moves towards 'modernisation' through new forms of urban managerialism may offer the prospect of a changed set of political relations precisely because control from above is no longer an option. It is possible to view self-management and self-discipline through a rather different lens, so that they become expressions of democratic involvement, rather than (or as well as) new forms of control.

Amin and Thrift (2002) suggest that the contemporary city is the prime site for the development of democratic citizenship. For them, it is "a place of becoming, and the fulfilment of social potential, of democratic experimentation through the efforts of citizens themselves, as free and socialized agents" (2002, p 143). They argue that the city and its institutions have the potential of "providing the opportunity for citizens to become something else and of mutuality to be strengthened" (2002, p 143). They believe that social progress can best be achieved "through a civic-minded and capable public" (2002, pp 141-2) and that such a public is most likely to be created in the crucible of a city. They stress the role of a wide range of non-state organisations – voluntary associations – in generating forms of politics beyond, alongside and sometimes linked to the state.

They take this notion further in their exploration of the 'distanciated' community, and identify the ways in which the very tracking and categorising of individuals helps to identify them as part of particular 'communities'. In other words, the bureaucratic systems of control themselves help to generate the social arrangements they seek to uncover. Amin and Thrift also point to the significance of social identity generated by rather 'lighter' forms of social interaction, as people come together for some activities and then disperse. Similarly, they highlight the importance of groups that come together by choice to pursue particular activities, from vegetarianism to heritage, angling to dance. This is a notion of community that incorporates rather more fluid and transient sets of relationships than the traditional model, which starts from an assumption of fixity and a culture of closure. This vision is reinforced by recognition of the role of diasporic communities both linked to place and to relationships across space. Some of these are localised or find localised expressions, but others are constituted by wider, flowing networks, of which they are part and which they in turn help to constitute (Amin and Thrift, 2002, pp 43-6).

Hirst (1994) sets out a manifesto for a future democratic polity based around a related vision of associative democracy. It builds on the notion that society is made up of plurality of associations through which individuals come together in a complex variety of ways that reflect their membership of multiple communities. These associations are not necessarily local, but many of them will find local expression and help to define places within cities in terms that recognise the importance of local diversity rather than homogeneity.

Hirst sets out a manifesto for a future. For him, the role of the state (that is, the role of urban policy) is to engage in the "orchestration of social consensus" (1994, p 118) and the regulation of distributional arrangements. It is a powerful and, in many respects, persuasive picture of what might be possible. However, it is less successful in charting the route by which we might be able to move from here to such an attractive future.

The question that remains, therefore, is whether these possibilities and potentialities implied by this vision are finding a reflection in the working out of the new urban policy. In her critically supportive discussion of Labour's urban policy, Hill (2000) indicates some ways in which the possibility of increased democratic participation might be achieved. She highlights what she sees as the various ways in which a broader notion of community might underpin a more democratic and participative approach. For her 'community' is best defined as "the actual network of social interaction ... not whether people have a sense of community in subjective terms" (Hill, 2000, p 103). So, while local community that is based around place may provide one means of enabling participation and involvement in policy, so might wider communities of interest that stretch across urban areas (and even between them). She recognises the complexities of 'community', emphasising that it is a social, rather than a physical, construct expanding beyond territorial jurisdictions.

> Grass-roots citizen action, community involvement in regeneration projects, and area decentralisation of decisions are all part of the renewed vitality of urban affairs. Clustered around these precepts are ideas – and ideals – of self-help and empowerment. (Hill, 2000, p 220)

Healey and her colleagues (Healey, 1997, 1998; Cars et al, 2002) also highlight some of the possibilities, exploring the making of new institutional arrangements, particularly in urban planning. They redefine the role of planners (classic street-level bureaucrats) as enablers of local residents to engage in planning their own neighbourhoods. And they look for ways in which the voice of local communities may more effectively be amplified and heard.

At the core of these democratic visions are a series of assumptions about the nature of the 'communities', or the sets of social relations, that exist within cities. Like Amin and Thrift, Hirst stresses their plurality. Healey and her colleagues suggest that it should be possible to utilise a participative framework to enable moves towards the building of agreement and consensus in the practice of urban development. There is an often unspoken assumption that it is either possible to manage potential conflict or to find ways of minimising its impact. Discussion may not bring rationality, but it does seem to have the possibility of reaching some sort of consensus or, at any rate, readiness to accept change. There also seems to be an assumption that there are few (if any) areas within which deep social divisions might fundamentally undermine the possibilities of urban democracy. Amin and Thrift acknowledge that they make little reference to issues of gender, race or the environment – and, it might be added, 'class'. They suggest that the absence of these issues from the text is largely explained by a lack of space (Amin and Thrift, 2002, p 5). But that absence also suggests that they do not view those divisions as playing a central part in shaping our lives in cities. The notion of 'power' that underpins these approaches is the power of various groups and individuals 'to do' certain things rather than the power of one group 'over' another.

Clearly, this is an important aspect of the way in which life is organised in cities. However, there is a real danger that it may understate the extent to which divisions within the city remain of fundamental importance. The search for agreement assumes that the differences are just superficial – we can all agree on the most rational way forward (on the basis of compromise and consensus). Or it is assumed that (pluralist) diversity in effect means accepting the existing divisions and many of their implications.

If there are still significant forms of social inequality that find their expression in our cities, then the practice of urban policy may reflect rather a different political process. So, 'community' may also work as the basis on which resistance can be constructed and alternative approaches to the shared understandings of progressive politics developed. In his exploration of contested communities, Hoggett asks whether or not community action may work as "the unhappy revenge of the socially excluded" (1997, p 11). Byrne, too, identifies the possibility that the 'community' can generate forms of what he calls "space-based solidarity", organised around a consciousness of "the communality that derived from common spatial experience and were willing to act communally" (1999, p 119). However, he draws rather more pessimistic conclusions for the possibilities of urban policy because of the way in which post-modern urbanisation (as he calls it) has generated communities that are "so fragmented and disorganised" (1999, p 123). The very features that the urban optimists see as creating new possibilities of democratic participation are those that Byrne identifies as undermining the possibility of community-based political challenges.

There is a fundamental ambiguity surrounding the democratic potential of the new urban policy. It offers both the prospect of increased self-discipline and the hope of greater participation, as well as greater influence for those whose concerns have traditionally been marginalised. The extent to which that participation is achieved and influence is applied remains uncertain, however. Paradoxically, a model that downplays the role of elected local government may reduce the scope for change. The active involvement of local government in sponsoring participation and seeking to represent and give voice to community in all its many expressions is likely to be a prerequisite for a more open democratic process. This requires a fundamental shift in attitude, since it fits uneasily with the 'modernisation' agenda currently being pursued for local government. However, without such involvement some voices will be given more status than others, and the power of some to determine their own lives will be more restricted than others (Cochrane, 1996). Instead of attempting to construct a new space for 'community' as an alternative to 'state', a more complex process, which brings them together, is a necessary basis for the development of a more democratic process of urban governance.

Notes

[1] This chapter concerns itself with contemporary developments in urban policy in England. Even before devolution, approaches to urban policy in the UK's component nations differed significantly and those differences have been reinforced by devolution. Clearly policy learning is taking place across the internal boundaries of the UK, and there are significant continuities in approach, but it is important to acknowledge that this chapter makes no claim to be considering new policy directions in Wales, Northern Ireland and Scotland.

[2] For example, see ODPM (2001) for a list of 96 separate programmes deemed to be relevant.

Further reading

Official publications are a valuable source of information on the perspectives, ideologies and understandings that underpin the new policies. Since policy is an area in which policy statements of one sort or another are frequently issued, it is important to be aware of the most recent ones. Newman (2001) provides a fascinating overview of the new social policy context, while Hill (2000) offers a more positive analysis of New Labour's engagement with urban policy specifically. Amin and Thrift (2002) present challenging ways of rethinking the understanding of the city, which have interesting implications for urban policy, citizenship and democracy; Pile et al (1999) offer a series of perspectives on the city that highlight its divisions as well as the connections that it creates.

TWELVE

New Labour, community and the future of Britain's urban renaissance

Mike Raco

Introduction

Integral to New Labour's vision for an urban renaissance is the belief that empowered and mobilised communities can and should play an enhanced role in the development and implementation of urban policy agendas. Modernising Britain, in New Labour terms, requires a rearticulation of active citizenship, with the state's role moving from that of a provider of (welfare) services, to that of a facilitator. The state will enable communities and individuals to take more responsibility for the conduct of their own lives.

The Blair government has embarked on a series of reforms that seek to reconstruct the relationships between civil society and the state based on new modern principles of flexibility, lean government, and a withdrawal of the state from particular territories of action (see Chapter One of this volume). This chapter draws on the contributions to this volume as well as research elsewhere to examine the status and meaning of the term 'community' in this new context, and the role that communities may play in the renaissance of Britain's cities. It argues that, despite the rhetoric of empowerment and capacity building that characterises urban policy discourses, the rise of community has to be understood, primarily, in *instrumental* terms. Community mobilisation is a means to an end for policy makers. It plays a key role in legitimising and facilitating regeneration programmes in a context where the role of the state is changing and communities and individuals are increasingly being forced to play a greater role in their own governance.

The chapter also interrogates the processes involved in defining communities. It argues that despite the complexities and contingencies of community formation, all communities are characterised by boundaries of inclusion and exclusion. As such, the potential for community-based agendas to provide inclusive and democratic forms of urban politics is relatively limited (see Chapters Seven and Eight of this volume). All too often, this inherent exclusivity is put to one side in policy and academic debates concerning urban governance and regeneration policy. Communities are often assumed to exist in particular places and the aim of policy is to help them to help themselves.

This chapter's discussion is divided into two sections, followed by some general conclusions. The first section examines the various definitions of community used by New Labour. It argues that, despite an enhanced awareness of the varying forms of urban community that exist, it is place-based communities that still represent the mainstay of policy programmes since they are best able to fulfil the instrumental role that policy makers design for them. The second section assesses the ways in which communities have become both the subjects and objects of urban policy in this new era of neoliberal government (Peck and Tickell, 2002). It examines the New Labour push towards a new localism and the impacts that this has had on urban policy. It also discusses the issue of policy transferability and best practice and highlights some of the institutional problems in implementing the new localism. The concluding section looks at the future of community in urban policy more generally and discusses possible future scenarios.

Empowering communities: New Labour and the discourses and practices of community construction

It is unsurprising, perhaps, that urban policy has been a key site for the articulation and implementation of reformist agendas, for it is in urban communities that the contradictions and impacts of neoliberal programmes on everyday lives are experienced most strongly (Brenner and Theodore, 2002; Jessop, 2002). Cities contain the highest concentrations of poverty and inequality. They have suffered from massive losses in manufacturing employment in recent decades and contain the highest relative and absolute levels of unemployment, crime and other socioeconomic indicators of deprivation (Turok and Edge, 1999; Robson et al 2000). There is also a widespread perception, reinforced and reproduced by the mass media and television soap operas such as *EastEnders* and *Coronation Street*, that strong, homogenous, urban communities exist in Britain's cities, which, if effectively nurtured and operationalised, could provide the basis for subsequent regeneration programmes (Burgess and Gold, 1985; Harvey, 1996).

Contributors to this volume have shown that there remains a number of tensions in the definitions of community offered by the Labour government in its various policy programmes. If the main objective of community involvement is to facilitate more efficient and effective forms of government, then how have communities been defined and identified and what have been the processes of community selection? Is it the role of policy makers, intent on implementing their policy programmes, to establish the boundaries of communities, or should they be constructed by local people using their own imaginations and frames of reference? What forms of community should be promoted and in whose interests? Should, for example, the focus be on place-based communities or should there be a greater emphasis on communities of interest, which may or not be congruent with development areas? Moreover, are there community groups that are more deserving of assistance than others, and what should be done with those who are characterised as undeserving or in some way degenerate?

As various chapters of this volume have demonstrated, in most urban policy initiatives it is communities of *place* (or those resident in bounded urban spaces) that represent the mainstay of policy initiatives. Communities of place are not only a priori assumed to exist but they are also given an ontological status as agents of (local) governance. They are relatively easy to define, in bureaucratic–administrative terms, and their inclusion is highly functional for policy makers working to bounded geographical areas. This functional role is of central importance, since, according to one government agency, "we know that successful regeneration *only* happens with active community involvement" (Active Community Unit, 2001, para 1.4; emphasis added). In other words, activating area-based communities is critical to policy effectiveness and should be promoted, not primarily to democratise policy processes, but to make programmes work more efficiently.

In this sense, despite the rhetoric of modernisation and the implementation of 'new' agendas, there are strong continuities with past efforts to establish community involvement in government programmes. Previous rounds of local government reorganisation across the UK have, similarly, tended to focus on the functionality of spaces of governance rather than their congruence with community imaginations. Both the Redcliffe-Maud and Banham Boundary Commissions of the 1970s and 1990s "concerned themselves with community as an issue in the creation of appropriate administrative units ... which have allowed them to concentrate their attention primarily on issues of service delivery and efficiency" (Barnett and Chandler, 1997, p 144).

New Labour has continued this tradition with the promotion of programmes of action that equate area-based problems with area-based communities (see Chapters Four and Five of this volume). Urban policy is driven by a core belief that there exists "different kinds of citizens who are recognised not for what they do or what they have been made into but for what they lack" (Cruikshank, 1999, p 123). Seemingly, it has been preoccupied with identifying the weaknesses, deficiencies and lack of social citizenship endemic in poorer, deprived communities. A lack of responsibility, obligation and citizenship on the part of those least able to change their circumstances is presented as the root cause of social exclusion, rather than a more rounded focus on the obligations of others, such as elite groups in society or resource-rich, powerful institutions. In Levitas' terms, the focus on an included social majority means that the very rich and other elites "are discursively absorbed into the included majority, their power and privilege slipping out of focus if not wholly out of sight" (1998, p 7). Instead, urban policy agendas closely mirror Cruikshank's (1998) description of voluntary governance:

> [Power is] articulated through the constitution and regulation of individual liberty ... [in order to] make good citizens out of poor ... to expand the limits and maximise the powers of government by making the people self-governing. (Cruikshank, 1999, pp 8-9)

By focusing on area-based excluded communities, urban policy is characterised by its tendency to pathologise certain identifiable groups. In doing so, it provides a perceived political dividend, in that state action does not appear to be directly assisting those categorised as undeserving. Instead, it rewards those who demonstrate that they have the will and motivation to help themselves, thereby relieving the state and civil society more broadly of their 'burden' (Galbraith, 1992; Schneider and Ingram, 1997). As the chapters in this volume have demonstrated, discursive and practical responsibility for the problems faced by communities has been moved away from government policies of the past and placed firmly with 'degenerate', targeted communities themselves, which are portrayed as somehow outside of (or excluded from) the normal values of civil society (see Chapters Five to Eight of this volume). Those who help themselves (and are, therefore, 'deserving' according to the government's criteria) require assistance to enhance their capacities and play a more active role in local politics.

Defining communities in area-based terms is a critical component of urban policy. It enables policy makers to 'fix' community – socially and spatially – in ways that make it visible and enable it to be worked on and shaped. It also promotes the norm of ideal, area-based cohesive communities in which:

> there is a common vision and sense of belonging for all communities; the diversity of people's different backgrounds and circumstances are appreciated and positively valued; those from different backgrounds have similar life opportunities; and strong and positive relationships are being developed between different people from different backgrounds in the workplace, in schools and within neighbourhoods. (LGA, 2002, p 6)

Such conceptions have informed policy responses to high-profile urban events (such as the riots that took place in Bradford, Oldham and Burnley in 2001 or the murder of Damilola Taylor in 2000) that were blamed on a lack of community cohesion and the existence of degenerate cultures in deprived urban areas (for discussion, see Amin, 2002a, 2000b).

However, this focus on creating functional, cohesive and spatially bounded communities has inherent limitations. Any attempt to equate the notion of community with particular geographical areas assumes a homogeneity of interests within them. Yet, geographical places do not represent single, uncontested entities and will "not necessarily be the spatiality of the internally coherent, spatially contiguous, local community" (Massey, 1997, p 112). A focus on 'place' communities is unable to capture the particular dynamics of places and communities that are constructed in and through "the simultaneous coexistence of social interrelations and interactions at all spatial scales" (Massey, 1994, p 264). Moreover, the form and character of social interrelations from which communities are developed are undergoing increasingly rapid change, over greater and greater spatial scales. A combination of economic restructuring, shifting social attitudes, and new technologies of interaction and communication are impacting on the scale and form of interaction between people and, in turn, are shaping the nature of community formation (Healey, 1997; Aart Scholte, 2000; Amin et al, 2000).

To some extent the Blair government has attempted to address these changes in its urban policy frameworks. New Labour thinkers such as Leadbeater (1999) and Mulgan (1998a) have been at the forefront of debates over emerging forms of community. There has been some shift in policy emphasis, with new agendas showing greater sensitivity to other forms of 'community', particularly non-place-based communities and communities of interest (see Figure 12.1 overleaf). The launch of Community Strategies in 2000, for example, required local authorities to "engage and involve local communities" and develop "a proper assessment of their needs" (DETR, 2001, p 3). Local authorities are expected to develop relationships not only with area-based communities but also with communities of interest, which may or may not cut across administrative boundaries. As the guidance states, local authorities and others should recognise that:

> individuals belong simultaneously to a number of communities of interest, of both place and interest, and will identify with different communities according to their circumstances and the issues under discussion. Community Strategies should reflect this complexity and ... accommodate it by putting in place a variety of routes into participation. (DETR, 2001, para 52)

To fulfil this multifaceted agenda, local agents are required to develop a range of locally defined mechanisms of consultation and inclusion. Yet, while Community Strategies exemplify an apparent new wave of thinking on community involvement in local policy making, recognition of the existence of different types of community runs up against the central objective of urban policy – that is, to develop communities as agents of government. Adopting new, broader definitions of community makes it extremely difficult to operationalise policy agendas. If communities can be variously described as place-based, interest-based, class-based, gender-based, and so on, then policy makers at the local level, often working with limited resources and in tightly controlled, centrally defined managerial frameworks, face an almost impossible task in resolving complex representational and practical issues.

Despite the rhetoric of community empowerment, the evidence presented in this volume highlights the limited devolution of powers to community organisations. This is due to a tendency of communities to come up with 'wrong answers' (in the government's terms) and a lack of trust in the representational legitimacy of community representatives (see Chapters Five, Six and Eight of this volume). For example, capacity building is defined as a

Figure 12.1: Definitions of key community terms

Community capacity building
A process that aims to ensure that individuals, groups and communities have access to the knowledge, skills and resources they need to take to action in their community.

Community development
A process that aims to promote the active involvement of people in the issuea that affect their lives. It is a process based on the sharing of power, skill, knowledge and expertise.

Community group/organisation
Informal groups or more formal organisations formed by people in a community of place or interest, in order to pursue a common interest, meet a shared need, or campaign for a common cause.

Community of place
A community whose members are defined geographically by their place of residence, as opposed to a community defined by common interests or characteristics.

Communities of interest
A community whose members have common needs or characteristics (such as ethnic origin, disability, gender, and so on), as opposed to a community defined geographically.

Virtual community
Communities that emerge from the internet when enough people carry on public discussions and that operate in ways that are completely decoupled from the need to meet physically.

Voluntary organisation
Formal non-profit distributing and non-statutory organisation, usually established as a charity, with the aim of providing a service or meeting a need of benefit to the public.

Sources: Adapted from Rheingold (1993); Stubbs (1998); Active Community Unit (2001, annex B)

process that "aims to ensure that individuals, groups and communities have access to the knowledge, skills and resources they need to take action in their community" (Active Community Unit, 2001, annex B). While this appears to be an approach that empowers community groups, the key determinant over capacity building concerns who in fact has the power to determine what capacities communities require and what 'knowledge, skills and resources' communities need to 'take action' in a particular policy context. Local authorities, for example, see community-based programmes as an opportunity to "consolidate their role as leaders of their local communities" (LGA, 2002, p 8), rather than representing a process that should be "predominantly bottom-up, rather than top-down" (DETR, 2001, para 16).

The emphasis on empowerment also requires the redefinition of communities and the inclusion and exclusion of particular groups. Chapter Eight of this volume, for example, highlights the ways in which the needs and aspirations of disabled communities have been marginalised from regeneration discourses. Local actors working to government agendas believed that the needs of various disabled groups would be met by 'others' and that, in practice, community inclusion meant only inclusion for those who could contribute to policy agendas or would be directly affected by them. Disabled people did not fit either category. In other contexts, such as Chapter Five's study of regeneration in

Plymouth, Chapter Six's research on London, or Chapter Seven's work on Oxford, community involvement is discursively structured in and through notions of 'responsible' and 'irresponsible' participation. If communities are seen to be positive in their attitudes towards development projects, then they are included and described as responsible bodies, representing community perspectives and needs in a positive and constructive manner. If, however, various community voices challenge the legitimacy of programmes or are overtly critical, then their views are dismissed as unrepresentative and motivated by other political agendas. Again, it is only particular types of deserving communities that can also play a part in implementing agendas that policy makers recognise as legitimate agents to be empowered.

This is exemplified by New Labour's unwillingness to include community groups that it sees as 'politically motivated' and critical of its wider agendas. For Labour, "*genuine* community engagement" involves "ensuring that all sections of the community have the opportunity to participate – not just the usual suspects" (DETR, 2001, para 51; emphasis added). Exactly 'who' the usual suspects are in such discussions is not clear. However, government programmes such as Community Development Funds and Community Chests have as one of their central aims the objective of funding and promoting a broad range of community agencies in an attempt to pluralise representation and shift influence away from what are perceived as politicised community activists. Pluralisation can also be seen as a mechanism for fragmenting local opposition to projects as it dissipates the power of local agents and communities to obstruct progress (see Chapter Six of this volume). As such, the findings presented here reflect those of other studies where community involvement has been shown to be discursively and institutionally structured by policy makers (see for example, Cochrane, 1986; Hastings, 1998; Raco, 2000).

Although community formation is a complex and contingent process, communities of all kinds possess one overriding characteristic – they are *exclusionary in their inclusiveness*. Defining communities always requires some form of social or spatial boundary drawing. These boundaries are neither natural nor rational, but are formed in and through broader relations of power, privilege and exclusion. This is evident in studies of community organisations, which can, for instance, be reactionary in promoting local agendas of discrimination and exclusion along ethnic or gender lines (see Young, 1990; Harvey, 1996; Chapter Three of this volume). At the same time, communities are riven by internal divisions of power so that efforts to encourage active citizenship and community mobilisation often result in the perspectives of those who represent themselves most effectively (that is, those in the most powerful positions) being most influential. This rarely equates with the views of those in greatest need. Community representatives can be just as narrow in their interpretation of broader views than the formally elected officials that the government says they should replace (DETR, 1999b).

Given the highly erratic and differential nature of community politics, the focus on community as an object of democratisation can be questioned. As

Amin and Thrift argue, the basis of an enhanced urban politics should be through the articulation of *universal* rights which "lies in a particular form of democracy – civic empowerment and participation – which has always been associated with cities" (2002, p 131). In essence, this involves "rights-based and other institutionalised actions at national and urban level to build capacity and capability across the social spectrum" (2002, p 154). If new discourses and practices of urban policy are to promote greater inclusion, tolerance and capacities, then 'community', with its exclusionary character, may be an inappropriate vehicle to undertake such a task.

This is demonstrated by the tendency of community mobilisation to be at its strongest when it takes on negative forms (for example, in providing opposition to a perceived threat to people or places), but weaker when it comes to developing community agendas of inclusiveness (Saunders, 1980; East, 2002). Imagined communities will always exist outside of the boundaries, imaginations and bureaucratic proceduralism of state agencies and it cannot be determined a priori whether or not a community exists in a regeneration area, or what form its needs and (political) aspirations will take (see Harvey, 1996; Dalby and MacKensie, 1997).

Neoliberalism, community and the new localism

The expansion of community in urban policy has not been a benign process, with policy makers and planners handing over the reigns of power to community groups and organisations. The rearticulation of community that has gathered pace during the 1990s and 2000s only partly consists of a challenge to the inflexible, bureaucratic structures of the existing welfare state[1]. Instead, community 'empowerment' has been re-established in a context of shifting relationships between the state and civil society, with community representing a convenient territory of action to be mobilised, shaped and activated in the pursuit of broader agendas.

The roots of these new state–society relationships can be found in the changing form and character of neoliberalism since the 1980s. As Peck and Tickell argue, the aggressive neoliberal Thatcherite programmes of the 1980s "have gradually metamorphosed into more socially interventionist and ameliorative forms" (2002, p 384), such as the Blair government's so-called Third Way (see Chapter One of this volume; Giddens, 2000a, 2000b; Rose, 2000c). As the social and economic costs of neoliberalism have begun to undermine the structures on which social and economic systems depend, so the role of governments has had to expand – or, in Peck and Tickell's (2002) terms, be 'rolled out' – and become surreptitiously more interventionist to ensure the long-term sustainability of strategies and programmes of action. A key element of this 'rolling out' has involved the mobilisation of active communities as "a flanking, compensatory mechanism for the inadequacies of the market mechanism" (Jessop, 2002, p 455). It might be added that the promotion of community is also a compensatory mechanism for the growing inadequacies and under-funding of the welfare state, particularly in urban areas.

Such notions of community are being actively promoted by the Blair government as it embarks on a new round of welfare reform. At the Labour Party Conference of October 2002, Tony Blair announced that reform was to be spearheaded by a 'new localism', based on the belief that:

> just as mass production has departed from industry, so the monolithic provision of services has to depart from the public sector. Out goes the big state. In comes the enabling state. (Prime Minister Tony Blair, quoted in Wintour, 2002, p 1)

Similarly, Chancellor Gordon Brown articulated:

> a new localism where there is flexibility and resources in return for reform and delivery .... [A] new era – an age of active citizenship and an enabling state – is within our grasp. And at its core is a renewal of civic society where the rights to decent services and the responsibilities of citizenship go together. (Brown, 2002, speech to New Deal for Communities project in Hull)

This adoption of new localist principles has in part been a consequence of the strong Atlantic focus of the Blair government. From 1997 to 2000, it propagated political and intellectual relations with the Clinton administration jointly to promote the concept of the Third Way as a new form of Anglo-American capitalism, which could be transferred to a range of different national policy contexts (see Giddens, 1998). Gordon Brown, for example, has used references to US welfare and urban programmes to justify a number of reforms. Similarly, at the Urban Summit in November 2002, John Prescott referred directly to selective regeneration projects in the US and Europe as integral to Britain's urban renaissance, which, he argued, is "about defining a new vision – what the Americans call a new urbanism" (Prescott, 2002, p 1). Key speakers at the event included Joan Clos, Mayor of Barcelona, and John Norquist, Mayor of Milwaukee (WI), both of whom spoke about the regeneration of their own cities and commented on the ways in which best practice could be transferred to the British context.

This internationalisation of regeneration discourses has influenced the character of British urban policy with its focus on Action Zones, area-based initiatives (ABIs), local business mobilisation, place marketing and community self-help. Such initiatives increasingly resemble those that took place in US cities during the 1980s and 1990s, where development agencies are often dealing with extreme inequalities and social divisions. It is perhaps a telling comment on the growth of inequality in Britain's cities that it is US-style local programmes, with their weak planning regimes and limited inputs of state resources, that appeal to the Blair government, rather than alternative agendas that rely on strong, redistributive welfare agendas. As Harvey's (1989a) research on waterside regeneration initiatives in Baltimore and other US cities shows, the speed and degree of urban policy transfer has been heightened by new forms of place competition, globalisation and a broad and uncritical acceptance of the managerial concept of 'best practice'.

However, there are structural problems in transferring policy 'solutions' from one context to another. Contrasting urban problems, welfare state traditions, relationships between the state and civil society, local social relations and a range of other contextual factors makes the 'successful' transfer of policy a process that is erratic, at best. At worst, it is a dangerous cul de sac that limits innovation and diversity and has the potential to stigmatise those places that are unable to emulate the success of foreign competitors. The 'successes' of regeneration projects in Milwaukee, for example, have been underpinned by vigorous and selective place marketing and significant investments in tourist and conference facilities. Recently, Milwaukee has also been at the forefront of Third Way-style welfare reforms in which education provision has become dominated by divisive selection procedures based on free-market principles. However, in implementing these agendas, alternative local histories and traditions, such as those of native American communities, have been marginalised and inequalities have risen (see Kenny, 1995; Greene et al, 1999). Despite these deficiencies, Milwaukee has become a model of regeneration that has been uncritically accepted as best practice.

Similarly, in Barcelona, the one European city that has been promoted as a role model for British cities, the benefits that regeneration has brought to local communities have often been exaggerated. Indeed, recent research indicates that the city is now facing many of the same problems that afflict Anglo-American cities – selective suburbanisation, deindustrialisation, the geographical concentration of deprived communities, rapidly escalating house prices, excessive profiteering by property developers, battles over public space and increasing rates of crime (see Munoz, 2000). Moreover, its regeneration was underpinned by significant state investment and interventionist planning, neither of which is likely to take place in most British cities, given the new localism's emphasis on local capacity building rather than direct state investment.

The social and economic histories of places also differ significantly so that the conditions that bring about regeneration in one place cannot simply be replicated elsewhere. In what ways can Barcelona or Milwaukee, for instance, represent a realistic role model for regeneration in Barnsley, Gateshead or Southend-on-Sea? Similarly, the 'new urbanism' of the US, championed by John Prescott at the Urban Summit has, in practice, involved the polarisation of urban communities, the formation of gated enclaves, the institutionalisation of punitive security strategies, and crude conceptions of the relationships between urban forms and human behaviour (Tallen, 1999; Smith, 2002). Such realities can be lost in the fevered pursuit of best-practice models and the implementation of off-the-shelf policy solutions. Indeed in Britain, US-inspired regeneration initiatives, such as the redevelopment of the London Docklands, could be characterised as examples of 'worst practice' in terms of their repeated failure to fulfil their policy objectives and their tendency to enhance urban socioeconomic inequalities.

There are also operational issues to overcome in implementing the new localism in urban policy. The government has committed itself to bending mainstream welfare spending to deprived areas through Public Service Agreements (PSAs) (see Chapter One of this volume). However, as the DETR's own assessment of PSAs points out, "it is as yet unclear how they will be implemented ... given generally limited resources" (HM Treasury, 2000, para 19). Large elements of government spending are channelled in and through institutions fixed in particular places, such as hospitals, schools and universities. How can money be targeted without the wholesale abolition of the principles of universal entitlement that underpin the welfare state? Recent government initiatives, such as the establishment of Foundation Hospitals, are in fact pushing agendas in the opposite direction by giving additional funds to those public-sector bodies that are already proving to be most successful in an attempt to prevent middle-class flight from the public sector (Dobson, 2002). Other key public-spending decisions, such as the awarding of contracts for the defence industry or the establishment of lucrative research institutions, are still being located in already affluent regions and locations (see Lovering, 1998; Massey, 2001).

Even in cases of increased spending in a particular local authority area, it does not necessarily follow that local people will benefit from it. Targeting resources raises a series of boundary questions over the definition of deprived areas and local delivery structures. Poorer wards currently receive above-average public spending. Bramley et al's (1998) study, for example, found that deprived wards in Liverpool received 29% more resources than the national average. However, the research also found that "the increment in public spending associated with higher levels of deprivation is modest rather than massive in scale" (quoted in HM Treasury, 2000, p 21). Much of this spending is ameliorative (such as social security), whereas in sectors such as education "there is relatively little difference in the levels of overall funding between schools in disadvantaged and advantaged areas" (HM Treasury, 2000, p 21). Targeting deprived wards and changing the balance of local spending priorities also has the potential to create local political tensions between different local interests. Even if extra money were to be provided to local authorities in deprived areas, there is little guarantee that the additional resources would be spent on the most deprived communities. Effective implementation would require the wholesale restructuring of the existing relationships between central and local government and the ways in which resources are collected and allocated.

Overall then, New Labour's urban policy represents a hybrid of new ways of thinking about state–civil relationships and existing traditions of state action. It has been influenced by the domestic politics and practices of welfare reform and broader international, particularly US, discourses of communitarianism, capacity building and empowerment. 'Community' has a key role to play in this new localist future, with local partnerships expected to become more involved in the development and implementation of regeneration initiatives.

'Community' and the future of Britain's urban renaissance

Where do all of these trends leave 'community', both as a concept and as a political force? On the one hand, it seems that communities, of one type or another, will continue to play a critical role in British urban policy. Following the publication of the Urban Task Force report (DETR, 1999a) and the Urban White Paper (DETR, 2000e), planning agendas are beginning to shift, albeit gradually, towards 'sustainability agendas', which involve the promotion of brownfield, urban development projects. A key element of sustainability discourses concerns the mobilisation and empowerment of communities, with communities again being defined in both instrumental and non-instrumental terms. There is a possibility that urban areas may undergo a prolonged and sustained round of public and private sector investment over the next 20 years or so. The roles and responsibilities of communities may then take on a new significance, since urban communities will be at the forefront of change and possess the capacity to legitimate and contribute to the implementation of new agendas. There could be a new urgency to involve communities on the part of policy makers; that may lead to new mechanisms and practices of consultation and inclusion.

On the other hand, if current trends continue, urban communities may well find themselves becoming detached from future policy-making processes and practices. As Chapter Three of this volume argues, the promotion of property- and design-led development agendas could marginalise urban communities, as they have in the past, as the urgency to attract developers to inner-urban locations outweighs the moral and practical need to involve those most affected by developments. Whatever the outcome, new development agendas will undoubtedly place new pressures on existing communities and create new conditions for urban conflict. Simultaneously, the relentless privatisation of the public services on which poorer communities depend is having a much bigger impact on the lives of many urban residents than any government regeneration scheme. As public transport networks and social housing supplies become increasingly expensive and fragmented in the cause of profiteering, so the social sustainability of urban communities comes under greater and greater threat. Add to this the government's determination to promote hi-tech industries at the expense of blue-collar manufacturing (on which many urban communities depend), ongoing and severe deindustrialisation, the deterioration of workers' pay and their working conditions, and an unwillingness to deal with the crises afflicting public services and house price inflation, and the outlook for many of Britain's poorest residents and communities is relatively bleak.

More broadly, the attention that the Labour government has devoted to urban issues has been subject to ongoing change and uncertainty since 1997. On the one hand, there has been a new urgency in debates on urbanism, quality-of-life issues, and the economic and environmental capacities of cities. However, there is a new discursive and, to a lesser extent, practical policy focus on the needs of cities, the problems facing urban communities and the need to develop broader definitions of urban problems (see, in particular, Chapters Two to Four of this volume). On the other hand, there has been precious little concrete action, and limited resources devoted to the task of regeneration. The Urban White Paper (DETR, 2000e), for example, is a relatively toothless piece of legislation – long on rhetoric, but short on substance. With the recent rise of the Countryside Alliance and the political mobilisation of selected, elite sections of rural society, there is also a danger that future government regimes will look to tackle urban issues with less urgency. It is possible that politicians may wish to avoid the charge of 'favouring' urban areas over rural, something that the Countryside Alliance and other Conservative interests have put at the heart of their concerted political campaigning.

For some, the very nature of community is also undergoing structural changes of such significance that the term 'community' in the traditional sense no longer possesses heuristic value. New technologies have enabled the formation of what Rheingold (1993) terms 'virtual' communities, or communities that "emerge from the internet when enough people carry on public discussions" (Rheingold, 1993, p 5). These new forms of placeless community have become increasingly popular with some writers who see them as the precursors of a more open, democratic and interactive future in which face-to-face communication gives way to virtual interactions conducted through information technology networks[2]. The Blair government, among others, has enthusiastically promoted the widespread adoption of new technologies in its attempts to democratise civil society. (Indeed, there have been suggestions recently that elections and political debates could be conducted through public internet stations.) Virtual communities offer new possibilities for policy makers to establish forms of interaction with communities and opportunities for individuals to establish new relationships with each other and with government agencies.

However, access to virtual communities is still highly structured and limited. A range of research demonstrates that activity rates are higher for certain groups: men rather than women; the middle classes rather than manual classes; and those involved in occupations in which they frequently use appropriate technology, as opposed to those that do not (see Dietrich, 1997; Watson, 1997). Also, the notion that such networks exist in a virtual space (or cyberspace), leaving individuals "completely decoupled from the need to meet physically" (Schmidtke, quoted in Stubbs, 1998, para 1.1), ignores the ongoing materiality of such networks. Users need locations for interaction, communications networks and infrastructure, and domain locations, forcing them to adopt material configurations in particular places (Bromberg, 1996; Stubbs, 1998)[3]. It is easy to exaggerate the decline of place communities, and while the Blair government has been keen to promote virtual communities as a part of its modernisation agendas, in practice area-based communities are still the objects of government.

If processes of community formation are undergoing change, so too, then, is the political context within which urban politics is being played out. The new localism requires places to develop competitive agendas in which they compete for mobile resources and investment (Hall and Hubbard, 1998). Tensions can develop over the ways in which community histories and realities are linked to particular narratives of places (Jessop, 1997). In regeneration areas such as Cardiff Bay in South Wales, regeneration programmes over a period of 20 years have had the implicit objective of displacing and relocating deprived local communities in an effort to gentrify areas of the city and make them more attractive to visitors and potential investors (Thomas and Imrie, 1999). Given the growing importance of place competition, it seems likely that battles over public space, histories and identities may become even more acute in future. This has implications for the role of urban researchers, as the processes involved in developing knowledge about places could become even more politically charged and sensitive. As Chapter Seven of this volume demonstrates, there will always be the tension in research that seeks to document what happens in a place or to a community, but not to stigmatise the community in question.

Across the UK, the devolution of power to the Scottish Parliament, Welsh Assembly, the Northern Ireland Assembly, and to a lesser extent the English Regions in 1999, has also brought a new dimension to the possible form and character of urban renaissance agendas. Decision-making processes and administrative regimes have long differed between different parts of the UK (Imrie and Thomas, 1993; Elcock and Keating, 1998; Greenhalgh and Shaw, 2002). Urban policy agendas have also varied significantly, with community-based area initiatives, for example, playing a particularly significant role in Scotland (see Midwinter et al, 1991; Raco et al, 2003: forthcoming). As Chapter Four of this volume demonstrates, devolution has created new possibilities for different policy agendas to be established for different UK cities. On the one hand, this has the potential to enable new forms of policy transfer to take place so that devolution encourages policy learning between towns and cities operating in similar, if varied, policy contexts. On the other hand, it may create unevenness in the priorities given to urban regeneration and simultaneously may increase competition between places to attract resources and personnel. Whatever the influence, it is clear that at the same time as the Blair government is seeking to centralise urban policy agendas, it has established new sites of resistance that can modify the tactics and practices of government.

In essence, what we see is communities of one form or another playing a key part in the New Labour project but, in turn, being subjected to contradictory roles, definitions and pressures. For policy makers, the instrumentalisation of communities is primarily a vehicle for the promotion of instrumental or governmental efficiency. It is this that drives reform and underpins the logic behind making communities both the subject and the object of policy agendas. In so doing, the complexities of community imaginations and perceptions become fixed and structured in policy-making terms. Yet, as Amin and Thrift argue, strategies of control and instrumentalism may represent "totalising projects but they are not totalisations" (2002, p 108). In different places, agendas will be operated in different ways in response to existing socio-political relations, imaginations of place and traditions of government. Where top-down definitions of urban communities have been imposed, new forms of resistance and ways of thinking often emerge to challenge or contest agendas. Perhaps the biggest challenge facing community activists lies in developing proactive – rather than reactive – community involvement and fostering new forms of engagement in which participation, rights and responsibilities can be developed.

Notes

[1] In some policy areas, new and more interactive relationships have been formed between experts and policy recipients. See Nocon and Qureshi (1996).

[2] For discussion of virtual networks, see Castells (1996); Shields (1996); Stubbs (1998); Urry (2002).

[3] Social relations still structure virtual communities, and this has significant material effects. For example, one trend is for extremist groups to use virtual networks as a vehicle for organising their activities, such as inciting violence against minority groups, through the promotion or racist or homophobic agendas.

Acknowledgements

I would like to thank Rob Imrie and two anonymous referees for their insightful comments on an earlier draft of this chapter. Thanks also to contributors to the Third Regeneration Management Research Workshop, 'Urban Renaissance in Question', (University of Durham, 15 November 2002), who made a number of constructive comments on a presentation based on this chapter.

Further reading

For a good discussion of democracy and urban communities, see Amin and Thrift (2002, pp 131-56). In terms of situating debates on community in the wider context of changes to the state, *Antipode* Special Volume 34 (Brenner and Theodore, 2002) provides an excellent summary of key debates. For a sophisticated discussion of New Labour and Third Way thinking, Rose (2000b) is well worth a read, as is the Community Links (2000) policy discussion book.

References

Aart Scholte, J. (2000) *Globalisation – A critical introduction*, Basingstoke: Palgrave.

Acheson, D. (1998) *Independent inquiries into inequalities in health*, London: The Stationery Office.

Action for Market Towns (1999) *Rural England – A discussion document*, Bury St Edmunds Action for Market Towns.

Active Community Unit (2001) *Funding community groups*, London: HMSO.

Aldridge, S., Halpern, D. and Fitzpatrick, S. (2002) *Social capital – A discussion paper*, London: Performance and Innovation Unit.

Alexander, J. (1998) *Real civil societies – Dilemmas of institutionalisation*, London: Sage Publications.

Amin, A. (2002a) 'Ethnicity and the multicultural city: living with diversity', *Environment and Planning A*, vol 34, pp 959-80.

Amin, A. (2002b) *Ethnicity and the multicultural city,* Liverpool: ESRC Cities Programme.

Amin, A. and Thrift, N. (2002) *Cities: Re-imagining the urban*, Cambridge: Polity Press.

Amin, A., Massey, D. and Thrift, N. (2000) *Cities for the many not the few*, Bristol: The Policy Press.

Anastacio, J.B., Hart, L., Keith, M., Mayo, M. and Kowartzic, U. (2000) *Reflecting realities: Participants perspectives on integrated communities and sustainable development*, Bristol/York: The Policy Press/Joseph Rowntree Foundation.

Arnstein, S. (1969) 'A ladder of citizen participation', *Journal of the American Institute of Planners*, vol 35, pp 216-24.

Atkinson, A. (1998) *Social exclusion, poverty and unemployment*, CASE Paper 4, London: London School of Economics.

Atkinson, D. (ed) (1995) *Cities of pride: Rebuilding community, refocusing government*, London: Cassell.

Atkinson, R. (1998a) 'Countering urban social exclusion: the role of community participation and partnership', in R. Griffiths (ed) *Social exclusion in cities: The urban policy challenge*, Occasional Paper no 3, Bristol: Faculty of the Built Environment, University of the West of England.

Atkinson, R. (1998b) 'Les aléas de la participation des habitants à la gouvernance urbaine en Europe', *Les Annales De La Recherche Urbaine*, vol 80, pp 75-83.

Atkinson, R. (1999a) 'Discourses of partnership and empowerment in contemporary British urban regeneration', *Urban Studies*, vol 36, pp 59-72.

Atkinson, R. (1999b) 'Countering urban social exclusion: the role of community participation in urban regeneration', in G. Haughton (ed) *Community economic development*, London: The Stationery Office.

Atkinson, R. (1999c) 'Contemporary English urban policy and the European Union', in M. Ilmonen, M. Johansson and H. Stenius (eds) *Helsinki–Berlin–Stockholm. 3 European capitals facing the future*, Helsinki: Helsinki University of Technology.

Atkinson, R. (2000a) 'Combating social exclusion in Europe: the new urban policy challenge', *Urban Studies*, vol 37, pp 1037-55.

Atkinson, R. (2000b) 'Narratives of the inner city: the construction of urban problems and urban policy in the official discourse of British government, 1968-1998', *Critical Social Policy*, vol 20, pp 211-32.

Atkinson, R. (2001) 'La nouvelle gouvernance urbaine et la régénération urbaine: gérer la participation des habitants', in T. Spector, J. Theys and J. Ménard (eds) *Villes du XXIe siécle. Quelles villes voulons – nous? Quelles villes aurons – nous? Tome II formes urbaines, mobilité, villes durables, gouvernance*, Ministère de l'Équipement et du Logement, Paris: Direction de la Recherche et des Affaires Scientifiques et techniques.

Atkinson, R. (2002) 'Does gentrification help or harm urban neighbourhoods? An assessment of the evidence-base in the context of the New Urban Agenda', CNR Paper 5 (www.neighbourhoodcentre.org.uk).

Atkinson, R. (2003: forthcoming) 'Urban policy and regeneration: bringing the fragments together?', in N. Ellison and C. Pierson (eds) *New developments in British social policy*, London: Palgrave Press.

Atkinson, R. and Cope, S. (1997) 'Community participation and urban regeneration in Britain', in P. Hoggett (ed) *Contested communities: Experience, struggles and policies*, Bristol: The Policy Press.

Atkinson, R. and Moon, G. (1994) *Urban policy in Britain: The city, state and market*, Basingstoke: Macmillan.

Audit Commission (1989) *Urban regeneration and economic development*, London, HMSO.

Audit Commission (2002) *Neighbourhood renewal*, London: HMSO.

Badcock, B. (2001) 'Thirty years on: gentrification and class changeover in Adelaide's inner suburbs, 1966-1996', *Urban Studies*, vol 38, pp 1559-72.

Bailey, N. (ed) (2002) *Better communities in Scotland: Will the community regeneration statement close the gap? Conference report*, Glasgow: Scottish Centre for Research on Social Justice, University of Glasgow (www.scrsj.ac.uk).

Bailey, N., Barker, A. and MacDonald, K. (1995) *Partnership agencies in British urban policy*, London: UCL Press.

Ball, M. (2002) 'Excuse me, but we have to live here', *The Guardian*, 7 July.

Barnes, C. (1991) *Disabled people in Britain and discrimination*, London: Hurst and Company.

Barnes, C. and Oliver, M. (1995) 'Disability rights: rhetoric and reality in the UK', *Disability and Society*, vol 10, pp 111-16.

Barnes, T. and Duncan, J. (1992) 'Introduction: writing worlds', in T. Barnes and J. Duncan (eds) *Writing worlds: Discourse, text and metaphor in the representation of landscape*, London: Routledge, pp 1-17.

Barnett, N. and Chandler, J. (1997) 'Local government and community', in P. Hoggett (ed) *Contested communities: Experience, struggles and policies*, Bristol: The Policy Press, pp 144-62.

Barr, A., Hashagen, S. and Taylor, P. (2000) *ABCD handbook: A framework for evaluating community development*, London: Community Development Foundation.

Beck, U. (1998) *Democracy without enemies*, London: Sage Publications.

Beckett, A. (2000) 'Colonising the night', *The Guardian*, Saturday Review, August 12, pp 1-2.

Bell, C. (1978) 'Studying the locally powerful: personal reflections on a research career', in C. Bell and S. Encel (eds) *Inside the whale*, Sydney: Pergamon.

Bender, T. (1975) *Towards an urban vision*, Baltimore, NJ: Johns Hopkins University Press.

Benington, J. (1972) *Strategies for change at the local level: Some reflections*, Coventry: Community Development Project.

Benjamin, A. (2001) 'Neighbourhood watch', *The Guardian*, 28 November.

Benn, M (2002) 'New Labour and social exclusion', *The Political Quarterly*, vol 71, pp 309-81.

Berk, R. and Rossi, P. (1990) *Thinking about program evaluation, Newbury Park and London*, London: Sage Publications.

Berry, B. (1985) 'Islands of renewal in seas of decay', in P. Peterson (ed) *The new urban reality*, Washington DC: The Brookings Institution, pp 69-96.

Bianchini, F. and Parkinson. M. (eds) (1993) *Cultural policy and urban regeneration. The West European experience*, Manchester: Manchester University Press.

Birch, A. (2000) 'A new face for the Elephant', *Building Design*, pp 16-19.

Blair, A. (1996) *Leading the way – A new vision for local government*, London: Institute for Public Policy Research.

Blair, A. (1997) 'The will to win', Speech at the Aylesbury Estate (Southwark, London), 2 June.

Blair, A. (1998a) 'Foreword', in Social Exclusion Unit, *Bringing Britain together – a national strategy for neighbourhood renewal*, Cmnd 4045, London: The Stationery Office, pp 1-2.

Blair, A. (1998b) *The third way: New politics for the new century*, London: Fabian Society.

Blair, A. (2001) 'The government's agenda for the future', Speech, 8 February, (www.number10.gov.uk).

Blunkett, D. (2001) *Politics and progress – Renewing democracy and civil society*, London: Politico Press.

Blunkett, D. (2002a) Speech at the relaunch of the Active Community Unit, (www.homeoffice.gov.uk).

Blunkett, D. (2002b) 'How government can help build social capital', Speech to the Performance and Innovation Unit, 26 March, (www.homeoffice.gov.uk/civil_renewal/piuspeech).

Boateng, P. (1999) 'Foreword', in Home Office, *Community self-help*, Policy Action Team Report no 9, Active Community Unit, London: HMSO, p 1.

Boddy, M. (2002) 'Linking competitiveness and cohesion' in I. Begg (ed) *Urban competitiveness: Policies for dynamic cities*, Bristol: The Policy Press, pp 33-53.

Boix, C. and Posner, D. (1998) 'Social capital: the politics behind', *ECPR Newsletter – Special feature on social capital and trust*, pp 13-19.

Bourdieu, P. (1985) 'The forms of capital', in J. Richardson (ed) *Handbook of theory and research for the sociology of education*, New York: Greenwood, pp 241-58.

Bourdieu, P. (1991) *Language and symbolic power*, Cambridge: Polity Press.

Bowring, F. (2000) 'Social exclusion: limitations of the debate', *Critical Social Policy*, vol 20, pp 307-30.

Boyle, P. and Halfacree, K. (1996) *Migration into rural areas*, Chichester: John Wiley.

Brace, C. (1868) 'The industrial school and its benefits', *New York Times*, 14 December, p 8.

Bramley, G., Evans, M. and Atkins, J. (1998) *Where does public spending go? A pilot study to analyse the flows of public expenditure to local areas*, London: DETR.

Brechin, S. (1999) 'Objective problems, subjective values, and global environmentalism: evaluating the postmaterialist argument and challenging a new explanation', *Social Science Quarterly*, vol 80, pp 793-809.

Breheny, M. (1992) *Sustainable settlement and urban form*, London: Pion.

Brennan, A., Rhodes, J. and Tyler, P. (1998) *Evaluation of the Single Regeneration Budget Challenge Fund: A partnership for regeneration*, London: DETR.

Brennan, A., Rhodes, J. and Tyler, P. (1999) 'The distribution of SRB challenge fund expenditure in relation to local-area need in England', *Urban Studies*, vol 36, pp 2069-84.

Brenner, N. and Theodore, N. (2002) 'Preface: from the "new localism" to the spaces of neoliberalism', *Antipode*, vol 34, pp 341-7.

Bridge, G. (2001) 'Bourdieu, rational action and the time–space strategy of gentrification', *Transactions of the Institute of British Geographers*, vol 26, pp 205-16.

British Colonial Office (1958) *Community development*, London: HMSO.

Bromberg, H. (1996) 'Are MUDs communities? Identity, belonging and conciousness in virtual worlds', in R. Shields (ed) *Cultures of the internet – Virtual spaces, real histories, living bodies*, London: Sage Publications, pp 143-52.

Brownill, S. (1990) *Developing London's docklands*, London: Paul Chapman.

Brownill, S. and Darke, J. (1998) *Rich mix: Inclusive strategies for regeneration*, Bristol: The Policy Press.

Brownill, S., Razzaque, K., Stirling, T. and Thomas, H. (1996) 'Local governance and the racialisation of urban policy in the UK: the case of Urban Development Corporations', *Urban Studies*, vol 33, pp 1337-55.

Buck, N. (2001) 'Identifying neighbourhood effects on social exclusion', *Urban Studies*, vol 38, pp 2251-75.

Burgess, J. and Gold, J. (eds) (1985) *Geography, the media and popular culture*, London: Croom Helm.

Burgess, J., Harrison, C. and Filius, P. (1998) 'Environmental communication and the cultural politics title of environmental citizenship', *Environment and Planning A*, vol 30, pp 445-60.

Burgess, S. and Propper, C. (2002) 'The dynamics of poverty in Britain', in J. Hills, J. Le Grand, and D. Piachaud (eds) *Understanding social exclusion*, Oxford: Oxford University Press, pp 44-61.

Burns, D., Hambleton, R. and Hoggett, P. (1994) *The politics of decentralisation: Revitalising local democracy*, Basingstoke: Macmillan.

Burton, E. (2000) 'The compact city: just or just compact? A preliminary analysis', *Urban Studies*, vol 37, pp 1969-2006.

Butler, J. (1998) 'Merely cultural', *New Left Review*, vol 227, pp 33-44.

Butler, T. (1997) *Gentrification and the middle classes*, Aldershot: Ashgate.

Butler, T. (2001) 'We won't make way for middle income key workers', *The Guardian*, 15 October.

Butler, T. and Robson, G. (2001) 'Negotiating the new urban economy – work, home and school: negotiating middle class life in London', Paper presented at the Annual Royal Geographical Society–Institute of British Geographers Conference, Plymouth, 2-5 January.

Byrne, D. (1999) *Social exclusion*, Buckingham: Open University Press.

Cabinet Office (2000) *Rural economies report*, London: HMSO.

Caborn, R. (1999) Speech to First National Regeneration Conference, 27 May, (www.regeneration.net).

Cameron, S. and Davoudi, S. (1998) 'Social exclusion, looking in or looking out', in A. Madanipour, G. Cars and J. Allen (eds) *Social exclusion in European cities*, London: Jessica Kingsley, pp 235-53.

Carley, M. (2002) *Community regeneration and neighbourhood renewal: A review of the evidence*, Edinburgh: Communities Scotland.

Carlton Smith, J. and Darke, J. (1998) *The Leys: Lessons from research*, Research Paper, Oxford: Oxford Brookes University.

Carmona, M. (2001) 'Implementing urban renaissance – problems, possibilities and plans in South East England', *Progress in Planning*, vol 56, pp 169-250.

Cars, G., Healey, P., Madanipour, A. and de Magalhaes, C. (eds) (2002) *Urban governance, institutional capacity and social milieux*, Aldershot: Ashgate.

Castells, M. (1977) *The urban question*, London: Edward Arnold.

Castells, M. (1996) *The internet galaxy*, Oxford: Oxford University Press.

Caulfield, J. (1989) 'Gentrification and desire', *Canadian Review of Sociology and Anthropology*, vol 26, pp 617-32.

Caulfield, J. (1994) *City form and everyday life: Toronto's gentrification and critical social practice*, Toronto: University of Toronto Press.

Cave, B. and Curtis, S. (2001) *Health impact assessment for regeneration projects – Volume III: Principles*, London: East London and The City Health Action Zone & Queen Mary, University of London.

Champion, T., Fotheringham, S., Rees, P., Boyle, P. and Stillwell, J. (1998) *The determinants of migration flows in England: A review of existing data and evidence*, Newcastle: University of Newcastle and University of Leeds.

Chanan, G., Garratt, C. and West, A. (2000) *The new community strategies: How to involve local people*, London: Community Development Foundation.

Clarke, J. and Newman, J. (1997) *The managerial state: Power, politics and ideology in the remaking of social welfare*, London: Sage Publications.

Clavel, P. and Kraushaar, R. (1998) 'On being unreasonable: progressive planning in Sheffield and Chicago', *International Planning Studies*, vol 3, pp 143-62.

Cochrane, A. (1986) 'Community politics and democracy', in D. Held and C. Pollitt (eds) *New forms of democracy*, London, Sage Publications, pp 51-77.

Cochrane, A. (1996) 'From theories to practices: looking for local democracy in Britain', in D. King and G. Stoker (eds) *Rethinking local democracy*, London, Macmillan, pp 193-213.

Cochrane, A. (1999) 'Just another failed urban experiment? The legacy of the Urban Development Corporations', in R. Imrie and H. Thomas (eds) *British urban policy – An evaluation of the Urban Development Corporations*, London: Sage Publications, pp 246-58.

Cochrane, A. (2000) 'The social construction of urban policy', in G. Bridge and S. Watson (eds) *A companion to the city*, Oxford: Blackwell, pp 531-42.

Cochrane, A. (2001) 'New Labour, new urban policy?', in H. Dean, R. Sykes and R. Woods (eds) *Social Policy Review 12*, Newcastle: Social Policy Association. pp 184-204.

Cochrane, A., Peck, J. and Tickell, A. (1996) 'Manchester plays games: exploring the local politics of globalisation', *Urban Studies*, vol 33, pp 1319-36.

Coleman, D. and Salt, J. (1992) *The British population*, Oxford: Oxford University Press.

Coleman, J. (1988) 'Social capital in the creation of human capital', *American Journal of Sociology*, vol 94, pp 95-120.

Coleman, J. (1994) *Foundations of social theory*, Cambridge, MA: Belknap Press.

Colenutt, B. (1999) 'New deal or no deal for people based regeneration?', in R. Imrie and H. Thomas (eds) *British urban policy – An evaluation of the Urban Development Corporations*, London: Sage Publications, pp 233-45.

Colenutt, B. and Cutten, A. (1994) 'Community empowerment in vogue or vain?, *Local Economy*, vol 9, pp 236-50.

Collins, M. (2001) 'The Elephant's graveyard', *The Observer Magazine*, 2 September, pp 20-4.

Commission for Social Justice (1994) *Social justice – Strategies for national renewal*, London: Vintage Press.

Community Development Foundation (1995) *Regeneration and the community in Wales*, London: Community Development Foundation.

Community Development Initiative (1999) *Community-based capacity building in Blackbird Leys, Oxford: A bid for support from the government's Single Regeneration Budget Challenge Fund*, Oxford: Community Development Initiative.

Community Links (2000) *What if…? Fifteen visions of change for Britain's inner cities*, London: The Short Book Company.

Cook, I., Crouch, D., Naylor, S. and Ryan, J. (eds) (2000) *Cultural turns/ geographical turns*, Harlow: Longman.

Countryside Agency (2001) *The state of the countryside 2001*, Cheltenham: Countryside Agency.

Countryside Agency (2002a) 'Market town regeneration in the West Midlands', Countryside Research Note 45, Cheltenham: Countryside Agency.

Countryside Agency (2002b) *Market towns healthcheck handbook*, Cheltenham: Countryside Agency.

Courtney, P. and Errington, A. (2000) 'The changing role of small towns in the rural economy and the implications for development policy', *Local Economy*, vol 15, pp 280-301.

Cousins, C. (1998) 'Social exclusion in Europe: paradigms of social disadvantage in Germany, Spain, Sweden and the United Kingdom', *Policy & Politics*, vol 26, no 2, pp 127-46.

Craig, G. (1998) 'Community development in a global context', *Community Development Journal*, vol 33, pp 2-17.

Crosby, D. (2002) 'Bus cuts are crippling us', *Sunderland Echo*, 28 August, p 1.

Crow, G. (1997) 'What do we know about the neighbours? Sociological perspectives on neighbouring and community', in P. Hoggett (ed) *Contested communities*, Bristol: The Policy Press, pp 17-30.

Cruikshank, B. (1999) *The will to empower – Democratic citizens and other subjects*, London: Cornell University Press.

Dabinett, G., Lawless, P., Rhodes, T. and Taylor, P. (2001) *A review of the evidence base for regeneration policy and practice*, London: DETR.

Dagger, R. (2000) 'Metropolis, memory and citizenship', in E. Isin (ed) *Democracy, citizenship, and the global city*, London: Routledge, pp 25-47.

Dalby, S. and Mackensie, F. (1997) 'Reconceptualising local community: environment, identity, and threat, *Area*, vol 29, pp 99-108.

Dalley, G. (ed) (1991) *Disability and social policy*, London: Policy Studies Institute.

De Souza Briggs, X. (1998) 'Brown kids in white suburbs: housing mobility and the many faces of social capital', *Housing Policy Debate*, vol 9, pp 177-221.

Deakin, N. (2001) *In search of civil society*, Basingstoke: Palgrave.

Deakin, N. and Edwards, J. (1993) *The enterprise culture and the inner city*, London: Routledge.

Dean, J. and Hastings, A. (2000) *Challenging images: Housing estates, stigma and regeneration*, Bristol/York: The Policy Press/Joseph Rowntree Foundation.

Dean, J., Hastings, A., More, A. and Young, R. (1999) *Fitting together? A study of partnership processes in Scotland*, Edinburgh: Scottish Homes.

Dean, M. (1999) *Governmentality: Power and rule in modern society*, London: Sage Publications.

DeFilippis, J. (2001) 'The myth of social capital in community development', *Housing Policy Debate*, vol 12, pp 781-806.

Department of Health (1998) *Our healthier nation: A contract for health*, London: The Stationery Office.

DETR (Department of the Environment, Transport and the Regions) (1997) *Regeneration: The way forward*, London: The Stationery Office.

DETR (1998a) *Modernising local government. Local democracy and community leadership*, London: The Stationery Office.

DETR (1998b) *Single Regeneration Budget bidding guidance: A guide for partnerships (Round 5)*, London: The Stationery Office.

DETR (1998c) *Single Regeneration Budget – Bidding guidance (Round 6)*, London: The Stationery Office.

DETR (1999a) *Towards an urban renaissance. Final report of the Urban Task Force, chaired by Lord Rogers of Riverside*, London: Spon/The Stationery Office.

DETR (1999b) *Involving communities in urban and rural regeneration*, London: The Stationery Office.

DETR (2000a) *Department of the Environment, Transport and Regions annual report 2000*, London: The Stationery Office.

DETR (2000b) *Living places – Urban renaissance in the South East technical report*, London: The Stationery Office.

DETR (2000c) *New Deal for Communities: Gathering baseline information*, London: The Stationery Office.

DETR (2000d) *New Deal for Communities: Monitoring, review and evaluation*, London: The Stationery Office.

DETR (2000e) *Our towns and cities – The future: Delivering an urban renaissance*, London: The Stationery Office.

DETR (2000f) *The state of the English cities*, London: The Stationery Office.

DETR (2001) *Local Strategic Partnerships. Government guidance summary*, London: The Stationery Office.

DETR and MAFF (Ministry of Agriculture, Fisheries and Food) (2000) *Our countryside: The future – A fair deal for rural England*, Cm 4909, London: The Stationery Office.

Development Board for Rural Wales (1995) *Rural Wales: The new directions*, Cardiff: Development Board for Rural Wales.

Devonport New Deal for Community (NDC) (2001) *Devonport people's dreams: New Deal for Communities delivery plan 2001-2011*, Plymouth: Devonport NDC.

DfES (Department for Education and Skills) (2002) *Community finance initiative*, London: The Stationery Office.

Diamond, J. (2001) 'Managing change or coping with conflict? Mapping the experience of a local regeneration partnership', *Local Economy*, vol 16, pp 272-85.

Dietrich, D. (1997) '(Re)-Fashioning the techno-erotic woman: gender and textuality in the cyberspace cultural matrix', in S. Jones (ed) *Virtual culture: Identity and communication in cyberspace*, London: Sage Publications, pp 65-84.

Disability Alliance (2000) *Social security committee report of the Benefits Agency Medical Services and submission by Disability Alliance and RADAR*, Briefing no 13, London: Disability Alliance.

Dixon, J. (1995) 'Community stories and indicators for evaluating community development', *Community Development Journal*, vol 30, pp 327-36.

Dobson, F. (2002) 'Dobson attacks elitist cabinet', *The Observer*, 3 November.

DoE (Department of the Environment) (1972) *Human habitat: How do you want to live?*, London: HMSO.

DoE (1977) *Policy for the inner cities*, London: HMSO.

DoE (1981) *The urban programme: The partnership at work*, London: HMSO.

DoE (1985) *Five year review of the Birmingham inner city partnership*, London: HMSO.

DoE (1995) *Involving communities in urban and rural regeneration: A guide for practitioners*, London: HMSO.

DoE (1997) *Bidding guidance: A guide to bidding for resources from the Government's Single Regeneration Budget Challenge Fund*, London: HMSO.

Doig, B. (1992) *Policy evaluation: The role of social research*, London: HMSO.

Dowling, R. (2000) 'Cultures of mothering and car use in suburban Sydney: a preliminary investigation', *Geoforum*, vol 31, pp 345-53.

Driver, S. and Martell, L. (1997) 'New Labour's communitarianisms', *Critical Social Policy*, vol 17, pp 27-46.

Driver, S. and Martell, L. (2002) 'New Labour, work and the family', *Social Policy and Administration*, vol 36, pp 46-61.

Duncan, P. and Thomas, S. (2000) *Neighbourhood regeneration: Resourcing community involvement*, Bristol/York: The Policy Press/Joseph Rowntree Foundation.

Dwelly, T. (2001) 'Reviewing the New Deal for Communities', *The Guardian*, 10 September.

Dwyer, P. (2002) 'Making sense of social citizenship: some user views on welfare rights and responsibilities', *Critical Social Policy*, vol 22, pp 273-99.

Eagleton, T. (1986) *Against the grain*, London: Verso Press.

East, L. (2002) 'Regenerating health communities: voices from the inner city', *Critical Social Policy*, vol 22, pp 147-73.

Edwards, B., Goodwin, M., Pemberton, S. and Woods, M. (2000) *Partnership working in rural regeneration: Governance and empowerment*, Bristol/York: The Policy Press/Joseph Rowntree Foundation.

Edwards, B., Goodwin, M., Pemberton, S. and Woods, M. (2001) 'Partnership, power and scale in rural governance', *Environment and Planning C: Government and Policy*, col 19, pp 289-310.

Edwards, B., Anderson, J., Fahmy, E., Gardner, G. and Woods, M. (2002) *Participation and power in rural community governance: Interim project report on voluntary sector engagement*, Aberystwyth: Institute of Geography and Earth Sciences, University of Wales.

Edwards, C. (2001) 'Inclusion in regeneration: a place for disabled people?', *Urban Studies*, vol 38, pp 267-86.

Edwards, C. (2002) 'Barriers to involvement: the disconnected worlds of disability and regeneration', *Local Economy*, vol 17, pp 123-35.

Edwards, J. (1995) 'Social policy and the city', *Urban Studies*, vol 32, pp 695-712.

Edwards, J. (1997) 'Urban policy: the victory of form over substance?' *Urban Studies*, vol 35, pp 825-43.

Eisenschitz, A. and Gough, J. (1993) *The politics of local economic policy: The problems and possibilities of local initiative*, Basingstoke: Macmillan.

Eisinger, P. (1973) 'The conditions of protest behaviour in American cities', *Political Studies*, vol 6, pp 11-28.

Elcock, H. and Keating, M. (eds) (1998) *Remaking the Union – Devolution and British politics in the 1990s*, London: Frank Cass Press.

Estates Gazette (2002) 'Sickening tale: an elephant shot for questionable spoils', *Estates Gazette*, pp 1-2.

Etzioni, A. (1996) *The new golden rule: Community and morality in a democratic society*, New York: Basic Books.

Fainstein, S., Gordon, I. and Harloe, M. (eds) (1992) *Divided cities: New York and London in the contemporary world*, Oxford: Blackwell.

Fairclough, N. (1992) *Discourse and social change*, Cambridge: Polity Press.

Fals-Borda, O. (1992) 'Evolution and convergence in participatory action research', in J.S. Frideres (ed) *A world of communities: Participatory research perspectives, North York*, Ontario: Captus University Publications.

Ferman, B. (1996) *Challenging the growth machine: Neighbourhood politics in Chicago and Pittsburgh*, Kansas: University Press of Kansas.

Fetterman, D. (1994) 'Empowerment evaluation', *Evaluation Practice*, vol 15, pp 1-15.

Fetterman, D. (2000) *Foundations of empowerment evaluation*, Thousand Oaks, CA: Sage Publications.

Fetterman, D., Kaftarian, S. and Wandersman, A. (1996) *Empowerment evaluation: Knowledge and tools for self-assessment and accountability*, New York: Sage Publications.

Fine, B. (2001) *Social capital versus social theory. Political economy and social science at the turn of the millennium*, London: Routledge.

Foley, M. and Edwards, B. (1999) 'Is it time to disinvest in social capital?', *Journal of Public Policy*, vol 19, pp 141-73.

Foley, P. (1999) 'New Labour: A new deal for communities?' *Public Money and Management*, January-March, pp 7-8.

Foley, P. and Martin, S. (2000) 'A new deal for community? Public participation in regeneration and local service delivery', *Policy and Politics*, vol 28, pp 479-91.

Foley, P., Hutchinson, J. and Fordham, G. (1998) 'Managing the challenge: Winning and implementing the Single Regeneration Budget Challenge Fund', *Planning, Practice and Research*, vol 13, pp 63-80.

Folkman, D. and Rai, K. (1997) 'Reflections on facilitating a participatory community self-evaluation', *Evaluation and Programme Planning*, vol 20, pp 455-65.

Fordham G., Hutchinson, J. and Foley, P. (1999) 'Strategic approaches to local regeneration: the Single Regeneration Budget Challenge Fund', *Regional Studies*, vol 33, pp 131-41.

Forester, J. (1999) *Planning in the face of power*, Berkeley: University of California Press.

Forrest, R. and Kearns, A. (1999) *Joined up places*, Bristol: The Policy Press.

Forrest, R. and Kearns, A. (2001) 'Social cohesion, social capital and the neighbourhood', *Urban Studies*, vol 38, pp 2125-43.

Foucault, M. (1977) *Discipline and punish: The birth of the prison*, London: Allen Lane.

Foucault, M. (1979) 'Governmentality', *Ideology and Consciousness*, vol 6, pp 5-21.

Foucault, M. (1980) 'Questions on geography', in C. Gordon (ed) *Power/knowledge – Selected interviews and other writings*, Brighton: Harvester Press, pp 63-77.

Foweraker, J. and Landman, T. (1997) *Citizenship rights and social movements: A comparative and statistical analysis*, Oxford: Oxford University Press.

Fraser, N. (1995) 'From redistribution to recognition? Dilemmas of justice in a 'post-socialist age', *New Left Review*, vol 212, pp 68-93.

Fraser, N. (1997) 'A rejoinder to Iris Young', *New Left Review*, vol 223, pp 126-9.

Fraser, N. (1998) 'Heterosexism, misrecognition and capitalism: A response to Judith Butler', *New Left Review*, vol 228, pp 140-9.

Fraser, N. (2000) 'Rethinking recognition', *New Left Review*, vol 3, pp 107-20.

Freeman, L. and Braconi, F. (2002) 'Gentrification and displacement', *The Urban Prospect: Housing, Planning and Economic Development in New York*, vol 8, pp 1-4.

Friends of the Earth (2000) *Press release: Urban White Paper – Drowning in a sea of carrots* (www.foe.co.uk/pubsinfo/infoteam/pressrel/2000/20001116170753.html).

Fukuyama, F. (1995) *Trust: The social virtues and the creation of prosperity*, New York: The Free Press.

Fukuyama, F. (1999) *The great disruption – Human nature and the reconstitution of social order*, London: Profile Books.

Furbey, R. (1999) 'Urban "regeneration": reflections on a metaphor', *Critical Social Policy*, vol 19, pp 419-45.

Fyfe, N. (1998) 'Reading the street', in N. Fyfe (ed) *Images of the street: Planning, identity and control in public space*, London: Routledge, pp 1-10.

Galbraith, J. (1992) *The culture of contentment*, London: Sinclair-Stevenson.

Geddes, M. (1997) 'Poverty, excluded communities and local democracy', in N. Jewson and S. MacGregor (eds) *Transforming cities: Contested governance and new spatial divisions*, London: Routledge, pp 205-18.

Geddes, M. (1997) *Partnership against poverty and exclusion?* Bristol/York: The Policy Press/Joseph Rowntree Foundation.

Giddens, A. (1984) *The constitution of society: An outline of the theory of structuration*, Cambridge: Polity Press.

Giddens, A. (1990) *The consequences of modernity*, Cambridge: Polity Press.

Giddens, A. (1991) *Modernity and self-identity: Self and society in the late modern age*, Cambridge: Polity Press.

Giddens, A. (1995) *A contemporary critique of historical materialism*, Cambridge: Polity Press.

Giddens, A. (1998) *The third way – The renewal of social democracy*, Cambridge: Polity Press.

Giddens, A. (2000a) *The third way and its critics*, Cambridge: Polity Press.

Giddens, A. (2000b) 'The second globalisation debate – a talk with Anthony Giddens', (www.edge.org/3rd_culture/giddens/giddens_index.html).

Ginsburg, N. (1999) 'Putting the social into urban regeneration policy', *Local Economy*, vol 14, pp 55-71.

Gould, P. (1999) *Analysis*, BBC Radio 4, broadcast 12 July.

Gould-Ellen, I., Mijanovich, T. and Dillman, K.-N. (2001) 'Neighbourhood effects on health: exploring the links and assessing the evidence', *Journal of Urban Affairs*, vol 23, no 3-4, pp 391-408.

Granovetter, M. (1973) 'The strength of weak ties', *American Journal of Sociology*, vol 78, pp 1350-80.

Grant, W. (1989) *Pressure groups, politics and democracy in Britain*, London: Philip Allan.

Greene, J., Peterson, P. and Du, J. (1999) 'Out of adversity, diversity in urban education', *Education and Urban Society*, vol 31, pp 190-213.

Greenhalgh, P. and Shaw, K. (2002) 'Regional Development Agencies and physical regeneration: can RDAs actually deliver the urban renaissance?', Paper presented at the Third Regeneration Management Research Workshop, 'Urban Renaissance in Question', University of Durham, 15 November.

Hackworth, J. and Smith, N. (2001) 'The changing state of gentrification', *Tijdschrift voor Economische en Sociale Geografie*, vol 92, pp 464-77.

Hall, D. and Hall, I. (1996) *Practical social research: Project work in the community*, London: Macmillan.

Hall, P. (1997) 'Regeneration policies for peripheral housing estates: inward – and outward – looking approaches', *Urban Studies*, vol 34, pp 873-90.

Hall, P. (1999) 'Social capital in Britain', *British Journal of Politics*, vol 29, pp 417-61.

Hall, S. (2000) 'The way forward for regeneration? Lessons from the Single Regeneration Budget Challenge Fund', *Local Government Studies*, vol 26, pp 1-14.

Hall, S. and Hickman, P. (2002) 'Neighbourhood renewal and urban policy: a comparison of new approaches in England and France', *Regional Studies*, vol 36, pp 691-707.

Hall, T. and Hubbard, P. (1998) *The entrepreneurial city: Geographies of politics, regime, and representation*, Chichester: Wiley.

Halpern, D. (1998) 'Poverty, social exclusion and the policy-making process: the road from theory to practice', in C. Oppenheim (ed) *An inclusive society – Strategies for tackling poverty*, London: Institute for Public Policy Research, pp 269-83.

Hambleton, R. and Thomas, H. (eds) (1995) *Urban policy evaluation: Challenge and change*, London: Paul Chapman Publishing.

Hamnett, C. (1973) 'Improvement grants as an indicator of gentrification in inner London', *Area*, vol 5, pp 252-61.

Hamnett, C. (2002) 'Gentrification and the middle class remaking of inner London', Paper presented to the 'Upward Neighbourhood Trajectories: Gentrification in a New Century Conference', University of Glasgow, September.

Hampton, W. (1970) *Democracy and community*, London: Oxford University Press.

Harley, B. (1992) 'Deconstructing the map', in T. Barnes and J. Duncan (eds) *Writing worlds: Discourse, text and metaphor in the representation of landscape*, London: Routledge, pp 231-47.

Harvey, D. (1989a) *The condition of postmodernity*, Oxford: Blackwell.

Harvey, D. (1989b) 'From managerialism to entrepreneurialism: the transformation of urban governance in late capitalism', *Geografiska Annaler*, vol 71B, pp 3-17.

Harvey, D. (1996) *Justice, nature, and the geography of difference*, Oxford: Blackwell.

Harvey, D. (2000) *Spaces of hope*, Oxford: Blackwell.

Hastings, A. (1998) 'Connecting linguistic structures and social practices: a discursive approach to social policy analysis', *Journal of Social Policy*, vol 27, pp 191-211.

Hastings, A. (ed) (1999a) 'Discourse and urban change', *Urban Studies* Special Issue, vol 36.

Hastings, A. (1999b) 'Discourse and urban change: introduction to the special issue', *Urban Studies*, vol 36, pp 1-17.

Hastings, A. (2002) *Community participation in urban and rural regeneration: A literature review*, Scottish Executive Social Inclusion Network Review Paper, (http://www.scotland.gov.uk).

Hastings, A., McArthur, A. and McGregor, A (1996) *Less than equal: Community organisations and estate regeneration partnerships*, Bristol: The Policy Press.

Healey, P. (1997) *Collaborative planning: Shaping places in fragmented societies*, London: Macmillan.

Healey, P. (1998) 'Building institutional capacity through collaborative approaches to urban planning,' *Environment and Planning A*, vol 30, pp 1531-46.

Henning, C. and Leiberg, M. (1996) 'Strong ties or weak ties? Neighbourhood networks in a new perspective', *Scandinavian Housing and Planning Research*, vol 13, pp 3-26.

Hibbitt, K., Jones, P. and Meegan, R. (2001) 'Tackling social exclusion: the role of social capital in urban regeneration on Merseyside – from mistrust to trust?', *European Planning Studies*, vol 9, pp 141-61.

Higgens, J., Deakin, N., Edwards, J. and Wicks, M. (1983) *Government and urban policy*, Oxford: Basil Blackwell.

Hill, D. (2000) *Urban policy and politics in Britain*, London: Macmillan.

Hillier, J. (1993) 'To boldly go where no planners have ever ...', *Environment and Planning D: Society and Space*, vol 11, pp 89-113.

Hinchcliffe, S. (1996) 'Helping the earth begins at home: the social construction of socio-environmental responsibilities', *Global Environmental Change*, vol 6, pp 53-62.

Hirst, P. (1994) *Associative democracy – New forms of economic and social governance*, Cambridge: Polity Press.

HM Treasury (1988) *Policy evaluation: A guide for managers*, London: HMSO.

HM Treasury (2000) *Government interventions in deprived areas (GIDA) cross-cutting review, spending review 2000*, London: HMSO.

HM Treasury (2002) *Spending review 2002*, London: HMSO.

Ho, S. (1999) 'Evaluating urban regeneration programmes in Britain: exploring the potential of the realist approach', *Evaluation*, vol 5, pp 422-38.

Hoban, M. and Beresford, P. (2001) 'Regenerating regeneration', *Community Development Journal*, vol 16, pp 312-20.

Hobson, T. (2000) 'The London Borough of Newham in facts and stats', in Community Links *What if...? Fifteen visions of change for Britain's inner cities*, London: The Short Book Company, pp 37-45.

Hoggett, P. (1997) 'Contested communities', in P. Hoggett (ed) *Contested communities*, Bristol: The Policy Press, pp 3-16.

Holloway, L. and Kneafsey, M. (2000) 'Reading the space of the Farmers' Market: a case study from the United Kingdom', *Sociologia Ruralis*, vol 40, pp 285-99.

Holman, B. (2000) 'A vision from Easterhouse', in Community Links *What if...? Fifteen visions of change for Britain's inner cities*, London: The Short Book Company, pp 27-36.

Home Office (1968) *Community development – Background paper for Community Development Projects*, London: HMSO.

Home Office (1999) *Community self help*, Policy Action Team Report no 9, Active Community Unit, London: The Stationery Office.

Home Office (2001a) *Neighbourhood renewal*, London: The Stationery Office.

Home Office (2001b) *Community cohesion: A report of the independent review team chaired by Ted Cantle*, London: Home Office.

Home Office (2001c) *Building cohesive communities: A report of the ministerial group on public order*, London: Home Office.

House of Commons Hansard Debates (2001) *Rural and Urban White Papers*, 26 January, Column 1187, UK (www.parliament.the-stationary-office.co.uk/pa/cm200001/cmhansrd/vo010126/debtext/10126-01.html).

House of Commons Public Accounts Committee (1989) *Twentieth report: Urban Development Corporations*, London: HMSO.

House of Commons Select Committee on Employment (1989) *Third report: The employment effects of Urban Development Corporations*, HC 327 I and II, London: HMSO.

Howarth, C. (2001) 'Towards a social psychology of community: a social representations perspective', *Journal for the Theory of Social Behaviour*, vol 31, pp 223-38.

Hughes, G. and Mooney, G. (1998) 'Community', in G. Hughes (ed) *Imagining welfare futures*, London: Routledge, pp 55-102.

Humphries, B. and Truman, C. (1994) *Re-thinking social research: Anti-discriminatory approaches in research methods*, Aldershot: Avebury.

Hutton, W. (2000) 'The economics of poverty', in Community Links *What if...? Fifteen visions of change for Britain's inner cities*, London: The Short Book Company, pp 15-26.

Imrie, R. (1996a) *Disability and the city: International perspectives*, London: Paul Chapman Publishing.

Imrie, R. (1996b) 'Transforming the social relations of research production in urban policy evaluation', *Environment and Planning A*, vol 28, pp 1445-64.

Imrie, R. and Hall, P. (2001) *Inclusive design: Designing and developing accessible environments*, London: Spon Press.

Imrie, R. and Thomas, H. (1993) 'The limits of property-led regeneration', *Environment and Planning C: Government and Policy*, vol 11, pp 87-102.

Imrie, R. and Thomas, R. (eds) (1999) *British urban policy and the Urban Development Corporations*, London: Sage Publications.

Imrie, R., Pinch, S. and Boyle, M. (1996) 'Identities, citizenship and power in cities', *Urban Studies*, vol 33, pp 1255-61.

Jacobs, J. (1961) *The death and life of great American cities*, New York: Random House.

Jenks, M., Burton, E. and Williams, K. (1996) *The compact city: A sustainable urban form?*, London: Spon.

Jessop, B. (1997) 'The entrepreneurial city: re-imagining localities, redesigning economic governance, or restructuring capital?', in N. Jewson and S. MacGregor (eds) *Transforming cities – contested governance and new spatial divisions*, London: Routledge, pp 28-41.

Jessop, B. (1998) 'The rise of governance and the risks of failure: the case of economic development, *International Social Science Journal*, vol 155, pp 29-45.

Jessop, B. (2000) 'Governance failure', in G. Stoker (ed) *The new politics of British local governance*, Basingstoke: Macmillan, pp 11-32.

Jessop, B. (2002) 'Liberalism, neoliberalism, and urban governance: a state-theoretic perspective', *Antipode*, vol 34, pp 452-72.

Jonas, A. and Wilson, D. (eds) (2000) *The urban growth machine: Critical perspectives two decades later*, New York: State University of New York.

Jones, C. and Novak, T. (1999) *Poverty, welfare and the disciplinary state*, London: Routledge.

Jones, J. (2001) 'Give them the money', *The Guardian*, 29 August.

Jones, M. (2001) 'The rise of the regional state in economic governance: "partnerships for prosperity" or new scales of state power?', *Environment and Planning A*, vol 33, pp 1185-211.

Jones, M. and Ward, K. (1998) 'Grabbing grants? The role of coalitions in urban economic development', *Local Economy*, vol 13, pp 28-38.

Jones, M. and Ward, K. (2002) 'Excavating the logic of British urban policy: neo-liberalism as the crisis of crisis management', *Antipode*, vol 34, pp 473-92.

Jones, O. and Little, J. (2000) 'Rural challenge(s): partnership and new rural governance', *Journal of Rural Studies*, vol 16, pp 171-84.

Jordan, B. (1996) *A theory of poverty and social exclusion*, Cambridge: Polity Press.

Kawachi, I. and Berkman, L. (2000) 'Social cohesion, social capital and health', in L. Berkman and I. Kawachi (eds) *Social epidemiology*, New York: Oxford University Press.

Kawachi, I., Kennedy, B. and Wilkinson, R. (1999) 'Crime: social disorganisation and relative deprivation', *Social Science and Medicine*, vol 48, pp 719-31.

Kawachi, I., Kennedy, B., Lochner, K. and Prothrow-Stith, D. (1997) 'Social capital, income inequality, and mortality', *American Journal of Public Health*, vol 87, pp 1491-8.

Kearns, A. and Forrest, R. (2000) 'Social cohesion and multilevel urban governance' *Urban Studies*, vol 37, pp 995-1018.

Kennedy, B., Kawachi, I., Prothrow-Smith, D., Lochner, K. and Gupta, V. (1998) 'Social capital, income inequality, and firearm violent crime', *Social Science and Medicine*, vol 47, pp 7-17.

Kennedy, S., Kiecolt-Glaser, J. and Glaser, R. (1990) 'Social support, stress and the immune system', in B. Sarason, I. Sarason and G. Pierce (eds) *Social support: An interactional view*, London: Wiley.

Kenny, J. (1995) 'Making Milwaukee famous: cultural capital, urban image, and the politics of place', *Urban Geography*, vol 16, pp 440-58.

King, T. (1980) 'Press notice', 18 August, Department of the Environment, London: HMSO.

Kleinman, M. (1998) *Include me out? The new politics of place and poverty*, CASE Paper 11, London: London School of Economics.

Kogan, M. (1999) 'The impact of research on policy', in F. Coffield (ed) *Research and policy in lifelong learning*, Bristol: The Policy Press, pp 31-46.

Kooiman, J. (ed) (1993) *Modern governance*, London: Sage Publications.

KPMG (1998) *What works? Learning the lessons: Final evaluation of City Challenge*, London: DETR.

Lang, R. and Hornburg, S. (1998) 'What is social capital and why is it important to public policy?', *Housing Policy Debate*, vol 9, no 1, pp 1-16.

Lawless, P. (1991) 'Urban policy in the Thatcher decade: English inner-city policy, 1979-90', *Environment and Planning C: Government and Policy*, vol 9, pp 15-30.

Leadbeater, C. (1999) *Living on thin air – The new economy*, London: Viking.

Lee, P. (1999) 'Where are the socially excluded? Continuing debates in the identification of poor neighbourhoods', *Regional Studies*, vol 33, pp 483-6.

Lees, L. (1994) 'Gentrification in London and New York: an Atlantic gap?', *Housing Studies*, vol 9, pp 199-217.

Lees, L. (1996) 'In the pursuit of difference: representations of gentrification', *Environment and Planning A*, vol 28, pp 453-70.

Lees, L. (2000) 'A reappraisal of gentrification: towards a "geography of gentrification"', *Progress in Human Geography*, vol 24, pp 389-408.

Lees, L. (2002) 'Rematerializing geography: the "new" urban geography', *Progress in Human Geography*, vol 26, pp 101-12.

Lees, L. (2003: forthcoming) 'The ambivalence of diversity and the politics of urban renaissance: the case of youth in downtown Portland, Maine', *International Journal of Urban and Regional Research*.

Lees, L. and Demeritt, D. (1998) 'Envisioning "The Liveable City": the interplay of "Sin City" and "Sim City" in Vancouver's planning discourse', *Urban Geography*, vol 19, pp 332-59.

Lefèbvre, C. (1998) 'Metropolitan government and governance in western countries: a critical review', *International Journal of Urban and Regional Research*, vol 22, pp 9-25.

Levitas, R. (1996) 'The concept of social exclusion and the new Durkheimian hegemony', *Critical Social Policy*, vol 16, pp 5-20.

Levitas, R. (1998) *The inclusive society? Social exclusion and New Labour*, Basingstoke: Macmillan.

Levitas, R. (2000) 'Community, utopia, and New Labour', *Local Economy*, vol 15, pp 188-197.

Ley, D. (1980) 'Liberal ideology and the postindustrial city', *Annals of the Association of American Geographers*, vol 70, pp 238-58.

Ley, D. (1994) 'Gentrification and the politics of the new middle class', *Environment and Planning D: Society and Space*, vol 12, pp 53-74.

Ley, D. (1996) *The new middle class and the remaking of the central city*, Oxford: Oxford University Press.

LGA (Local Government Association) (2000) *Preparing community strategies: Government guidance to local authorities*, London: LGA.

LGA (2002) *Draft guidance on community cohesion*, London: The Stationery Office.

Liverpool City Council (1991) *The Liverpool quality of life survey*, Liverpool: Chief Executive's Department, Liverpool City Council.

Local Economic Policy Unit (2001) *Elephant and Castle community profile household survey*, London: South Bank University.

Loftman, P. (2001) 'Ethnic minority experiences of the Single Regeneration Budget – issues for capacity building', Paper presented to the 'Capacity Building and Inclusion Seminar', South Bank University, London, 26 September.

Logan, J., Taylor-Gooby, P. and Reuter, M. (1992) 'Poverty and income inequality', in S. Fainstein, I. Gordon, and M. Harloe (eds) *Divided cities: New York and London in the contemporary world*, Oxford: Blackwell, pp 129-50.

London Borough of Lambeth (2000) *Vauxhall regeneration – The tenants decide*, Press Release, London: London Borough of Lambeth.

London Borough of Southwark (1999) *Elephant Links: A bid for Single Regeneration Budget Funding*, London: London Borough of Southwark.

Lovering, J. (1995) 'Creating discourses rather than jobs: the crisis in the cities and the transition fantasies of intellectuals and policy makers', in P. Healey, S. Cameron, S. Davoudi, S. Graham and A. Madani-Pour (eds) *Managing cities: The new urban context*, London: Wiley, pp 109-26.

Lovering, J. (1998) 'Labour and the defence industry: allies in "globalisation"', *Capital and Class*, vol 65, pp 9-20.

Lovering, J. (1999) 'Theory led by policy: the inadequacies of the new regionalism (illustrated from the case of Wales)', *International Journal of Urban and Regional Research*, vol 23, pp 379-98.

Lyons, M. (1996) 'Employment, feminisation, and gentrification in London, 1981-93', *Environment and Planning A*, vol 28, pp 341-56.

MacGillivray, A. (2002) *The glue factory – Social capital, business innovation and trust*, London: New Economics Foundation.

Mackian, S. (2002) 'Complex cultures: re-reading the story about health and social capital', *Critical Social Policy*, vol 22, pp 203-25.

Macnaughten, P. and Urry, J. (1998) *Contested natures*, London: Sage Publications.

Maloney, W., Smith, G. and Stoker, G. (1999) 'Social capital and urban governance', mimeo, Glasgow: Department of Government, University of Strathclyde.

Maloney, W., Smith, G. and Stoker, G. (2000) 'Social capital and associational life', in S. Baron, J. Field and T. Schuller (eds) *Social capita – Critical perspectives*, Oxford: Oxford University Press, pp 212-25.

Marshall, T., Woodburn, S. and Miller, J. (1997) *Comparing the areas LOVAS sweep 1: Variation in the size of sectors, volunteering, staff and incomes*, LOVAS (Local Voluntary Activity Survey) Paper 3, London: Home Office, Research and Statistics Directorate.

Massey, D. (1994) *Space, place and gender*, Cambridge: Polity Press.

Massey, D. (1997) 'Space/power, identity/difference: tension in the city', in A. Merrifield and E. Swyngedouw (eds) *The urbanisation of injustice*, London: Lawrence & Wishart, pp 100-16.

Massey, D. (2001) 'Geography on the agenda', *Progress in Human Geography*, vol 25, pp 5-17.

Mattson, G. (1997) 'Redefining the American small town: community governance', *Journal of Rural Studies*, vol 13, pp 121-30.

Mayo, M. (1997) 'Partnerships for regeneration and community development', *Critical Social Policy*, vol 17, pp 3-26.

McCrone, D. (1991) 'Urban renewal: the Scottish experience', *Urban Studies*, vol 28, pp 919-38.

McDonald, B. (2000) *Elephant boys*, London: Mainstream Publishing.

McGregor, A. (1992) *A review and critical evaluation of strategic approaches to urban regeneration*, Edinburgh: Scottish Homes.

McKie, L., Barlow, J. and Gaunt-Richardson, P. (2002) *The evaluation journey: An evaluation resource pack for community groups*, Edinburgh: ASH Scotland.

McNay, L. (1994) *Foucault – A critical introduction*, New York: Continuum Press.

Merridew, T. (2001) 'Learning and locality: a research agenda for exploring the role of regeneration consultancies', Paper presented at the 'Area-based Initiatives in Contemporary Urban Policy' conference, Danish Building and Urban Research/European Urban Research Association, Copenhagen, 17-19 May.

Merrifield, A. (1996) 'Social justice and communities of difference: a snapshot from Liverpool', in A. Merrifield and E. Swyngedouw (eds) *The urbanisation of injustice*, London: Lawrence & Wishart, pp 200-22.

Merrifield, A. (2000) 'The dialectics of dystopia: disorder and zero tolerance in the city', *International Journal of Urban and Regional Research*, vol 24, pp 473-89.

Midwinter, A., Keating, M. and Mitchell, J. (1991) *Politics and public policy in Scotland*, Macmillan: Basingstoke.

Miller, P. and Rose, N. (1990) 'Governing economic life', *Economy and Society*, vol 19, pp 1-31.

Ministerial Group on the Family (1998) *Supporting families*, London: The Stationery Office.

Monbiot, G. (2001) *Captive state – The corporate takeover of Britain*, London: Pan.

Morgan, K. (2002) 'The new regeneration narrative – local development in the multi-level polity', *Local Economy*, vol 17, pp 191-9.

Morrison, Z. (2003: forthcoming) 'Recognising recognition: social justice and the place of the cultural in social exclusion policy', *Environment and Planning A*.

Moynihan, D. (1969) *Maximum feasible misunderstanding: Community action in the war on poverty*, New York: The Free Press.

Moyser, G. and Parry, G. (1989) 'Community, locality and political action', in A. Mabileau, G. Moyser, G. Parry, P. Quantin and T. Shaw (eds) *Local politics and participation in Britain and France*, Cambridge: Cambridge University Press.

Mulgan, G. (1998a) *Connexity: Responsibility, freedom, business and power in the new century*, London: Vintage.

Mulgan, G. (1998b) 'Social exclusion: joined up solutions to joined up problems', in C. Oppenheim (ed) *An inclusive society – Strategies for tackling poverty*, London: Institute for Public Policy Research, pp 259-68.

Mulgan, G. (2001) 'Joined up government: past, present and future', Paper presented to 'Joined-Up Government', British Academy Conference, 30 October.

Mumford, L. (1938) *The culture of cities*, New York, NY: Harcourt.

Mumford, L. (1961) *The city in history: Its origins, its transformations, and its prospects*, San Diego: Harvest Books.

Munoz, P. (2000) 'The Olympic Urbaism and the new scale of metropolitan Barcelona: the Olympic Village in Poblenou', Working Paper, Department of Geography, Universitat Autonoma de Barcelona.

Murdoch, J. (1997) 'The shifting territory of government: some insights from the Rural White Paper', *Area*, vol 29, pp 109-18.

Murray, C. (1990) *The emerging British underclass*, London: IEA Health and Welfare Unit.

Murtagh, B. (2001) 'The politics and practice of urban policy evaluation', *Community Development Journal*, vol 36, pp 223-33.

Nash, V. (2002) 'Why community matters', in V. Nash (ed) *Reclaiming communities*, London: Institute of Public Policy Research.

NCVO (National Council for Voluntary Organisations) (2000) *New Deal for Communities: Phase 2 report*, London: National Council for Voluntary Organisations.

Neighbourhood Renewal Unit (2002) *Evidence into practice: New Deal for Communities national evaluation*, London: Neighbourhood Renewal Unit.

Nevin, B. and Shiner, P. (1995) 'The Left, urban policy and community empowerment: the first steps towards a new framework for urban regeneration', *Local Economy*, vol 10, pp 204-17.

Newman, J. (2001) *Modernising governance: New Labour, policy and society*, London: Sage Publications.

Newman, J., Sullivan, H., Barnes, M. and Knops, A. (2002) 'Power, participation and political renewal', Paper presented to the Social Policy Association Conference, Teesside, July.

Nocon, A. and Qureshi, H. (1996) *Outcomes for community care for users and carers*, Milton Keynes: Open University Press.

North, P. (2000) 'Is there space for organisation from below within the UK Government's Action Zones?: A test of "collaborative planning"', *Urban Studies*, vol 37, pp 1261-78.

North, P. and DeFilippis, J. (2003: forthcoming) 'The emancipatory community? Place, politics and collective action in cities', in L. Lees (ed) *The emancipatory city: Paradoxes and possibilities*, London: Sage Publications.

North, P. and Winter, A. (2002) *Project Vauxhall review*, London: South Bank University.

Nottinghamshire County Council (2000) *Health strategy*, Nottingham: Nottinghamshire County Council.

Oatley, N. (ed) (1998a) *Cities, economic competition and urban policy*, London: Paul Chapman Publishing.

Oatley, N. (1998b) 'Transitions in urban policy: explaining the emergence of the "Challenge Fund" model', in N. Oatley (ed) *Cities, economic competition and urban policy*, London: Paul Chapman Publishing, pp 21-38.

Oatley, N. (2002) 'The Community Finance and Learning Initiative', *Local Economy*, vol 17, pp 163-9.

ODPM (Office of the Deputy Prime Minister) (2001) Information on programmes relevant to urban policy, (www.urban.odpm.gov.uk/whitepaper/progs/index.htm).

ODPM (2002) *Community Chests*, (www.urban.odpm.gov.uk/whitepaper/progs/comchest.htm).

Ogden, P. (1992) (ed) *London Docklands: The challenge of development*, Cambridge: Cambridge University Press.

Oliver, M. (1990) *The politics of disablement*, Basingstoke: Macmillan.

Oliver, M. (1992) 'Changing the social relations of research production', *Disability, Handicap and Society*, vol 72, pp 101-14.

Oppenheim, C. (1998) 'Poverty and social exclusion: an overview', in C. Oppenheim (ed) *An inclusive society – Strategies for tackling poverty*, London: Institute for Public Policy Research, pp 11-28.

Osborne, M. and Rose, N. (1999) 'Governing cities: notes on the spatialisation of virtue', *Environment and Planning D: Society and Space*, vol 17, pp 737-60.

Owens, S. (1986) *Energy, transport, and urban form*, London: Pion Press.

PA Cambridge Economic Consultants (1987) *An evaluation of the Enterprise Zone experiment*, London: HMSO.

PA Cambridge Economic Consultants (1990) *An evaluation of garden festivals*, London: HMSO.

PA Cambridge Economic Consultants (1991) *An evaluation of the government's Inner-City Task Force initiative*, London: DTI.

PA Cambridge Economic Consultants (1995) *Final evaluation of Enterprise Zones*, London: HMSO.

Pacione, M. (ed) (1997) *Britain's cities: Geographies of division in urban Britain*, Harlow: Longman.

Packman, C. (1998) 'Community auditing as community development', *Community Development Journal*, vol 33, pp 249-59.

Paddison, R. (2001) 'Communities in the city', in R. Paddison (ed) *Handbook of urban studies*, London: Sage Publications, pp 194-205.

Painter, C. and Clarence, E. (2001) 'UK local Action Zones and changing urban governance', *Urban Studies*, vol 38, pp 1215-32.

Parkinson, M. (1998) *Combating social exclusion – Lessons from area-based programmes in Europe*, Bristol/York: The Policy Press/Joseph Rowntree Foundation.

Parry, G., Moyser, G. and Day, N. (1992) *Political participation and democracy in Britain*, Cambridge: Cambridge University Press.

Paxman, J. (1998) *The English – A portrait of a people*, London: Penguin.

Peck, J. and Tickell, A. (1994) 'Too many partners...the future for regeneration partnerships', *Local Economy*, vol 9, pp 251-65.

Peck, J. and Tickell, A. (2002) 'Neoliberalising space', *Antipode*, vol 34, pp 380-404.

Pennington, M. and Rydin, Y. (2000) 'Researching social capital in local environmental contexts', *Policy & Politics*, vol 28, pp 233-49.

Perri 6 (2002) 'Governing friends and acquaintances: public policy and social networks', in V. Nash (ed) *Reclaiming communities*, London: Institute of Public Policy Research.

Petersen, T., Saporta, I. and Seidel, M.-D. (2000) 'Offering a job: meritocracy and social networks', *American Journal of Sociology*, vol 106, pp 763-816.

Peterson, P. (1981) *City limits*, Chicago: University of Chicago Press.

Pile, S., Brook, C. and Mooney, G. (1999) *Unruly cities?: Order–disorder*, London: Routledge.

Piven, F. and Cloward, R. (1977) *Poor people's movements: Why they succeed, how they fail*, New York, NY: Routledge.

Plant, R. (1974) *Community and ideology*, London: Routledge & Kegan Paul.

PLCRC (Pan London Community Regeneration Forum) (1999) *Capacity building: The way forward*, London: London Regeneration Network.

Plymouth 2020 (1999) *Pathfinder strategy and action plan: Plymouth's submission to the Local Government Association under its Pathfinder New Commitment to Regeneration,* Plymouth: Plymouth 2020 Partnership.

Plymouth 2020 (2000) *The new plan for Plymouth: A consultation paper on the 2020 Vision for Plymouth and the city's planning strategy,* Plymouth: Plymouth 2020 Partnership and Plymouth City Council.

Plymouth City Council (2002) *Neighbourhood renewal strategy 2002-2007. 'Narrowing the gap',* Consultation Draft, Plymouth: Plymouth City Council.

Popular Housing Forum (1998) *Kerb appeal: The external appearance and site layout of new houses,* Winchester: The Popular Housing Forum.

Portes, A. and Landolt, P. (1996) 'The downside of social capital', *The American Prospect,* vol 26, pp 18-21.

Postone, M. (1993) 'Introduction: Bourdieu and social theory', in C. Calhoun (ed) *Bourdieu: Critical perspectives,* Cambridge: Polity Press, pp 1-13.

Powys County Council (1996) *From rural market towns to international market places,* Powys: Powys County Council.

Prescott, J. (2000) '£800 million boost for deprived areas', News Release 2000/ 0636, Department of Transport, Local Government and the Regions, 10 October, at www.press.dtlr.gov.uk/pns/

Prescott, J. (2002) *Lessons from the past to guide our future,* www.urbansummit.gov.uk

PSMRU (Public Sector Management Research Unit) (1988) *An evaluation of the Urban Development Grant Programme,* London: HMSO.

Purdue, D., Razzaque, K., Hambleton, R., Stewart, M., Huxham, C. and Vangen, S. (2000) *Community leadership in area regeneration,* Bristol/York: The Policy Press/Joseph Rowntree Foundation.

Putnam, R. (1993) *Making democracy work: Civic traditions in modern Italy,* New Jersey: Princeton University Press.

Putnam, R. (1995) 'Tuning in, tuning out: the strange disappearance of social capital in America', *Political Science and Politics,* vol 28, no 4, pp 664-83.

Putnam, R. (1996) 'Political attitudes and the local community', *American Political Science Review,* vol 60, pp 640-54.

Putnam, R. (1998) 'Foreword', in *Social Capital: Its importance to housing and community development, Housing Policy Debate,* vol 9, no 1 (Special Issue), pp v-viii.

Putnam, R. (2000) *Bowling alone: The collapse and revival of American community,* New York: Simon and Schuster.

Putnam, R., Kettle, P. and Taylor, F. (eds) (1970) *The geography of urban places*, Toronto: Methuen.

Quintanilla, G. and Packard, T. (2002) 'A participatory evaluation of an inner-city science enrichment programme', *Evaluation and Programme Planning*, vol 25, pp 15-22.

Raco, M. (2000) 'Assessing community participation in local economic development – lessons for the new urban policy', *Political Geography*, vol 19, pp 573-600.

Raco, M. and Imrie, R. (2000) 'Governmentality and rights and responsibilities in urban policy', *Environment and Planning A*, vol 32, pp 187-204.

Raco, M., Turok, I. and Kintrea, K. (2003: forthcoming) 'Local Development Companies and the regeneration of Britain's cities', *Environment and Planning C: Government and Policy*.

Radcliffe, P. (1999) 'Housing inequality and "race": some critical reflections on the concept of 'social exclusion', *Ethnic and Racial Studies*, vol 22, pp 1-22.

Rahman, M., Palmer, G., Kenway, P. and Howarth, C. (2000) *Monitoring poverty and social exclusion 2000*, York: Joseph Rowntree Foundation.

Redclift, M. (1987) *Sustainable development: Exploring the contradictions*, London: Methuen.

Renaisi (2002) *The Shoreditch New Deal for Communities project*, www.renaisi.com/local/shord.htm

Rheingold, H. (1993) *The virtual community: Homesteading on the electronic frontier*, Reading: Addison Wesley.

Rhodes, R. (1988) *Beyond Westminster and Whitehall: The sub-central governments of Britain*, London: Routledge.

Rhodes, R. (1995) *The new governance: Governing without government*, London: Economic and Social Research Council.

Rhodes, R. (1997) 'From marketisation to diplomacy: it's the mix that matters', *Public Policy and Administration*, vol 12, pp 31-50.

Richards, D. and Smith, M. (2002) *Governance and public policy in the UK*, Oxford: Oxford University Press.

Roberts, P. and Sykes, H. (2000) *Urban regeneration: A handbook*, London: Sage Publications.

Robins, K. (1995) 'Collective emotion and urban culture', in P. Healey, S. Cameron, S. Davoudi, S. Graham and A. Madani-Pour (eds) *Managing cities: The new urban context*, London: Wiley, pp 45-62.

Robson, B. (1994) 'No city, no civilisation', *Transactions of the Institute of British Geographers*, vol 19, pp 131-41.

Robson, B., Parkinson, M., Boddy, M. and McLennan, D. (1994) *Assessing the impact of urban policy*, London: HMSO.

Robson, B., Parkinson, M., Boddy, M. and McLennan, D. (2000) *The state of the English cities*, London: DETR.

Robson, C. (1993) *Real world research*, Oxford: Basil Blackwell.

Robson, G. and Butler, T. (2001) 'Coming to terms with London: middle-class communities in a global city', *International Journal of Urban and Regional Research*, vol 25, pp 70-86.

Roger Tym and Partners (1998) *Urban Development Corporations: Performance and good practice*, London: DETR.

Rogers, R. and Gumuchdjian, P. (1997) *Cities for a small planet*, London: Faber and Faber.

Room, G. (ed) (1995) *Beyond the threshold: The measurement and analysis of social exclusion*, Bristol: The Policy Press.

Rose, N. (1993) 'Government, authority and expertise in advanced liberalism', *Economy and Society*, vol 22, pp 283-99.

Rose, N. (1996a) 'The death of the social? Re-figuring the territory of government', *Economy and Society*, vol 25, pp 327-56.

Rose, N. (1996b) 'Governing "advanced" liberal democracies', in A. Barry, T. Osbourne and N. Rose (eds) *Foucault and political reason*, London: UCL Press, pp 37-64.

Rose, N. (2000a) 'Governing cities, governing citizens', in E. Isin (ed) *Democracy, citizenship, and the global city*, London: Routledge, pp 95-109.

Rose, N. (2000b) 'Community, citizenship and the Third Way', *American Behavioral Scientist*, vol 43, pp 1395-411.

Rose, N. (2000c) 'Government and control', *British Journal of Crimonology*, vol 40, pp 321-39.

Rose, N. and Miller, P. (1992) 'Political power beyond the state: problematics of government', *British Journal of Sociology*, vol 43, pp 173-205.

Ross, M. (1955) *Community organisation – Theory, principles, and practice*, New York: Harper and Row.

Routledge, B. and Amsberg, J. (1996) *Endogenous social capital*, Washington: Graduate School of Industrial Administration/World Bank.

Routledge, P. and Simons, J. (1994) 'Embodying spirits of resistance', *Environment and Planning D: Society and Space*, vol 13, pp 471-97.

Rubington, E and Weinberg, M. (eds) (1995) *The study of social problems: Seven perspectives*, Milton Keynes: Open University Press.

RDC (Rural Development Commission) (1995) *Rural challenge bidding guidance*, Salisbury: RDC.

Russell, H. and Killoran, A. (2000) *Public health and regeneration: Making the links*, London: Local Government Association/Health Education Authority.

Russell, H., Dawson, J., Garside, P. and Parkinson, M. (1996) *Interim evaluation of City Challenge*, London: HMSO.

Sampson, R., Raudenbush, S. and Earls, F. (1997) 'Neighbourhoods and violent crime: a multilevel study of collective efficacy', *Science*, vol 277, pp 918-24.

Sandercock, L. (1998) *Towards cosmopolis*, London: Wiley.

Sanhu, B. (2002) 'After Oldham and September 11th – capacity building for stronger diverse communities', *Local Economy*, vol 17, pp 90-5.

Sassen, S. (2000) 'Analytical borderlands: economy and culture in the global city', in G. Bridge and S. Watson (eds) *A companion to the city*, Oxford: Blackwell, pp 168-80.

Saunders, P. (1980) *Urban politics – A sociological approach*, London: Penguin.

Schneider, A.-L. and Ingram, H. (1997) *Policy design for democracy*, Kansas: Kansas University Press.

Schofield, B. (2002) 'Partners in power: governing the self-sustaining community', *Sociology*, vol 36, pp 663-83.

Schoon, N. (2001) *The chosen city*, London: Spon.

Schuller, T., Baron, S. and Field, J. (2000) 'Social capital: a review and critique', in S. Baron, J. Field and T. Schuller (eds) *Social capital – Critical perspectives*, Oxford: Oxford University Press, pp 1-38.

Scott, G., Campbell, J. and Brown, U. (2002) 'Childcare and urban regeneration', *Critical Social Policy*, vol 22, pp 226-46.

Scottish Executive (2002a) *Better communities in Scotland: Closing the gap – The Scottish Executive's community regeneration statement*, Edinburgh: The Scottish Executive.

Scottish Executive (2002b) *Local Government in Scotland Bill*, Edinburgh: The Stationery Office.

Scottish Office (1995) *Programme for partnership: Announcement of the outcome of the Scottish Office review of urban regeneration policy*, Edinburgh: The Scottish Office.

SEATO (South East Asian Trading Organisation) (1966) *Proceedings on the SEATO conference on sustainable development*, Bangkok: SEATO.

Select Committee on Environment, Transport and Regional Affairs (2001) *Minutes of evidence*, 24 January (www.parliament.the-stationary-office.co.uk/pa/cm200001/cmselect/cmenvtra/166/1012402.html).

SEU (Social Exclusion Unit) (1998) *Bringing Britain together – A national strategy for neighbourhood renewal*, Cmnd 4045, London: Stationery Office.

SEU (2000) *National strategy for neighbourhood renewal: A framework for consultation*, London: The Cabinet Office.

SEU (2001) *A new commitment to neighbourhood renewal: National strategy action plan*, London: The Cabinet Office.

Shakespeare, T. (1993) 'Disabled people's self-organisation: a new social movement?', *Disability, Handicap and Society*, vol 8, pp 249-64.

Shaw, C. and McKay, H. (1942) *Juvenile delinquency and urban areas*, Chicago: University of Chicago Press.

Sherman, J. (2002) '£25 billion of public projects built with private cash', *The Times*, 26 September.

Shields, R. (ed) (1996) *Cultures of the internet – Virtual spaces, real histories, living bodies*, London: Sage Publications.

Shucksmith, M. (2000) *Exclusive countryside?*, York: Joseph Rowntree Foundation.

Silver, H. (1994) 'Social exclusion and social solidarity: three paradigms', *International Labour Review*, vol 133, pp 531-77.

Simons, J. (1995) *Foucault and the political*, London: Routledge.

Six, P. (1997) *Escaping poverty – From safety nets to networks of opportunity*, London: Demos.

Slowey, J., Potter, T., Sullivan, H., Burrows, D. and Severn, A. (2001) *Response to the Social Exclusion Unit's Strategy Action Plan, Neighbourhood Initiatives Foundation*, www.nifonline.org.uk

Smith, N. (1996) *The new urban frontier: Gentrification and the revanchist city*, London: Routledge.

Smith, N. (2002) 'New globalism, new urbanism: gentrification as global urban strategy', *Antipode*, vol 34, pp 427-50.

Smith, S. (1993) 'Bounding the Borders: claiming space and making place in rural Scotland', *Transactions of the Institute of British Geographers*, vol 18, pp 291-308.

Smith, S. (1999) 'Arguing against cuts in lone parent benefits: reclaiming the desert ground in the UK', *Critical Social Policy*, vol 19, pp 313-34.

SWERDA (South West of England Regional Development Agency) (no date) *Rural programme: Market and coastal towns*, (available from SWERDA, Sterling House, Dix's Field, Exeter EX1 1QA).

Southern, A. (2001) 'What matters is what works? The management of regeneration', *Local Economy*, vol 16, pp 264-71.

Sparkes, J. and Glennerster, H. (2002) 'Preventing social exclusion: education's contribution', in J. Hills, J. Le Grand and D. Piachaud (eds) *Understanding social exclusion*, Oxford: Oxford University Press, pp 52-78.

Stepney, P., Lynch, R. and Jordan, B. (1999) 'Poverty, exclusion and New Labour', *Critical Social Policy*, vol 19, pp 109-27.

Stewart, J., Spencer, K. and Webster, B. (1976) *Local government: Approaches to urban deprivation*, Home Office Urban Deprivation Unit, Occasional Paper no 1, London: HMSO.

Stewart, M. (2002a) *Collaboration and co-ordination in area-based initiatives*, Research Summary no 1, London: Neighbourhood Renewal Unit and Regional Co-ordination Unit.

Stewart, M. (2002b) *Issues for community-led regeneration. Communities at the heart? Lessons from the New Deal for Communites*, London: South Bank University.

Stewart, M. and Taylor, M. (1995) *Empowerment and estate regeneration: A critical review*, Bristol: The Policy Press.

Stoker, G. (1998) 'Governance as theory: five propositions', *International Social Science Journal*, vol 155, pp 17-28.

Stone, D. (1989) 'Casual stories and the formation of policy agendas', *Political Science Quarterly*, vol 104, pp 281-300.

Stubbs, P. (1998) 'Conflict and co-operation in the virtual community: email and the wars of the Yugoslav Republic', *Sociological Research Online*, (www.socresonline.org.uk/socresonline/3/3/7.html).

Sullivan, H. and Potter, T. (2001) 'Doing 'joined up' evaluation in community based regeneration', *Local Governance*, vol 27, pp 19-31.

Swann, C. and Morgan, A. (eds) (2002) *Social capital for health – Insights from qualitative research*, London: Health Development Agency.

Tallen, E. (1999) 'Sense of community and neighbourhood form: an assessment of the social doctrine of the New Urbanism', *Urban Studies*, vol 36, pp 1361-79.

Tarrow, S. (1994) *Power in movement*, Cambridge: Cambridge University Press.

Tatchell, P. (1982) *The battle for Bermondsey*, London: Heretic Books.

Taylor, M. (1995) 'Unleashing the potential: bringing residents to the centre of regeneration', *Housing Summary*, vol 12, York: Joseph Rowntree Foundation.

Taylor, M. (1997) 'The impact of local government changes on the voluntary and community sectors', in R. Hambleton (ed) *New perspectives on local governance*, York: York Publishing Services.

Taylor, M. (2000a) 'Communities in the lead: power, organisational capacity and social capital', *Urban Studies*, vol 37, pp 1019-35.

Taylor, M. (2000b) *Top down meets bottom up: Neighbourhood management*, York: Joseph Rowntree Foundation.

Taylor, M. (2001) 'The new public management and social exclusion: cause or response?', in K. McLaughlin, S. Osborne and E. Erlie (eds) *The new public mangement: Current trends and future prospects*, London: Routledge.

Taylor, M. (2002a) 'Community and social exclusion', in V. Nash (ed) *Reclaiming communities*, London: Institute of Public Policy Research.

Taylor, M. (2002b) 'Is partnership possible? Searching for a new institutional settlement', in G. Cars, P. Healey, A. Madanipour and C. De Magalhaes (eds) *Urban governance, institutional capacity and social milieux*, Aldershot: Ashgate, pp 106-24.

Taylor, M., Craig, G. and Wilkinson, M. (2000) 'Co-option or empowerment? The changing relationship between the state and the voluntary and community sectors', *Local Governance*, vol 28, pp 1-11.

Taylor, P. (1999) 'Places, spaces and Macy's: place–space tensions in the political geography of modernities', *Progress in Human Geography*, vol 23, pp 7-26.

Temkin, K. and Rohe, W. (1998) 'Social capital and neighbourhood stability: an empirical investigation', *Housing Policy Debate*, vol 9, pp 61-88.

Tewdwr-Jones, M. and Allmendinger, P. (1998) 'Deconstructing communicative rationality: a critique of Habermasian collaborative planning', *Environment and Planning A*, vol 30, pp 1975-89.

Tewdwr-Jones, M. and McNeill, D. (2000) 'The politics of city-region planning and governance: reconciling the national, regional and urban in the competing voices of institutional restructuring', *European Urban and Regional Studies*, vol 7, pp 119-34.

Thatcher, M. (1987) 'There's no such thing as society', *Women's Own*, 3 October, p 8.

Thatcher, M. (1993) *The Downing Street years*, London: Harper Collins.

Thomas, A., Karn, V. and Gibson, M. (1984) *Research on urban renewal*, Swindon: Economic and Social Research Council.

Thomas, H. and Imrie, R. (1999) 'Urban policy, modernisation, and the regeneration of Cardiff Bay', in R. Imrie and H. Thomas (eds) *British urban policy – An evaluation of the Urban Development Corporations*, London: Sage Publications, pp 106-27.

Thompson, G. (1993) 'Network coordination', in R. Maidment and G. Thompson (eds) *Managing the United Kingdom*, London: Sage Publications, pp 51-74.

Thornley, A. (1993) *Urban planning under Thatcherism*, London: Routledge.

Tiesdell, S. and Allmendinger, P. (2001) 'Neighbourhood regeneration and New Labour's third way', *Environment and Planning C: Government and Policy*, vol 19, pp 903-26.

Topping, P. and Smith, G. (1977) *Government against poverty, 1970-1975: Liverpool CDP*, Oxford: Social Exclusion Unit.

Townley, B. and Wilks-Heeg, S. (1999) 'Democratic evaluation: putting principles into practice', *Local Economy*, vol 14.

Toynbee, P. and Walker, D. (2001) *Did things get better? An audit of Labour's successes and failures*, London: Penguin.

Tsouvalis, J., Seymour, S. and Watkins, C. (2000) 'Exploring knowledge-cultures: precision farming, yield mapping, and the expert-farmer interface', *Environment and Planning A*, vol 32, pp 761-950.

Turok, I. (1989) 'Evaluation and understanding in local economic policy', *Urban Studies*, vol 26, pp 587-606.

Turok, I. (1991) 'Policy evaluation as science: a critical assessment', *Applied Economics*, vol 23, pp 1543-50.

Turok, I. and Edge, N. (1999) *The jobs gap in Britain's cities*, Bristol: The Policy Press.

United Nations (1967) *Local participation in development planning – a preliminary study of the relationship of community development to national planning*, New York, NY: United Nations.

United Nations (1980) *Urban renewal and the quality of life*, New York: United Nations.

Urban Forum (1997) *Urban clearway*, Urban Forum Newsletter, no 3, London: Urban Forum.

Urban Task Force (1999) *Towards an urban renaissance. Final Report of the Urban Task Force, chaired by Lord Rogers of Riverside*, London: Spon.

URBED, MORI and the School for Policy Studies, University of Bristol (1999) *But would you live there? Shaping attitudes to urban living*, London: Urban Task Force.

Urry, J. (2002) 'Mobility and proximity', *Sociology*, vol 36, pp 255-74.

Valler, D., Wood, A., Atkinson, I., Betteley, D., Phelps, N., Raco, M. and Shirlow, P. (2003: forthcoming) 'Business representation and the UK regions: "Mapping" institutional change', *Progress in Planning*.

van Weesep, J. (1994) 'Gentrification as a research frontier', *Progress in Human Geography*, vol 18, pp 74-83.

Walker, P., Lewis, J., Lingayah, S. and Sommer, F. (2000) *Prove it! Measuring the effect of neighbourhood renewal on local people*, London: New Economics Foundation.

Ward, K. (1997a) 'The Single Regeneration Budget and the issue of local flexibility', *Regional Studies*, vol 31, pp 78-80.

Ward, K. (1997b) 'Coalitions in urban regeneration: a regime approach', *Environment and Planning A*, vol 29, pp 1493-506.

Watson, N. (1997) 'Why we argue about virtual community: a case study of the phish.net Fan Community', in S. Jones (ed) *Virtual culture: Identity and communication in cyberspace*, London: Sage Publications.

Watt, P. and Jacobs, K. (2000) 'Discourses of social exclusion – an analysis of Bringing Britain Together: A National Strategy for Neighbourhood Renewal', *Housing Theory and Society*, vol 17, pp 14-26.

Weaver, M. (2001a) 'Housing row threatens pioneering regeneration project', *The Guardian*, 3 October.

Weaver, M. (2001b) 'Friction slows New Deal', *The Guardian*, 20 February.

Weaver, M. (2002) 'What's the big deal in the end?', *The Guardian*, July 7.

Webster, D. (1994) *Home and the workplace in the Glasgow conurbation: A new analysis and its implications for urban regeneration and regional employment policy*, Glasgow: City Housing Glasgow.

Welsh Office (1996) *A working countryside for Wales*, Cm 3180, London: HMSO.

Wilkinson, R. (1994) *Unfair shares*, London: Barnardo's.

Wilkinson, R. (1996) *Unhealthy societies: The afflictions of inequality*, London: Routledge.

Wilks-Heeg, S. (1996) 'Urban experiments limited revisited: urban policy comes full circle', *Urban Studies*, vol 33, pp 1263-79.

Wilson, W.J. (1987) *The truly disadvantaged: The inner city, the underclass and public policy*, Chicago: University of Chicago Press.

Wintour, P. (2002) 'Parties consign welfare state to history – "new localism" seen as key to providing services', *The Guardian*, 12 October.

Wirth, L. (1938) 'Urbanism as a way of life', *American Journal of Sociology*, vol XLIV, no 1, pp 1-24.

Wood, M. (2000) 'Community involvement and capacity building', in J. Low (ed) *Regeneration in the 21st century*, Bristol: The Policy Press, pp 12-20.

Woods, M. (1999) 'Performing power: local politics and the Taunton pageant of 1928', *Journal of Historical Geography*, vol 25, pp 57-74.

Woods, M. (2002) 'New Labour's countryside: the re-description of a policy space', Paper presented to the Annual RESSG Conference, 18-19 September, Cardiff University.

Woods, M. (2003: forthcoming) 'Political articulation: the modalities of new critical politics of rural citizenship', in P. Cloke, T. Marsden and P. Mooney (eds) *The handbook of rural studies*, London: Sage Publications.

Woods, M., Fahmy, E., Anderson, J., Edwards, B. and Gardner, G (2003: forthcoming) 'Electoral participation in town, parish and community councils: a new critical analysis', *Local Government Studies*.

Woolcock, M. (2001) 'The place of social capital in understanding social and economic outcomes', *Canadian Journal of Policy Research*, vol 2, pp 11-17.

Wyly, E. and Hammel, D. (1999) 'Islands of decay in seas of renewal: housing policy and the resurgence of gentrification', *Housing Policy Debate*, vol 10, pp 711-98.

Wyly, E. and Hammel, D. (2001) 'Gentrification, housing policy, and the new context of urban redevelopment', in K. Fox (ed) *Critical perspectives on urban redevelopment*, vol 6, London: JAI Press/Elsevier Science, pp 211-76.

Young, I. (1990) *Justice and the politics of difference*, Princeton, NJ: Princeton University Press.

Young, I. (1997) 'Unruly categories: a critique of Nancy Fraser's dual systems theory', *New Left Review*, vol 222, pp 147-60.

Index

A

Action on Smoking and Health 214
Area based initiatives and:
  community participation 87-8, 95-6
  constructing neighbourhoods 110-12
  critique of 87-9
  cycle of decline 90
  deliberative democracy 98
  English regeneration 89-100
  failure of local governance 97
  integrated approaches to regeneration 85
  Local Strategic Partnerships 85-6, 89, 94, 95, 97-8, 108
  loss of jobs 90
  nature of community 91
  neighbourhood decline 90
  neighbourhood management 94
  network poverty 93
  Plymouth, UK 108-18
  regeneration discourses 243-4
  renewal policy 85, 86
  Scottish regeneration 89-100
  social capital 88, 96, 99
  Social Exclusion Unit 89-100
  weaknesses of 86-7
  worklessness 90-1
action at a distance 104, 112, 115
Action for Cities 207, 209
action plans 21, 48, 49, 89, 108, 163, 166, 171, 185, 189-190, 191, 194, 227, 229
action zones 19, 20, 24-25, 57, 114, 243
active citizens 6-7, 32, 105, 180, 182, 189, 192-4, 197-203, 215, 235, 241, 243
Active Community Unit 21, 22, 240
Adelaide, Australia 74
advocacy 97, 126, 213, 216
affordable housing 11, 175
alienation of local communities 215-16
Amsterdam, the Netherlands 76
argumentation 136-7
associationalism 40, 45, 52, 53, 56, 93
associative democracy 93
Audit Commission 16, 27, 29, 31, 43-4, 93
Australia 74
Aylesbury Estate, London 134

B

Baltimore, USA 71, 224, 244
Banham (Boundary Commission) 237
Barcelona, Spain 76, 224, 244
bidding; see competitive bidding
biotechnology 72
Birmingham, UK 134, 181, 213, 220
Blackbird Leys, UK 139-61
Blair, T. 4, 5, 6, 7, 9, 11, 13, 26, 37, 54, 124, 141, 178, 182, 210, 225-226, 235, 239, 242, 243, 247, 248
Blunkett, D. 12-13, 21
Boateng, P. 21
Boston, USA 71
Bourdieu, P. 40, 44
Brace, C. 8-9
Bradford, UK 29, 49, 238
Bristol, UK 112
Brixton, London 78
bureaucrats 226, 232
Burnley, UK 29, 49, 238
business community 30

C

Cabinet Office 188
Caborn, R. 5
capacity building 21, 47, 48, 99, 115, 122, 139-40, 146, 154-5, 210, 214, 240
Cardiff Bay, UK 248
Chicago School 77
child neglect 9
children 8, 58, 71, 73-4, 152, 155
citizenship 4, 5, 11-12, 32, 61, 62, 65, 182, 189, 191, 225, 231, 235, 237, 241
City Challenge 12, 25, 171, 189, 207, 208
civic participation 24, 42
civil society 7, 44-5, 98, 225-6, 235, 238, 242, 244, 245-6, 247
class 9, 25, 26, 28, 29-30, 33, 43, 45-6, 61, 70-2, 73, 74, 75, 80, 87, 91, 115, 116, 136, 137, 144, 157, 158, 159, 187, 224, 233, 239, 245, 247
Clinton, W. 243
collaborative 60, 98, 123, 198, 216
Commission for Social Justice 225

communitarianism 4, 5, 53-4, 79, 99,
  193, 210, 225-6, 245-6
community and:
  active citizens 6-7, 24, 196-7
  breakdown of 8
  building confidence of 47
  capacity of 10, 31, 47, 140, 155-6
  cohesion of 49-51, 52-3
  competitive bidding process; *see*
    competitive bidding
  conflict 124-38
  constructing neighbourhoods 110-12
  constructing partnerships 197-200
  criticisms of 78-80, 184-7
  cultural (in) justice 139-61
  cultural stigmatisation of 34, 139-61
  definitions of 26, 55-6, 78-80, 91,
    102-6, 227-8, 232-3, 235-6, 238-42,
    243, 246-9
  deliberative democracy 98
  democratic vision 231-4
  development of 10, 45, 48-9
  disabled people 34, 163-81
  discourses of 4, 5, 6-12, 33, 101, 123-
    4, 179-80, 205-6, 226, 228-9
  empowerment of 32, 36, 48, 94-5, 97,
    193-6, 210-14, 217-19, 223-4,
    236-42
  engagement of 200-3
  estrangement from policy 153-7
  evidence-based policy 210-11
  functioning of 47-8, 124-38
  governance 5, 7-8, 33-4, 102-6, 107,
    118
  governmentality 102-6, 117-18
  health 56-7
  individual deficiency 24
  involvement in policy 4, 32, 102, 113,
    121-38, 145-61, 209, 237-42
  lack of skills 92-93
  language of 61
  management of 228-30
  mutilevel governance 93-100
  neo liberalism 12, 242-6
  network deficiencies of 92-3
  object of policy 6, 26, 167-70
  obligations and responsibilities of 5,
    21, 30, 33, 172, 225-6, 237
  organic conceptions of 8-9, 185-6
  participation 87-8, 93-9
  pathology of 25-6, 89, 93, 95, 238
  payment for participation 158-60
  policy evaluation 35, 205-20

  policy initiatives 14-15, 22-3
  professional expertise 153-7, 214, 217
  relations with developers 131-2
  rescaling of government 31
  resistance 121-38
  resources of 6, 121-2, 194-5
  role of councillors 97-8
  safety 15
  self help 21, 30, 39, 47-8, 87, 91, 93,
    227
  small towns 181-204
  social capital 43-4, 47, 55-60, 92, 96,
    99
  social entrepreneurs 229
  social exclusion 106, 143-5
  social inclusion 123-4, 134, 182-3
  social injustice 139-61, 167-70
  stereotypes of 145-61
  stigmatisation of 145-61
  stock transfer 133-4
  targeting of 29
  targets 176-80
  technical fix 135
  urban renaissance 75, 78-80
  Urban Task Force 80, 227
  Urban White Paper 64, 80
  virtual spaces 247
  welfare of 46
Community Chests 21, 22, 241
Community Development Foundation
  197, 214
Community Development Projects
  9-10, 29, 163, 217
Community Development Venture
  Fund 22
Community Empowerment Fund 21,
  22, 137
Community Finance and Learning
  Initiative 22, 24
compact urban form 75-8
competitive bidding 12, 145-6, 150-2,
  153-8, 159, 164-5, 166-7, 168,
  171-2, 176-80, 188, 191, 196, 198
competitive individualism 7
Conservative Party 10-11, 12, 52, 53,
  66, 87, 101, 145, 166, 182, 189-90,
  192, 196-7, 210, 246
Continental attitude 65
cooperation
councillors 97-8, 114, 131, 186,
  198-201
councils 21, 153, 185, 186-7, 198, 230
countryside 64, 181-204, 247

Countryside Agency 181, 182, 185, 188, 189, 190-1, 203
Countryside Alliance 247
Coventry, UK 9
Community Planning Partnerships (Scotland), 86, 89, 94, 95, 98, 99
crime 4, 8, 9, 13, 18, 19, 24, 28, 39, 40, 46, 47, 48, 49, 53, 55, 56, 64, 67, 90, 91, 142, 143, 144, 148, 151, 217, 228, 236, 244
crime initiatives 15, 18
Crossman, R. 10
cultural domination 140
cultural injustice 139, 140, 143-5, 146, 150-1, 156-7, 159-61
cultural justice 139-61
cultural politics 62
cycle of decline 90

D

degenerate policy 6, 12-26, 115, 237, 238
deindustrialisation 244
deliberative democracy 98, 112
delivery (of policy) 8, 13, 17, 21, 32, 39, 45, 53, 54, 108, 111, 113, 114, 183, 187, 193, 199, 209, 226, 230, 237, 243, 245
democracy 21, 36, 40, 44, 55, 58-59, 65, 77, 79-80, 97-8, 99, 103, 123-4, 137, 190, 197, 203, 212, 213, 217-19, 224, 225, 231-4, 235, 241-2, 249
democratic agents 21
democratic renewal 58-9
densification 67, 75-6
Department for Work and Pensions 170
deprivation 12, 13, 17, 19, 21, 24, 25, 28, 30, 31-8, 39, 43, 47, 48, 49, 51, 52, 54, 57, 59, 86-7, 91, 92-4, 97, 100, 101-2, 106, 108-19, 124-5, 139, 140, 141, 145-61, 163-4, 166, 173, 179, 183, 184-5, 208-9, 210, 214, 216, 228, 236, 237, 238, 244, 245, 248
Development Board for Rural Wales 92, 193, 194, 196, 204
development process 128, 192
devolution 5, 6, 17, 234, 239-40, 248
Devonport NDC, UK 112-19, 213
Department for Education and Skills 24, 170
disability 34-5, 157, 163-81, 240-1
Disability Alliance 174

disabled people 34-5, 150, 157, 163-81, 240-1

E

economic injustice 140, 141, 152, 157, 158, 160-1
economic justice 141, 146, 152, 160
education 4, 10, 13, 19, 24, 28, 30, 38, 40, 46, 49, 53, 55, 57-8, 64, 67, 71, 73-4, 90, 91, 99, 107, 113, 115, 143, 166, 170, 182, 225, 244, 245
education and training initiatives 15
education policy 73
educational disadvantage 30, 151
Education Zones 19, 20
educational attainment 4, 13, 57, 90
elderly 9, 228
Elephant and Castle, UK 124-37
Employment Zones 126
empowerment 7, 12, 26, 52, 25, 48, 54, 59, 94, 95, 97, 100, 123, 136, 137, 179, 183, 196-7, 198-9, 203, 204, 205, 206, 217-19, 223, 228-30, 232, 236-42, 245, 246
Empowerment evaluation 217-19
empty homes 73
England 48, 49, 61, 63, 64, 67, 70, 71, 75, 77, 86, 89, 94, 108, 112, 167, 182, 183, 188, 189, 193, 223, 234
English Heritage 189
English Partnerships 14, 16
enterprise zones 207
entrepreneurialism 103, 192, 226
environmental policies 16
equity 205
ethnic minorities 46, 49, 57, 122, 148, 150, 159, 164, 168, 169, 170, 180, 226
ethnicity 25, 228
Etzioni, A. 5, 7, 13
Europe 62, 63, 75, 141, 142, 182, 192, 243, 244
European Commission 142
European Union 182
evaluation fatigue 215-16
Evaluation for Real 213-14
expertise 7, 25, 26-27, 34, 63, 80, 97, 116-17, 153-7, 176, 198, 214-17, 230, 240, 242

F

Faith Groups 127
family 7, 8, 9, 24, 39, 40, 44, 54, 90-1,
    142, 143-4, 195, 218
fear of crime 8, 47, 49, 53, 151-2
flats over shops 73
Foucault, M. 6, 21, 103-6
Friends of the Earth 73

G

Garden City 77
garden festival 207
gender 25, 142, 143-4, 157, 199, 233,
    240, 241
gentrification 11, 33, 34, 61-82, 116
Giddens, A. 13, 45, 52-3, 123, 176, 225,
    242, 243
Glasgow, UK 181, 224
global warming 75
globalisation 52, 78, 244
governance 5, 6-7, 27, 33-4, 36, 45, 59,
    62, 66-7, 85-6, 88, 93-100, 101-19,
    123, 183, 185, 187, 197, 199, 203,
    229, 230, 231, 234, 235-6, 237-42
Government Office for London 127,
    130, 168, 175
Government Offices 86, 92, 122, 127,
    130, 146, 148, 154, 164, 166, 168,
    169, 173, 175, 211
governmentality 73, 102-6, 117-18
grant coalitions 171
Greater London Action on Disability
    165, 175
greenbelt 67, 75
Groundwork 213

H

Habermas, J. 135-6
Harvey, D. 61, 103, 236, 241, 242, 243-4
Health Action Zones 19, 20, 24-5
health 7, 13, 16, 19, 20, 22, 24, 25, 28,
    30, 31, 39, 46, 55, 56-7, 64, 67, 73,
    85, 90, 91, 99, 113, 142, 143, 182,
    185, 189-91, 200, 202-3
Health Development Agency 56-57
Health Improvement Programmes 22
health policies 16, 18, 22
Healthy Living Centres 22
Heseltine, M. 3, 13, 189
Heygate Estate, London 126-30

Home Office 8, 9, 13, 21, 30, 49, 50, 51,
    186
Home Zones 20
housing 4, 11-12, 13, 19, 25, 26, 27, 28,
    31, 47, 51, 64, 67, 71, 74-5, 77, 78,
    90, 110, 112, 114, 116, 126, 127-9,
    130-7, 142, 143, 144, 145-61, 182,
    188, 227, 246
housing policies 16, 18
Howard, E. 77
Huddersfield, UK 224
Hutton, W. 30

I

identity 45, 60, 142, 186, 187, 190, 195,
    225, 227-8, 231
imagined neighbourhoods 111
incorporation 10, 34, 122, 223-34
index of deprivation 110
indicators 60, 110, 151, 152, 155, 169,
    170-9, 184, 212, 236
information technology 72, 247
inner cities 3, 4, 10, 33, 45, 61, 63-4, 74,
    75-76, 110, 188, 223
Inner City 100 Project 4
internet 126, 240, 247

J

joined up 37, 54, 141-2, 171
Joint Mobility Unit Access Partnership
    170, 174

K

Kensington, London 211, 213
King, T. 10

L

labour mobility 71
Lambeth, London 130-7
land policies 16
leadership 4, 34, 35, 124, 133-6, 154,
    187, 199, 205, 206, 210, 211-12, 214,
    218, 219, 227
Learning Network 191
Leeds, UK 71, 181
leisure and sports policies 16
leverage 42
liberal rhetoric 65
liveable cities 62, 72, 76

Liverpool, UK 3, 9, 10, 181, 211, 213, 245
local government 3, 9-10, 28, 39, 89, 93-100, 101, 102, 164, 172-5, 179, 185, 186-7, 226, 230, 233-4, 237, 245
Local Government Association 51, 108
Local Strategic Partnerships 17, 19, 86, 89, 94, 95, 97-8, 99, 108, 137, 163, 171, 230
localism 36, 236, 242-6, 247-249
London 3, 27, 28, 29, 34, 66, 78, 124-37, 165, 168, 173, 174-5, 181, 188, 241
London docklands 66, 244
lone parents 143-4, 151

M

Ministry of Agriculture, Foods and Fisheries 182, 184
mainstream spending 17-19, 40, 56-7, 85-6, 88, 93-4, 96-100, 107, 113, 124, 245
managerialism 176-80, 231
Manchester, UK 181, 224
manufacturing 184-5, 188, 236, 246
Market Town Healthcheck 185, 189-91, 200, 202-3
market towns 181-204
media 71, 148, 152, 200, 201, 236
Millennium Communities 23
Milwaukee, USA 218, 243, 244
modernisation 12-13, 21, 39, 54, 59, 93-100, 107, 117-18, 224-5, 231, 233, 235, 237, 247
moral decay 8-9
moral responsibility 65
Morrell, D. 10
mortality 4, 56
Mulgan, G. 5, 7, 13, 21, 37, 38, 54, 239

N

National Childcare Strategy 24
National Strategy Action Plan 23, 48, 89-100, 163, 164, 166-7, 171, 173, 179
natural sciences 216-17
National Council of Voluntary Organisations 205, 212-13
New Deal for Communities 19, 23, 27-9, 106-19, 164, 211-14

Neighbourhood Initiatives Foundation, USA 214
neighbourhood renewa, 4, 5, 13, 15, 17, 19-26, 27-31, 40, 47-9, 51, 59, 85-100, 110-19, 144, 163, 164, 166-7, 211, 212-14, 227
Neighbourhood Renewal Fund 19, 21, 23, 119, 167
Neighbourhood Renewal Team 17
Neighbourhood Renewal Unit 17, 51, 119, 211, 230
neo-liberalism 78, 225, 242-6
network poverty 57, 93
New Economics Foundation 213
New Labour and:
  agenda for change 12-13
  area based initiatives 19
  break with special initiatives 85
  business community 30
  citizenship and rights 5, 182, 191
  coming to power 4, 118-19
  commitment to urban regeneration 4, 246-7
  community cohesion 49-51
  community construction 236-42
  community leadership 205
  consensus 29-30
  democratic renewal 58-9, 235
  devolution 248
  election victory 39
  government through community 7-8
  joined-up policy 54, 101, 141
  managerial solutions 26-7
  middle classes 72
  multilevel policies 85-100
  new technology 247
  obligations and responsibilities 5, 13, 30, 59, 102, 225-6, 237-8
  partnerships 7, 163, 179
  policy programmes for cities 4-5, 6, 13-26
  public services 13-14
  public spending 72-3
  rejection of market and state 6-7
  renewal policies 85-6
  rescaling of government 31
  restoration of the family 8
  reviving communities 47-8, 235-236
  Single Regeneration Budget 145-6; also see entry for SRB
  social capital 47-9, 51-9, 60
  social exclusion 31; *see also* entry for social exclusion
  social justice 66

Third Way 39-40, 52-4, 243
understanding of communities 7, 8-9,
  26-35, 78-80
urban policy evaluation 210-14
New Opportunities Fund 23
New Right 192
new technology 239, 247
New Urbanism 243, 244
New York, USA 71
Newcastle, UK 224
nonrecognition 140
norms 42, 43, 46, 49, 55, 56, 58, 143
Northern Ireland 234, 248
Nottingham, UK 25

O

obligations 5, 7, 12, 225-37
Office of the Deputy Prime Minister
  17, 21, 23, 146, 166-7, 223, 230
Oldham, UK 29, 49, 238
open space 75, 126
organic society 8
Out of Schools Childcare Initiative 24
output, 27, 129, 137, 154, 155, 166, 167,
  168, 169, 171, 176-9, 201
owner occupation 77
Oxford UK, 34, 139-61, 241

P

parenting 8, 71
participant evaluation 217-19
participation 11, 12, 24, 34, 35, 39, 42,
  58-9, 62, 79, 87-8, 93-100, 106, 123,
  124-37, 141, 142, 145-61, 169,
  178-9, 181-201, 209, 212, 217-19,
  224, 231-4, 239, 241, 249
partnerships and:
  civil society 7
  community capital 43-4
  community-led example of 28, 108-
    18
  conflict 124-37
  consensus 29, 122-3, 171
  construction of 197-9
  corporate interests 11
  criticisms of 171-80
  disabled people 34, 163-80
  empowerment 12, 179
  engaging with local people 6, 123,
    167-8, 200-2
  evaluation of 10
  examples of 124-37, 145-61, 188-204

funding of 122, 150, 187
governing through communities
  192-6
Health Action Zone 25
ineffectiveness of 94
multilevel governance 33, 85-100
new philanthropy 12
policy development 17
private sector 66, 230
raison d'être 123-4
resisting gentrification 34
rhetoric of 34, 122, 123, 171
social capital 39
social network 7
struggle 123-4
successful bids 12
trust 53
pathology 6, 24, 25-6, 33, 87, 89, 91, 93,
  95, 100, 105, 238
Piccadilly Circus, London 126
place marketing 244
planning for real 190, 200
Plymouth, UK 33, 102, 108-18, 213,
  241
polarisation 11, 49, 64, 77, 87, 116, 139,
  140, 244
policy design 6, 25-26, 30-1, 205
policy evaluation 35, 205-21
political rationalities 104
pollution 25, 64, 65, 67, 75
positivism 176, 178-9, 216-19
poverty 3, 9, 11, 13, 19, 21, 26, 28, 30,
  37-8, 46, 57, 85, 87, 93, 110, 114,
  115, 139,141-2, 144, 148, 236
power 4, 5, 8, 10, 12, 13, 19, 29, 31, 34,
  35, 37, 38, 40, 43, 44-6, 53, 59, 62,
  63, 76, 94, 102, 103-7, 115, 118, 129,
  136, 142, 143, 144, 145, 171-5, 179,
  187, 197-204, 206, 210-20, 223-34,
  237-8, 240, 248
Prescott, J. 19, 63, 65, 243
private sector 10, 11, 12, 27, 30, 31, 35,
  63, 66, 69, 73, 85, 106, 108, 114,
  126, 130-1, 172, 189, 226, 227, 230,
  246
privatisation 31, 53, 122-3, 132, 134,
  246
professionals 7, 9, 10, 48-9, 72, 116,
  136-7, 146, 150-1, 153, 154, 155-61,
  219, 224, 226, 229, 230
property development 71, 52, 115
property-led 3, 11
prosperity 64, 74, 187
Public Accounts Committee 11

public life 8, 186, 187
Public Service Agreements 17, 18, 86, 245
public services 7, 13, 17, 30, 31, 39, 48, 59, 65, 90, 93-4, 96, 97, 184, 245
public space 51, 77, 79-80, 244, 248
public transport 31, 64, 191, 246
Putnam, R. 8, 40, 42, 44-5, 46, 49, 52, 58, 78, 81, 99, 185

Q

quality of life 60, 64, 92, 190, 195, 223, 246
questionnaire fatigue 216

R

race 142, 150, 157, 170, 233
reciprocity 42, 56
Redcliffe-Maud 237
Regional Development Agencies 17, 18, 86, 114, 137, 148, 166, 173, 182-3, 214-15
responsibilities 5, 13, 17, 19, 27, 28, 30, 32, 33, 59, 63, 65, 93, 98, 99, 101-2, 106, 113, 115, 118, 128, 166, 171-2, 179, 182, 193, 210, 217, 224-6, 227-8, 230, 235, 237, 243, 246, 249
Reviving Communities 47
rights and responsibilities 5, 26, 33, 36, 61, 128, 142, 178, 179, 182, 225-7, 242, 243, 249
risk 13, 59, 107, 155, 180, 219
Royal National Institute for the Blind 164, 170, 174,
Royal National Institute for the Deaf 164
Rogers, R. 63, 64, 65, 70
Rotary Club 186, 187
Round Table 186
Rural Action Areas 193, 194
Rural Challenge 188-9, 193
Rural Development Agencies 182, 189, 190, 191, 203
Rural Development Commission 189

S

Schoon, N. 3, 4, 12, 31, 224
Scotland 48, 49, 86-100, 188, 214, 234, 248
Scottish Executive 48, 85, 86, 89, 92-3, 94, 95, 97

Scottish Local Government Bill 97
segregation 29, 50, 60, 77, 79, 87, 170
self help 6, 9, 10, 21, 30, 39, 48-53, 59, 87, 88, 90, 93, 95-6, 99, 192, 210, 227, 232, 243
self-management 227, 229, 231
Shore, P. 63
Shoreditch, London 27, 28
short-termism 65
Single Regeneration Budget 12, 19, 23, 27-8, 34-35, 106, 112, 121-2, 124-37, 139-61, 163-80
small towns 35, 181-204
social capital 26, 32-3, 37-60, 80, 88, 90, 91, 92, 95, 96, 99, 101, 116, 123, 194, 202-3, 210
social disadvantage 11, 151
social division 4, 6, 52, 141, 142, 143, 215, 232-3, 243
social entrepreneur 7, 226, 229-30
social exclusion 33, 34, 37-40, 46, 54, 56, 60, 74, 75, 77-8, 87, 91, 92-3, 139-61, 163-4, 166, 167, 180, 182, 225, 227, 237
Social Exclusion Unit 4, 17, 21, 33, 37, 47, 48, 54, 64, 70, 72, 74, 85, 86-7, 89, 90, 91, 97, 110, 122, 141-2, 143, 144-5, 148, 163, 164, 171, 179, 210, 227
social glue 42, 43
social housing 28, 112, 127-8, 132, 133-5, 148, 158, 246
social inclusion 4, 38-9, 45, 53-4, 66-7, 72, 77, 79, 101, 122, 137, 139, 141, 143, 145, 146, 154, 156, 159, 160, 167
social justice 66, 79-80, 139, 142, 160, 225
social mix 47, 72, 74, 116, 117, 203
social order 5, 9, 40
Soho, London 78
South Bank, London 126, 130
Southend-on-Sea, UK 244
Southwark, London 9, 126, 130, 131, 133, 134, 135, 136
Sports Action Zones 20
stakeholder 35, 53-67, 178, 198-99, 202, 211, 213, 217-18, 227
stamp duty 73
Straw, J. 8
Sunderland, UK 31
surveillance 79
sustainability 30, 33, 61, 62, 63, 64, 66, 67, 72, 75-6, 78, 79, 80, 88, 130, 195, 246

symbolic capital 40

T

targets 10, 13, 17, 18, 19, 25-6, 27, 29, 30, 34, 54, 86, 89, 94, 102, 111, 113, 141, 154, 155, 164, 168, 169, 171, 173, 176-80, 193, 226, 238, 245
technologies of government 27, 33, 102, 104, 106
terrain of governance 33, 102,
territory 53, 105, 203, 242
Thatcher, M. 3, 11, 12, 17, 52, 66, 176, 182, 197-8, 208, 242
Third Way 39, 52-4, 242-3, 244, 249
traffic congestion 64, 75
training 21, 24, 38, 59, 87, 115, 155, 159, 172, 173, 175, 177, 180, 191, 213, 225
Transport 16, 30, 31, 64, 73, 76, 87, 126, 170, 175, 184, 190, 191, 240
Treasury 17, 19, 21, 73, 113, 207, 211-12
trickle down 3, 11, 184
trust 29, 40, 42, 43, 44, 45, 49, 51, 52, 53, 55, 56, 58, 59, 178, 239

U

Urban Development Corporations 11, 163, 180, 207
underclass 26, 87, 91, 115
unemployment 58, 85, 110, 115, 142, 144, 151, 158, 184, 211, 236
United Kingdom 9, 31, 52, 57, 58, 61, 64, 71, 80, 102, 108, 117, 121, 126, 218, 219, 234, 237, 248,
United Nations 9
United States 40, 52, 57, 63, 115, 206, 217-19, 243-244
urban decline 3, 4, 8, 19, 40, 47, 63-6, 70, 87, 88, 89, 90-3, 99-100, 101-2, 108, 114-15, 118, 122, 188, 248
urban development grant 207
urban intensification 67
Urban Programme 10, 208, 243
Urban Regeneration Companies 17
urban renaissance 6, 12, 24, 26-31, 33, 35, 61-81, 110, 226, 235-49
Urban Splash 71
Urban Summit 243, 244
Urban Task Force 17, 26-27, 33, 61-82, 227-8, 246

Urban White Paper 13, 21, 26-7, 61-82, 107, 246, 247
use value 45

V

value for money 111, 173, 176, 178, 208
VAT reforms 73
Vauxhall, London 130-7
virtual communities 240, 247
voluntary associations 8, 11, 12, 45, 59, 231
Voluntary Sector 122, 126, 145, 156, 168, 172, 196, 213, 218, 219, 220, 226
voluntary work 158-60
volunteering 21, 47, 186-7
vulnerable community 151

W

Wales 183, 187, 191, 192-204, 234, 248
wealth creation 66
welfare state 12, 13, 26, 30, 36, 53, 101, 225, 242-6
welfare to work 4, 13, 170
Welsh Assembly 248
Welsh Development Agency 182, 192, 193, 194
Welsh Office 194
Westminster 126, 174
what works 4, 131, 211-12, 226
Wirth, Louis 8
workfare 12
Working Families' Tax Credit 24
worklessness 28, 52, 90-1, 115, 210